DATE DUE

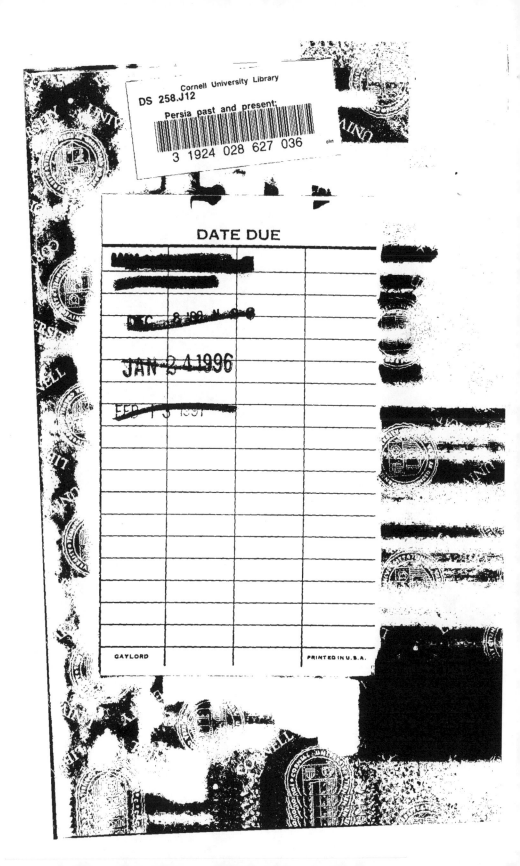

PERSIA PAST AND PRESENT

From a painting by Jay Hambidge.
Courtesy of the Century Co.

KING DARIUS OFFERS SACRIFICE UNTO ORMAZD

(See page 303)

'A great god is Auramazda, who created this earth,
who created yonder heaven, who created man, who
created Peace for man, who made Darius king.'
:- — OLD PERSIAN INSCRIPTION.

THE illustration, for which I have to thank the courtesy of *The Century Magazine*
and of Mr. Jay Hambidge, who drew it to illustrate an article of mine, has been
made with especial regard to archæological accuracy. The details are taken largely
from the Old Persian sculptures at Persepolis, Susa and Behistun, supplemented by
material from the Avesta and other ancient writings. The figure floating in the sky
represents the god Auramazda, girt with the wings of divinity and circle of eternity
and holding in his hand the ring of sovereignty. The priest serving at the Fire Altar,
which is still to be seen on the rocks at Nakshi Rustam, wears the veil *paitidāna*
before his lips as he chants the invocation. The king with his army has ridden across
from the palace at Persepolis, six miles distant. The groom Oibares holds his
favorite horse. The soldiers stand in an attitude of devotion while the king pro-
claims his faith and offers worship to the god to whom he ascribes all good.

PERSIA PAST AND PRESENT

A BOOK OF TRAVEL
AND RESEARCH

WITH MORE THAN TWO HUNDRED ILLUSTRATIONS AND A MAP

BY

A. V. WILLIAMS JACKSON

PROFESSOR OF INDO-IRANIAN LANGUAGES, AND SOMETIME
ADJUNCT PROFESSOR OF THE ENGLISH LANGUAGE
AND LITERATURE IN COLUMBIA UNIVERSITY

New York
THE MACMILLAN COMPANY
LONDON: MACMILLAN & CO., Ltd.
1906

Norwood Press
J. S. Cushing & Co. — Berwick & Smith Co.
Norwood, Mass., U.S.A.

TO MY MOTHER

' More is thy due than more than all can pay.'

—SHAKSPERE.

PREFACE

THE preparation of this volume has been a work after my own heart for the past three years, and I am now almost sorry that it is finished, although it has been carried forward amid many distractions of an official and public nature besides my regular duties at the University. I have entitled it a book of travel and research, having essayed the somewhat difficult task of combining these two themes into a union which I hope will be found true, at least in spirit, even if imperfect when judged by the standards that I should like to uphold.

I was tempted at first to label some of the chapters, like those on Takht-i Suleiman, Kangavar, Ragha, and a part of the section on the Old Persian Inscriptions, with a warning, 'this chapter is dedicated to the student,' and to prefix to other chapters, like those on the different cities, By Caravan and Cavalcade, Pasargadæ, and Persepolis, a prefatory line, 'dedicated to the general reader.' I decided against such a procedure, because I believe that the interests of both are ultimately one, and if the general reader enjoys a comfortable forty winks while certain technical matters are being discussed, he will awaken refreshed to resume his interest at a point where the specialist may begin to nod. But these very comments may have in themselves a somnolent effect and defeat their own end by superinducing the results they are seeking to avert. For that reason I shall refrain from adding others, and shall proceed rather to bring out the points which I wish to emphasize.

By hard work during my stay in Persia, I succeeded in seeing a good deal of the country and observing Persian life

with that keenness of interest which enthusiasm for the subject produces and that closeness of application which years of
preparation tend to cultivate. I could have wished that the
time and means at my disposal had been more abundant, but
'half a loaf is better than no bread at all,' and years of experience in travel have taught me that impressions gained in a
few months are often more vivid than when the stay in the
country is prolonged indefinitely. Of course, there is the
well-recognized danger of receiving wrong impressions and of
generalizing from insufficient data, but I have tried to reduce
the factor of error as far as possible by seeing as much of the
country as I could, so as to be able to distinguish between
local and general conditions, and by subjecting my observations
to the test of comparison with the history of the country from
the earliest times. How far I have succeeded or failed must
be decided by those who are competent to judge. I can only
plead in my own behalf that I have worked conscientiously
throughout to make the book as good as I was able, and one
example of this will be found in the attention given also to
illustration. The illustrations that are ordinarily presented
I have supplemented by pictures of subjects that are rarely
chosen, and I have done this mainly from a collection of photographs taken by myself on the journey or by friends in Persia.

How little can be done without the aid of one's predecessors,
when writing a book, will be best appreciated by those who
have aimed, like myself, at adding a mite to the body of knowledge already existing. On that account I have constantly
and without hesitation consulted the works of my fellow-
laborers in the field during the past three thousand years, from
Zoroaster and Herodotus, through the Arab writers, to Ker
Porter, Browne, and Curzon. I have been careful everywhere
to quote my sources for any special piece of information and
to acknowledge my indebtedness without hesitation. If the
footnotes seem more abundant than usual, it is because of
this desire faithfully to provide the reader with the means of

consulting the material used at each particular point or to enable him to call into question a view I have expressed, because I have frankly stated the fact when the authorities are at variance.

There are several respects in which I should have liked to be able to bring the book nearer to completeness, but I think I may say with all modesty that some compensation for this will be found in the suggestiveness of the volume because of the light it throws upon certain historical points which were not previously clear or even known before; and I also believe that many readers will welcome a new presentation of matters that were already familiar to them. The student of Zoroastrianism, moreover, will find many points to consider in connection with his own work, especially the numerous identifications suggested for ancient sites, or explanations proposed for doubtful passages in the literature, as I have always kept that in view.

I have spoken of my indebtedness to those of the past; I have also an obligation to the present which I deeply feel. First of all, I am indebted to President Nicholas Murray Butler and the Trustees of Columbia University for granting me leave of absence to visit Iran. Then, I am grateful to the many friends, as well as officials, who gave me suggestions and aid in regard to my journey. The Christian missionaries at home were especially helpful in this respect, and in Persia they welcomed me at their homes with a hospitality for which I shall ever be grateful.

In the preparation of the book on my return, I received many serviceable hints from Mr. Frank E. Morgan, of Bennington, Vermont, and I owe a special debt of gratitude to two of my student friends. To my pupil, Dr. Louis H. Gray, former Fellow in Indo-Iranian Languages at Columbia, I wish to express my sincere thanks for generous assistance rendered in reading over the manuscript of a large part of the book before it went to the press and for his counsel with regard

to matters of general presentation.   To my younger pupil,
Mr. George C. O. Haas, A.M., Fellow in Indo-Iranian, I am
especially grateful for help from the beginning.   Hardly a
day has passed since the first chapter was written without
his giving me some aid, either by going through the entire
manuscript with an eye to matters of detail, or by correcting
with me every page of proof as it came from the compositor,
or by preparing the Index, the value of which the reader will
easily recognize.   There are many other friends whose kindness I recall, but if their names be missing in print, it is not
because they are forgotten, but because they are 'registered
where every day I turn the leaf to read them,' including among
this number the publishers, whose generous attitude toward
the subject has enabled me to present the work in a way that
I hope may find favor with the reader, general and special,
for whom the book is written.

A. V. WILLIAMS JACKSON.

COLUMBIA UNIVERSITY,
    May 7, 1906.

CONTENTS

xi

LIST OF ILLUSTRATIONS

LIST OF WORKS OF REFERENCE

This list includes only the works most often referred to. Detailed information concerning other books and papers is given in the footnotes.

Adams, Isaac. Persia by a Persian. (Grand Rapids, Michigan), 1900.

Barbaro, Josafa. Travels to Tana and Persia by Josafa Barbaro and Ambrogio Contarini, tr. William Thomas. London, 1873. (Hakluyt Society publications, vol. 49.)

Barbier de Meynard. See Mas'ūdī and Yāḳūt.

Bartholomae, Christian. Altiranisches Wörterbuch. Strassburg, 1905. [Air. Wb.]

Bell, John. Travels in Asia. In Pinkerton, General Collection of Voyages and Travels, 7. 273–516, London, 1811.

Benjamin, S. G. W. Persia and the Persians. Boston, (1886).

Bharucha, Sheriarji Dadabhai. A Brief Sketch of the Zoroastrian Religion and Customs. Bombay, 1893.

Bishop, Mrs. (Isabella L. Bird). Journeys in Persia and Kurdistan. 2 vols. New York, 1891.

Browne, Edward G. A Year Amongst the Persians. London, 1893.

Browne, Edward G. A Literary History of Persia from the Earliest Times until Firdawsí. New York, 1902.

Brugsch, Heinrich. Im Lande der Sonne: Wanderungen in Persien. 2d ed. Berlin, 1886.

Chardin, Sir John. Voyages en Perse et autres lieux de l'Orient. 4 vols. Amsterdam, 1735.

Clavijo, Ruy Gonzalez de. Narrative of the Embassy to the Court of Timour at Samarcand A.D. 1403–6, tr. C. R. Markham. London, 1859. (Hakluyt Society publications, vol. 26.)

Contarini, Ambrogio. Travels to Tana and Persia by Josafa Barbaro and Ambrogio Contarini, tr. William Thomas. London, 1873. (Hakluyt Society publications, vol. 49.)

Ctesias. The Fragments of the Persika of Ktesias, ed. John Gilmore. London, 1888.

Curzon, George N. Persia and the Persian Question. 2 vols. London, 1892.

Darmesteter, James. Le Zend-Avesta, traduction nouvelle. 3 vols. Paris, 1892–3. (Annales du Musée Guimet, vols. 21, 22, 24.) [Le ZA.]

De Goeje, M. J. Bibliotheca Geographorum Arabicorum. 8 vols. Leiden, 1870–94.

della Valle, Pietro. Viaggi di Pietro della Valle il Pellegrino. 2 vols. Brighton, 1843.

della Valle, Pietro. Extracts from the Travels of Pietro della Valle in Persia. In Pinkerton, General Collection of Voyages and Travels, 9. 1–137, London, 1811.

Dieulafoy, Marcel A. L'Art Antique de la Perse. 5 vols. Paris, 1884–5.

Ethé, Hermann. Neupersische Litteratur. In Grundriss der Iranischen Philologie, 2. 212–368, Strassburg, 1896–1904.

Firdausī. Firdusii Liber Regum qui inscribitur Shah Name, ed. J. A. Vullers (et S. Landauer). 3 vols. Leiden, 1877–84.

Firdausī. Le Livre des Rois, traduit et commenté par Jules Mohl. 7 vols. Paris, 1876–8.

Firdausī. Il Libro dei Re, poema epico, recato dal Persiano in versi Italiani da Italo Pizzi. 8 vols. Turin, 1886–8.

Flandin, E. N., and Coste, X. P. Voyage en Perse. 8 vols. Paris, (1843–54). (Relation du Voyage, 2 vols.; Perse Ancienne, texte, 1 vol., planches, 4 vols.; Perse Moderne, 1 vol.)

Gordon, Sir Thomas Edward. Persia Revisited (1895). New York, 1896.

Gottheil, R. J. H. References to Zoroaster in Syriac and Arabic Literature. In Classical Studies in Honour of Henry Drisler, pp. 24–51, New York, 1894.

Haug, Martin. Essays on the Sacred Language, Writings, and Religion of the Parsis. 3d ed., edited and enlarged by E. W. West. London, 1884.

Horn, Paul. Geschichte Irans in Islamitischer Zeit. In Grundriss der Iranischen Philologie, 2. 551–604, Strassburg, 1896–1904.

Ibn Ḥauḳal. The Oriental Geography of Ebn Haukal, tr. Sir William Ouseley. London, 1800.

Jackson, A. V. Williams. Zoroaster, the Prophet of Ancient Iran. New York, 1899.

Justi, Ferdinand. Geschichte Irans von den Ältesten Zeiten bis zum Ausgang der Sasaniden. In Grundriss der Iranischen Philologie, 2. 395–550, Strassburg, 1896–1904.

Justi, Ferdinand. Empire of the Persians. In History of All Nations, vol. 2, Philadelphia and New York, 1905.

Justi, Ferdinand. Iranisches Namenbuch. Marburg, 1895.

Karaka, Dosabhai Framji. History of the Parsis. 2 vols. London, 1884.

Kārnāmak-ī Artakhshīr-ī Pāpakān. The original Pahlavi Text, edited (and translated) by Darab Dastur Peshotan Sanjana. Bombay, 1896.

Ker Porter, Sir Robert. Travels in Georgia, Persia, Armenia, Ancient Babylonia, etc. 2 vols. London, 1821.

Knanishu, Joseph. About Persia and its People. Rock Island, Illinois, 1899.

Korān. The Koran, tr. George Sale. London, no date. (Chandos Classics.)

Landor, A. Henry Savage. Across Coveted Lands. 2 vols. New York, 1903.

Lynch, H. F. B. Armenia, Travels and Studies. 2 vols. New York, 1901.

Malcolm, Napier. Five Years in a Persian Town. New York, 1905.

Marquart, J. Ērānšahr nach der Geographie des Ps. Moses Xorenac'i. Berlin, 1901. (Abh. d. Kgl. Ges. d. Wiss. zu Göttingen, Phil.-Hist. Klasse, new series, vol. 3, no. 2.)

Mas'ūdī, al-. Maçoudi, Les Prairies d'Or, ed. et tr. C. Barbier de Meynard. 9 vols. Paris, 1861-77.

Morgan, J. de. Mission Scientifique en Perse. Vol. 2, Études géographiques, Paris, 1895. Vol. 4, Recherches archéologiques, Paris, 1896.

Nöldeke, Theodor. See Tabarī.

Odorico da Pordenone. Les Voyages en Asie du bienheureux frère Odoric de Pordenone, publié par Henri Cordier. Paris, 1891. (Recueil de Voyages, vol. 10.)

Ouseley, Sir William. Travels in Various Countries of the East, more particularly Persia. 3 vols. London, 1819-23.

Perkins, Justin. A Residence of Eight Years in Persia. Andover, Mass., 1843.

Perrot, G., and Chipiez, C. Histoire de l'Art dans l'Antiquité. Vol. 5, Perse, etc., Paris, 1890.

Pietro della Valle. See della Valle.

Polo, Marco. The Book of Ser Marco Polo the Venetian concerning the Kingdoms and Marvels of the East, tr. and ed. Sir Henry Yule. 3d ed., revised by Henri Cordier. 2 vols. London, 1903.

Rawlinson, George. The Five Great Monarchies of the Ancient Eastern World. 4 vols. London, 1862-7.

Rawlinson, George. The Sixth Great Oriental Monarchy. London, 1873.

Rawlinson, George. The Seventh Great Oriental Monarchy. London, 1876.

Rosenberg, Frédéric. Le Livre de Zoroastre (Zarātusht Nāma) de Zartusht-i Bahrām ben Pajdū. St. Petersburg, 1904.

Sādik Iṣfahānī. The Geographical Works of Sádik Isfahàni, tr. by J. C. from original Persian Mss. in the collection of Sir William Ouseley, the editor. London, 1832.

Schwarz, Paul. Iran im Mittelalter nach den Arabischen Geographen, 1. Leipzig, 1896.

Shāh Nāmah. See Firdausī.

Shatrōīhā-ī Aīrān. In Pahlavi Texts, 1, edited by Jamaspji Dastur Minocheherji Jamasp Asana, pp. 18–24, Bombay, 1897.

Shatrōīhā-ī Aīrān. In Aiyādgār-i-Zarīrān, Shatrōīhā-i-Airān, etc., translated with notes by Jivanji Jamshedji Modi, pp. 50–180, Bombay, 1899.

Spiegel, Friedrich. Érānische Alterthumskunde. 3 vols. Leipzig, 1871–8.

Spiegel, Friedrich. Die Altpersischen Keilinschriften. 2d ed. Leipzig, 1881.

Stolze, F., and Andreas, F. C. Persepolis. 2 vols. Berlin, 1882.

Sykes, Percy M. Ten Thousand Miles in Persia, or Eight Years in Irán. New York, 1902.

Ṭabarī, al-. Geschichte der Perser und Araber zur Zeit der Sasaniden, aus der Arabischen Chronik des Tabari, von Theodor Nöldeke. Leiden, 1879.

Tavernier, Jean Baptiste. Six Travels through Turkey and Persia to the Indies, tr. J. Philips. London, 1684.

Texier, C. F. M. Description de l'Arménie, la Perse, et la Mesopotamie. 2 vols. Paris, 1842–52.

Thaʿālibī, al-. Histoire des Rois des Perses. Texte Arabe publié et traduit par H. Zotenberg. Paris, 1900.

Tomaschek, Wilhelm. Zur Historischen Topographie von Persien. In Sb. d. Phil.-Hist. Classe d. kais. Akad. d. Wiss. zu Wien, 102 (1883), pp. 145–231.

Weeks, Edwin Lord. From the Black Sea through Persia and India. New York, 1896.

Weissbach, F. H., and Bang, W. Die Altpersischen Keilinschriften. 1. Lieferung. Leipzig, 1893.

Weissbach, F. H. Die Achämenideninschriften Zweiter Art. Leipzig, 1890.

West, E. W. Pahlavi Literature. In Grundriss der Iranischen Philologie, 2. 75–129, Strassburg, 1896–1904.

West, E. W. Pahlavi Texts. 5 vols. Oxford, 1880–97. (Sacred Books of the East, vols. 5, 18, 24, 37, 47.)

Wilson, Charles. Handbook for Travellers in Asia Minor, Transcaucasia, Persia, etc. London, 1895.

Wilson, S. G. Persian Life and Customs. New York, 1895.

Yākūt. Geographisches Wörterbuch, ed. Wüstenfeld. Leipzig, 1866.

Yākūt. Dictionnaire géographique, historique, et litteraire de la Perse, extrait du Módjem el-Bouldan de Yaqout, par C. Barbier de Meynard. Paris, 1861.

Zotenberg, H. See Thaʿālibī.

ABBREVIATIONS

Abh.	= Abhandlung.
A.H.	= (*Anno Hegirae*), Mohammedan era.
AJP.	= American Journal of Philology.
Artax. Pers.	= inscriptions of Artaxerxes at Persepolis.
Av.	= Avestan.
Bd.	= Būndahishn.
Bh.	= Behistan inscription of Darius.
BYt.	= Pahlavi Bahman Yasht.
c.	= (*circa*), about.
d.	= died.
Dar. Alv.	= inscription of Darius on Mt. Alvand (Elvend), near Hamadan.
Dar. Pers.	= inscriptions of Darius at Persepolis.
ed.	= edition of, edited by.
Gk.	= Greek.
ibid.	= (*ibidem*), in the same work.
id.	= (*idem*), the same author.
IF.	= Indogermanische Forschungen.
JAOS.	= Journal of the American Oriental Society.
JRAS.	= Journal of the Royal Asiatic Society.
JRGS.	= Journal of the Royal Geographical Society.
KZ.	= Kuhn's Zeitschrift für Vergleichende Sprachforschung.
l.c.	= (*loco citato*), at the place previously cited.
MKh.	= Dīnā-ī Maīnōg-ī Khirad.
Mod. Pers.	= Modern Persian.
Nir.	= Nīrangistān.
NR.	= inscriptions of Darius at Naksh-i Rustam.
Ny.	= Nyāish.
OP.	= Old Persian.
op. cit.	= (*opus citatum*), the work previously cited.
Pers.	= Persian.
Phl.	= Pahlavi.
pl.	= plate.

Sb.	= Sitzungsberichte.
SBE.	= Sacred Books of the East.
seq.	= (*sequentia*), and the following.
Sir.	= Sīrōzah.
s.v.	= (*sub verbo*), under the word.
tr.	= translation of, translated by.
Vd.	= Vendīdād.
v.l.	= (*varia lectio*), variant reading.
Vsp.	= Visperad.
WZKM.	= Wiener Zeitschrift für die Kunde des Morgenlandes.
Xerx. Pers.	= inscriptions of Xerxes at Persepolis.
Ys.	= Yasna.
Yt.	= Yasht.
ZDMG.	= Zeitschrift der Deutschen Morgenländischen Gesellschaft.
Zsp.	= Zātsparam.
Zt.	= Zeitschrift.
Zt. f. Assyr.	= Zeitschrift für Assyriologie.

PERSIA PAST AND PRESENT

CHAPTER I

EN ROUTE FOR THE LAND OF THE LION AND THE SUN

'I am bound
To Persia, and want guilders for my voyage.'
—Shakspere, *A Comedy of Errors*, 4. 1. 3.

It was at the end of January, 1903, that I received leave
of absence from Columbia University for half a year to enable
me to visit the Orient again. The previous voyage had been
to India and Ceylon, two years before; my present goal was
Persia and Central Asia. The purpose of my journey was
antiquarian study and scholarly research, especially with
regard to Zoroaster and the ancient faith of the Magi, for
I had come early under the spell of those Wise Men from
the East and had long felt the charm drawing me toward the
Province of the Sun; but I hoped also to contribute something
to our knowledge of Persia's present, as well as past, and to
a better understanding of the relations existing between them.

My plan was to traverse as much of the territory known
to Zoroaster as I could, including Transcaspia and Turkistan,
and to visit the places most celebrated in the history of Persia.
The route which I marked in advance on the map, and was
able to accomplish, carried me from the Caucasus on the north
nearly to the Persian Gulf on the south, thence to Yezd in
the central desert and back northward to Teheran and the
Caspian Sea. Crossing this, I continued the journey into the
heart of Asia, to Merv, Bokhara, and Samarkand.

It is a far cry from New York to the Caspian — more than seven thousand miles — but this distance had first to be covered before the real journey began. The first four thousand miles of the trip by steamer and rail were uneventful. At Berlin I stayed a few days to see my teacher, Professor Karl F. Geldner, whose writings first inspired me with an interest in Persia, and to make some visits among old friends, as well as calls upon officials, before starting on my forty-eight-hour journey to St. Petersburg, where I found my friend and former pupil Mr. Montgomery Schuyler, Jr., then a secretary at the American Embassy. I had brought with me official letters of recommendation from Washington to St. Petersburg, as well as to Teheran and Tabriz, which proved an open sesame to the Ministers of State, and I shall not forget the kindness of the various official representatives, Russian and American, at the capital of the Tsar. Besides this I met with courtesies from scholar friends both there and at Moscow; they had not only been in Persia, but were well acquainted with Transcaspia and Turkistan and could give valuable suggestions for the journey.

At Moscow, rich in historic memories, I had an excellent opportunity to inspect the interesting Verestchagin collection of paintings in the Tretiakoff Gallery. This collection is particularly rich in paintings which illustrate Central Asian life, and they gave me a glimpse in advance of the scenes which I should see at Merv, Bokhara, and Samarkand. After a day's stay I took the weekly *train de luxe* bound southward toward the Caucasus, the Caspian, and the highway to Persia.

For three full days the train rolled on through the steppe-country, level, and uninteresting when covered with snow. The stops were infrequent but long, and I welcomed each time the third of the set of bell signals which the Russian railways employ at their stations, because it was a sign for the journey to be resumed toward the goal I had in view.

At Vladikavkas, on the morning of the fourth day — it was

OLD FORTIFICATIONS AT ELIZABETPOL, THE ANCIENT GANJAH

Thursday, I remember — I caught my first sight of the giant barrier of the Caucasus towering against a cloudy sky and frowning down on the white plain beneath. Its beetling cliffs were bare of snow in places, and here and there a deep gorge or ravine looked like the scar of some Titan wound upon its sullen face. The lonely scene grew in impressive grandeur as the day wore on. The old myth of Prometheus rose before my imagination. Far in the distance I could picture the desolate vulture-peak where the demigod lay chained in fetters because he had stolen fire from heaven as a boon for men. Well might the suffering benefactor of mankind have longed for the sun to rise and 'dispel the hoar frost at dawn,' or, when scorched by the heat and torn by the ravening bird, have yearned for 'starry-kirtled night to hide day's sheen.'[1] I could hear faint echoes of the dialogue with Io and mutterings of the Titan's curse against the wrath of Zeus. Little did I dream when I read *Prometheus* in college days that I should ever see the place where Æschylus had laid his tragic scene.

The streams rushing from the mountains and the flocks of sheep huddled together in the open places of the snow recalled to my mind the story of Colchis and the Golden Fleece. I learned *en route* that tradition tells how the shepherds of by-gone days were wont to find grains of gold clinging to the new-shorn fleece when they lifted it from the stream where it was washed, because the mountain torrent had left a golden deposit amid the woolly strands. The legend of the rich reward seems not to be quite forgotten.

For a moment, Greek mythology, classic reminiscences, and thoughts of college days made me forget that the land of my quest was Iran, not Hellas, and that I was seemingly deserting the Orient for Greece. I had to recall myself once more to the East.

All day the railway skirted the great plain beneath the Caucasus, which was never more than twenty miles distant.

[1] Æschylus, *Prometheus Bound*, 20 seq.

The scenery at this time of the year was barren and dreary. Hardly a trace of vegetation was visible except where the wind had blown a space bare in the snow and revealed a possible promise of verdure when spring should come. Flocks of sheep and goats were to be seen wherever a bit of fodder could be found, and scant herds of rugged cattle lounged disconsolately about.

I was interested in watching the changes in the types of the people as the journey progressed. Some of the natives represented to perfection the type of the Scythian shepherd in antiquity; they wore huge sheepskin coats and had their feet wrapped in coarse bagging which was lashed about the legs with thongs; their heads were covered with a cap of heavy fur which was almost indistinguishable from the shock of hair and heavy beard. A few looked a little more modern because of the long rifle with which they stood guard over their flocks. Most of them had the shambling gait of the East and the Oriental fashion of squatting, which was particularly noticeable around the railway stations. All of them had dark complexions which looked weather-beaten and coarse. The Iranian type of features grew more and more pronounced as the Caspian was approached, and I could recognize distinct likenesses to the Pathans and Waziris, those Afghan tribesmen of Iranian blood, whom I had seen in the Khaiber Pass two years before. It is clear that Iran begins ethnologically with the Caucasus and the Caspian, the historic borderland between Europe and Asia, although the Russian frontier line to-day has encroached a hundred or two miles over the old Persian border.

Darkness had fallen when the train arrived at Petrorvsk, but through the gloom I could catch sight of the white waves of the Caspian lashed into foam by the wintry winds. Before daylight the next morning, Friday, March 6, I had reached Baku. Instead of proceeding thence across the Caspian to Teheran, which would have been more convenient in many ways, I decided to continue the journey to Tiflis in order to

The Old Citadel of Tiflis

General View of Tiflis

enter Persia through Azarbaijan, the region which gave birth to Zoroaster, as I believe.

The journey from Baku to Tiflis by rail occupies about fourteen hours. A great part of the route traverses the southern side of the Caucasus range along whose northern base we coasted the day before. The scenery is less magnificent, but the plain is rich, and the mountain range on the south running parallel with its sister chain on the north, from the Caspian to the Black Sea, looks higher because of its proximity to the railway. The cattle visible on the plain were of the same general character as the day before, but troop after troop of camels showed that the East had been reached. Some of these had rough blankets thrown over their backs to protect them from the rigors of the weather, as the climate was a contrast to that of the desert where they had been bred. The Persian buffalo could be seen here and there, and all were busily engaged in nibbling the few traces of prospective grass that could be found in the plain.

There is little of interest to note on the way from Baku to Tiflis, but about halfway between the two cities the railroad passes the town of Elizabetpol, which was originally the Persian town of Ganjah, its name having been changed when the Russians took possession of the place in 1804. Its mosque near the bazaar is said to have been erected by the Persian monarch Shah Abbas in the seventeenth century, and numerous ancient remains in the neighborhood show the antiquity of the city. Its chief claim upon our interest perhaps is the fact that Ganjah was the home of the Persian poet Nizami, who died there about the year A.D. 1203. This romantic minstrel sang of the love of Khosru Parviz for the Armenian princess Shirin and the tragic passion of her artist lover Farhad, besides telling the legendary adventures of Alexander in epic strain and recounting old tales with imaginative grace.[1]

That whole afternoon of my journey the sky had for me a

[1] See p. 226, below.

poetic coloring; the sunshine was tempered by clouds which imparted a tinge of melancholy; there was a faint suggestion of spring in the air; but dusk and its accompanying chill came early, and evening had already closed in before Tiflis was reached. The night turned out clear and cold. The lamps of the terraced town shone bright like a myriad lights in the blue, and gave a fairy-like effect to the scene. Much of this impression was dispelled by day, but this was not due to lack of good accommodations at the Hotel de Londres, which is one of the last places for bidding adieu to Western comforts before entering Persia.

The Michaelis Bridge over the Kura at Tiflis

The Caucasian Museum, Tiflis

CHAPTER II

TIFLIS, THE CAPITAL OF TRANSCAUCASIA

'Parthians, and Medes, and Elamites, and the dwellers in Mesopotamia, and in Judæa, and Cappadocia, in Pontus, and Asia.'
— NEW TESTAMENT, *Acts* 2. 9.

TIFLIS is a combination of Orient and Occident. It is one of those cities in which Western civilization has been welded on to Eastern custom, but the signs of the joining will never disappear. Its languages are as many as those at the gift of tongues at Pentecost, and its types are as multifarious as a union of ancient and modern life can bring together. Along its crowded thoroughfares the sheepskin-clad dweller of the Caucasus rubs elbows with the Armenian, Georgian, Persian, Kurd, Turk, and Tartar, or moves side by side with the European dressed in broadcloth. The ever shifting groups and constantly changing colors rival a kaleidoscope in variety. The winding alleys of the native quarters, the mazes of the bazaars, and the crowded passages between the booths are quite Oriental, but the European sections of the town, with broad streets, long avenues, and large squares, are Occidental and show the evidences of Russian advance.

Being the capital of Transcaspia, Tiflis is the head of the civil and military authority, as well as the seat of government. Its growth commercially has been remarkable in recent years; its busy heart throbs with the double pulse of East and West, and its claim to one hundred and sixty thousand inhabitants seems not at all exaggerated.

Historically Tiflis is a place of interest also, as it was the capital of ancient Georgia. It is said to have owed much of

7

its original renown to the Georgian emperor Vakhtang Gurgas-
lan, in the fifth century of our era, who was attracted to the
place by the health-giving properties of its sulphur baths. The
qualities of these hot springs are especially mentioned by the
Arab traveller Ibn Haukal, in the tenth century, who states
that 'the water is warm without fire,' and adds, 'Tiflis is
a pleasant place and abounds in provisions; it has two walls
of clay and produces much fruit, and agriculture is practised
in its territories.'[1]   In the latter part of the fourteenth century it suffered, in common with most cities of Asia, the misfortune of being plundered by Timur Lang, or Tamerlane.   Its
general development as a metropolis, though menaced at times
by the Turks, went on under Persian rule until 1801, when the
Russians took possession of Tiflis, and it has remained ever
since under the sway of Russian authority, although riots and
uprisings, due to the unruly character of the mixed population
of the Caucasus, have occurred from time to time.

The town is situated partly upon a hill, the site of the
ancient citadel, and approaches another elevation to the north
and east, so that the city has a somewhat terraced effect.
Through the middle of it, running from northwest to southeast and roughly dividing it in half, flows the river Kura, the
Cyrus of the ancients.   On either side of this rapid stream,
and forming the southern part of the town, are the native
quarters of Tiflis, the Georgian section (Avlabar) being on
the east, or left, bank, the bazaars on the west, or right, bank.
Adjoining the bazaars as we look northward, and still on the
same side of the river, is the Russian quarter, with its fine
edifices, broad avenues, and imposing Alexander Garden as a
centre.   Crossing the river from this point by one of its
several bridges, we enter the German district, which extends
northward from the Georgian quarter and owes its name to
a colony of sturdy dissenters from Würtemberg, who were
among a number that left the Fatherland early in the last

[1] Ibn Haukal, tr. Ouseley, p. 160.

century because of certain religious differences of opinion and made Tiflis their adopted home.

In the Russian quarter are stately buildings devoted to administration, the post, and banking, together with churches, theatres, clubs, shops, hotels, residences official and private, parks, and gardens, all of which show the introduction of Western ideas. One of the most interesting edifices is the Caucasian Museum with its rich collection of illustrative material relating to the region lying between the Caspian and the Black Sea. Here the student will find a storehouse of antiquarian wealth amassed with care and judgment by Dr. Gustav Radde, who devoted years of his life to the cause. When I arrived at Tiflis, I learned that this enthusiastic and scholarly collector was seriously ill with what eventually proved to be his last sickness. Despite his feeble condition he insisted upon my coming to call at his bedside and sent a special guide to conduct me around the museum. The kindly greeting which he gave me and the gentle farewell that followed I shall always remember.

The museum well repays a careful visit. As a special collection to illustrate the natural history, flora and fauna, ethnology, and archæology of the Caucasus region — a region particularly interesting as being the bridge between Asia and Europe — it is unmatched. Two exhibits of aquatic life and land animals around the Caspian Sea particularly interested me because of their being referred to in the Avesta, or Zoroastrian Bible. One of these was a fine specimen of the giant sturgeon, known as the *accipenser huso*, a fish fifteen feet or more long, and mentioned in the Avesta, as I believe, under the name of *kara masya*, or *kar*-fish.[1] The other was a group of wild boars, admirably mounted by the taxidermist so as to display all the fierceness and combativeness of the *varāza*, or wild boar, described in the Zoroastrian texts.[2]

To us of the West the chief attraction of Tiflis lies not in its

[1] See Vd. 19. 42 ; Yt. 14. 29 ; Pahlavi Vsp. 1. 1 ; Bd. 18. 3 ; etc.   [2] See Yt. 14. 15 seq.

European features, but in its Oriental side and the remains which it shows of an older civilization. A survival of Oriental mediævalism is seen in the fortress which crowns the height overlooking the city and commands the town with its old-time battlements. Still older are the remains of a tower and ruined aqueduct which overlook the Botanical Garden to the south of Tiflis. The bridges that cross the river Kura (Cyrus) and connect the two halves of the city are partly old and partly new. The most interesting, perhaps, because most crowded, is the bridge of the Tartar Meidan, which leads to one of the sections of the native bazaars. These bazaars are not so Oriental as the Persian bazaars, but their crowded booths, the variety of wares displayed, and the bargains they offer in Daghistan rugs and Caucasian armor, afford an attractive place of visit for those who have not travelled in the East before.

During my stay of three or four days at Tiflis I gathered some additional information regarding the Yezidis, or Devil-Worshippers, a people to whom my attention had previously been drawn in connection with my studies about Zoroaster and the religion of ancient Persia. A Swedish missionary, the Rev. E. John Larson and his wife, who have done much evangelistic work among the Yezidis of Tiflis and the vicinity and have thus become familiar with their manners, customs, and beliefs, were my informants.

The Yezidis are chiefly found in the Caucasus, Armenia, and Kurdistan, although they are scattered over a considerably wider territory, their headquarters being in the province of Mosul, Mesopotamia. Owing to the persecutions which they have suffered throughout their history, their number is not large; nevertheless they are said to number twelve thousand in the region of the Caucasus alone, and there are at least several hundred Yezidis living in the immediate vicinity of Tiflis. They do not speak of themselves ordinarily as Yezidis, but employ the names of their respective tribes or adopt by preference the term Dasni, a tribal designation in the neighborhood of

RUINED TOWER AND AQUEDUCT OVERLOOKING THE BOTANICAL GARDEN

THE TARTAR MEIDAN AT TIFLIS

Mosul, close to the site of ancient Nineveh, which was one of the original homes of the religion. Various explanations have been proposed for the name *Yezīdī*, among them one which associates it with *Yazdān*, the Persian word for God, as the Yezidis undeniably believe in a god, although they do not ordinarily speak of him. A second suggestion is to connect it with the town of Yezd. A third seeks to derive the name from Yezid, the detested Mussulman Kaliph who slew Husein, the grandson of Mohammed, for Yezid is fabled to have been a champion of their faith. But none of these suggestions seem very satisfactory.[1]

According to the belief of the Yezidis, God, the creator of heaven and earth, first made from his own essence six other divinities, the sun, the moon, and the principal stars, and these joined with him in creating the angels. The devil, who was God's own creation, rebelled against his lord and was cast into hell. He afterward repented of his sin, did penance for seven thousand years, and shed tears of contrition which fill seven vessels that will be used at the Day of Judgment to quench the fires of the seven hells. God in his mercy pardoned the recreant, restored him to heavenly rank, made him one with himself, and forbade the angels to look with scorn upon their reinstated brother. Inasmuch as God's grace thus forgave and exalted even Satan himself, man should not look with hatred upon this so-called representative of evil. On this account the Yezidis never allow the name of Satan to pass their lips, avoiding even a syllable that suggests the word, and shrinking with horror from any mention of the devil by others. They venerate his sacred majesty under the name of *Malik Ṭā'ūs*, 'King Peacock,' a title which they apply to the holy

---

[1] For further details on this and the general subject of the Yezidis, see my article 'Yezidi' in the *New International Encyclopædia*, 17. 939; my note in *JAOS*. 25. 178–181; Spiro, *Les Yezidi*, Neuchatel, 1900 (in *Bulletin Soc. Neuchâtel. Géog.* 12. 275 seq.); Adams, *Persia by a Persian*, pp. 497–509, Grand Rapids, Mich., 1900; Layard, *Nineveh and its Remains*, part 1, ch. 9, pp. 270–325, London, 1854; id. *Nineveh and Babylon*, London, 1853.

standard (*sanjak*) or symbol of their religion, which is a peacock, conventionalized in their art so as almost to resemble a cock. Malik Taus revealed himself in the form of a handsome youth with a peacock's tail when he appeared in a vision before Sheikh Aadi, the prophet of the faith.

I have sometimes thought that this reverence shown for the power of evil may be similar in character to the propitiatory sacrifice offered in ancient times to the divinity beneath the earth by Amestris, the wife of Xerxes, according to Herodotus and other authorities.[1] It seems possible also that the *daēva-yasna*, or 'Devil-Worshippers,' anathematized in the Avesta may have entertained kindred ideas about venerating the realm of darkness, and that the Yezidis and their strange beliefs preserve traces of the devil-worship in Mazandaran which Zoroaster so bitterly denounced.

It is clear that the Yezidi faith shows some ancient Iranian traits, such as certain marked dualistic features, a reverence for the elements, fire, water, and earth, and a belief in a father primeval, who lived before Adam and did not fall in sin. This latter belief appears to be a reminiscence of the Avestan Gaya-maretan, who lived before Mashya and Mashyoi, the Iranian Adam and Eve. The Yezidis likewise refrain from spitting upon the ground — an observance as old as the Magi[2] — nor will they pour boiling water upon the earth for fear of scalding the face of the little devils. I have often been told that if a circle be drawn on the ground around a Yezidi he will stand for hours in the middle of it without venturing to step over the charmed line, which reminds one of the *karshvars* drawn in Avestan rites of exorcism according to the Vendidad. It is thought, moreover, that the Yezidi religion shows distant survivals of the old Assyro-Babylonian worship of the sun, moon, and stars, for the faith appears to have retained the sun-god Shamash under the form of Sheikh Shems and the

[1] Herodotus, *Hist.* 7. 114 ; cf. 3. 35.   *paedia*, 8. 1. 42. See also Adams,
[2] *Ibid.* 1. 99, 138 ; Xenophon, *Cyro-*   *Persia*, pp. 497, 499.

Yezidis, or so-called Devil-Worshippers, in Tiflis

moon-god Sin as Sheikh Sinn, an emanation of God himself.[1]

In many respects the Yezidi doctrines have been influenced
by Manichæism, and its doctrines of purity, by Nestorian
Christianity and especially by Mohammedanism. With each
of these religions the Yezidis have come into contact. They
recognize Mohammed as a prophet of equal rank with Abraham
and the patriarchs, and they believe that Christ was an angel
in human form. One curious statement that I heard is that
the Yezidis sacrifice one sheep every year to Christ and thirty
to the devil. The rite of baptism is practised among them,
and circumcision is general, but not universal. A part of their
marriage ceremony consists in the bridegroom and bride dividing a piece of bread between them, but the Yezidis also allow
Mohammedan priests formally to officiate at their weddings
and even at their funerals. They recognize, however, a regular system of priesthood of their own, headed by a Myr, or
high priest, together with various ecclesiastics and clerical
functionaries, and including an order of mendicant devotees,
male and female, *fakīr* and *fakīriah*. The Yezidis have no sacrifices or temples in the true sense of the term, but they have
a number of religious ceremonies and observe several fasts and
festivals, most important among the latter being the autumnal
worship of the effigy of Malik Taus, an occasion which is
accompanied by offerings and prayers. Among their peculiar
superstitions is a curious abhorrence for the color blue.

In their daily life the Yezidis are not forbidden the use of
wine, as the Mohammedans are, but they do not indulge in
it to excess. Nor is polygamy prohibited, although it is apparently not much practised on account of the poverty of the
people. The belief in a future life, and a system of rewards
and punishments hereafter, forms part of their faith. Among
these punishments is the condemnation to assume in another
existence the form of some animal, for the doctrine of trans-

[1] Spiro, *Les Yezidi*, pp. 20, 25.

migration is a recognized one.[1] The Yezidis have a book of
divine revelation, which they call Al-Yalvah, and they name
as its great expounder their sainted head Sheikh Aadi, who
lived about A.D. 1200.[2]

As to their social status I was informed that the Yezidis
around Tiflis and Erivan occupy an inferior position, and I
understand that the same is true elsewhere. Their occupations
at Tiflis are largely menial, as they are employed chiefly in
drudgery work and as scavengers. For that reason they go
clad in the meanest rags. The stories which were told me
about them reminded me somewhat of the 'sweeper class' in
India; but recent Russian municipal ordinances at Tiflis have
partly transferred the duties of the Yezidis to other hands, so
that their occupations have varied considerably within the past
year or two. In general they are accustomed to live outside
the town and come into the city for work during the day. The
wife carries on the household duties and does the agricultural
work connected with the soil. The wants of the Yezidi and
his family are meagre, and they appear to lead contented lives.
Around Tiflis, moreover, there are said to be a considerable
number of Yezidis who, despite their impoverished appearance,
possess considerable money.

Most of the last day in Tiflis was devoted to making final
preparations for my journey and to completing the necessary
outfit, for Persia is still without railroads and hotels, except at
Teheran, and travelling through the country is synonymous
with roughing it.

For caravan transport the 'kit' should be as light and com-
pact as possible, but a folding cot, serving alike as bed, desk,
and dining-table, is indispensable. A European saddle and
bridle, boots or riding-leggings, will also be found to be a *sine*

---

[1] For general details see my note,
JAOS. 25. 181; Adams, *Persia*, pp. 499,
505–506; Spiro, *Les Yezidi*, pp. 14 (286),
16 (288), 29 (301).

[2] So my informant; but Adams,
Persia by a Persian, p. 501, says
'about the middle of the tenth century.'

TYPES OF YEZIDIS, OR DEVIL-WORSHIPPERS, AT TIFLIS

TIFLIS CITADEL (ANOTHER VIEW)

qua non. As for clothing, it is well to remember that the cold in the mountains is intense in winter and the heat of the deserts is equally extreme in summer. In either case dark smoked glasses will be found to be a great protection against the snow, sun, or dust. Besides the necessary cooking utensils and travelling articles, I took also an extra supply of straps, padlocks, two cameras, some books, including a map, several knick-knacks for gifts, and sundry other things which one is likely to need on a long journey. For packing this outfit my experience showed that two stout leather suit-cases and a portmanteau were sufficient, if supplemented by some native pouches. It is important above all in caravaning to have several small bundles, rather than one or two large ones, for the parcels can thus be more easily distributed so as to balance equally on the packhorse.

At the hotel I engaged the services of a Georgian guide, old Rustom, to conduct me to the frontier; his name pleased me because of its historic associations with Rustam, the Persian hero. As a guide he was well informed and reliable, and well equipped linguistically, since he spoke no less than six languages. French was our medium of communication.

The luggage, including camp-bed and saddle, was dexterously packed, the final arrangements were all completed, and before many hours I was on the train, started for a trip of fifteen more hours to Erivan, where the railroad now ends beneath the shadow of Mount Ararat.

CHAPTER III

ERIVAN, MOUNT ARARAT, AND THE ROAD TO THE PERSIAN BORDER

'The ark rested upon the mountains of Ararat.'
— OLD TESTAMENT, *Genesis* **8**. 4.

TOWARD sunset on the following day, as the train approached the ancient town of Erivan, I caught my first view of Mount Ararat, crested with clouds and wrapped in snow over which the sun shed a soft roseate hue. Rising solitary from the plain, not backed by ranges of lesser hills, Ararat possesses a lonely grandeur which makes it a fitting place for the ark to have rested upon at the solemn death-hour of an older race and the birth of a new generation.

This stupendous mountain, which comprises two contiguous bases, lifts its huge mass nearly seventeen thousand feet above sea-level, or fourteen thousand above the surrounding plain. The summit of the larger peak, known as Great Ararat, is 16,916 feet high, and is crowned with eternal snow; the crest of Little Ararat, seven miles distant, is 12,840 feet, and it is hardly less impressive. Both peaks owe their origin to forces of a volcanic nature, and a great chasm, thousands of feet deep, torn in the northwestern side of Great Ararat, lays bare the dead giant's heart.[1]

The Avesta mentions Ararat, it is thought, under the name of Mazishvant (Yt. 19. 2), a term which recalls Masis, the designation given it by the Armenians, who believe it to be the mountain on which the ark rested, having taken over the tradition of the deluge with their acceptance of Christianity.

[1] For an excellent description of Ararat and an account of an ascent to its top, see Lynch, *Armenia*, 1. 142–199, London, 1901.

16

MOUNT ARARAT, NEAR ERIVAN

RUSTOM, MY GEORGIAN GUIDE TO THE FRONTIER

The Persian name for it is Koh-i Nuh, 'Noah's Mountain,'[1] while the Tartars merely call it Aghri Dagh, 'Steep Mountain,' the name given to the range running eastward. The old superstition current among the natives, to the effect that its summit cannot be reached by man, has long been dispelled, since no less than sixteen different ascents by Europeans have been recorded within the past hundred years.

Legends about Noah naturally cluster around Ararat and its vicinity. The place where the patriarch planted the vine and partook to excess of the juice of the grape was formerly shown near the village of Akhuri (Akori), or Arguri — a hamlet whose name, by popular etymology in Armenian, is supposed to mean 'he (Noah) planted the vine' (*ark uṙ*),[2] whence the modern form Arguri. In like manner the spot where he built an altar and offered burnt sacrifices to Jehovah used to be pointed out, as well as a stunted willow sprung from a plank of the ark.[3] These relics were swept away by a terrific earthquake which took place in the chasm near Akori, July 2, 1840, overwhelming the village and destroying its inhabitants. From the descriptions by those who survived the cataclysm it must have resembled the terrors of the Day of Judgment.

For two nights I slept a frozen sleep at Erivan beneath the heights of Ararat. The so-called 'hotel' at which I lodged was one merely in name and sign, and I almost perished with the cold. I look back with a shiver at the experience in those uncomfortable quarters; but later, when I became acquainted with exposure in Persian mud hovels, I thought that the hostelry may not actually have been so bad as it seemed.

Erivan is the capital of Russian Armenia and a place of nearly thirty thousand inhabitants. Its history is obscure, but local tradition is naturally not loath to carry the origin of the

---

[1] The ark is alluded to in the Koran, ch. 29.

[2] On this mistaken folk-etymology, see Hübschmann, *Die altarmenischen Ortsnamen*, in *Indogermanische Forschungen*, 16. 395, Strassburg, 1904.

[3] See Wilson, *Persian Life*, p. 46; Lynch, *Armenia*, 1. 182.

c

town back to the days of Noah.   The name Erivan, according
to some authorities, stands for Erevan and is derived from the
Armenian *erevan*, 'appearance,' since 'dry land first made its
appearance here after Noah's flood.'   According to others, it
owes its origin to the legendary king or heros eponymus Erovand, or to the Armenian leader Erovant or Ervand, who was
overthrown by the Persians in the first century of our era.[1]
The one etymology is as unlikely as the other.[2]   According
to the Armenian historian, John Katholikos, Erivan was a
place of considerable size in the seventh century, although we
know little if anything about it till the sixteenth, when the
possession of Erivan became a bone of contention between the
Persians and the Ottoman Turks.[3]   The question was finally
settled in 1827, when the Russians took possession of the city.
The bazaars accordingly show abundant evidence of the Russian occupation and advance in trade, and I was able at Erivan
to add to my kit a number of European necessaries not ordinarily found in Asiatic marts.

   In its general characteristics Erivan is Oriental, not Occidental, but it does not show the many signs of antiquity which
might be expected of its age.   This is largely due to the
frequent wars between the Turks and the Persians — wars
rendered more cruel by reason of the bitter hatred that exists
between the rival Mohammedan sects of Sunnis and Shiahs
to which the two nations respectively belong.   These conflicts
have helped to destroy numerous monuments which Erivan
must have boasted in the past.   There are still some mosques
and minarets worthy of attention, but the chief memorial of
the Persian period is the palace of the governors, or *sardārs*,

---

[1] See Lynch, *Armenia*, 1. 209 seq.
For the name Erovand, see Justi,
Iranisches Namenbuch, p.89.

[2] Hübschmann, *IF.* 16. 425.

[3] John Katholikos wrote in the
eleventh century, compiling the annals of his country down to the year
A.D. 925 (Lynch, *Armenia*, 1. 210,
n. 2).   The fact that the Arab traveller
Ibn Haukal does not mention Erivan
in the tenth century, nor Yakut in the
twelfth, can hardly be used as an
argument, as John Katholikos flourished between these two writers.

ERIVAN

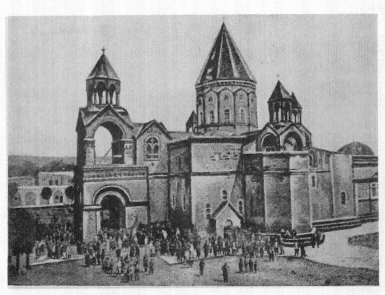

ARMENIAN CHURCH AND MONASTERY AT ECHMIADZIN

adjoining a mosque whose dome is decorated with colored tiles and inlaid arabesques. The palace itself forms part of a fortified enclosure overlooking the Zangi River, which sweeps beneath its mud walls. Although falling into decay, the audience-hall of the palace still shows signs of former splendor, with fretted ceilings inlaid in Persian style with tiny mirrors, and with walls adorned by historic paintings. Among the more modern portraits is that of Fath Ali Shah, the great-great-grandfather of the present Shah; but the paintings which interested me most were those of Sohrab and Rustam, whose fatal conflict Matthew Arnold has retold from Firdausi, and of Feramurz, Rustam's second son. At the end of the great chamber was a huge latticed window, whose panels were inlaid with small patines of colored glass, through which the sun shone with a rich iridescence. The view through this dazzling frame as the afternoon faded was fine. Far in the distance, but ever close at hand, loomed snow-clad Ararat; beneath the palace walls and the buttresses of the fort swept the river Zangi, held in check only by its precipitous banks; a caravan wended its way slowly across the bridge; and through the deserted hall of princes shone a gleam of sunlight reflecting the splendor of by-gone days.

The greater part of my second day at Erivan was spent in a visit to the Armenian church and monastery of Echmiadzin, about thirteen miles distant, near the village of Vagharshapat. This celebrated cloister is the seat of the Katholikos, or patriarch, of the Armenian church. It is said to have been founded by Gregory the Illuminator, who converted the Armenians to Christianity early in the fourth century, and relics of the saint are preserved among its treasures. The library contains a valuable collection of Armenian manuscripts, among which I noted some particularly fine copies of the gospels,[1] some

---

[1] The most recent notes on these are by Meillet, *Journal Asiatique*, 165 (10th ser. 14), pp. 487–507, Paris, 1904; id. *Quelques Évangéliaires Arméniens Accentués*, extr. from *Des Mémoires Orientaux*, Paris, 1905.

ancient boundary stones inscribed with cuneiform characters
(not Persian), a rich assortment of Parthian, Roman, and
Sasanian coins, and many other objects of interest to the
archæological student.   The priest who conducted me through
the various buildings had studied Oriental languages under
my teacher Geldner in Berlin, so that we had a bond of
sympathy at once, and excellent opportunities were afforded
me to see the collections.

The next afternoon I arranged to leave Erivan for Julfa on
the Persian border.   It was now necessary to procure a post-
chaise, as the railroad had been laid no farther than Erivan,
but I had the greatest difficulty in obtaining any sort of
conveyance.   A party of Russian engineers had first claim
on all horses, as they were on their way to Persia to build
for the government macadamized roads, over which the railway lines can be laid down later.   At last a vehicle was
secured; it was a heavy phaeton, with a large leather hood
over the back, and it was drawn by four horses.   There was
much ado in getting the baggage lashed securely on behind,
and after many delays and petty annoyances the journey was
finally begun.

Progress was difficult and slow.   Ice, snow, and slimy mud
filled the roads and rendered speed impossible.   The inner court
of the first caravansarai at which we halted looked like a lake,
although the room on each side of the entrance was habitable.
I took the one on the right, as the left was already occupied by
rough natives who wore heavy sheepskin caps and were armed
with daggers and long guns.   If there had been any Armenians among them, I presume my Georgian guide Rustom would
have called them hogs, for he muttered *cochon* every time we
passed a group of Armenians on the road.   I was too tired to
take particular notice of my surroundings and was glad at
the haste with which Rustom arranged my camp-bed.   In an
instant I was asleep.

Shortly after midnight I awoke with a start.   A dark figure

ECHMIADZIN IN THE SNOW

BAZAAR OF ERIVAN

with long ebon beard and black cowl concealing the face stood at the foot of my cot. In the uncertain light the form looked like that of a giant. I grasped instinctively for my revolver, but a salutation came from the muffled lips, and I saw that the newcomer had no malicious intent. He was accompanied by an elderly woman, robed partly in black, and she nodded a silent greeting. Both used Russian, but spoke very little. We interchanged civilities and cigarettes, but I did not inquire about the purpose of their journey, nor they about mine. As we were to start before daylight, I made no attempt to sleep again, and in a couple of hours I had resumed my seat in the post-chaise, followed by the vehicle of my fellow-travellers. The darkness was thick, the snow blinding, and the road was continually blocked by trains of camels, caravan succeeding caravan in endless procession. I counted two hundred of these dromedaries in less than a quarter of an hour. They were chained in strings of eight, ten, or a dozen, and their heavy bells, donging monotonously as each one passed, made the count easy.[1]

Toward dawn I could catch a glimpse of the wagon of our companions following through the snow. Across the front of their vehicle was a long, narrow box, and I then learned that it was an empty coffin in which the woman was to bring back the body of one of her sons, who had died ten days before in a remote district. I now knew the reason for her travelling through the storm. The return journey must have been even more sad for her.

The sunless day was passed driving mile after mile in the teeth of biting sleet and hail. My face was frost-bitten, my hands were chapped, and altogether I suffered severely from the cold, relieved only when we halted at a post-house for a change of horses. I did not, however, mind the discomforts so much as might be expected, since something new was constantly occurring in this desolate region shrouded in snow,

[1] The Persian camel bell dongs rather than dings.

and I enjoyed the novelty of the experiences.   Once a wolf skulked across the plain near our path, but it was too dark for a shot, and he disappeared into the gloom.

We travelled on through the night until we reached Nakhi-chavan, or Nakhjavan, where there was a chance for a slight rest.   This place was known to the Greek geographer Ptolemy, in the second century A.D., as Naxouana[1]; but it lays claim to far greater antiquity, since tradition and popular etymology make it 'Noah's first station' (Armenian *nakh-ijevan*) after he came from the ark, and his reputed tomb is shown as a sacred shrine.[2]   Ibn Haukal, among others, mentions Nakhjavan in the tenth century of our era, and Yakut, two hundred years later, tells something of its history,[3] for events of considerable moment have taken place there, and we know that, situated near the river Aras, it has been several times the scene of bloody encounters between warring armies.[4]   Ridiculously enough, my recollections of Nakhichavan are chiefly associated with the excellent bread I found at the rest-house, in contrast to the Persian bread on which I had afterward to subsist.   Finally, in the forenoon of Saturday, March 14, I reached Julfa, on the Aras, the ancient Araxes.   In the classic writers this river was proverbial for its swift current, whose rushing descent from the Armenian mountains carried away the bridges in the winter time, so that Vergil calls it 'the stream intolerant of any span' —*pontem indignatus Araxes.*[5]   The river is now the boundary between Persia and Russia, although historically the confines of Iran have always extended far beyond the Aras.

At Julfa an incident occurred in connection with the Russian export customs for which I was not prepared.   The customs officers when examining my baggage kept asking only one

---

[1] Ptolemy, *Geog.* 5. 13 (941).

[2] See Wilson, *Persian Life*, p. 47; Perkins, *Eight Years in Persia*, p. 134, Andover, 1843; and, on the fanciful etymology, consult Hübschmann, *IF.* 16. 455.

[3] Ibn Haukal, p. 165; Yakut, tr. Barbier de Meynard, pp. 561, 565, n. 1.

[4] Cf. Lynch, *Armenia*, 1. 345.

[5] Vergil, *Æneid*, 8. 728.

A CARAVAN IN THE SNOW

question, but I did not understand Russian, nor did they know either French, German, or English. The inspection came to a standstill, therefore, until old Rustom, who had not previously been allowed to enter the customs lines, was summoned. In answer to the inspector's query he promptly asserted that I was not carrying arms, to which I responded as promptly that I had a revolver at my belt. My straightforward reply cost me the pistol, as a new tariff law forbade the exporting of firearms to Persia; but my honesty was repaid by my not having to see the weapon confiscated, and permission was granted me to send it back to Tiflis by Rustom. The person to whom I consigned it afterward presented the weapon to an American missionary whose revolver had been stolen on a journey. I parted with the pistol with regret, and afterward when alone in remote places in Persia I several times missed this steel companion with heart of lead.

The customs examination being finished, I said good-by to Rustom, since he could accompany me no farther, being a Russian subject and therefore not allowed to leave the Tsar's kingdom without permission. I had to cross the Aras alone. Standing on the shore and awaiting some means of transport, I felt with Troilus 'like a strange soul upon the Stygian bank, staying for waftage.' Charon's boat, which was to ferry me over this Persian Styx, arrived at last. It came in the form of a rude scow made of coarse planks knocked together in the roughest possible fashion. Fiends clamoring for obols held the oars, dropping them eagerly to grasp bakhshish or clenching the fist to demand more. Fortunately the crossing was quickly effected, and when we reached the Iranian 'Lethe's wharf' I quite forgot the dark past, remembering only the joy of awakening in the longed-for paradise of the Province of the Sun.

CHAPTER IV

PERSIA, THE LAND AND ITS HISTORY, AND OUR INTEREST IN THE COUNTRY

'What have we to do
With Kaikobád the Great, or Kaikhosrú ? '
—FitzGerald, *Rubaiyat of Omar Khayyam*, 10.

'My father's kingdom,' said Cyrus the Younger, 'extends so far to the south that men cannot live there because of the heat, and northward to where they cannot exist because of the cold.'[1] This proud boast may be taken almost literally, for Persia is a land of extremes, from the frigid winters of the high altitudes of Azarbaijan to the torrid summers of the Persian Gulf ; but the climate in the interior as a whole is temperate when we consider the latitude — Shiraz, for example, being farther south than Lahore in upper India. This fact is sometimes lost sight of.

Geographically the country of Persia is a great tableland — the plateau of Iran — which extends beyond its eastern borders into Afghanistan and covers altogether an area nearly one-fifth as large as the United States. Mountains with rocky passes guard the approach at almost every point of the frontier and run their barriers into the interior to hold back the great deserts which threaten to invade from the east. A part of the vast tableland is well watered, but there are no rivers in Persia that are worthy of the name, and most of them lose their streams in the soil before becoming tributary to other bodies. In many parts of the kingdom, therefore, owing to the dearth of water, it is necessary to resort to irrigation in order to convert other-

[1] Xenophon, *Anabasis*, 1. 7. 6.

24

THE DIEULAFOY FRIEZE OF ARCHERS FROM SUSA

wise arid districts into arable lands or to prevent them from sinking back into barren wastes. Irrigation was synonymous with righteousness in the old Zoroastrian religion, and agriculture a religious duty. The soil of the country responds rapidly to tillage, and there are districts in Persia which are accounted among the most fertile in the world.

Over this wide and varied expanse of territory there is spread a population which is estimated at more than ten million souls. The number is not large for the area occupied, and Persia is not counted as a densely settled country. Ethnologically the people are of Aryan stock, but they show an admixture of foreign blood introduced by conquest or due to contact with border nations. This latter is especially true in the case of the strong infusion of Turkish and Tartar blood in the northwest and northeast. In general the inhabitants of Farsistan, the original Persis, have remained freest from foreign elements and have preserved more nearly the Persian type of Darius, who boasts in his inscription that he is 'a Persian, the son of a Persian, an Aryan and of Aryan blood.'[1] Purest of all, perhaps, though few in number, are the Zoroastrians, who have maintained the old Iranian religion and have never intermarried with alien races.

Historically Persia is one of the great nations of antiquity. Of all the Eastern countries which came into contact with Greece and Rome, Persia alone has preserved her independence. Her monarchs have been rulers for three thousand years, and the Shah on the Peacock Throne to-day may boast his claim as inheritor of King Jamshid's legendary rule as well as the sceptre of the Median Deioces and the crown of Cyrus the Great.

Bactria, Media, and Persia were the three historic kingdoms of Iran. Bactria, whose dynasties are partly legendary, was subjugated by Media after the latter, under Deioces, had thrown off the Assyrian yoke about B.C. 708. Phraortes, his

---

[1] Inscr. Nakhsh-i Rustam, a 13–15.

son and successor (B.C. 647–625), and Cyaxares, his grandson
(B.C. 625–585), were wise and powerful rulers, extending the sway
of Media as far as Egypt; but Astyages, the son of Cyaxares,
proved a feeble monarch, and Media forfeited her supremacy.
The province of Persia, led by Cyrus, revolted against her;
Astyages was defeated in battle, and Cyrus became king of the
united Medo-Persian empire (B.C. 558–530), and founder of the
Achæmenian dynasty. Then followed Cambyses, his mad son,
whose misrule lasted for eight years, ending in death by his
own hand (B.C. 522) on the way back from Egypt to recover
his crown, which had been seized by a Magian priest, Gaumata,
called Smerdis the Usurper, from his impersonating the king's
dead brother. The imposture was discovered, and the false
Smerdis was slain by Darius Hystaspes, who now ascended the
throne (B.C. 522). This able monarch reorganized the empire
on broad and far-reaching lines and ruled with great ability
for more than thirty years (B.C. 522–486). Signs of weakness
had already shown themselves, however, in the unsuccessful
attempt of Darius to invade Greece, but these marks of decadence became more and more manifest in the reigns of Xerxes
and Artaxerxes, until the tottering throne of the Achæmenidæ
fell when Darius III (Codomannus) was conquered by Alexander the Great and afterward perished (B.C. 323). The Grecian
arms thus proved triumphant over the Persians within the
borders of Iran, as they already had at Marathon, Salamis, and
Platæa.

The invasion and partial subjugation of Persia by Alexander
resulted in the establishment of the Græco-Bactrian government of the Seleucidæ, which lasted for seventy years and was
followed by the Parthian dynasty, which ruled the fortunes of
Persia for five centuries (B.C. 250–A.D. 226). They in turn
yielded to the triumphant ascendancy of the Iranian house of
Sasan, who restored the Zoroastrian faith as state religion and
dreamed of forming a great national power. Their rule lasted
over four centuries (A.D. 226–651), but their hope of establish-

DARIUS III DEFEATED BY ALEXANDER IN THE BATTLE OF ISSUS
(Pompeian Mosaic in the Naples Museum)

YAZDAGARD III SLAIN IN A MILL AT MERV
(From the Columbia University Manuscript of the Shah Namah)

ing a world-empire was shattered by the Arab invasion, which resulted in the conquest of Persia and the overthrow of the Zoroastrian dynasty of the Sasanidæ, A.D. 651. With the death of Yazdagard III, who was treacherously slain in that year after being defeated in battle, the Sasanid line came to an end, the Zoroastrian faith, which had been the state religion for more than a thousand years, was deposed, and Islam took its place as the national religion of Iran.

The centuries which followed were often marked by misrule, invasion, and even foreign rule. A succession of longer or shorter lived dynasties, like the Ommiads (A.D. 661–749), Abbasids (749–847), Ghaznavids (961–1186), Seljuks (about 1030–1200), the Mongols under Jenghiz Khan (1162–1227) and under his grandson Hulagu (d. 1265), who maintained his court at Maraghah, and the Tartars under Timur Lang (d. 1405) and his successors, fill the pages of Persia's history until the fifteenth century. At the end of the sixteenth, Persia saw the rise of a great sovereign, Shah Abbas (1585–1628), who wielded the sceptre alike with regal power and magnificence, and at his court representatives of European potentates were received and entertained with pomp. His successors unfortunately proved inferior in ability, and the Afghans invaded Persia in the eighteenth century and contributed to the general disorganization that lasted until about the year 1789. The Kajar dynasty was then established by Agha Mohammed Shah, the eunuch monarch, who was succeeded by his nephew Fath Ali Shah (1798), and he in turn by Mohammed Shah (1835), and this line has held the Persian throne ever since.

The scope of this book does not permit my touching upon the past or present relations between Persia and the Occident, or making any forecasts as to the future. I shall also forego saying anything about the social institutions of modern Persia as compared with ancient Iran. In religion, however, Persia has played so important a part, a part not wholly laid aside, that some idea of her religious history must be given in order to make clear many points in the chapters which follow.

Zoroastrianism was the ancient faith of Iran and is important because of the likenesses which it presents to Judaism and Christianity.[1] A phase of this religion known as Mithraism penetrated into the Roman world during the early Christian ages and spread so rapidly in many parts of Europe that altars were set up and cave-temples built to celebrate the mysteries of the Persian divinity Mithra and to glorify this personification of light, the sun, and truth. Furthermore, the system of Manichæism, which sprang up on Persian soil, was powerful enough to compete for a time with Neo-Platonism and Christianity for the religious and intellectual supremacy of the Roman Empire. Mohammedanism is the religion of Persia to-day, as she accepted Islam at the time of the Arab conquest, but Persia belongs to the Shiite sect of the faith and acknowledges Ali, Mohammed's first cousin and son-in-law, as the Prophet's successor in opposition to the Sunnite branch of Islam. She is in fact the chief representative of Shiism and has been largely instrumental in the growth of this factional movement which divides the Mohammedan world with a bloody schism. In Persia, moreover, within the last seventy years a new religious movement, eclectic in its character and known as Babism, has sprung up and assumed such proportions as to menace the universal supremacy of Mohammedanism in Iran and even to attract attention and some followers in the Occident.

In art and architecture Persia is renowned for the grandeur of some of her ancient monuments and for the beauty and decorative design of much of her later work. In both these fields she is believed to have borrowed in early times largely from Assyria and Babylon and slightly from Egypt, and later also from Greece, Rome, and Byzantium, as well as somewhat from China. Nevertheless she has dealt with the importations

[1] See pp. 57–69, below.

The Portal of Xerxes at Persepolis

freely, added much, and made the production so characteristically her own as often to bring forth a new creation; and
if she has accepted gifts in artistic lines from China, it was
only in part return for generous loans previously made to /
Chinese art by herself.

In the domain of linguistics there are a number of points
which are interesting to consider in connection with Persia.
For the older languages I need only refer to the contributions
which were made to comparative philology, as well as religion
and history, when the Zoroastrian scriptures were discovered
and the cuneiform inscriptions deciphered. The study of the
Pahlavi, or Middle Persian, texts, inscriptions, coins, and gems
has yielded valuable results for general history as well as for
linguistic science. The modern language of Persia has an
interest even for the student of English who is not an
Iranian specialist, because the loss of inflections and the
admixture of Arabic words in Modern Persian, due to the
Mohammedan conquest, may be paralleled with similar phenomena in our own tongue with its levelled case-endings,
analytic structure, and its vast infusion of words brought in
by the Norman invasion. In the matter of linguistic purity
and the avoidance of foreign words in a national epic, Firdausi's
Shah Namah, Book of Kings (A.D. 1000), affords an excellent
parallel to Layamon's poetic chronicle, the Brut (A.D. 1200).
The Iranian poet is as free from the contamination of Arabic
words, which later became fashionable, as the British bard
from elements of Norman-French origin.

Our ordinary vocabulary of to-day owes something to
Persia.[1] So common a word as *van*, a heavy vehicle, is an
abbreviation of *caravan* (which has been etymologized in the
folk-speech as 'carry-van'), and is as Persian as *Shah, tiara*,

---

[1] I am indebted for suggestions to
the sketch by my friend, Professor
Horn, *Was verdanken wir Persien*,
in *Nord und Süd*, Heft 282, p. 379,
Breslau, 1900. See also Skeat, *Ety-
mological Dictionary*, p. 759, Oxford,
1882 ; and my address in *Congress of
Arts and Science*, St. Louis, 1904.

bakhshish, and *magic* (from *Magi*).   The Persian term *bazaar*
is current in English, and *shawls, sashes, awnings, turquoises,*
and *taffeta* are standard articles in our linguistic stock in trade
as the goods themselves in our markets.   Products so common
in America as the *orange, lemon, melon,* and *peach* (the last
word being a disguised form of the Latin *malum Persicum,*
which has come to us through the French) are Iranian in name
as well as in origin.   The vegetable *spinach* is Persian, and the
word *asparagus* also traces its lineage apparently through the
Greek ἀσπάραγος ultimately to Avestan *sparegha,* 'shoot, stalk.'
I must add, however, that this vegetable has gained much in
delicacy by being transplanted to the West, if I may judge by
the asparagus which now grows in Persia.   The list of our
linguistic indebtedness might be increased by including a score
of words like *julep* (familiar in 'mint julep'), which is really
an arabicized form of the Persian *gulāb,* 'rose-water'; *hazard,*
applied to taking the one chance in a 'thousand' (Pers.
hazār); and last but not least, *Paradise,* which has come to us
from Persian through the Greek, while *gul* and *bulbul,* the
Persian 'nightingale and rose,' are familiar to all readers of
Eastern poetry.

   The title of Persian literature to a place among the great
literatures of the world is a recognized one, and it is in this
domain perhaps that Persia makes the greatest claim upon our
interest.   In age the Avesta and the Old Persian Inscriptions
carry us back at least to the sixth century before Christ and
possibly earlier; the Pahlavi literature belongs to the Sasanian
period from the third to the sixth century after Christ; and
the Modern Persian began within the last thousand years.   It
sprang up a century or two after the Arab conquest as a re-
naissance movement with the revival of the old national feeling;
and this period is certainly the most interesting of all.   Some
knowledge of Firdausi, Saadi, and Hafiz belongs to true culture, and Omar Khayyam has become an English classic
through FitzGerald's version.   The less-known names of the

His Royal Highness Muzaffar ad-Din, Shah of Persia

romantic poetic Nizami, the dervish Jalal ad-Din Rumi, and the mystic Jami (d. 1492), the last classic poet of Persia, should be mentioned as deserving to be known to lovers of literature.

Little space remains for writing about the influence of Persia upon our own poetry. Persia was hardly known to England before the sixteenth century, yet Chaucer alludes to Persian blue, ' pers,' in the Prologue. Among the Elizabethans, Preston dramatized the story of 'Cambises,' Marlowe has Persian names and Persian scenes in his *Tamburlaine*, and Shakspere alludes to ' Persian attire ' in *King Lear*, to ' a Persian prince ' in *Merchant of Venice*, and to a voyage to Persia in his *Comedy of Errors*. Milton summarizes the early history of Persia in the third book of his *Paradise Regained*, besides referring to ' Ecbatan,' ' Hispahan,' ' Tauris,' and ' Casbeen ' in *Paradise Lost*. Shelley appears to have a faint reminiscence of the pillared halls at Persepolis in his *Alastor*, and Byron in the *Giaour* and Landor in the *Gebir* hark back to the old Zoroastrian faith of Iran. Matthew Arnold and Edmund Gosse, as poetical writers, came under Firdausi's spell, and a dozen other instances might be mentioned where Persia has influenced English poets, one of the best known being Tom Moore, whose *Lalla Rookh* is full of the melody, perfume, color, beauty, tenderness, and tremulous ecstasy which imagination associates with the East.

In the realm of English prose the two volumes of *Persian Tales* by Ambrose Philips, after a French version, were widely read in the latter part of the eighteenth century, and the familiar *Arabian Nights* are really largely Persian. The inimitable Persian novel *Hajji Baba of Isfahan*, by Morier, is so thoroughly Oriental that Persians who read English mistake it for a serious composition and take umbrage at some of its amusing accounts. One of our American contemporaries, moreover, the novelist Marion Crawford, chose Zoroaster as a character around which to weave a romantic story. To these examples I might add dozens of others if I chose to go outside of English and speak of the influence of Persia upon French, German, and other European literatures.   I shall restrict myself, however, and return to my main theme, resuming the journey through the country whose history and position in the world I have briefly sketched.

THE PERSIAN INN AT JULFA, WITH THE CUSTOM HOUSE ON THE LEFT

A PART OF THE 'ROAD' BETWEEN JULFA AND MARAND

CHAPTER V

THROUGH THE SNOW FROM THE ARAS TO TABRIZ

'They proceeded thence all the next day through the snow.'
— XENOPHON, *Anabasis*, 4. 5. 7.

IMMEDIATELY after crossing the Aras at Julfa I had to proceed to the custom house. There I was received by the Director of the Persian Customs, a Belgian gentleman, who was in charge of the frontier at this point. After scanning my letters of introduction and my official papers, he made an inquiry only as to whether I carried arms and ammunition. I told about the episode across the river with my revolver. When the formalities were over, he extended to me a cordial invitation to be his guest at dinner that evening, an invitation which I gladly promised to accept as soon as I could dispose of my luggage at the Persian rest-house across the way.

This lodging-place was a house founded literally upon the sand, for it was built near the low bank of the Aras; it was long, but not deep, had two stories and fairly large rooms, a double veranda across the front, and a flag-pole on top — the latter a mark of Western influence. About the entrance were strewn bales of cotton, which a caravan had just unloaded, and in the rear was the camel train. The dromedaries were being quartered for the night in the open. They were forced to kneel down in a circle around a bundle of fodder, which helped to keep them in order. The shouts, kicks, blows, and punches of the drivers, which accompanied this proceeding, called forth a score of inarticulate growls, protests, and objections on the part of the camels. It was fortunate perhaps that I did not understand either camel language or camel-driver jargon.

D

33

At the telegraph office adjoining the rest-house I received a message from the head of the American Christian Mission at Tabriz saying he had despatched an Armenian servant to meet me, and sent a wagon drawn by four horses, with a Turkish driver named Meshad Seyid Ullah. I welcomed this assurance of a conveyance to take me to Tabriz, found my attendants had arrived, and then enjoyed a delightful evening with my host, who gave me much information regarding the route over which I was to travel. I rested well in my Persian quarters except at intervals when the camels set up a cry of protest against some wrong, real or imaginary.

It was ten o'clock next morning before I succeeded in getting everything ready to start on what proved to be a two days' journey through the snow, and altogether the worst experience I had yet encountered; but when travelling in Persia we become accustomed to discomforts and inconveniences which otherwise would seem unbearable. Two quotations from Hamlet kept recurring to my mind: one was, 'the hand of little employment hath the daintier sense;' the other, 'thus bad begins, but worse remains behind' — and worse did remain behind.

For part of the first day the route was through the exposed bed of a river filled with boulders of stone and blocks of ice. Now we were sinking in the water, next plunging into a snow-bank, and again extricating the wagon from a deep gulch. The mud on the side hills was nearly up to the hubs, so there was no chance for progress with a vehicle there; nevertheless I was glad to climb up on the heights for a while, and try walking, in order to lighten the load for the struggling horses below.

At distant intervals along the trail there were mud cabins which served as tea-houses (*chāi khānah*). These gave a welcome excuse for a halt and refreshment. The tea was good, but dirt was plentiful, yet I soon began to be accustomed to that, for the descent to Avernus is easy. The delays in getting started again were exasperating, and I had to keep incessantly

Mountain Village buried in Snow between Marand and Sofian

urging, scolding, begging, and bribing the driver to make haste in order to reach Marand that night. The device of the bribe proved the more effective, and resulted in a series of lashes, plied savagely upon the tired horses and accompanied by a succession of encouraging shouts, whistles, grunts, cries, squeals, yells, and chirrups, infinite in variety, but of endless weariness, and alternating with the humming of a tune which might have been the Turkish equivalent of that of which the old cow died.

We managed to keep fairly well in the caravan trail (I cannot call it a road), but once in the darkness we lost it, and a violent collision with a telegraph pole was the result. Fortunately only the harness was broken, not our bones. After making repairs we proceeded tolerably until the village of Marand was reached ; there on the bank of a stream the wagon suddenly upset, and I was sent sprawling into the mud, amid bags, boxes, and bundles. The only thing to do was to take the matter good-naturedly and laugh ; this cheered the situation immediately, and the villagers came out in a friendly manner from their simple homes, helped me to replace my scattered belongings, and guided us to a place of lodging.

The upper room where I spent the night was fairly comfortable, thanks to a blazing fire, but the heat had the disadvantage of bringing out from the cracks and crevices scores of huge vermin, descendants, perhaps, of the noxious *khrafstras* of the Avesta. I slept soundly, nevertheless, for a journey of eleven hours is conducive to weariness, although the distance covered, despite all my efforts, was only forty-five miles.

As a place, Marand is no longer of any consequence, although it was once an important town. Yakut says that even in his time, seven centuries ago, it was partly abandoned and falling into ruins because of the ravages of the Turkish tribes who swept down upon it, carrying off the inhabitants and leaving desolation in their wake.[1] It is clear from his account that

[1] Yakut, p. 524.

religiously Marand must have been a stronghold of Islam at his
time, and no longer Zoroastrian, as he states that it was the
birthplace of a number of eminent Mohammedan teachers. At
the time of my visit I did not know that at Marand there are
the remains of an ash-hillock which is believed to go back to the
days of Zoroastrian fire-worship, and, like the mounds at Urumiah, to owe its origin to a vast accretion of ashes from a
fire-temple. If I had known of this fact at the time, I should
have examined the mound. The antiquity of the town, as it
was once the capital of the Sasanian canton of Vaspurakan,
would favor the likelihood of a reward for undertaking excavations in the vicinity for Zoroastrian researches ; but as far as
biblical matters are concerned, there is nothing except the fanciful etymology of the name as *Mair-and*, 'the Mother is there,'
to support the tradition that Noah's wife is buried at Marand.[1]

The next morning the weather was dull and dreary, and it
was nine o'clock before I could start. A few minutes later we
were crossing a ford of the stream on whose bank the wagon
had upset the night before, and whose water we had drunk for
breakfast with the assurance that it was 'most excellent'
(*āb-i khailī khūb*). I now saw a dead cat floating on its surface and the villagers washing their dirty clothes in the stream.
A short drive through slush and mud, after crossing the ford,
brought us to the foothills, and all that day the route lay
up steep mountains and down into deep valleys, although the
altitude of the latter was rarely less than four thousand feet
above sea-level, as the tableland is high at this point. The
mountain scenery looked like a sea of gigantic billows raised
by some Titan storm that had torn up its surface. And snow
was everywhere. The depth of the snow made progress very
slow, and once our vehicle became hopelessly stuck in a huge
drift, and I had to pay handsomely for extra horses to pull
it out. The country was sparsely settled, and many of the

[1] On the name Marand see the article by Hübschmann, *Die altarmen-*
ischen Ortsnamen, in *IF.* 16. 347,
451.

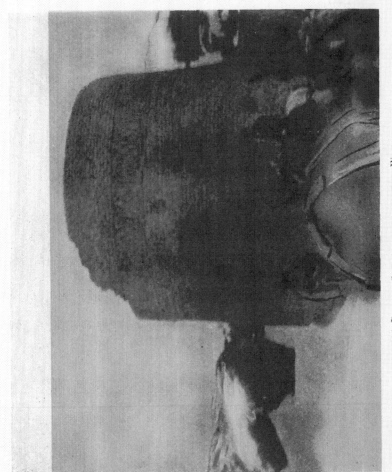

A Ruined Caravansarai on the Way

hamlets were buried in the snow, one or two on the mountain-
side (like the one in my picture) looking as if their occupants
had hibernated all winter, so completely was their communication cut off. Most desolate among all the sights, however,
was a ruined caravansarai, which, like a hundred others in
Persia, was attributed to Shah Abbas the Great as builder.
The magnificence of its founder and the former splendor of
its many kingly occupants, in contrast with its present ruinous
condition, struck me as an illustration of Omar Khayyam's
familiar quatrain : —

> 'Think, in this batter'd Caravanserai
> Whose Portals are alternate Night and Day,
> How Sultán after Sultán with his Pomp
> Abode his destined Hour, and went his way.'

It was late in the afternoon when we finally drew near the
village of Sofian, or Zofian, which had been the scene of a bloody
battle between the Turks and the Persians in the latter part of
the sixteenth century.[1] As there is a post-house at Sofian, I
proceeded to arrange for hiring horses, since those of my
driver were completely fagged out. The master of the post,
with whom I had to bargain, had a nose shaped like a carrot,
and evidently Turanian blood in his veins; the Persian lineaments seemed to be almost wanting in his face. In his manners, however, he was kindly ; in his movements, Orientally
slow ; but with much dignity he conducted me to his own room,
which was warm and comfortable and furnished with some
good rugs and divans. Two Persian merchants were lolling
on cushions, drinking tea, and seemed to have so much time
at their disposal that they were willing to spend more of it
in asking questions of the newly arrived *farangī*, than I had
time to spend in answering.

A start was made at last, and as I left Sofian I got a good
view of the northeastern shore of Lake Urumiah and of Mount
Sahand. Both of these places were for me historic landmarks,

---

[1] See Ker Porter, *Travels*, 1. 219.

the former as a lake which Zoroaster knew well, and the latter possibly, I believe, as Mount Asnavand of the Avesta, on which it is said that Zoroaster beheld a vision of heaven and conversed with Haurvatat, the guardian angel that presides over waters.[1] To me the sight of the mountain and the lake was a joyful one, because I felt as if I had met friends whom I had longed to see; this made the journey for the remainder of the day seem shorter.

It was between eight and nine in the evening when I finally reached Tabriz and found a welcome at the mission house. I became a 'Fire-Worshipper' in earnest, as my hosts laughingly said, when I greeted the blazing logs whose cheery flame brought back the blood to my face, which had been cracked in deep gashes by the cold. I had been for two full days on the road through the snow, having taken all that time to accomplish a journey of eighty-five miles. It was a pleasant prospect now to be able to look forward to a rest for several days, and that in one of the largest of the cities of Persia.

[1] See the suggestions in my *Zoroaster*, pp. 48, 100, 207, although other identification may be suggested, cf. p. 141, below.

TABRIZ

CHAPTER VI

TABRIZ, THE RESIDENCE OF THE CROWN PRINCE

'In his retreat to Tauris or Casbeen.'
— MILTON, *Paradise Lost*, **10**. 435.

TABRIZ, the residence of the heir apparent to the Persian throne, and the commercial centre of Azarbaijan, is a city whose age and birthplace are not known, but it may count a thousand years as but a fraction of its life. The Persian tradition which ascribes its founding to Zobeidah, the wife of Harun al-Rashid (better known as the Caliph Haroun Alraschid of the Arabian Nights, A.D. 800), sets its date too late, as in the case of Kashan and other cities which are said to have been built by this heroine. It is true that a fountain at Tabriz is called after her name, but the city can be shown to have existed under the Sasanians, four centuries before her time.[1]

Tabriz has been identified with the ancient Gaza, Ganzaca, by some scholars, but this identification is not accurate,[2] nor are we positive that it was formerly called Shahistan,' King's-town,' by the Persians and had its name changed to Tabriz ('this revenge,' *ta-vrezh*) by the Armenian king Khosru I, who sacked the city, A.D. 346, in revenge for the death of his brother, and then called the place 'this revenge,' a name which the city has

---

[1] The tradition of Zobeidah as founder is given by Mustaufi, *Nauzhat al-Kulūb* (A.D. 1340), and he gives the Mohammedan year of the founding as A.H. 175 = A.D. 790; see Barbier de Meynard, *Dict. géog. de la Perse*, p. 132, n. 2. For a sketch of the history of Tabriz I would refer to Rev. S. G. Wilson, *Persian Life and Customs*, pp. 323–325, New York, 1895. To Mr. Wilson, who was my host during a stay of five days in Tabriz, I am indebted for much information regarding the city.

[2] For the more likely association of Gaza with Shiz, see p. 131, below.

39

borne ever since as a memorial of the event.[1]   The Persians
again recovered possession of Tabriz from its Armenian conquerors, but owing to its exposed position on the frontier the
town has frequently been subjected to foreign invasion and occupation, by Arab, Seljuk, and Mongol, one of the fiercest of the
stormings being that by Timur Lang (Tamerlane), who sacked
it with his Tartar hosts in the latter part of the fourteenth
century.   Terrific earthquakes also have shattered it again
and again, A.D. 858, 1041, 1721, and 1780, killing thousands
of people and destroying its main buildings.   Nevertheless
the city has maintained its position as a great Persian metropolis, inherited from its rank as a capital under the Mongols, and
has enjoyed prosperity as a centre of trade and commerce, so
that Tabriz remains to-day what the Arab traveller Yakut
called it when he visited it in 1203 (A.H. 610), 'the principal
city of Azarbaijan, flourishing and well populated.'[2]   The
number of its inhabitants is not less than one hundred and
seventy thousand.

A view of the city is disappointing if we expect to find lofty
buildings and that variety of color which we associate with the
Orient.   Instead of this, there is a monotonous expanse of flat-
roofed, single-storied houses, broken only by the domed arches
of the bazaars and the high wall of the ancient citadel.   Clay
and mud plaster, for the most part, are used in the construction
of buildings, and these give a dull appearance to the unimposing architecture.   The houses, with windowless outer walls,
turn their backs on the street and show their faces only to the
exclusive brick courtyard in the interior.   The entrance is made
through an unpainted wooden door, studded with heavy nails,
like the portal of a Norman keep, and having a small grating
above to admit light and air.   In the courtyard we may find
a small garden, and, if so, a tank for preserving that precious
commodity, water ; but the general appearance of the interior,
like its unattractive entrance, is not such as to lead one to

[1] Wilson, *Persian Life*, p. 323.   [2] Yakut, p. 132.

The Ark, or Citadel, of Tabriz

suppose how handsomely the house may be decorated on the inside with rugs, old tapestry, pieces of Persian armor, and faïence.

As we walk about the town we have to find our way through a labyrinth of streets, narrow passages, and side alleys, some of the latter being less than six feet wide, and ultimately we reach the outskirts of the city. Walls surround Tabriz, as they have from the earliest times, and their circuit has gradually increased with the compass of the town. Gardens border these walls, with vineyards and orchards lying beyond, and Tabriz has been famous for its fruits and vegetables for over a thousand years.[1] But there was little to suggest this abundance. The suburbs, when I saw them, were buried in snow, and so also were low hills adjacent to the plain on the north and northeast, which looked dwarfed in comparison with the heights of Mount Sahand that rise to an altitude of nearly twelve thousand feet on the south and are clad in ermine most of the year round.

As a municipality, Tabriz has more pretence to government than any other Persian city except Teheran, although there could be no comparison, of course, with a well regulated European city in the matter of efficiency. Twenty-four different wards are recognized, each managed by a magistrate (*kad-khudā*), who is responsible to the burgomaster (*baglār-bagī*), and he in turn to the governor of the province (*ḥākim*), and thus ultimately answerable to the Shah.[2] The streets are generally unpaved, except in a few places where cobble-stones are laid, and when I was at Tabriz in March, little attempt was made to remove the snow and slush, and I understand that the dust and dirt in summer are equally intolerable. As the streets are not regularly lighted, persons who go out after dark carry huge cylindrical lanterns, resembling our Chinese

[1] See the praise of its apricots by the Arab geographers Yakut (A.D. 1200) and Mustaufi (A.D. 1340) given in Bar- bier de Meynard, *Dict. géog. de la Perse*, p. 132.

[2] Cf. Wilson, *Persian Life*, p. 66.

lanterns, but made of thin muslin. The size of these luminous transparencies is in proportion to the dignity and position of the person escorted (for in Persia one generally goes out with a servant as an escort), and a grandee may be recognized by a giant lantern, three feet high and twenty inches in diameter, carried before him.

The water-supply of the city interested me, because this problem is often more difficult to solve in Persia than elsewhere. Most of the water in Tabriz is carried in underground channels from the outlying districts and distributed through the town by means of cemented conduits and clay pipes. During one of the days of my stay the garden of the mission was irrigated, so I had an opportunity of seeing how the water was distributed. The plug of the pipe leading from the street into the yard, which in many cases is a mass of clay or waste rags to serve as a stopper, is removed, and the water allowed to stream through the channels of the courtyard and into a reservoir (*ambār*) in the cellar of the house. The gardener superintends the distribution of the stream, which is allowed to run for several hours, depending upon the contract, and then the waterman again shuts off the supply and opens it in turn for the next house. In the management of the water system, however, little attention is paid to matters of hygiene, and the water becomes much polluted by surface drainage, so that it is easy to see how an epidemic like cholera can spread.[1]

The two architectural monuments in Tabriz which have a special claim to interest are partly in ruins. The most conspicuous of these is the Ark, or citadel, which may be seen from almost every part of the town. This massive structure probably occupies the same position as the old building which Yakut described seven hundred years ago as ' the Palace of the Amir, built of red brick artistically set, and very solidly constructed.'[2] The people call the citadel the Arch of Ali Shah (*Tāḳ-i Alī Shāh*), after the name of Taj ad-Din Ali Shah, who

---

[1] See also Wilson, *Persian Life*, p. 70.　　　[2] Yakut, p. 133.

THE BLUE MOSQUE, TABRIZ

was the grand vizir of the Mongol ruler Ghazan Khan, at the beginning of the fourteenth century, and built the mosque which once formed a part of the structure.[1] The battlements of the Ark rise more than a hundred feet in height, and the walls are fully twenty feet in thickness. The forbidding appearance of the solemn pile agrees well with the story that criminals were formerly executed by being thrown from its summit. Local accounts add a narrative of a curious escape of a woman who was condemned to this horrible death ; her skirts and balloon-like pantalets acted as a parachute to break the fall, so that she received no injury.

As I surveyed the towering wall and observed its ancient style of architecture, I could not help thinking that it probably did not differ much from that on the top of which a tragic scene was enacted in the days of the tyrant Cambyses, son of Cyrus, as told by Herodotus. According to the famous historian, the king's grand vizir Prexaspes determined that the truth about the usurpation of the False Smerdis should be known, though his own life be forfeited in the cause. He therefore ascended the tower of the palace and began to harangue the people who were gathered below to listen, telling them of the glorious reign of their former king, Cyrus, the atrocities committed by Cambyses, and describing how treachery had brought Smerdis and the Magians into power ; then, before he could be seized, he flung himself headlong from the summit to destruction.[2]

Far more interesting from the architectural standpoint is the second monument of Tabriz, the well-known Masjid-i Kabud, or Blue Mosque. This fine specimen of Mohammedan art, dating from the middle of the fifteenth century, is now falling into utter decay, but its crumbling walls and arches still show graceful lines and are encrusted with tiles of a rich blue color, set

[1] See the statement of Mustaufi, cited by Barbier de Meynard, *Dict. géog.* p. 132, n. 1, and compare also Wilson, *Persian Life*, p. 64, and Curzon, *Persia*, 1. 522.
[2] Herodotus, *History*, 3. 75.

off by exquisite faïence of yellow, salmon, white, and black, interwoven with patterns and arabesque scrolls. It is fortunate that the French archæologist and artist Texier preserved some of its perishing beauty in his handsome reproductions published nearly three quarters of a century ago, and that the younger German scholar Sarre, in his fine photographs and colored engravings, has also contributed his share toward saving more of the Blue Mosque, for it will probably have fallen into utter decay before another hundred years are past.[1]

The other buildings in the city require only brief mention. There are said to be no less than three hundred and eighteen mosques in Tabriz, but none of them can bear comparison with the Blue Mosque.   The religious merit of the city is enhanced by the fact that it can boast of having the tombs of eight Imamzadahs, sainted followers of Mohammed and of his son-in-law Ali ; while some 'companions of the Prophet' are said also to be interred on Mount Sahand.[2]   These facts bear out the proud title 'Cupola of Islam,' which Tabriz bore even six centuries ago,[3] and the city is so bigotedly Mohammedan that Jews are said not to be ordinarily tolerated in the town.

The oldest portion of the city is known as the Kalah, or Fortress, although its walls have practically disappeared and the moat has been largely filled in and built upon.   The central part of this old-time fortified section is occupied by the bazaars.   These marts of trade are among the finest in Persia, if not in all the East, and are a source of endless interest to the traveller.   In construction they are of the characteristic Oriental type, consisting of acres of vaulted arches built of brick and masonry, roofed over and divided by long narrow passageways, with shops and alcoves on each side.   At occasional intervals large portals lead out into square courts en-

[1] See Texier, *Description de l'Arménie, la Perse*, etc., Paris, 1842-1845 ; Sarre, *Denkmäler Persischer Baukunst*, Berlin, 1901.

[2] Mustaufi, cited by Barbier de Meynard, *Dict. géog.* p. 133, n. 1.   'Companions' (*ashāb*) is a technical term in Islam.

[3] Mustaufi, *op. cit.* p. 132, n. 1.

INTERIOR OF BAZAAR AT TABRIZ

closed to serve as places for the caravans to unload and lodge. The light in the bazaar is generally dim except where holes pierce the domes at regular intervals and let in shafts of sunshine, which serve also to reveal the dirt below. The passageways of the bazaars always seem crowded; camels, donkeys, and pack-mules add to the confusion of the disordered mass of buyers and sellers, and the incessant cry *khabardār! khabardār!* 'take care! take care!' ejaculated by the drivers, becomes exasperating, especially when you have to crowd against the wall to let some grandee pass. This local notable may be mounted on horseback and preceded by a lackey called a *farāsh*, who clears the way with a mace; but sometimes the noteworthy is seated in a carriage and preceded by outriders.

The bazaars open shortly after sunrise and do not close until sunset, at which time the shops are shut with wooden shutters and the gates of the bazaar barred and locked. The booths in which the goods are displayed measure scarcely more than ten or twelve feet square, and often much less. The customers do not enter the shop, but walk along the narrow passageways and bargain with the salesman, who squats lazily on the brick ledge in front of his store or sometimes rises slowly to bring from the rear of the booth an article which the prospective purchaser wishes to examine. If the price cannot finally be agreed upon after long bartering, the face of the merchant assumes a look of stolid indifference or Oriental disdain, and the customer passes along to the next shop. Beyond a rough grouping of industries there is little order or arrangement in the distribution of the booths. Here may be a fruit-stall with a rich supply of melons, which are kept on sale even in winter; there an Armenian silversmith doing fine filigree-work by hand; on this side a cap-maker busy with finishing a lambskin hat or a black Persian fez; yonder a baker flapping huge sheets of dough against the sides of an earthen oven (*tandūr*). The oven itself is simply a hollow scooped in the earth and lined on the sides with pebbles, which

absorb the heat and bake the giant flap-jack, but impart to
the bread a peculiar pitted appearance and often a gritty taste.
We can well understand why this bread is called 'pebble-
bread' (*nān-i sangak*).   During my stay at Tabriz, bonbons and
tinsel decorations were much in evidence in the bazaars, as
the season of No-Ruz, the Persian New Year, was approaching.

In making purchases in the bazaars the monetary unit is
the 'kran' (*ḳrān*), or rather the two-kran bit, the latter being
equivalent, roughly speaking, to twenty cents in American
money.   The kran itself is made up of twenty *shāhīs*, each
worth half a cent, and ten krans make up the 'toman' (*tōmān*),
something less than a dollar.   As an actual coin, however, the
toman no longer exists except in rare gold pieces, although
the Imperial Bank of Persia has issued paper tomans, which
are handsomely engraved notes, but are little current outside
of Tabriz and Teheran, being exchanged at a considerable loss
in other towns.   For this reason the traveller has to go weighted
down with bags of silver, when he starts on a journey, and
they make a heavy addition to his load.

As Tabriz is the commercial centre of northwestern Persia
and its trade with Europe is constantly growing, I may appro-
priately add a few words regarding the commercial relations of
Persia and the United States.[1]   The 'Treaty of Friendship and
Commerce' between the United States and Persia was concluded
December 13, 1856, and came into force in the following year.
The phrasing of its opening paragraph is interesting, as it gives
the royal titles of the Shah.   I reproduce it verbatim.

'IN THE NAME OF GOD, THE CLEMENT AND MERCIFUL—

'The President of the United States of America and His Majesty,
as exalted as the planet Saturn; the Sovereign to whom the Sun
serves as a standard; whose splendor and magnificence are equal to
that of the skies; the Sublime Sovereign and the Monarch whose

[1] For various printed reports on   kindness of Mr. David C. Beatty, of
Persian trade I am indebted to the   Yonkers, N.Y.

A Courtyard adjoining the Bazaar, Tabriz

armies are as numerous as the stars; whose greatness calls to mind that of Jemshid; whose magnificence equals that of Darius; the Heir of the Crown and Throne of the Kaianians; the Sublime Emperor of all Persia: being equally and sincerely desirous of establishing relations of friendship between the two governments which they wish to strengthen by a treaty of commerce and friendship and useful to the citizens and subjects of the two high contracting parties — have for this purpose named for their plenipotentiaries . . .'

Then the names of the respective appointees are given and these are followed by a series of eight articles regarding the friendly and diplomatic relations of the two countries and treating of matters of trade and commerce, as well as the obligations to be fulfilled by both parties and the privileges to be enjoyed. The various items of the treaty contain the 'most favored nation clause' throughout, so that the United States is entitled to the same rights and privileges in commercial matters as any other nation.

Trade between our country and Persia is yet in its infancy, as is shown by the Consular Reports; but there are several points to which attention may be called as significant. Russia has the bulk (about fifty per cent) of Persia's export and import trade; Great Britain comes next with about twenty-five per cent; the remainder goes to 'other countries,' under which general heading the United States is also included. The lately appointed Persian Minister to Washington emphasizes the possibility of an extensive increase in the trade between his country and our own; and Mr. John Tyler, our Vice-Consul-General at Teheran, shows in his recent reports that there is at least a prospective opening for American manufactures, especially for agricultural machinery, and a growing demand for American merchandise.

'American lamps, clocks, matches, and locks have a steadily increasing sale in the Teheran bazaars, especially locks, which excel in mechanical complexity, combined with lightness and convenience of handling (important considerations), anything hitherto put on sale. American hand pumps and cooking and warming stoves find appreciative purchasers and should, with proper management and competitive enterprise, soon monopolize the market.'

From experience I can understand how so indispensable an article as the padlock is in Persia might find a ready market. The wholesale introduction of clocks, I believe, is one of the greatest needs in timeless Persia, but I fear that their general use will depend largely upon the introduction of railroads, which would help to spread more widely the idea that time and money are synonyms. I might add that the admiration shown by the natives for the leather articles in my travelling-outfit leads me to think that American straps, clasps, buckles, riding-leggings, and top-boots would find a good sale, for the Persians themselves are capable workers in leather and know how to appreciate a good calfskin product. The time, there-fore, may not be distant when we shall see a larger sale both of American merchandise and of 'Yankee notions' in the bazaars of Persia and a complimentary import in return of precious stones, like the topaz, pearls from the Persian Gulf, silks, shawls, and embroideries, besides the well-known con-signments of carpets and rugs.

Not far from the bazaars is a large public square to which a particular interest attaches, not because of the armory and the gunsmiths' shops, the arsenal, prison, royal stables, and buildings belonging to the Crown Prince, but because it was the scene of the execution of the Bab, a Persian reformer, on July 9, 1850. This religious enthusiast and moral teacher, whose real name was Mirza Ali Mohammed, was born in Shiraz about the year 1820. He was trained at first to commer-cial life, but a pilgrimage to Kerbela and Najaf, and after-ward to Mecca, awakened in his heart the religious enthusiasm which made him devote his life henceforth to developing the tenets which he held. Upon his return to his native city, about 1844, he assumed the title of *Bāb*, or ' Gate ' leading to the spiritual life. His religious views were somewhat eclectic ; his doctrines leaned toward a mystic pantheism, with elements of gnosticism, and were of a highly moral order, and so liberal as to include steps toward the emancipation of woman.

In the eyes of the strict Mohammedan, however, the tenets upheld by the Bab were rank heresy. Nevertheless, they spread rapidly and awakened such intense sympathy among those who were dissatisfied with the régime maintained by the Persian mullahs, on the one hand, and raised such bitter opposition, on the other, among those who were pronouncedly conservative, that they led finally to bloody conflicts which resulted in the imprisonment of the Bab. He was ultimately taken to Tabriz and there condemned to be shot. The place of execution was this very square of the arsenal and gunsmiths which I am describing. Cords were passed under his arms, and he was suspended from the wall above a small shop which was pointed out to me. By his side was suspended also a devoted disciple, a young merchant of Tabriz, and orders were given to the soldiers to fire their volley. When the smoke cleared away, the body of the young follower of the Bab was discovered, riddled with bullets ; but by some strange hap the Bab had escaped. The shots had simply cut the cords that held him, so that he fell to the ground unhurt and took refuge in the shop below. He was probably dazed ; for had he retained his presence of mind, he might at once have turned the incident into a miracle before the astonished multitude. He was seized, however, dragged forth from the shop and again suspended, and shot to death by a different company of soldiers, since the first absolutely refused to fire another volley. The bodies of the two religious martyrs were then cruelly dragged through the streets and thrown to the dogs and birds, but they were afterward taken up and buried by sympathetic Babis, as the movement had gained a large number of adherents. It still has many followers, despite the persecution to which the sect has been subjected.[1]

---

[1] See Browne, *A Year Amongst the Persians*, pp. 58–64, and espe- cially the same author's translation of the *Tārīkh-i-Jadīd, or New History of*

E

Babism, in fact, is not confined to Persia, but has adherents in Mesopotamia, Syria, Egypt, India, and even in America, where some of its believers have tried to disseminate their doctrines.[1]

On the opposite side of the same public square, in the prison, another religious martyr was executed some years ago. This was a Mohammedan priest who had abjured Islam and adopted Christianity. He was cast into prison, confined in an upper room which looks out upon the square, and, after being nearly starved to death, was finally strangled by a bowstring, refusing to the last to renounce his belief in Christ.

One afternoon of my stay in Tabriz was devoted to a visit to the gardens and summer palace of the Vali Ahd, or Crown Prince, who makes this city his chosen place of residence, as his predecessors have done for the past hundred years. This summer abode, with its fine garden, lies on the southern side of the city, although it is called 'Northern Garden' (*Bāgh-i Shamal*), having taken that name from an older residence on the north side which it replaced. The snow lay so deep when I saw it that I could gain no real impression of what the park might be in spring and summer, but the driveways and avenues of trees were attractively laid out, the arched gateway of brick was effective as an entrance, and the palace itself more worthy of the name than some of the so-called palaces in Persia, which are not always kept up well.

In paying visits in the city I learned something of the native etiquette, which has a great deal of charm as well as formality. The Persians are distinctly a social people and their manners in company are extremely polite. Their vo-

---

[1] *Mīrzā 'Alī Muḥammad the Bāb, by Mīrzā Ḥuseyn of Hamadān*, pp. 299–312, especially pp. 303–306, Cambridge, 1893 ; compare also Browne, *The Episode of the Bāb*, 2. 43–45, 182, 190, 321–322, Cambridge, 1891.

[1] There is a society of Babists in Chicago who call themselves Behaists, after Beha Ullah, who claimed to be the successor of the Bab and a manifestation of the glory of God. See *Open Court*, 18. 355 seq., 398 seq., Chicago, 1904.

AN ACHÆMENIAN SEAL: THE KING SLAYING A MONSTER
(Exact Size)

THE CROWN PRINCE'S GARDEN
(Bāgh-i Shamal, Northern Garden)

cabulary of etiquette is rich in courteous phrases and complimentary terms, and the *salāms*, or benedictions of peace,
which form part of the greeting to the visitor, serve as a
charming introduction to conversation.

When a visit is to be paid to a person of rank, it is customary
for the visitor to send word in advance to inquire of the dignitary what hour would be convenient for receiving the call.
The response comes back couched in some courteous phrase and
names the time, 'two hours before sunset,' or perhaps earlier, as
the case may be. On being ushered into the reception chamber,
we find ourselves in a large room, richly carpeted with soft rugs
and lined with divans, but otherwise little furnished except with
a few chairs for Europeans when they are received. The host
enters a moment later and comes forward to greet his guest.
As an Oriental he appears in his stockinged feet, for shoes are
forbidden indoors, and wears his black lambskin cap (*kulāh*),
as it would be bad form to have the head uncovered. His polite
salām aleikum, ' Peace be unto you,' is responded to in kind, with
a mutual inquiry about the ' august health' of each, after which
the talk proceeds easily and unaffectedly.

In a few minutes one of the troop of servants enters, bringing
the *kaliān*, or water-pipe, as an added mark of hospitable
attention. This pipe stands about two feet high and is somewhat elaborate in its structure. The base is a large glass
vessel of a graceful shape, holding a quart of water. From
this vase there rises the tube of the pipe, which is about fifteen
inches long, made of dark wood, sometimes elaborately carved,
and capped by a China bowl, which is usually decorated with a
picture of the Shah and a fringe of silver chains hanging from
its rim. The tobacco is placed in this bowl, after the leaves
have been moistened and squeezed out, and a square piece of
charcoal is used to light it and left burning on the top while
the pipe is in use. The stem itself is about eighteen inches
long, and is inserted into the water-vase at a convenient angle.
It is made of the same dark wood as the tube and is capped

with a mouthpiece of silver.   In using the pipe the smoke is
not drawn by whiffs into the cheeks, as in the case of a cigar, but
is inhaled in long draughts directly into the lungs, the strength
of the nicotine being diminished somewhat in passing through
the water, which is occasionally also scented.   After three or
four long puffs it is *en règle* to pass the pipe to the next person
at the right and so on throughout the company.   A tray of
sweetmeats and some tea served in tiny glasses form an additional course and complete the hospitality, and then the guest
asks permission to 'remove the cause of trouble to the host,'
and take his leave, which is finally granted after a variety of
protests.   Formality is resumed at the final leave-taking, and
many compliments are passed in saying good-by.

The Persians at their banquets, I am told, show the same
grace in entertaining, and the conversation is easy, bright, and
witty.   There is a great variety of courses, if we count the
sweets, dried fruit, and other delicacies, which are partaken
during the evening before the solid dishes are served.   This
takes place before the company is to break up, so that the latter
are hardly more than a supplement to the lighter delicacies
which precede them.   The custom with the ancient Persians
was the same.   Herodotus says that 'the Persians indulge in
very few solid dishes, but they eat many desserts, which are not
served up on the table all together at the same time.'   He adds,
'the Persians are very much addicted to wine.'[1]   Since the time
of Mohammed this abuse has been forbidden, but the injunctions
of the Koran in this respect are not so strictly complied with
as they might be.   I was informed also that an occasional
feature of lavish entertainments is an exhibition of dancing
boys, somewhat similar to the nautch girls of India.   These
boys are said to be handsome youths, but spoiled and effeminate,
like those at Bokhara and Samarkand, and it may have been

---

[1] Herodotus, *History*, 1. 133, cf.   *Persians*, pp. 108–111 ; Wilson, *Per-*
Rawlinson, *Herodotus*, 1. 219, n. 6.   *sian Life*, p. 243 seq.
See also Browne, *A Year Amongst the*

against such minions as these that some of the shafts of Zoroaster's invective in the Avesta were launched.[1]

Although situated in a region which was historically connected with Zoroaster's name, Tabriz yielded little for my
researches in that respect : first, because Mohammedanism has
obliterated the traces of Zoroastrianism ; second, because
the winter season prevented my making investigations in
the mountains, which possibly might have yielded some results.
I was particularly anxious, for example, to ascend Mount
Sahand, the mountain which possibly may be identical with
Asnavand of the Avesta, but the heavy snows cut off all
approach.   Still more inaccessible at this time of year was
Mount Savalan, near Ardabil, three or four days' journey distant from Tabriz.   This is the mountain which I think is to be
identified with the ' Mount of the two Holy Communicants '
in the Avesta, where Zoroaster communed with Ormazd.   A
number of the Oriental writers, such as Ibn Haukal (tenth
century), Kazvini (1263), Mirkhond (1474), and others, expressly record the tradition that Zoroaster received a revelation from Ormazd on the heights of the Iranian Sinai and that
he wrote the Avesta there.[2]   Among these authorities is the
author of the *Suvar Aklāīm Sab'ah*, or ' Outline of Countries,'
who, writing in Persian, about A.D. 1400, attributes the tremen-
dous snows around Ardabil, near which Mount Savalan rises, to
a curse uttered against the people by Zoroaster because they
rejected his faith.   The fulfilment of this anathema seemed
to me a veritable fact, for I had to abandon all hope of reaching Savalan, owing to the snow-bound roads, and to content
myself with a distant view of this sacred mountain from the
Caspian Sea when I returned to Baku in June.   One of the

[1] Avesta, Ys. **51**. 12 ; Vd. **8**. 26, 27,
32, etc.; see also Herodotus, *History*,
1. 135.

[2] See my *Zoroaster*, pp. 34, 195 ;
consult also Stackelberg, *Persische
Sagengeschichte*, in *Wiener Zeitschrift*

für Kunde des Morgenlandes, 12. 230–
234, Wien, 1898, and Brunnhofer, *Vom
Pontus bis zum Indus*, p. 182, Leipzig,
1893 ; see also Ibn Haukal, tr. Ouseley, p. 173.

native lords of the district about Tabriz, Anton Khan, an Armenian, gave me some description of the crater of Mount Savalan and of the hot springs which Kazvini mentions, but he said there is no tradition that he knew of, regarding the Fire-Worshippers in this region.[1] Another lord, Sadir Khan, a Persian, informed me about an ash-hillock of a fire-temple at Marand which I had missed on my way to Tabriz.

My inquiries regarding inscriptions or sculptures in the vicinity of Tabriz did not result in eliciting any information,[2] but I found that coins and gems are occasionally unearthed in the neighborhood. I purchased several specimens of coins dating from the Parthian and Sasanian periods, and a seal which is of considerable interest because of its age, as it is certainly to be attributed to the Achæmenian era. The seal is oval in shape, flat on the carved face and rounded at the back, and it measures one inch by three fourths of an inch (twenty-five centimeters by twenty centimeters). The stone is a blue chalcedony or sapphirine, which came into use during the early Persian period. It is carved with the figure of a king or warrior, slaying a monster with his dagger, somewhat after the manner of the sculptures at Persepolis. The working out of the design, in my judgment, shows too much originality to be a mere later imitation of this motive, and there is no evidence to show that the seal is a forgery. I am supported in my view that it belongs to Achæmenian times by other scholars who have seen it, among them Dr. William Hayes Ward, of New York, an authority on seals and cylinders.

The last day of my stay at Tabriz, which I should gladly have prolonged in order to enjoy the hospitality extended from many sides, was spent in making visits among friends in the

[1] It was still famed as a seat of Magism in the tenth century of our era, according to Ibn Haukal, tr. Ouseley, p. 173.

[2] I saw at the French Consulate at Tabriz a fragment of an Ancient Persian cuneiform inscription, but it had been brought from Susa by M. de Morgan and, I believe, already published.

SAFAR AWAITING DIRECTIONS

European section, which forms a part of the Armenian quarter of the town. A final tour of the bazaars had also to be made to secure a stock of provisions to carry 'on the road,' and an extra supply of warm clothing had to be purchased, for the cold was still intense. The evening was passed at a dinner party given by my host and hostess, with a final good-by to American and European friends.

At the eleventh hour, when the dinner was over (and it was literally eleven o'clock), I learned that the Armenian servant whom I had engaged, and to whom I had paid part of his month's wages in advance, had 'decided not to go on the journey.' This placed me in a great predicament: the horses had been hired and preparations made for an early start in the morning, so that postponement even for a day meant a serious change in my plans. A ray of light, however, shone through the darkness. I bethought myself of a young Persian, named Safar Adilbeg, a convert from Mohammedanism, whom I had noticed working about the mission grounds. I had been attracted by his honest face and demeanor, and after a hurried conference with my host and mission friends, to ask if the young man might be allowed to go, I received hearty approval on their part, and Safar was aroused from bed to be questioned on the subject. He accepted the proposal at once, hesitating only lest his lack of experience should disqualify him. I felt sure, however, that he would fill the post well, for I was convinced of his merit, and we struck a bargain on the spot. My confidence was rightly placed, and although I used occasionally to wonder whether some serious blemish in his character might not develop, it never did, and I sometimes amusingly thought that wings would sprout and that his name would have to be changed to Raphael, after the story in Tobit. His true worth grew more and more in my esteem as time went on, and I am glad to be able to add that he has since then happily realized the ambition of his life in studying medicine at

Teheran, in order to become a physician and practise among his people.

Before proceeding with the narrative of my journey after leaving Tabriz it may be advisable in the next chapter to give some account of Zoroaster and the Avesta, as these names have often been mentioned already and will frequently be referred to hereafter.

CHAPTER VII

ZOROASTER AND THE AVESTA

'At whose birth and growth all creatures of the holy creation cried, " Hail ! " '
— AVESTA, *Yasht* **13**. 93.

' TELL me how it comes to pass,' says one of the fathers of
the early Christian church, 'that the majority of people know
nothing more about Zoroaster than the name.' And yet there
is a tradition that the wise men who came from the East to
worship at the manger cradle in Bethlehem were led to undertake their pious journey ' by reason of a prophecy of Zoroaster.' The name, moreover, of this forerunner of the Magi
has been used in literature of later times as a synonym for
wisdom. To Byron, Zoroaster was a 'sage'; to Shelley he
appeared as 'the Magus' or as 'Earth's dead child'; and the
German writer Nietzsche chose to veil his recently published
thoughts under the title 'Thus Spake Zarathushtra.' It is
the more interesting to know something about the life and
character of this Persian lawgiver and philosopher of old, this
religious teacher of ancient Iran, because much has been added
in the last few years to our knowledge of Zoroaster as a historical personage — a man to whom we may perhaps be justified
in assigning, indirectly at least, a place in the line of prophets
that have been since the world began.[1]

In the early dawn of the seventh century before Christ he
appears as a star on the horizon, remotely a heathen herald of
the Christian day to come. He comes as an elder contemporary

[1] I am indebted to Mr. J. B. Walker
for permission to reprint with additions
and alterations my article on Zoroaster
in the *Cosmopolitan Magazine*, 28.
349–357, New York, 1900. For a
detailed life of the teacher see my
Zoroaster, the Prophet of Ancient Iran,
New York, 1899.

of the Grecian sages Thales and Solon. If our calculation
be right, he must still have been living when the Jews were
carried up into captivity at Babylon. His birthplace was
the district to the west or southwest of the Caspian Sea, not far,
apparently, from the city of Urumiah, which we are approaching on our journey, and the scene of a part of his early missionary preaching and teaching was the territory south of this
very sea. The crest of Mount Alborz gilded with God's eternal
sunrise — for Alborz is a holy mountain in the Avesta — may
have suggested the theme for more than one inspired discourse.
The wellsprings of blazing oil and phenomena of igneous origin
familiar in the volcanic regions of Iran may have seemed to
him a symbol of the source of the Fire Divine.

Dressed in white flowing robes we may picture him preaching before his people. The priestly vestments of the Parsi
dastur to-day, and the Gheber mantle and belt of the fire-
worshipper in *Lalla Rookh* are lineal descendants, no doubt,
of the ancient Median garb which he wore. Herodotus tells us
that the Persians took their style of dress from the Medes
because they thought it handsomer than their own. The form
of worship and manner of chanting the ritual which the great
historian describes is largely kept up in the Zoroastrian religion
to-day. In speaking, Zoroaster used a language akin to the
ancient Sanskrit, but more abounding in long final vowels, as he
lifted up his voice in exhortation of the masses or sang the
praises of the god Ahura Mazda.

In his youth, so far as we can gather, he must have been
reared in a state of society that showed marked and paradoxical
extremes. From the ancient records we may judge that the culture, such as it was in those early times, was offset by extraordinary crudeness and barbarism ; and Media in some respects
has changed but little since then. Zoroaster was well acquainted, we may believe, with the civilization of the ancient
cities, but better acquainted with the gross ignorance and base
superstition of unlettered country life. These two widely

A PERSIAN PAGE

separated stages may be seen in the Avesta itself. The
wattled hut of the peasant or the temporary habitation of
the marauding nomad form a contrast to the 'palace of a
thousand columns' which is incidentally referred to in the
sacred text. The rude hovels are still perpetuated in the mud
dwellings of the poor ; and the ruins of Susa and of Persepolis,
with their pillared courts, best seen in the restorations of
Dieulafoy or of Perrot and Chipiez, bear witness to how noble
the grander architecture of the Persians must have been. The
ancient city of Ecbatana, known as Achmetha in the Bible,
possessed a pile of buildings of no mean order, if we may judge
from the Father of History, who tells of its seven concentric
walls, painted each in a different color and crowned by a
citadel whose battlements shone with silver and gold. It is
true that Zoroaster never mentions this city, but we are
justified in regarding it as a type of the cities which he
knew.

In contrast to this possible approach to luxury we must place
the other view ; for whatever may have been the higher civilization, or whatever there may have been of incipient culture,
in Zoroaster's day, we have in his own words evidence enough
of a prevailing density of superstition and of a mist of religious
unbelief that hung like a pall over the benighted people whose
eyes and ears he came to open and whose hearts and minds he
came to illumine and enlighten. Messiahlike he appears, and
the land of Iran rings with his clarion note of reform. He is
born as one out of the fulness of time. He arises to revolu-
tionize the religious thought of Iran, to stir the soul of Media
and Bactria, and to form for the coming nation of Persia a
creed that is to boast a Cyrus, 'the shepherd of the Lord,' and
a Darius who shall give command for rebuilding the Temple of
Jerusalem. The details of Zoroaster's life may be in a measure
legendary, but behind them all we can see the figure of a great
historic personage, whose actual existence we have no longer
any reason to doubt.

The year B.C. 660 was perhaps the date of Zoroaster's birth, although much uncertainty has prevailed on the subject and some scholars argue that he flourished a century or two earlier. The Avesta and the Middle Persian books known as the Pahlavi writings describe the prophecies that foretold his coming and the signs and wonders that heralded his entrance into the world. Some idea of the youth and personality of this future master may be gathered from these texts, which the reader may easily consult in translation in Max Müller's series of *Sacred Books of the East.* In reading of his life we cannot help feeling that we are in the presence of a person whose character even in youthful years combines vigorous thought with speculative imagination. It is instinctive for such spirits to act as guides. We may be certain that Zarathushtra early heard the call that spoke to his heart and made him feel an individual fitness, a peculiar consecration, for his hallowed office. His person is sanctified; his bearing is that of one who is to receive a weighty charge.

The extravagant stories of plots against his life by sorcerers and demons, which the old books of Iran enjoy repeating, or of his disputes with perverted and crafty ministers of a false creed, under whose blinding influence even his own father lived, present a dark picture of a foul religion and a depraved priesthood, which he felt himself destined to combat and overthrow. 'Tell me,' he later says in one of his Gathas, or Psalms, in which he alludes to the false priests and devils, 'tell me truly, O Lord, have such demons ever been good rulers?' It is precisely these who, to quote his own words used on another occasion, 'have united themselves with power for the purpose of destroying the life of man by their evil deeds; but their own soul and their own conscience will make them howl when they come to the Bridge of Judgment, to be inmates forever and ever of the House of Falsehood [*i.e.* hell].' And again he exclaims, 'Tell me truly how we shall banish Falsehood from ourselves even unto those who, full of unbelief, take no thought which accords with Righteousness, nor have felt delight in the communion of Good Thought.'

On the other hand, a moment after these anathemas or impassioned utterances against the wicked, we find evidence of Zoroaster's mild-heartedness and of his loving-kindness toward the good. In the liberality of his spirit, if we are to believe tradition, he was so broad-minded as to show a willingness to pick out and adopt what was noble even in the corrupt existing faith.

But the path for full inspiration must first be prepared, and the way to enlightenment must previously be laid open, before the revelation comes to a man of Zarathushtra's nature. Tradition says that Zoroaster retired from the world when he came of age and that he lived for some years upon a remote mountain in the silence of the forest or taking shelter in a lonely cave. In this connection I have already referred to Mount Savalan (p. 53), and in Mount Sahand there is a cavernous vault which is said to be Zoroaster's cave, and a subterranean chamber near Maraghah, with a fire-altar, is attributed to his worship.[1] It was the solemn stillness of such surroundings that lifted his soul into direct communion with God. A divine vision is accorded him, apparently on the occasion of some religious conference, and at the age of thirty, after leaving the Iranian Sinai, he is prepared to teach a new law. 'Righteousness is the best good' — *ashem vohū vahishtem astī* — is his watchword; but he finds little fruitful soil for his theme. He wanders over the land of Iran and through the territory that is now Afghanistan, and even tarries for a time in the country of Turan. But it is to deaf ears that he preaches, and his inspiration seems almost destined to be in vain.

The rulers harden their hearts before the newly inspired prophet; the people fail to accept the message of the god

---

[1] Mr. Arter, of Ziegler & Co., Teheran, told me that there is some such story about a cave in Mount Sahand. For the cave at Maraghah consult Ker Porter, *Travels*, 2. 495–497. See also p. 103, below.

Ahura Mazda. And yet Ahura Mazda, or Ormazd, is the 'Lord Wisdom, the Sovereign Knowledge.' It is doubtless true, moreover, that many persons were deterred from adopting the faith because of the doctrine of next-of-kin marriage, which Zarathushtra seems to have upheld because he felt that this would serve as a means of preserving in its purity and integrity the community of faithful adherents and advancing the struggling creed of his church militant.

For ten years, dervishlike, he is a wanderer. This we know also from the tone of dejection which still echoes in some of the Zoroastrian Psalms. In his peregrinations he appears to have found his way once more to the region of the Caspian Sea. The darkness of these sad years is illumined, however, by visions which help to make strong his faith and to give form to his religious system and creed. Seven times the mysteries of heaven are revealed to his transported soul; and a number of the places where these visions were beheld may be identified with a fair degree of certainty. Most of them are to be located in Azarbaijan not far from Lake Urumiah. He converses with Ormazd and is also privileged to interview the Archangels of Good Thought (Vohu Manah), Best Righteousness (Asha Vahishta), Wished-for Kingdom (Khshathra Vairya), Holy Harmony (Spenta Armaiti, guardian spirit of the earth), Saving Health (Haurvatat), and Immortality (Ameretat). Such are the names of the Persian hierarchy of Amshaspands, and these allegorical figures or personified abstractions stand in waiting about the throne of Ahura Mazda with a company of attendant angels. From these divine beings Zarathushtra receives commands and injunctions which he is to convey to mankind. They inculcate the doctrine of purity of body as well as of soul; they enjoin the care of useful animals, especially the cow and the dog; they emphasize the necessity of keeping the earth, the fire, and the water undefiled; and from several of their ordinances we can see that Zoroaster was a civil reformer as well as a

IDEALIZED PORTRAIT FROM A SCULPTURE SUPPOSED TO REPRESENT ZOROASTER

spiritual guide. Foremost among the commandments is the abhorrence of falsehood, the universal obligation to speak the truth. This is one of the most fundamental of the ethical tenets which form the basis of the entire ancient Persian religious system.

A revelation of the future is also vouchsafed to the soul of the Prophet during his sojourn in the celestial council, and one of the most precious boons which it is the privilege of his rapt spirit to receive in these moments of ecstasy is a premonition of the resurrection and of the future life. Unlike the Mohammedan visions of ethereal bliss, there is no jarring note of pleasures of a physical kind to mar the harmony and spirituality of this glimpse into the world beyond. But before the ecstatic Messenger is allowed to return to the world of material things, one word of warning is given to guard him against the guile and deceit of the Spiritual Enemy, Angra Mainyu, or Ahriman, as the devil is called. At this moment, as he turns from the dazzling splendor of heaven, a glimpse of the darkness, filth, stench, and torment of the 'Worst World' is disclosed. There in the murky depths of hell, with mocking howls and ribald jeers, huddle together and cower the vile crew of the archfiends and whole legions of demons, or 'devs,' as they are still named in Persian.

Nor is this caution any too timely, for at once upon the hallowed Seer's return to earth there occurs the temptation by Ahriman. Like the wily Mara seeking to beguile the newly enlightened Buddha, or the tempter Satan striving to betray the Saviour of mankind, the maleficent Ahriman endeavors to cause the righteous Zarathushtra 'to renounce the good religion of the worshippers of Mazda.' This moment is a crisis; it is one of the turning-points in the history of the faith. The foul fiend is repulsed and vanquished, and the victorious upholder of righteousness chants a kind of Te Deum — *yathā ahū vairyō* — as a pæan of his triumph. But he has to face many discouragements in his work; only one

convert to his faith is won during the first ten years of his
preaching.   This is his own cousin Maidhyoi-Maonha, the St.
John of the Religion.   In the twelfth year of his mission, however, came an achievement which made a crowning glory to
his career ; this was the conversion of King Vishtaspa, who
became the Constantine of the faith.

Exactly who this Vishtaspa, or Gushtasp, was, we cannot
with certainty say.   His name is the same as that of Hystaspes,
the father of King Darius, but there is no convincing ground
for identifying him with that personage.   Whether he was a
vassal king in Media itself or a monarch in eastern Iran, Bactria, or more probably the region corresponding to Afghanistan
and Persian Seistan to-day, belongs to scholars to discuss.[1]   It
suffices here simply to present this pious ruler, whom the Avesta
portrays as the nonpareil of kings, and to recall how his strong
arm made Zoroaster's religion current in the Province of the
Sun.

Vishtaspa is converted only after a long struggle, hesitancy,
and deliberation ; but when once convinced, he exhibits all the
zealous enthusiasm that is characteristic of a new convert.
His queen, Hutaosa, whose name at least recalls the name of
Atossa in Persian history, likewise accepts the faith and joins
the struggling church.   The nobles of the court follow the
high example.   Zoroaster's own family becomes a sharer in the
royal favor.   His third wife — for he was married three times
— is a sister of the king's grand vizir.   His favorite daughter
in turn is given in marriage to the other chief councillor of the
sovereign.   A number of relatives of the priest unite in the
confession of the faith.   Converts become many.   The spark
of religious enthusiasm kindled in the palace spreads like a
mighty flame throughout the land.   The people press to hear
Zarathushtra speak.   We can still listen to the verses of his
Gathas (Psalms) that served as texts for sermons.   Here is the
opening of one of his discourses, in which he tells of the two

---

[1] See my *Zoroaster*, pp. 205–225.

great opposing principles of Good and of Evil. The verses are
rhythmical, and in translating we may follow the order of the
lines : —

> ' Now shall I preach, and do ye give ear and hear,
> Ye who hither press from near and from afar!
> Now mark him all, for the Devil has been disclosed
> And nevermore shall he, Vile Teacher, the world destroy,
> Wicked Avower, he, of a sinful faith with his tongue.

> ' Now shall I preach of the world's Two Primal Spirits,
> The Holier One of which did thus address the Evil:
> " Neither do our thoughts, our teachings, nor our minds,
> Wishes, nor words, nor works, no, nor our religions,
> Nor do our souls agree in anything at all." ' [1]

On another occasion the same theme is taken up again by
Zoroaster in a Psalm (Gatha) which may be termed an Iranian
Sermon on the Mount. In this the priest bids his listeners to
be mindful of these Two Spirits which divide the universe
between them. People must not be deceived into making
a false choice, as the demons have done ; but they must
follow spiritual guidance, so as to be on the right side when
the judgment shall come ; for annihilation shall then overtake
Falsehood (Druj, Satan) and ruin shall attend upon the demons
and upon all who ally themselves with them. Let every man,
therefore, seek to make the world prepared. In the eighth
verse the Prophet breaks out into a fervent expression of hope
of a regenerate world and a new kingdom : —

> ' Therefore at the time when the retribution of the sinful shall come to pass
> Good Thought [Vohu Manah] shall dispense Thy Kingdom
> To the joy of those who deliver over Falsehood [Druj] into the hand of
> Righteousness [Asha].

> ' And so may we be such as make the world renewed,
> And do ye, Lord Mazda and Righteousness, bear your company,
> That our thoughts may wholly be where wisdom is abiding.

> ' For at the [final] Dispensation the blow of annihilation of Falsehood
> [Druj] shall come to pass,
> But those who share in a Good Report shall speedily unite together
> In the happy abode of Good Thought, of Mazda, and of Righteousness.

[1] Ys. 45. 1-2.

F

'If, O ye men, ye mark the doctrines which Mazda gave,
And [mark] the weal and the woe—namely, the long torment of the
wicked
And the welfare of the righteous—then in accordance with these [doc-
trines] there will be happiness hereafter.' [1]

Light begins to dawn upon the people. If good and evil,
god and devil, are in constant warfare with each other, what
is to bring about the ultimate solution of the conflict, what is
to give the victory to Ormazd and to put an end to the strife?
It is man. Man, a free agent, shall solve the problem by elect-
ing right and choosing goodness, if he follow Zoroaster's lead,
and as his reward he shall win joys eternal at the resurrection, 'when the dead again shall rise up, the quick be made
immortal, and the world, as desired, made perfect.'

But, exalted and spiritual as these religious tenets were,
not everything in the faith occupied so lofty, so perfect, so
transcendental a plane. It is difficult for a people to maintain
the high and ideal level of the leader. The knowing and enlightened may accept advanced theological doctrines, but the
masses require that which is more practical, more tangible.
Temporal considerations and material things cannot be left
out of sight by any reformer when he is founding his religion.
There is evidence of concessions being made in Zoroastrianism
to previous religious views or time-honored practices. The
glorification of the sun, moon, and stars as part of God's universe could not be omitted from the popular creed. The
ancient divinity Mithra, an embodiment of light and of the
sun, as we know from Tom Moore's *Fire-Worshippers*, is
canonized to stand beside Ormazd. The elements earth, fire,
and water are idealized as manifestations of purity. Xerxes
did pious homage to the vegetable kingdom when he decked
the plane-tree as a solemn rite on his way to Greece. Matters
and details of this kind were unquestionably recognized by
Zoroaster himself as elements to be accepted into his creed, as

---

[1] Ys. 30. 8-11.

he labored and taught, preached and converted, counselled and encouraged, during a ministry that lasted more than thirty years. His was a long life. Forty years of age or over when he first converted Vishtaspa, he lived until he was seventy-seven. Death came to him by violence in the holy wars which arose as a consequence of crusading for the faith, about the year B.C. 583. Such at least is the tradition, or legend, for there is a story that he was slain by the fanatical Turanians when they invaded Iran.

But the faith did not perish with the founder. We know from history how Zoroaster's creed was able to withstand the mighty shock given to it three centuries later when Alexander invaded Iran and at the request of the frail but beautiful Thais allowed the palace at Persepolis to be burned. It is claimed that the Avesta perished in the flames; but the Magian priest still held in memory the sacred texts, clung to the creed, and upheld the tottering rites. The faith revived once more and regained its pristine glory and flourished at the very time when the Roman wars with Persia fill the pages of history and the Zoroastrian heresy of Manichæism threatens to shake the Christian church. The final blow, however, came to Zoroastrianism in the sixth century from Islam. From that moment Persia practically adopted Mohammedanism and ceased to be Zoroastrian. Only a handful remained faithful to the old creed and were destined to endure countless sufferings from persecution in their native land. Another band, equally stubborn, refused to be converted, and chose exile in India, finding a place of refuge in Bombay and its vicinity, and thus becoming the ancestors of the present Parsis. Owing to their favorable surroundings among the Hindus they have prospered more than their Persian brethren, and like the latter they have remained genuine followers of the old-time faith of Zoroaster.

It is these two communities that have preserved for us until to-day the remnants of the ancient Zoroastrian scriptures, the Avesta and the Pahlavi books. In its present form the

Avesta is only a fragment of the original Zoroastrian scriptures. Tradition tells of twenty-one books, or a million of verses, composed by Zarathushtra and inscribed in letters of gold at the order of King Gushtasp, the patron of the faith. The destruction of the two archetype copies, the one at Persepolis, the other at Samarkand, is attributed to Alexander the Great.[1]

Only imperfect remnants of these originals have been preserved; in compass they would equal about one tenth of our Bible, and as in the latter we may recognize several subdivisions with reference to their contents. Most important is the *Yasna*, lit. 'sacrifice,' a liturgical work, comprising also the *Gāthās*, or Psalms of Zoroaster, the most sacred part of the Avesta, and supplemented by a series of minor litanies known as the *Visperad*, 'all the lords,' both works being used in the ritual and forming a sort of manual of devotion which corresponds to our prayer-book. Second in interest are the twenty-one *Yashts*, lit. 'praises,' a collection of metrical hymns in praise of the ancient divinities and mythical heroes of the religion. Third, and interesting in comparison with the Pentateuch, is a priestly code comprising twenty-one chapters and entitled *Vendīdād*, 'law against the demons,' a series of sacerdotal rules for the purification, and some miscellaneous matter of a legendary character. The remaining portion of our present Avesta is composed of minor prayers, invocations, and miscellaneous fragments.[2]

The loss of some parts of the Avesta is made up for in part by versions or summaries in the Pahlavi language of the Middle

---

[1] See p. 306, below, and my article *Some Additional Data on Zoroaster*, in the volume *Orientalische Studien* in honor of Professor Nöldeke, pp. 1031–1038, Strassburg, 1906.

[2] The best English translation of the Avesta is by Darmesteter and Mills, *Zend-Avesta*, 3 vols., in the *Sacred Books of the East*, Oxford, 1880–1887. There are French translations by Darmesteter, *Le Zend-Avesta*, Paris, 1892–1894, 3 vols., and by de Harlez, *Avesta*, Paris, 1881, a German one by Spiegel, and reference will be made hereafter to German renderings of selections by Geldner and by Bartholomae.

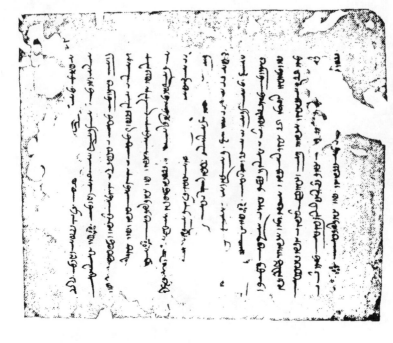

An Ancient Magian

(From Hyde's *Religio Vet. Pers.*)

Persian Empire, or supplemented again by later Persian writings on Zoroastrian subjects or by traditions which the priests have preserved. Most important among the Pahlavi texts is a work entitled *Būndahishn*, ' Original Creation,' a sort of Iranian Genesis founded on one of the original books of the Avesta which has been lost.[1]

An acquaintance with the ancient Zoroastrian literature and its language, and a familiarity with the history of the people that have preserved it, made me anxious to make the journey around Lake Urumiah, which Zoroaster himself must have made, and I used my own volume on the Prophet's life as a sort of handbook for the journey in laying out my route from Tabriz along the shores of the historic lake.

[1] Most of the Pahlavi books have been translated into English or summarized by West, *Pahlavi Texts*, 5 vols., in the *Sacred Books of the East*, Oxford, 1880–1897.

CHAPTER VIII

AROUND LAKE URUMIAH

'Wer den Dichter will verstehen
Muss in Dichters Lande gehen.'
— GOETHE, *Westöstlicher Divan.*

IN spite of rumors of deep snow I ventured to undertake the journey around Lake Urumiah from Tabriz to the city of Urumiah by wagon. I was warned in advance by one of my friends that if I tried to drive, I should be sure to wish I had ridden, and if I started on horseback, I should be certain to regret not having gone by carriage. Events proved the truth of his words. The 'roads' were in a vile condition, and the journey, which ordinarily occupies three or four days, took me six.

For the first forty-eight hours I had the companionship of two Persians whom we overtook on the road; they were also driving. One of them was a native of the village of Khosrova, near Dilman, northwest of the lake, and was on his way home from Meshad in eastern Persia.[1] The other was connected with the bank at Teheran. The latter was a particularly fine-looking fellow, with handsome eyes, clear-cut features, and a tall, well-developed frame. He wore on his head a hood, the ends of which formed a scarf to wrap about his face as a protection against the cold. This made him look like a veritable

---

[1] Is it possible that Khosrova preserves a lingering reminiscence of the Avestan king Haosravah, who sacrificed 'on the other side of Lake Chaechista' (Lake Urumiah), Yt. 5. 49, or does it owe its name to the later Sasanian king Khosru Parviz? I find that this suggestion has been previously made by Darmesteter, *Le ZA.* 2. 632, n. 92.

portrait of Darius Codomannus at the battle of Issus, a reproduction of which has been given above.

The temperature must have registered nearly zero during the
first two days of the trip, although I never had the courage to
consult the thermometer which was stowed away somewhere in
my baggage. In the daytime I was compelled to wear my sleep-
ing-jacket over my head to shield my frost-bitten face from the
congealing wind, and as evening fell I muffled a bathrobe over
this to add some warmth. I envied any one whose lot it might
be to make the journey in midsummer instead of in winter, and
I understood why the Avesta regarded winter as 'the work of
demons' and said that it was created by Ahriman as a blight to
mar the perfection of Airyana Vaejah, the Azarbaijan of to-day,
which otherwise would have been a paradise.[1] In this land the
Vendidad says 'there are ten months of winter and two months
of summer.'[2] A gloss, it is true, changes the text to 'five
months of winter and seven months of summer,' but judging
from my own discomfort (for March seemed in the Avestan
words to be the very 'heart of winter,' *zimahe zaredhaēm*), I
felt inclined to agree with the original reading. My discomfort was tempered, however, by the thought that the region
through which I was travelling had probably once been traversed by Zoroaster, and this added a zest to my observations
en route as the trail meandered forward along the northern
shore of the lake.

Lake Urumiah is the largest body of water in Persia,
although not quite so large as our Great Salt Lake in Utah,
which is about seventy-five miles long and from thirty to fifty
broad, the Persian lake being about eighty miles in length
and averaging twenty-four miles in breadth. Both of these
bodies of salt water lie about four thousand feet above the level

---

[1] See Vd. 1. 2, *zyąmča daēvō-
dātəm*. The heat near the northern
shore of Lake Urumiah is corre-
spondingly great in midsummer: 'no
place shows better than this the contrast between summer and winter in
Azarbaijan' (Wilson, *Persian Life*,
p. 83).

[2] Vd. 1. 3.

of the sea, and neither has any outlet. The waters of both are intensely saline and vary considerably in volume according to the condition of the mountain streams that feed them; but the average depth in each case is considerably less than twenty feet. Other resemblances might be pointed out, but enough have been indicated to show the parallel between the two.

About the shores of Lake Urumiah there are level plains, sometimes covering an area of many square miles, such as the great Plain of Urmi on the western border, and there are high mountains lying beyond them on all sides of the lake. These sometimes thrust their spurs down to the very edge of the water, as does the ridge of the Karabagh mountain on the northwest (six thousand feet high), and the offshoots of the great mountain of Sahand on the east (over eleven thousand feet). A few small islands dot the surface of the lake toward the south-central part, and from the middle of the eastern shore the mountain peninsula of Shahi, or Shah Kuh, juts out. This tongue of land was once an island twenty-five miles in circumference, but it has become a part of the mainland, because the lake has lowered somewhat.[1] Of recent years, however, the volume of water has tended again to increase, so that considerable fluctuations in the outline of the shores are still taking place. To-day there is no navigation on Lake Urumiah except what is carried on by means of clumsy scows propelled by primitive oars and sails.

We can trace the history of Lake Urumiah far back into antiquity, even to Zoroaster's time and still earlier. The region was familiar to the Assyrian kings as the scene of some of their active campaigns, and the lake appears in their inscrip-

---

[1] Yakut, who passed by Lake Urumiah twice (A.H. 612, 617 = A.D. 1215, 1220), speaks of the mountain island in the midst of the lake (see Barbier de Meynard, *Dict. géog.* p. 86), and Sir J. Macdonald Kinneir reports it as an island in his day (1810–1830); cf. Curzon, *Persia*, 1. 532. Similarly, Perkins (1843) calls it an island, 'which is much of the year a peninsula' (*Eight Years in Persia*, p. 170).

tions as the 'lake of the land Nairi.'[1]   It was known in the
Avesta by the name of Chaechasta, which the Arab geographers corrupted through Chiz into Shiz.[2]   The Avesta calls it
'deep' (*jafra*), which may be an appropriate epithet according to the ideas of the ancient Persians, who were unacquainted
with our great lakes; but its average depth hardly exceeds
fifteen feet.   The characteristic Avestan attribute, however,
which is applied likewise to the Caspian, is *urvāpa, uruyāpa,*
'whose water is salt.'[3]   Lake Urumiah is so briny that fish are
not found in its waters, and the only occupant appears to be a
small crustacean.   The Pahlavi treatise Bundahishn, which
several times mentions Lake Chechast, expressly states that
'there is nothing whatever living in it.'[4]   Ibn Haukal, in the
tenth century, makes a similar statement.[5]   As for the modern

---

[1] So Schrader, *Die Namen der Meere in den assyrischen Inschriften*, in *Abh. d. Akad. d. Wiss. zu Berlin*, 1877, pp. 184-193. For the relations between Lake Urumiah and Lake Van, see Streck, *Armenien, Kurdistan und Westpersien*, in *Zt. f. Assyriologie*, 13. 11. The fact that the region of the lake and city of Urumiah is alluded to in the Assyrian inscriptions is accepted by Ward, *Notes on Oriental Antiquities* in *American Journal of Archæology*, 6. 286, and by others. We might be tempted to seek the name of Urumiah, or Urmi, in the Assyrian *Urume*, but see Streck, *op. cit.* pp. 23-24.

[2] See p. 131. The actual Avestan form is *Vairi Čaēčasta* (or *Čaēčista*), Yt. 5. 49; Ny. 5. 5; Sir. 2. 9. On the name *Šīz* (*Čīz*) see my *Zoroaster*, pp. 195, 197, 201-202, 204.

[3] Such seems to be the force of Av. *urvāpa, uruyāpa,* as first pointed out by Darmesteter, *Études Iraniennes*, 2. 179. See also Geldner, *Vedische Studien*, 2. 270, Stuttgart, 1897, despite Bartholomae, *Altiranisches Wör-*

terbuch, p. 404, Strassburg, 1905. The Pahlavi tradition sees in this epithet 'warm water,' *garmāb, garmiā.* Shall we venture to compare Avestan *Uru-āpa, Uruy-āpa,* 'having salt (or warm) water,' with the modern name *Ur-mī, Ur-miā(h),* 'Urumiah,' which the natives commonly understood as 'place of water' (the last element being the Semitic word for water)? On Pahlavi *Čēčast* see also Rosenberg, *Livre de Zoroastre*, pp. xxviii, 74.

[4] Bd. **22.** 2; cf. **17.** 7; **23.** 8; and Bahman Yasht, **3.** 10.

[5] Ibn Haukal, tr. Ouseley, p. 162: 'There is a lake in Azarbaijan called the Lake of Armiah (Urumiah); the water is salt or bitter and contains not any living creature. All round this lake are villages and buildings; from the lake to Maraghah is a distance of three farsang; to Armi (Urmi, Urumiah), two farsang. The length of this lake is five days' journey by land; and by water, with a fair wind, a person may traverse it in the space of one night.'

name of the lake, the natives generally term it Dariah-i Shahi, or ' Royal Sea,' after the mountain peninsula of Shahi, or Shah Kuh, mentioned above. The early Greek geographer Strabo mentions it under the name of *Spauta* (written Σπαῦτα in the Mss.), which is supposed to be an error for *Kapauta*, the Persian *Kabūda*, lit. ' blue, cerulean '; [1] but since my return to America I heard two natives of Urumiah apply the name ' Spaut' to the lake, although I did not hear it so called while I was in Azarbaijan. [2] The Arab writer Masudi uses the name *Kabūdhān*, saying the lake is so called after the village of Kabodhan on an island in the lake ; [3] but the attribute ' cerulean' is more probably due to the color of the water, which presents a succession of blues melting into purples, mingled with ultramarine and green — hues which were all the more conspicuous against a background of snowy mountains and a shore whitened with crystals of salt due to the incrustation of saline deposits. The old name Shiz, or Chaechasta, seems absolutely to have disappeared, as I could find no trace or reminiscence of it among the people, although I inquired again and again during the two weeks or more which I spent in the vicinity of the lake. [4]

The heavy floods and inundations through which we had to make our way during a part of the journey around Lake Urumiah made the Avestan word *vōighna*, ' inundation, overwhelming flood, deluge,' a living reality. [5] The disasters and misery which follow in the wake of these winter freshets are as evident to-day as they were in ages past. Twice we had to descend to help the horses, which had been carried off their feet

[1] So, for example, Marquart, *Ērānšahr*, p. 143.

[2] They were Nestorians, and the designation may be Syriac.

[3] Marquart, *Ērānšahr*, p. 143.

[4] For additional details regarding Lake Urumiah see Barbier de Meynard, *Dict. géog. de la Perse*, pp. 85–86, who cites the authority of Saint-Martin, *Mém. sur l' Arménie*, 1. 56 seq. Compare also Bittner, *Der Kurdengau Ushnūje und die Stadt Urūmije*, in *Sb. Akad. Wiss.* 133, Abh. 3, pp. 1–97, Wien, 1895 ; Marquart, *Ērānšahr*, p. 143 ; Curzon, *Persia*, 1. 532–534.

[5] Vd. **1.** 3; Ys. **57.** 14.

by the treacherous caving-in of the bank of a stream. It was often a matter of the greatest difficulty to find a safe ford, but the natives seemed to have a remarkable instinct for discovering crossings. There were few bridges, if any, and I could understand why it was a pious act, according to the Zoroastrian faith, to build a bridge, and why this practice was enjoined also upon the worshippers of Ormazd as one means of penance for expiating the sin of having killed an otter — a sacred animal in the eyes of Zoroaster.[1]

Wherever there was a trace of stubbly grass, large flocks of sheep and goats were cropping it. The color of most of these was black or brown; the few white sheep among the number were conspicuous in contrast to the others. This made clear to me a Zoroastrian simile which had always been a puzzling one. The Pahlavi book of the Bundahishn, in describing the Day of Judgment, says that at the last day, when the souls are gathered together in a great assembly after the resurrection, 'a wicked man shall be as conspicuous in that assembly as a white sheep among the black.'[2] The white sheep was certainly the marked one in the flocks I saw on this journey.

My observations of some of the birds of Azarbaijan, the lark, thrush, and long-tailed magpie, were only incidental, but I took more careful note of the crow, raven, eagle, and vulture, because those are especially mentioned in the Avesta. The crow is seen everywhere. The raven is still more plentiful and flies in enormous flocks. On one occasion I counted over a thousand of these birds in a field near Lake Urumiah. So far as my observations went, the raven appears to be more common in northern Iran than it is in the south, but this fact may have been due to migration at the time when I made my notes, or to some accidental cause. The bird is large in size,

[1] Vd. **14**. 16.

[2] Bd. **30**. 10, *andār ān anjuman darvand aētūnŏ pētak cīgūn gōspand ī spēt andar ān sīāk bēṭ.* See the text of Justi, *Bundehesh*, p. 73, Leipzig, 1868; Westergaard, *Bund.* p. 73, Copenhagen, 1851; Unvalla, *Bund.* p. 85, Bombay, 1897; and the translation of West, *Pahlavi Texts*, in *Sacred Books of the East*, 5. 123, Oxford, 1880.

with a glossy bill and sleek wings. I wondered whether the martial bird *vāreghna*, *vārenjina* in the Avesta, a feather of whose wing was used by the warrior as an amulet, might possibly be identified with the raven.[1] The raven was the bird of battle among the Anglo-Saxons and other Germanic peoples, and the symbol upon the crest of Verethraghna, the Iranian Mars, on the coins of the Indo-Scythian kings, may be the raven.[2] The only other bird that would answer well to the description of the *vārenjina* is the peregrine falcon, which is noted for its swiftness of flight and habits of prey. It can hardly be the ordinary falcon, as that was a bird of sport in Persia, as elsewhere; nor was it the eagle, for that is called *saēna* in the Avesta.[3] The eagle, however, abounds in the mountainous regions of Iran, and I could understand why Xenophon should have represented Cyrus as taking omens from eagles.[4] Moreover, as I watched the soaring flight of this king of birds above the peaks, I was forcibly reminded of the name of that lofty range in eastern Iran, *Upāiri-saēna*, 'Above-the-Eagle,' whose height, according to the Avesta, surmounted even the eagle's flight.[5] The vulture (to which bird as well as to the dog the Magians used to throw the bodies of their dead to be torn) is found in Azarbaijan, but in numbers it did not seem so plenti-

---

[1] Yt. **14**. 19–22; **14**. 35–40. I find that this view has the support of the authority of Darab, as cited by Justi, *Handbuch der Zendsprache*, s.v., and of Tir Andaz and Darmesteter, *Le ZA*. 2. 566, n. 29 (which Bartholomae, *Air. Wb*. pp. 1411, 1412, brands as 'falsch'). Geldner, *Drei Yasht*, p. 65, n. 1, suggests the hawk, 'habicht,' as a possibility. The Bundahishn, **14**. 23, calls the raven *varāk* (the Modern Persian word for crow, *kalāgh*, is not to be confounded with this), and this is apparently the bird of victory which accompanied King Ardavan according to the Pahlavi *Kārnāmē-i Artakhshīr-i Pāpakān*,

ed. Darab D. P. Sanjana, pp. 16–17, Bombay, 1896, although Darab Sanjana (*loc. cit.*) calls it an 'eagle' (reading *lūk*), and Peshotanji, Nöldeke, and Antia (the latter, *Kārnāmak*, p. 16, Bombay, 1900) interpret the Pahlavi word in this passage as 'ram' (reading *varāk*).

[2] See Stein, *Zoroastrian Deities on Indo-Scythian Coins*, in *Indian Antiquary*, 17. 207, London, 1877 = reprint, p. 14, Bombay, 1888.

[3] From *saēna mərəya* comes the name of the mythical bird Simurgh.

[4] Xenophon, *Cyropaedia*, **2**. 1. 1; **2**. 4. 19.

[5] Yt. **19**. 3; Ys. **10**. 11.

My Guide to the Sasanian Sculpture

The Typical Village Dog of Azarbaijan

ful as I expected, perhaps owing to the cold season at the
time when I was there.[1]

The dogs formed a special object of notice because of the
esteem in which they were formerly held among the ancient
Zoroastrians, although now despised by the Mohammedans
except for hunting and as watch-dogs. So far as my knowledge goes, the Avesta is the only Oriental work which is highly
complimentary to the dog. It is true that he was venerated in
Egypt, but in India the Sanskrit writers usually speak of him
in derogatory terms, and so do the Hebrews in the Bible.[2] A
special sanctity, however, is attached to the animal in the Vendidad, and three chapters of this sacerdotal work are devoted
to the faithful friend of man.[3] Amid the high praises of the
canine virtues, the text does not hesitate to call attention to
certain vices, so that the eulogy does not degenerate into mere
flattery.[4] My observations of dogs were not confined to Azarbaijan, but were continued throughout the journey, south, east, and
north.

The typical dog of northern Iran, Transcaspia, and Turkistan is a large brute, resembling the mastiff in size, tawny in
color, and roughish in coat, although the hair may be thinner
and smoother in summer. In appearance he is somewhat wolfish, and in temper extremely savage. These wolfish characteristics corroborate the allusions in the Vendidad to the
nature of the hybrid sprung from a dog and a wolf.[5] Most of
the village dogs in the outlying districts of Azarbaijan have
their ears cropped quite close to the head, their masters adopting

---

[1] Vd. **6.** 45, 46; **7.** 30; **3.** 20; Herodotus, *Hist.* 1. 140; **3.** 16; Cicero,
Tusc. Disput. **1.** 45.

[2] An exception may perhaps be
found in Vedic times, when the dog
seems to have enjoyed a better reputation; cf. Hopkins, *The Dog in the
Rig-Veda*, in *Am. Journ. Philol.* 15.
154–163, Baltimore, 1894. Compare
also Watson, *The Dog Book*, 1. 15–20,

New York, 1905. Among Occidental
writers Dante and Shakspere do not
hesitate occasionally to give the dog a
metaphorical kick.

[3] See Fargards 13, 14, 15 of the
Vendidad, and consult Hovelacque, *Le
Chien dans l'Avesta*, Paris, 1876.

[4] See especially Vd. **13.** 44–48.

[5] Vd. **13.** 41–43.

this practice to prevent the ears of the creatures from being torn in the fierce fights in which they constantly indulge.

One of the best opportunities which I had for noticing dogs was later at the city of Urumiah itself, where I once saw a motley collection of a dozen or more dogs gathered about the slaughter-house. Here I observed a good specimen of the 'white dog with yellow ears,' which the Vendidad enjoins as one of the two dogs to be used in the *sag-dīd* ceremony of exorcising the spirit of death.[1] The second kind of dog required for the Avestan rite, namely a ' yellow dog with four eyes ' — that is, with two spots above the eyes — I did not specifically see. The spots over the eyes are apparently less common, which may account for the value of such dogs in the ancient ceremonies, and some European friends gave me the interesting information that the German dachshund loses the tan spots over his eyes after a generation or two in Persia.

Besides the tawny or yellowish village dog, the black, white, and parti-colored dog is also to be seen, especially in the towns. As a rule they are smaller in the cities than in the country and partake more of the mongrel type. Curiously enough, the village dog, despite his savage courage, especially toward strangers, proved to be in absolute dread of being 'shot' by the snap of a camera. It took me nearly a week before I succeeded in getting a photograph of the typical village dog of Azarbaijan, but I finally succeeded at a hamlet between Dilman and Guchi, by decoying the animal with egg-shells that I had thrown away after a hasty meal.

The stages of my journey as far as Dilman in the Plain of Salmas, northwest of the lake, were slow, averaging not more than twenty-five or thirty miles a day, with stops for the night at the villages of Dizah-Khalil[2] and Tazvich. Dilman was reached in the afternoon of Sunday, March 22. This town is one of the largest places in the plain, but its *manzil* seemed

---

[1] Vd. **8**. 16 ; see my article in *JAOS*.   [2] See p. 91, n. 1, below.
25. 182–183, and cf. p. 388, below.

little more than a shelter, nor was I attracted by an invitation to visit the tea-house near-by, which I later learned was an opium den. The carcass of a dead horse lying in the stream that runs through the town seemed characteristic of the place, but the people appeared to be kindly disposed to a stranger and showed something of a holiday spirit, as they had put on their best clothes to celebrate the season of No-Ruz and also Sunday, which is always a special 'bazaar-day,' the regular Mohammedan Sabbath being Friday.

I left Dilman the next morning at eight, with the weather bleak and dreary. In about two hours we came to an interesting old Armenian cemetery which is situated on a hillock near a small village. To reach this graveyard I had to leave the wagon and wade through snow and water for nearly half a mile. An inscription on a large monument near the summit ascribes the founding of the burying-ground to the Mamikonians, an ancient heroic family of Armenia, and I observed a number of grave-stones rudely shaped like a ram, a common image in old Armenian burial-places. I noticed also one long Syriac inscription, but the letters were almost illegible.

After a short stay on the hillock I proceeded on my journey to see the Sasanian bas-relief of the horsemen, which I knew was carved on the side of a rocky hill called Surat Daghi, 'Picture Mountain,' somewhere on the road between Dilman and Guchi. Shortly before noon we reached a tiny hamlet and found that we had passed the hill of the sculptures, having met no one on the deserted plain who knew precisely where the carvings were located. Accordingly I took a guide and returned on foot through mud and snow for a distance of nearly three miles in order to examine the bas-reliefs.

The sculptures are carved about a hundred feet above the plain on the face of a somewhat precipitous rock, and are undoubtedly Sasanian in origin, as they present all the characteristic features of the bas-reliefs at Tak-i Bostan, Naksh-i

Rustam, and Naksh-i Rajab.   The group is composed of four figures, two mounted and two standing.   The equestrian figures are royal personages, apparently represented in the act of receiving crowns from the two unmounted figures, which look like vassals and almost resemble grooms.   The first of the mounted individuals appears to be older than the other and wears a mustache and apparently also a beard; the second is younger and looks almost smooth-faced, but on closer examination this absence of the beard is only apparent, not real, being due to a mutilation of the lower part of the face by some iconoclast.[1] Both figures wear the familiar balloon-shaped head-gear with streamers floating out behind and a scarf or veil fluttering from below the shoulders.   The cloak about the shoulders of each is clasped in an easy manner, the garment of the elder personage being the more elaborate.   Each horseman grasps the reins of his steed with the left hand, which rests at the same time upon the hilt of a long, straight sword; while the right hand is extended to receive some proffered gift, which is hidden behind the horse's head in the first case, but looks like a chaplet in the case of the second cavalier.   The close-fitting coat or tunic, the baggy trousers flowing in rich drapery from the knees, and more elaborately carved in the case of the elder personage than in that of the younger, together with the heavy caparison of the horses, which includes a massive chain and ball swinging at the left flank, are typical of sculpture of the Sasanian dynasty.   The pose of the two horsemen is lifelike and spirited, although the workmanship is imperfect.

The men on foot are represented as bareheaded and with beards, mustaches, and hair bushy at the sides.   The face of the left figure is much mutilated, but that of the right is pre-

[1] My note-book has the memorandum ' smooth-faced ' corrected to ' no, hardly ' upon a more careful inspection of the stone, and this is confirmed by the photograph, which shows the mutilation of the rock, and by Ker Porter's sketch, which represents the figure as having a full beard (*Travels in Persia*, 2. 597, pl. 82), as well as by the drawing of Flandin and Coste, *Voyage en Perse, Ancienne*, 4. pl. 204–205, and Texier, *Description*, 1. pl. 40.

SASANIAN BAS-RELIEF, NEAR THE PLAIN OF SALMAS

served with sufficient clearness to show details, including what seems to be a collar or band about the neck.   Both individuals are clad in a simple manner, the upper garment being a tunic-like coat, the lower being huge bulging trousers.   There is a double belt about the waist of each, but no sword is noticeable, nor is there any characteristic accoutrement or decoration, but from the forearm of the figure on the right there hangs a pendant that looks like a circlet suspended by a short band.

The generally accepted identification of the group is that the bas-relief represents Ardashir Papakan, the first Sasanian king, and his son Sapor, receiving the submission of the Armenians, an event that occurred about A.D. 230, to which period the sculptures approximately belong.[1]

My examination of the sculptures took me some time, and on the way back I became separated from my servant and the guide, who had gone to search for an article I had lost on the way, so that I had some anxiety about finding the road to the hamlet alone ; but the servants finally came up, and we all returned together to the little settlement of mud hovels, and there I had something to eat, and succeeded in getting with my camera a snapshot of the Azarbaijan dog to which I have already referred.

The afternoon was well advanced when the journey was resumed, and we turned our faces southward to cross the Karabagh ridge, over six thousand feet above the sea.   The snow lay almost as deep as it did in the Avestan winter of Yima (Jamshid),[2] and it grew heavier and heavier as we ascended the mountain, until about half-past four the track was finally

[1] So Justi, *Empire of the Persians*, 2. 259 ; Wilson, *Persian Life*, p. 91. We have an incidental allusion also to the opposition of Armenia to Ardashir's authority in the Karnamak-i Artakhshir-i Papakan, 6. 2 (ed. Darab Sanjana, p. 24, Bombay, 1896). A different explanation of the scene is given by Ker Porter, *Travels*, 2. 599, who attributed an Armenian origin to the sculpture, and saw in the two horsemen the Roman emperor Galerius and the Persian king Narses, the latter making concessions to the Armenian prince Tiridates. But this explanation of the sculpture seems doubtful.

[2] See Vd. 2. 22.

lost in drifts as high as the horses' backs. We could proceed no farther for the nonce, and there seemed a good prospect of spending a freezing night on the mountains at an altitude of several thousand feet. At last traces of the path were discovered, and the guide went forward to secure horses and assistance from a post-house which was said to be some distance beyond. The falling snow and the biting cold made the delay seem long, but the messenger returned within an hour, leading three horses ; I was able, therefore, to dismiss the wagon, giving directions to the driver to return to the hamlet as best he could. I never heard how he reached his destination; but I imagine he arrived safely, *inshāllah*, 'by the Grace of God,' a Deo Volente phrase which the Persians employ in connection with everything they do.

The horses that came from the hill post looked thin and poorly kept, but we placed the load upon the back of the strongest ; the second animal was assigned to my servant Safar, and I mounted the third myself. Away we started through the snow.

As we crossed the first ridge there was still enough light to see, on the edge of a stream below, the fresh carcass of a horse that appeared to have fallen over the edge into the gorge, and from which a huge shaggy dog was tearing strips of fast-disappearing flesh. Dusk fell, and darkness closed in rapidly as we began the wild ride over the pass and through the gorges of the Karabagh mountain toward Guchi.[1] The native guide inquired ominously for our guns, which we did not have, and I thought lovingly of my revolver, which by this time was peacefully reposing at Tiflis. The night seemed too stormy, however, for robbers, but as I now look back on it and think of the murder of my friend Mr. Labaree and his servant on the same road from Khoi to Urumiah a year later,[2] and the pillaging of a party of ten in this region by a band of

---

[1] Or *Ḳuchi*, as the name is more accurately rendered.   [2] See p. 90, n. 1.

THE GREAT PLAIN OF URUMIAH

PLOWING WITH BUFFALOES NEAR URUMIAH

Kurds some months after I passed through it, the risk of the journey seems very real.[1]

The wind was high, and it drove sheets of blinding snow from the north, which we fortunately escaped whenever the path veered southward, although the drifts were often up to the horses' bellies. Over streams we proceeded and along precipices which seemed more sheer in the darkness, until the night became so pitchy black that there was nothing for us to do but throw the reins on the necks of the horses, swing our arms to keep from freezing, and trust to the horses' instincts to find the way. All this while my cane, umbrella, and hat-box with top hat were trundling at the side of my saddle and seemed ludicrously out of place amid these surroundings ; but I had had no chance to get rid of them (except by throwing them away as useless appendages) since I bade adieu to the last traces of civilization, where I had needed them in paying official visits. To cheer the situation and brighten my own spirits as well as those of the men, I whistled a tune and began to sing. All I could think of at the moment was the 'Star-Spangled Banner' — a strangely democratic pibroch for the highlands of Iran ! The guide responded with a Turkish ditty, which I answered in turn by a few lines of Hafiz that I knew in Persian, to the apparent entertainment of our leader, and thus we made the dark journey through what seemed to be the valley of the shadow of death. The lights of the mud houses on the outskirts of Guchi at last began to twinkle through the gloom, and it was not long before we had descended from the only remaining hill, crossed a level stretch, and found ourselves lodged in the best house in the village.

The master of the house was a tall, muscular man with heavy mustachio eyebrows which would have given his face a look of fierceness had it not been for his well-shaped nose and the kindly expression about his mouth. He was entertaining No-

[1] The Avesta alludes to such highwaymen, bandits, and assassins in Zoroaster's time under the designations *tāyu, hazaṅhan, gada.*

Ruz guests, as the New Year season was approaching its height, and although the company was composed of a set of rough-looking fellows, resembling tramps and bandits, they seemed to have good hearts, and ' I was of their felaweshipe anon.'

Some simple food and New Year's sweetmeats were provided for refreshment; my camp-bed was set up to furnish me a seat, while the guests squatted around the steaming *samovar* and enjoyed hot tea sweetened to a syrup by masses of sugar. Two little boys came in after the repast was over. They were clad in dirty rags, but were brothers of our host, who had summoned them to sing for our entertainment. Their bright faces beamed as they sang, which they did lustily and shrilly, beating time rhythmically upon a rough tambourine, while the host joined with a zest in the music. Finally he passed the tambourine to me with a request to sing. I chose 'Yankee Doodle' in preference to 'Home, Sweet Home,' because of the tune, and not the sentiment, for in general I believe the Persian would prefer the 'chop-sticks waltz' to a melody of Rubinstein or a symphony of Beethoven. Apropos of song, I asked the company if they knew the story of Shirin and her sculptor-lover Farhad, so beautifully told by Nizami.[1] Several knew it well and recited portions both in Persian and Turkish.

It was past midnight when the company broke up for the night and I found that I was to be one of five to occupy the rough-raftered, mud-walled room. I felt that I was in Media Past, for the Avesta presumes a condition of society in which a number shall occupy the same room, since it speaks of 'men lying down to rest in the same place, on a rug together, or a pillow together, whether there be two men by one another, or five, or fifty.'[2] The preparation of the natives for retiring consisted chiefly in loosening their belts and curling themselves up under a blanket, resting then undisturbed until the time came to give a shake, like a dog, in the morning. Three of the party who had not yet gone to bed remained squatting near

[1] See pp. 188, 226.   [2] Vd. 5. 27 = 7. 5.

A GLIMPSE OF URUMIAH

NORTHERN END OF LAKE URUMIAH

me and watched the proceedings with interest, first examining
my pistol-belt as I unclasped it (now minus the revolver),
admiring the leather, especially the mechanism of the clasp,
then commenting on the quality as a whole, and passing the
belt to the next. My russet riding-leggings, with their practical
Yankee fastenings, called forth special approval, so I passed
these around as further exhibits, and each of the three guests
who were awake gravely tried one on. This done, we all fell
asleep and remained undisturbed till after daylight. The
inspection of exhibits was then renewed as I unpacked my
dressing-case, brought out my folding mirror for shaving,
and proceeded to load my camera with fresh films. These
stages furnished exhibits X, Y, and Z, and I was glad when
I could pack up again and escape from being stared at.

Despite my oft-repeated *zūd, zūd, tēz, tēz,* 'quick, hurry up,
the sun had nearly reached the zenith before I succeeded in
getting two horses and a cart with which to resume the journey
to Urumiah, hoping to reach it that night. When I walked
out from the lodgings where we had spent the night, I found
we were on the edge of the great Plain of Urumiah, having
descended into it after the wild ride over the Karabagh passes
the night before. To hurry matters up for departure I started
to enter the courtyard where the men were engaged in hitch-
ing up the cart which was to be our next means of transportation. One of the servants rushed forward to urge me
not to enter because of the savage dogs. In the best Persian
I knew I protested that I was not afraid of dogs, but discovered in an instant that these dogs were of a most vicious
kind, and was forced to beat a retreat. The cart was finally
ready, and we started.

In the noonday air there was a slight suggestion of spring,
and I noticed that the peasants were making a first attempt
to turn up the soil with their plows. The Persian plow is a
very primitive sort of affair. It consists of the crotch of
a tree cut in such a manner that one of the two branches

may be sharpened and shod with iron to serve as a plowshare, while the other, or main trunk, serves as the beam.   Bullocks or cows are hitched to the unwieldy implement, and wheels are sometimes added to lighten the lumbersome affair.   The soil of the great alluvial plain, however, yields readily to such primitive implements, because it is one of the most fertile districts in all Persia and justifies its right to the title ' Paradise of Iran.' The entire district, in fact, merits the praise which the Avesta bestows on the larger region of Airyana Vaejah, or Azarbaijan, when it calls this 'the first and best of places created by Ormazd.' [1]

My efforts to reach Urumiah by nightfall failed signally at Karmabad, for there the guide absolutely refused to proceed farther on account of the dreadful state of the roads, which made it impossible to reach the city before dark.   I tried every device from coaxing and bribery to commanding, but he and his companions were obdurate.   Finally I had to yield and spend a cold night at the uncomfortable *manzil*, receiving a promise, however, that the start should be made at daylight on horseback.   Only twice in my Persian experience, besides this occasion, did I fail to carry my point about proceeding on the march when the natives objected; but this time I found that the men were right, as the guide, with some satisfaction, showed me next day when we floundered through seas of mud and slush which might have proved dangerous to life in the darkness. It was with a veritable feeling of joy, toward noon that day, March 25, the sixth of my journey from Tabriz, that I neared the walls of the city of Urumiah, one of the several towns that lay claim to having been the birthplace of Zoroaster.

[1] Vd. 1. 2. All writers, ancient and modern, speak of the richness of the soil and the abundance of the crops about Urumiah. See, for example, Mustaufi, cited in Barbier de Meynard's translation of Yakut, p. 26, n. 3, and also Curzon, *Persia*, 1. 535.

A Butcher and a Cobbler, Urumiah

Women washing Clothes, Urumiah

CHAPTER IX

URUMIAH, A SUPPOSED EARLY HOME OF ZOROASTER

'And there I shaped
The city's ancient legend into this.'
— TENNYSON, *Godiva*, 3-4.

'THEY claim that Urumiah was the city of Zardusht and that it was founded by the Worshippers of Fire,' so writes the Arab traveller Yakut, who visited the city in A.D. 1220, and a still earlier author Ibn Khordadhbah (about A.D. 816) calls it 'the city of Zaradusht,' while Al-Baladhuri (A.D. 851) also notes that 'Urumiah is an ancient city of Azarbaijan, and the Magians think that their master, Zaradusht, came from there.'[1] A half dozen other Oriental writers make similar statements associating Zoroaster's name directly or indirectly with Urumiah and pointing to its antiquity. Nevertheless the city is not mentioned in the Avesta or in the Pahlavi literature, for Anquetil du Perron was wrong in fancying that he recognized the name of Urumiah in the Zoroastrian prayer *Airyema Ishyō;*[2] although it does seem possible, as suggested in the preceding chapter, that its present name *Ur-mī, Uru-miah,* the latter element of which the natives often associate with *mā*, 'water,' may in some distant manner perpetuate the Avestan attribute *uruy-āpa, urv-āpa,* 'having salt (or warm) water,' which is applied to it in the ancient texts.[3] Most of the inhabitants, especially the Nestorians, call the city Urmi, the Persians Urumiah or Urmia, while European books employ

---

[1] See my *Zoroaster*, pp. 197–198; also pp. 17, 30, 38, 48, 49, 96, 165, of the same work.

[2] Cf. my *Zoroaster*, p. 97, n. 1.

[3] See p. 73, n. 3.

Ouroomiah, Oroumiah, Urumiyyeh, and Urumia, besides other spellings.

In its geographical situation the city is fortunate, lying in the alluvial plain of the 'Paradise of Iran,' and the climate is salubrious, though sometimes hot in summer after the rigorous winter. The river, which flows past the city on its southern side, and the abundant streams formed by the snow melting on the Kurdish hills to the west, assure a plentiful water-supply and excellent facilities for irrigation except during the extreme heat of summer. It is true that famine visited the city in 1879, but that was at a time when the scourge swept over a large part of Iran. Systematic cultivation in recent years has done much to obviate for all time the recurrence of such a disaster. The country, for miles around, is covered in summer with gardens that produce melons and cucumbers in abundance ; with orchards laden with apples, pears, peaches, plums, apricots, quinces, cherries, and mulberries; while the grapes of the vineyards are proverbial for their excellence. Wheat, barley, rice, and millet are among the products of the fields, and tobacco has been grown for many years, but its quality is suited rather for the common pipe, *chibūk*, than for the *ḳaliān*, in which the natives smoke rather the tobacco of Shiraz.

When I first saw Urumiah, at the end of March, there was nothing indicative of seed-time and harvest. The snow had only just begun to melt, deluging the plain with floods of water and converting large areas into seas of mud. Through this slough of despond we had slowly to wade our horses, and it needed the sharp ring of the guide's song to which I often echoed a bravo, *khailī khūb*, to cheer us on and keep the struggling animals in their course. A glimpse of the disappearing traces of the muddy way may be seen in the picture I took of a caravan of camels near the gate of Balau, as we entered the city from the north. They were stringing their way along, with dull-toned heavy bells, toward the caravansarai where they were to lay off their loads. I felt a special interest in these dromedaries near Zoroaster's city because the prophet's name, *Zarathushtra*, is said to mean some sort of a camel (*ushtra*).[1]

The city of Urumiah is girt by a wall some three or four miles in compass, pierced by seven gateways and strengthened by a moat at the more vulnerable points. The value of this double defence had something of a test during the memorable Kurdish raid upon Urumiah in 1880, when the city was besieged and threatened with destruction through an attack by the hostile descendants of the ancient Carduchi, who had plundered the surrounding villages, burned, ravaged, and murdered throughout the entire borders and were checked only after much bloodshed and considerable damage to property.[2]

As one enters the town, Urumiah gives the impression of most Persian cities. Some of the streets are fairly broad, and a rough attempt has been made, here and there, to pave them with large round stones from the river-bed. There is no system of drainage, save the water-channels from the moat and river, which serve alike to receive refuse and furnish a washing-place for the women to launder their clothes. A hopeful sign, however, that better municipal ordinances may some day be established, with efficient authority, is seen in the fact that the butchering of animals in the public streets has been forbidden and a public slaughterhouse has been built near the Hazaran gate in the northeastern part of the city. No provision, however, seems to be in force against shovelling the snow off the roofs into the streets and heaping up barriers that make the thoroughfare at times impassable; nor is there any restriction against the use of burying-grounds in the city, where economy of space, time, and labor leads to using the same grave two or three times. The quick and the dead are one kin, and the Persian has little idea of hygiene in such respects; I noticed especially in the hamlets of the rural districts that a preference

---

[1] The meaning 'plowing camel' has even been suggested; see my *Zoroaster*, pp. 147–149.

[2] For a full account of the events connected with the Kurdish raid, see Wilson, *Persian Life*, pp. 109–124.

was shown for placing the graveyard on the nearest hill, at the foot of which the village well was dug. As I followed the main street into Urumiah it led directly across a cemetery. There was no way of avoiding the graves, and the horses' hoofs often beat hollow over the excavation beneath the sod. In an adjoining plot a burial was in progress, and the mourners were still gathered about the half-filled grave, at the head of which was placed a rough stone without any inscription. It chanced to be the only funeral I saw during my stay in Persia, where the population is less dense and vitality less low than in plague-stricken India.

Another quarter of an hour's ride, and I found myself dismounting before the door of the American Presbyterian Mission, as the guest of the Rev. Dr. Benjamin Labaree. A welcome there awaited me which those can best appreciate who, weary, mud-bedraggled, chilled, and out of sorts, have endured the discomforts of 'the road' for six hard days through snow, slush, mire, and storm.[1]

In less than two hours after my arrival my host had arranged for my first afternoon of research among the ash-hills, which was to be an excursion with his son to Degalah, the largest mound near the city. There are more than a dozen of these elevations directly in the vicinity of Urumiah, and it is stated that there are as many as sixty-four about the lake. The larger number of them are scattered over the Urumiah

---

[1] I shall never forget this meeting with Dr. Labaree Sr. and young Mr. and Mrs. B. W. Labaree. Almost exactly one year later, March 9, 1904, Mr. Labaree Jr. was brutally murdered by bandits and fanatics on the road from Dilman over which I had passed. His servant, a bright young native, was shot, and the body robbed even of the clothes, and Mr. Labaree was carried away to a mountain ravine, where he was savagely stabbed to death with daggers and swords. His remains were stripped of everything of value, and the assassins escaped over the Turkish border. The bodies of these two martyrs to the Christian cause were afterward discovered and conveyed to Urumiah, where they were buried in the same grave. The United States government followed up the matter of the murder to its source and obtained from the Persian government some reparation for the heinous crime, and a guarantee for the greater safety henceforth of American citizens in Persia.

EXCAVATIONS IN DEGALAH ASH-HILL, NEAR URUMIAH

SPECIMEN OF ANCIENT POTTERY FROM URUMIAH
(In the author's collection)

plain and the plain of Sulduz to the south, but not to the north in Salmas.[1] They are all composed of immense deposits of ashes mixed with earth, the ashes having been added in many cases to a natural small elevation. 'In fact, there is scarcely an eminence on the plain which has not been increased, usually to a very great extent, by this means.'[2] The natives all agree in calling them ' hills of the Fire-Worshippers.' One must be careful, however, not to mistake for ash-mounds some of the numerous hillocks (*tapah*) about the lake, like the Gum Tapah at Mayan, not far from Tabriz, which imagination might easily crown with a fire-shrine. My first guide, knowing my interest in the subject, obligingly called the Gum Tapah an Atash Gah (fire-temple), but it is a mere sand-heap and was probably never one of the Zoroastrian pyræa.

The village of Degalah directly adjoins Urumiah. The ash-hill is three or four hundred yards long, nearly as many broad, and a hundred feet or more in height ; but its dimensions are constantly being reduced, as the peasants within the past century have discovered the value of the alkaline quality of the ashes for fertilizing purposes and for producing saltpetre. As a consequence the hill has been burrowed into, tunnelled, trenched, undermined, and cut down in scores of places, and the soil carried off to spread upon the adjoining farms. The photographs taken by Mr. Labaree and myself will show some of the pits and hollows resulting from these excavations. The structure of the mound was therefore easy to examine. It consists of soft earth with stratum upon stratum of solid ashes at varying depths and several feet thick. There is little stone in the mass, but in former times some stone buildings stood on the top of the hill, and the village of Degalah is built largely from the stones of these, as I am informed by my colleague,

---

[1] On Gaur Tapah, 'Unbeliever's Hill,' near Dizah-Khalil, on the north shore of the lake, see Ker Porter, *Travels*, 2. 606.

[2] This statement is quoted from a missionary among the Nestorians of Persia, Mr. E. C. Shedd, cited by Dr. W. H. Ward, *Notes on Oriental Antiquities*, in *Am. Journ. Archæology*, 6. 286.

Dr. A. Yohannan, who was born there. I understand also that a foundation-wall of burnt brick was discovered some time ago near the bottom of the hill, 'the bricks measuring at least six inches thick by eighteen to twenty-four inches long'—a statement which would agree with the so-called 'Gabar bricks' of Zoroastrian structures which I found elsewhere in Persia.[1]

In their excavations the workmen are constantly unearthing fragments of pottery, sometimes whole vessels, terra-cotta figurines, coins, and other remains which show signs of considerable antiquity. The specimens of earthenware are usually of a reddish or brownish clay, the commonest being a round pot with small handles or with a spout. They are generally without decoration, although a few have figures of men and horses, crudely drawn, or bands of color and other marks of ornamentation upon the surface.[2] Some of the jars are two feet or more in height; I saw such an amphora at a depth of more than twenty feet below the surface in one of the pits into which I went down. It was buried in an upright position in the earth, but was partly broken, so that we did not disturb it, except to scrape some of the débris from around it, which disclosed a few pieces of bones, grains of parched corn, and ashes in abundance. Potsherds by the hundreds were lying at the bottom and about the mouth of every pit, but I could not learn of a single instance where any inscribed tablet or cylinder had been found among the layers of earth and ashes.

It is common, when speaking of this and the other ash-hills around Urumiah, to say that they are composed 'entirely of ashes,'[3] but from my examination in the present instance, and my investigations in others, this term is to be taken relatively.

---

[1] See the quotation by Mr. Shedd in Dr. Ward's article (p. 286) previously cited, and cf. p. 255, below.

[2] A good collection of specimens may be seen in the museum room of the American Missionary College at Urumiah, and many individual samples may be found in the hands of the villagers or of residents in the city.

[3] Mr. Shedd, *op. cit.* p. 286; and a native of Urumiah, Jonathan Badall, now in Yonkers, informed me that the hill of Lakki, thirteen miles north of Urumiah, is composed 'wholly of ashes.'

POTTERY FROM THE TERMANI ASH-HILL, URUMIAH

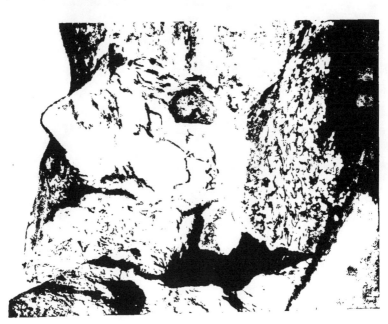

A PIT EXCAVATED IN THE DEGALAH ASH-MOUND

I believe therefore that Dr. Ward, even though he had not seen them, was right in his impression that they are composed rather 'of clay which has become mixed with ashes and saturated with nitrous salts of organic composition'; and he shows from an old Babylonian sculpture how such mounds could be built up.[1] There is every reason to assume that these elevations were surmounted by sanctuaries dedicated to the worship of fire, even if we do not agree in every detail with the natives, who unanimously attribute the vast accumulation of ashes to the accretions from the fire-temples, the ashes having been scattered over the hill age after age.[2]

On the following day a party was formed to visit another ash-hill and we rode out to Termani, six miles east of Urumiah. This mound culminates in an elevation some-what resembling a cone. A short distance from the conical rising it was possible to trace the general outline of what was once the foundation of an old building. The large size of the stones called forth comments from the natives, who expressed surprise as to how such large blocks could have been conveyed to the site where they stood. The hill itself has not been much excavated, but about fifteen or twenty years ago, when a well was being sunk near the top, an image of consider-able size was found. Unfortunately it was destroyed by the iconoclastic workmen, who were Mohammedans, as image-making is forbidden by the Koran.[3] On the hill I could see abundant traces of ashes everywhere, although they were not quite so plentiful as at Degalah. My judgment in this case, however, is based only upon an examination of the surface of the ground, as the mound had not been trenched and excavated like the other ; but the ground was strewn with potsherds which incidental diggings had brought to light, and the natives

[1] Ward, *op. cit.* p. 287.

[2] There is nothing of a volcanic nature in the deposit, so far as my limited geological knowledge allowed me to judge.

[3] See Koran (tr. Sale), chap. 2, pp. 18, 23, etc., and the Mohammedan tradition against pictures and images in Mishkat, bk. 12, chap. 1, pt. 1, and bk. 29, chap. 5.

had numerous specimens of earthenware vessels thus unearthed. One of these, which is shown in the photograph, had lost part of its spout, but kept its small handle; another presented a slight attempt at artistic finish, as the handle was twisted in a curious but rather graceful shape; still another, which did not look quite so old as the specimen that I selected, somewhat resembled a modern teapot with holes perforated in the spout to serve as a strainer.

A third mound which I visited was the hill of Ahmat, a short distance southeast of Termani. In one of the trenches there were fragments of a rather large urn, and I am told that specimens as large as a man are sometimes exhumed and that skeletons have been found buried in them.[1] The natives also informed me that, in excavating, they sometimes come across neatly made graves in these ash-mounds, with a stone slab covering the place where the body lay. The truth of this I afterward proved.

The following day spent among the ash-hills was devoted to the mound at Geog Tapah, or Gög Tepe, which lies a little east-southeast from Urumiah. It was the fourth ash-mound that I visited, and was one of the largest. A Christian church, erected by the Nestorians, now crowns the summit of this ancient ash-hill, and the minister, Mr. Morehatch, an Assyrian Christian born near Urumiah, told me that when the workmen were excavating for the foundations of the church they came across an underground chamber built of stone and containing a carved hollow cylinder three or four inches high. The stone vault, he explained, had been filled up in order to make the foundation of the building more secure, and the image had been purchased and sent to America. On my return home I found that this cylindrical bas-relief is now preserved in the Metropolitan Museum of Art in New York City, and that my friend Dr. William Hayes Ward had given a detailed descrip-

---

[1] See also a similar statement made by Mr. E. C. Shedd, cited in the article, already quoted, by Ward, *Am. Journ. Archæology*, 6. 287.

A Typical Mud Hut at Termani, near Urumiah

An Old Mill near Urumiah

tion of it in the publication referred to in the notes, supplemented by Mr. Shedd's account of the chamber where the object was found.[1] I have examined the cylinder a number of times, and through the courtesy of the Museum authorities I am able to give a reproduction of it.[2]

In shape it resembles a large napkin-ring made of translucent alabaster, and it measures $3\frac{1}{4}$ inches (94 millimeters) in height by $2\frac{1}{4}$ inches (59 millimeters) in diameter, the walls being about a quarter of an inch (6 millimeters) in thickness. The surface of the alabaster has been rendered somewhat opaque by exposure, as Dr. Ward observes in his description, from which I freely draw. The design of the carvings, in the opinion of this authority, is archaic Babylonian, and the figures represent the sun-god, Shamash, emerging from the portals of the east and accompanied by other divine personages. The god (the second figure on the right in the reproduction) carries a club on his right shoulder and holds a weapon in his left hand, as he mounts with his left foot the crest of a low hill. The hill is conventionally indicated by several rectangular blocks, which are multiplied also for the other figures to stand upon, and they form at the same time an ornamental base for the cylinder. Two bearded porters, with flowing hair and wearing low double-horned caps, fling open the gates through which the god advances. Behind the left-hand gate-keeper stands the demigod, Ea-bani, half man, half bull, facing full front and holding in his two hands a standard. Behind him again are three figures, on the other side of the cylinder, approaching the sun-god. The first of these is a man ; the second a woman in a flounced robe, who is considered by Dr. Ward to be the sun-god's wife ; and the third, a bearded divine figure clothed in a long skirted mantle. In the garments of all the figures I would call attention to the border of fringe, characteristic of the Median robe and noticeable on the sculptures of

---

[1] See Dr. Ward's article, *Notes on Oriental Antiquities*, in *American* *Journal of Archæology*, 6. 286–301.
[2] One third of the actual size.

the archers discovered by Dieulafoy at Susa and on the effigy
of Cyrus at Persepolis. Dr. Ward believes that this cylindrical bas-relief found at Geog Tapah is at least as old as
B.C. 2000, and probably older, and in his opinion it is 'a
purely Babylonian product, which was conveyed, probably
in some conquest of a very early period, to this distant land
of the Minni.

Beneath the sandstone floor of the chamber where the
cylinder was discovered some fragments of bones were found,
but they were so decomposed that it was impossible to make
anything out of them.[1] It is not infrequent, Mr. Morehatch
told me from his own observations, to unearth from the Geog
Tapah mound large earthen jars containing bones, which show
that the custom of urn-burial was sometimes resorted to, or
else that the use of *astōdāns* was in vogue, as explained below.
Malik Shimmon, my native host, at whose house we lunched,
stated that on his own property two skulls had been dug up
with brass nails driven into the ears. If this is to be taken as
indicating death by execution, added light may be thrown on
the interpretation of a passage in the Vendidad, where, among
other comparisons of torture and punishment, the torments of
hell are described as being as painful 'as if one should nail
the bones of his perishable body with iron nails.'[2]

It is quite evident, from what has been said, that Geog
Tapah was not only an ancient settlement, but that a part of
the mound served also as a cemetery. At one place, where a
deep road had been cut in the hill, I saw a number of graves
exposed, but they were near the surface and apparently not
very old, although in a ghastly condition to behold. Choosing
a spot on the other side of the hill, where it was possible to
excavate at a lower level on account of the conformation of the

[1] See Shedd, quoted by Ward, *op. cit.* p. 287.

[2] So Vd. 4. 51, *fšbiš . . . ava-pašāt*, is probably to be understood; see Darme-steter, *SBE.* 4². 48; *Le ZA.* 2. 63, n. 43; and consult also Bartholomae, *Air. Wb.* p. 879.

BAS-RELIEF CYLINDER FOUND NEAR URUMIAH
(Now in the Metropolitan Museum, New York)
(Two thirds actual size)

OPENING AN ANCIENT GRAVE IN THE SIDE OF THE GEOG TAPAH ASH-HILL

mound, we proceeded to examine an ancient grave or sepulchre that had already been laid partly bare. Malik Shimmon summoned an old man to open the grave, and in a few minutes his long shovel had laid the sepulchre fully unclosed to view. It was a rough sarcophagus of stone, a part of the upper slab and a portion of the side slab of which (both whitish in color) were intact. The head of the grave appeared to be located toward the right, as I looked into the opening. There was a large jar deep in the earth above what was presumably the foot of the grave, but we preferred not to remove it, as it was broken and apparently quite empty. The grave itself was likewise empty, except for a few fragments of bones scattered about; in fact in most cases where the interment shows the greatest signs of antiquity the skeletons have been reduced to dust, or at most a few pieces of bones remain. Yet Mr. Shimmon, who had seen a number of these stone receptacles opened, said that sometimes three or four skeletons are preserved in a single sarcophagus, and the digger recalled an instance where as many as six were found. I had the same assurance also on other authority.

Regarding the age and true nature of these repositories I am wholly undecided at the present time. If they were pre-Mohammedan and pre-Nestorian, as seems probable, it is open to question to which era we are to assign them, whether to a time when the Zoroastrian religion prevailed or to a still earlier date. If we assign them provisionally to the Zoroastrian period, we can only explain them as *astōdāns*, or stone receptacles constructed to receive the bones after the flesh had been denuded from the body by the vultures, in accordance with the tenets of the Zoroastrian religion.[1]

Leaving this opened grave and passing by another which had recently been discovered a few rods distant, but not fully laid bare, we turned our attention to other sights and ascended

[1] For this custom in regard to the bones, see Vd. **6**. 44–51, and consult Modi, *Astōdān, a Persian Coffin*, Bombay, 1889 (brochure).

the brow of the hill to view the surrounding country.   In the
near foreground still another ash-mound, a small elevation, was
pointed out; it was apparently the one called Chachili Hill,
which I passed two days later on my journey southward from
Urumiah.   The village of Saralan, built partly on an ash-hill,
lay on the same road, and there I saw the remains of a building
that had been exposed in digging, and likewise pieces of a large
oven (*tandūr, tanūr*, Av. *tanura*), together with fragments of
a huge amphora, or wine-jar (*līna*).   Not far from there, in
the same general southerly direction, lies the village of Dizach-
Takiah, or Diza-Takiah, built on one of the very largest of the
hills that show traces of ashes in this neighborhood.   My Nestorian friend, Rev. Yaroo M. Neesan, at whose uncle's house we
spent the night, told me that he himself had found at Diza-
Takiah a small statuette with Assyrian affinities.   In looking
over some of the specimens of pottery that had been unearthed
there in digging the foundations of his house, I noticed one
particularly interesting old piece; it was a large terra-cotta pot,
evidently very antique and probably used as a milking vessel,
according to my native host.[1]

It was at Geog Tapah, at the house of Malik Shimmon,
whose hospitality I enjoyed, that I had my first truly Persian
dinner.   We partook of this meal seated on the floor in
Eastern fashion, bolstered up by soft cushions and lost amid
a wilderness of dishes with a variety of viands characteristic of the country.   Among these was the clabber (*māst*), a

[1] The general subject of the ash-
mounds around Lake Urumiah was
treated many years ago, I believe, in
a sketch by Mr. Abbott, but I have
not been able to find the brochure or
even to discover its exact title.   Drs.
Lehmann and Belck gave some attention to the matter of the ash-mounds
in their recent scientific tours through
Armenia and northwest Persia.   Some
information regarding their finds of
pottery has been published by Virchow,
*Fundstücke aus Grabhügeln bei Ur-
mia, Persien*, in *Zt. f. Ethnol. (Verh.
d. Berliner Anthrop. Gesellsch.*), 30
(1898), pp. 522–527; 32 (1900), pp. 609–
612.   My own notes, though imperfect, will suffice to call the attention of
Zoroastrian scholars anew to this field
for archæological research in northwestern Persia.

caseous mixture that recalled to my mind the milk and cheese
diet upon which the classical writers say that Zoroaster lived
for years in the desert.[1] On our way back to the city we
passed a number of interesting sights, one of which was an old
mill, which interested me because of the primitiveness of its style
and structure.

As I happened to be in Urumiah before the season of the
Nō-Rūz festival, or Persian New Year, was over, I had an
excellent opportunity of becoming still better acquainted with
the social life of the people. No-Ruz, 'new day,' the oldest of
all Persian festivals, does not fall in January, like our own New
Year's, but comes in the springtime when the sun enters the
sign of Aries at the vernal equinox. Iranian tradition dates
the festival back thousands of years and says that it was first
celebrated in the golden age by Jamshid, who lived before the
Deluge. It was he who established the solar year ; and although the Persians, as Mohammedans, have otherwise adopted
the lunar calendar current among the Arabians, they have never
given up No-Ruz and its observances. The festival lasts over
a fortnight and is celebrated with as much spirit as it was a
thousand years ago in the time of Harun al-Rashid, when we
find it alluded to in the story of the Enchanted Horse in the
Arabian Nights as ' an ancient and solemn feast throughout all
Persia, which has been continued from the time of idolatry
and is observed not only in the great cities, but celebrated with
extraordinary rejoicings in every little town, village, and hamlet.'[2] Holiday attire, the interchange of gifts, congratulations,
and good wishes, together with merry-making, are the order of
the season. Nor has fashion allowed the time-honored custom
of paying visits on glorious Jamshid's day to lapse. The
callers are welcomed with large trays of sweetmeats and sugar

[1] See my *Zoroaster*, p. 34, n. 2,
where the classical references are
given.

[2] Compare *Arabian Nights*, p. 462,
Philadelphia, 1835 ; and for legends
connected with No-Ruz and the origin
of New Year's presents, see Albiruni,
Chronology of Ancient Nations, tr.
Sachau, pp. 199–204, London, 1879.

confectionery ; and favors of this sort are sent from friends to friends, because tradition says that 'he who tastes sugar on the morning of No-Ruz before speaking, and anoints himself with oil, will keep off all sorts of mishap during the greater part of the year.' Sugar and confectionery, of which the Persians are so extremely fond, have also ancient authority and royal sanction, since among other good things associated with the first New Year's Day and the inauguration of the solar calendar by King Jamshid was the happy discovery of the sugar cane, and the king ' ordered the juice to be pressed out and sugar to be made thereof.'

In making New Year's calls I had the pleasant privilege of going in the company of Dr. J. P. Cochran, the missionary physician at Urumiah, and our first visit was paid to Majidi Sultana, the newly appointed Vice-Governor, who two days before had received from the Shah his official appointment and the accompanying gift of a superb sword. He received us with formal ease and grace and, after the customary bows and salutations of etiquette had been made, conversed freely and pleasantly in Turkish, which the other visitors spoke well, but he addressed me in French, as I was not familiar with Turkish.

In his personality Majidi Sultana may be said to combine the soldier, courtier, and scholar, for he is a man of great personal bravery, a stern commander, yet extremely gentle and finished in his manners, endowed with great fondness for history and literature. His soldierly qualities are looked upon by the people with a respect approaching awe, and his military ability, quickness of decision, and promptness of action have won for him the post he holds. Urumiah is close to the Turkish border and the territory of the Kurds, and this district is particularly subject to danger from outlaws and marauding freebooters, as the Kurdish raid in 1880 proved. The Kurds in fact are even now a constant menace, and Majidi adopted the policy of employing a company of these warlike hillsmen themselves for the purpose of keeping order. Yet I have since

MART MARIAM CHURCH, URUMIAH
(Where one of the Magi is said to be buried)

A TYPICAL GROUP OF MULLAHS AND SEIDS

learned that he nearly lost his life in holding a conference with
the representatives of a rebel Sheikh from over the border.
A parley had been agreed upon, but in the midst of it some
threat of violence was made by the rebels; before the band
could carry out their purpose Majidi Sultana shot the leader
on the spot and had the rest seized and blown from the cannon's mouth in the public square of Urumiah.

In extending hospitality to us, Majidi Sultana was the
polished gentleman above the soldier, and his home bore evidences of culture and scholarly tastes.   Besides finely bound
Persian and Arabic works his library contained a few standard
French books, and he seemed to take a real interest in history.
Knowing his breadth of view and freedom from fanaticism I
had no hesitation in making inquiries about the Zoroastrian
religion, and I soon found, from the questions which he himself
put to me regarding the association of Zoroaster's name with
Ardabil and Mount Savalan, that his range of reading in the
Oriental writers on his shelves must have been considerable.
The decoration of his rooms showed taste, and his collection
of curios and antiques was an interesting one.   At my departure he promised to send two Kurdish guards to accompany
me for three days when I should start on my journey southward toward Hamadan.

After paying this visit to the governor the next ceremony
was to call upon one of the native Khans, a lord of several
villages.   Tea, tobacco, and sweetmeats formed part of the entertainment.   Following that came a visit to a Mullah, or Mohammedan ecclesiastic, which completed the afternoon, for Persian
calls last long.   The Mullah was a kindly old fellow and knew
two words of French, *bon jour*, which he followed up with a
Persian greeting, 'Your Worship is an illumination to my
eyes!'   In this latter salutation, however, there was an element of pathos, for the poor man had become almost totally
blind a few weeks before.   He had been suffering from cataract
and had submitted to an operation at the hands of a native

itinerant quack which had cost him his sight.   I could but
admire his nerve and courage as he quietly told how he held
his head perfectly still without flinching while the charlatan
thrust a needle into the pupil.   We prolonged for some time
our visit with the Mullah and his company of Seïds, or Descendants of the Prophet, until it was time to go, and then we
walked on foot through the streets, in order that I might see
more of the town.

Urumiah has no public edifice of any importance, but it has
a church of great antiquity associated with the Biblical story
of the Magi and indirectly with Zoroaster.   This is the old
Nestorian church of Mart Mariam, the Blessed Virgin, now
a Russian sanctuary.   Popular tradition says that in the crypt
lie buried two, or at least one, of the Magi who came to worship the infant Christ at Bethlehem.   The church may, therefore, be regarded as an Eastern rival of the Cathedral of
Cologne, besides having Persian competitors in Savah, Avah,
and perhaps Kashan.[1]

A legend regarding these Wise Men and the origin of the
church was told me by one of the ladies of the American Mission, who had it from her Syriac teacher at Urumiah.   I recognized it at once as a form of the story which is found in the
apocryphal New Testament Gospel of the Infancy, recounting
how the Wise Men received from Mary the swaddling-clothes
of the infant Christ as a gift, and on returning to their country
made a fire with which to worship and consume the clothes according to their religion, but the blessed garments remained un-
seared in the flames and became a sacred relic.   A church was
built in commemoration of the miracle, and it is this edifice
that serves as the burial-place of the Magi.   For convenience I
reproduce the narrative as it appears in the New Testament
Apocrypha, since it is also of interest because of the express statement that the Wise Men came from the East in accordance with a prophecy delivered by Zoroaster (Zoradascht).

[1] See p. 412, below.

'1. And it came to pass, when the Lord Jesus was born at Bethlehem, a city of Judæa, in the time of Herod the King; the wise men came from the East to Jerusalem, according to the prophecy of Zoradascht, and brought with them offerings: namely, gold, frankincense, and myrrh, and worshipped him, and offered to him their gifts. 2. Then the Lady Mary took one of his swaddling clothes in which the infant was wrapped, and gave it to them instead of a blessing, which they received from her as a most noble present. 3. And at the same time there appeared to them an angel in the form of that star which had before been their guide in their journey; the light of which they followed till they returned into their own country.

4. On their return their kings and princes came to them inquiring, What they had seen and done? What sort of journey and return they had? What company they had on the road? 5. But they produced the swaddling cloth which St. Mary had given to them, on account whereof they kept a feast. 6. And having, according to the custom of their country, made a fire, they worshipped it. 7. And casting the swaddling cloth into it, the fire took it, and kept it. 8. And when the fire was put out, they took forth the swaddling cloth unhurt, as much as if the fire had not touched it. 9. Then they began to kiss it, and put it upon their heads and their eyes, saying, This is certainly an undoubted truth, and it is really surprising that the fire could not burn it, and consume it. 10. Then they took it, and with the greatest respect laid it up among their treasures.'[1]

This story of the Gospel of the Infancy and the legend connected with the church in Urumiah seem to be old Nestorian traditions.[2]

Still another legend connecting Zoroaster's name with Urumiah is recorded. It is referred to by Spiegel, who states that in the mountain of Buzo-daghi, 'Calf Mountain,' to the northeast of the city, a cave is shown in which the Prophet

---

[1] New Testament Apocrypha, Infancy, **3**. 1–10. See also Walker, *Apocryphal Gospels*, pp. 100, 103, Edinburgh, 1870.

[2] The Gospel of the Infancy is current, for example, among the Nestorians in India, and Hone, *Apocryphal*

New Testament, p. 38, London, 1820, states that 'La Crosse cites a synod at Angamala, in the mountains of Malabar, A.D. 1599, which condemns this Gospel as commonly read by the Nestorians in that country (*i.e.* India).'

Zardusht is said to have lived.[1]   This would point apparently
to the tradition of Zoroaster's living for a time as a hermit in a
cave in the Persian mountains, but I myself have not been able
to get any direct information regarding this story, and a native
of Urumiah has since told me that he knows of the place only
as sacred in the eyes of the Mohammedans as 'Ali's Spring.'
I was later informed, however, that there is a rock cavern
near Maraghah on Mount Sahand which is pointed out as the
cave of Zardusht.[2]

Among the observances at Urumiah is one which the natives
regard as a reminiscence of ancient sun-worship — the blowing
of a horn and the beating of a kettle-drum at sunset.   The
place where this curfew signal is given is called the *Naḳārah
Khānah*, 'Band-Tower,' and is situated near the Darwaz-i
Ark, the gate where a citadel once stood.   The horn that is used
is more than six feet in length, and after the drum is beaten
for the third time (*üch tabil* in Turkish), no person is allowed abroad in the streets except under liability of arrest.
A similar custom is in use also at Isfahan, Teheran, Meshad,
Bokhara, and elsewhere, and I am inclined to think that it has
nothing more to do with sun-worship than has a sunset gun or
a curfew bell.[3]

The bazaars in Urumiah are in no way remarkable ; but
some of the shops carry a fair supply of European articles, one
of the best shops being kept by an Armenian.   The streets
have none of the press and throng of people that mark the
more densely populated towns.   The number of inhabitants is
variously estimated between fifteen thousand and forty thousand,
the difference in the estimates being largely due to whether the
surrounding villages are taken into account or not.   The majority of the population are Persians ; the remainder is composed

---

[1] Spiegel, *Ērānische Alterthumskunde*, 1. 131, n. 3, Leipzig, 1891.

[2] For traditions regarding Zoroaster's hermit life, see my *Zoroaster*,
pp. 34, 189 *e*, 194, n. 1.   With regard

to the caves see p. 61, n. 1, above, and
p. 173, n. 1, below.

[3] For the usage in Teheran and other
places, see p. 267, below, and Curzon,
Persia, 1. 164, 174, 309, 350 ; 2. 27.

of Turks, Afshars, Assyrian Nestorians, some Armenians, a few Jews, and a colony of Europeans.

A special historic interest is attached to the so-called Nestorian Christians. They are not of Persian blood, but originally Syrians, or rather Assyrians, a term which they themselves prefer, or Chaldæans, as the French call them. They are descendants of the ancient followers of the Christian bishop Nestorius, who was excommunicated in the fifth century for holding unorthodox views concerning the divinity of Christ, not regarding him as the God-man, but separating his human personality from his divine nature. The adherents of Nestorius spread first into Persia, then far and wide through Asia, carrying their sectarian doctrines with them. In recent years a number of these Persian Nestorians from Urumiah have come as immigrants to America, which they regard as a second Eldorado, and where they have found occupation in carpet shops, hat factories, and other industries. There is a colony of them in New York and in Yonkers, and as a rule they have proved themselves honest and faithful workers, anxious to avail themselves of the educational opportunities offered by the night-schools, and keeping up their connection with the Christian church.

A description of Urumiah would be incomplete without a notice of the Christian missions and their work in this difficult and dangerous field. America, France, England, and Russia are all represented in the cause, and some work is done by Germans and Swedes in the villages of the Urumiah plain. The Americans were the first on the ground, in 1835, under the American Board of Foreign Missions. For seventy years they have labored with devoted zeal, teaching, preaching, helping the poor, and ministering to the sick, for the medical dispensary plays an important part in the activity of the Mission. The buildings and grounds of the Mission itself, though simple and unassuming, are an object-lesson in making a place neat, homelike, and attractive ; and a separate department is set

aside as an office for the printing-press which aids in the evangelical and educational work. Special facilities for female education are given in the Fiske Seminary, where girls receive a
good schooling ; and opportunities for higher study are offered
to young men in Urumiah College, which was founded by
the missionaries many years ago. It is situated outside the
city, about twenty minutes' ride to the southwest, in a richly
wooded enclosure, like a park, which served as a place of
refuge for a large number of native Christians during the
Kurdish raid. Here are gathered the various buildings of the
institution — halls, plain but serviceable, recitation-rooms, simple
but neat, a small museum, a library and offices, and last but not
least the clinic and medical dispensary under Dr. Cochran's
supervision.

The hospitality which I enjoyed also at the English Mission
gave me an opportunity to judge of that good work as well,
and the same may be said of the representatives of the other
Christian creeds in their respective spheres. At the cost of
great personal sacrifice, and even risk of life, they are doing
their share to fulfil the commandment which bids them to
preach the gospel to all nations. To the Mission friends, one
and all, who were so kind to me during my stay I feel deeply
grateful.

My heart was quite full as I mounted my horse to join
my pack-caravan, led by Shahbas, the *chārvādār*, Safar, my
faithful servant, some attendants, and the two guards provided
for my safety on the journey by the governor, Majidi Sultana.
They were both well mounted, but Safar's horse resembled the
rake which the Clerk rode in the *Canterbury Tales*. The
horse upon which Shahbas sat cushioned — for his pack-saddle
(*pālān*) was a heavy mattress of stuffed straw — looked better
fed, but he had an uncanny fashion once in a while of getting
his left forefoot out of joint, then hobbling a few feet till
he stopped or fell, unless chance meanwhile twisted the dis-
located joint back into place. The pack-horse was a sturdy

gray stallion, and his color led to our calling him Kabud, literally 'blue.' My own animal was a small but good horse, so I dubbed him Rakhsh, after the famous charger of Rustam, much to the amusement of the Persians that heard the name. When all was ready the signal was given, and away our cavalcade started on the twelve days' journey to Hamadan.

CHAPTER X

BY CARAVAN AND CAVALCADE

'Where beasts and men together o'er the plain
Move on — a mighty caravan.'
— WORDSWORTH, *Descriptive Sketches*, 8.

'MESHADI, Mesh-a-di, Mesh-a-a-d-i-i !' in a gentle crescendo and with musical accent cries the voice of our Persian servant to awaken the *nā'ib*, or master of the caravansarai. A muffled *bali, bali,* 'yes, yes,' responds from a distant corner of the walled enclosure, and in a few minutes from somewhere in the darkness there peers into the mud-built sleeping-room the owner of this Oriental title. In reality the appellative Meshadi designates a Moslem who has made the pilgrimage to Meshad, if not to Mecca. In practice, however, it is often applied loosely, like our colonel, major, or professor, and frequently has little more dignity than the colloquial American 'boss.' Yet Meshadi, Husein, or whatever his name may be, is probably a tall, dignified individual, often handsome, with rather fine features, a chiselled nose, and a broad forehead surmounted by a high Persian cap. In his veins still flows some of the blood that made great the race of Cyrus; but he is slow, frequently shiftless, at the same time generally possessed of an eye to the main chance, but always kindly in his quiet way.

The camel-drivers are already up and starting before daylight. It is high time to be off. The dull dong, dong — not ding, dong, for there is no variety — coming from the huge bells attached to the dromedaries and mules, tells that the caravan-train, or Persia's Twentieth Century Express, is on the move. But he who wishes to travel 'fast,' as there are no

PACKING BAGGAGE BEFORE SUNRISE

(An incident of caravan travel)

AN APPROACHING CAMEL TRAIN

railroads in Persia, must have his own cavalcade of horses, as I did, eked out sometimes by mules or even by donkeys. If the route lies on the beaten tracks, one may resort to post-horses and go *chāpār*. But posthaste in the kingdom of the Shah does not mean much, as a rule, and patience unbounded is a necessary prerequisite for the traveller who does not wish to grow gray with anxiety and loss of temper at delays.

The sun is not yet up; murky darkness still floods the caravansarai. The small sleeping-room above, or *bālā khānah*, as the upper chamber is called, is lighted by the flicker of a primitive palm-oil lamp, or by a candle, if the voyager has had the forethought to purchase one at the last bazaar. All this while, however, the man in charge of the wretched hostelry has been silently standing at the rickety door waiting for orders. But your first inquiry is 'Where are the horses; are they ready?' — *asphā kujā and, asphā hāzir hastand?* The unfortunate necessity of asking this question early will be learned with time, if time exists in almost clockless Persia. Only too often it happens, unless one has taken the precaution to have the animals tied or properly hobbled, that the horses have wandered off during the night to a distance of three or four miles, grazing on the plain. With camels there is perhaps less chance of this, as the wary camel-driver has forced his ungainly beasts to lie down in a crowded circle around the bundles of hay that serve as a magnet to keep the nose of the ship of the desert duly pointed toward the fodder pole. With the fleet little Persian horses the case is different. The keen strain of Arab blood keeps up their love of the desert, and at the slightest provocation, unless controlled, they scamper miles away on the plain.

The horses must, therefore, be recovered, and the *nā'ib* of the caravansarai summons his head man to perform the task. He responds with the conventional *chashm*, implying, 'My eyes are the forfeit if I fail to do your Worship's bidding,' and disappears in the darkness. By experience it will be found

well to promise a silver tip to the whipper-in's lash, if he will
only secure the renegade horses betimes, so that the day's
journey may begin.   This attractive promise is sufficient to
call forth a lazy stretching also on the part of a second, a third,
or a fourth attendant, each of whom slowly throws off the
lethargy of sleep and declares that he stands ready to saddle
and give extra barley to the horses on their return.   In fact,
one of the group gives assurance that the animals are already
near-by. God save the phrase ! 'Near-by' may mean half
an hour or an hour or more of the traveller's patience, who
thinks vainly of American speed and the time-table rush of
the latest Chicago Limited.

The intervening time, however, has not been vacant, though
darkness still prevails.   Our own excellent and faithful man-
servant Safar, who has learned through Western contact the
meaning of the word 'hustle' and has caught the enigmatic
force of its indefinable spell, has been busy every moment.   In
an instant he has kindled a fire with a skill that is the despair
of one who looks upon the combustionless combination of damp
fagots, sedge grass, brier bush, and perhaps pancakes of manure
fuel.   Fresh water (*āb-i tamīz*) has been brought by invisible
hands evoked out of the darkness.   The *samovar*, or Russian
tea-urn, which forms part of the advance guard of encroaching
Russian civilization, is already simmering.   A moment later,
while you are adjusting your riding-leggings, the faithful Safar
has an improvised breakfast of some sort ready to be served on
the mud floor of the room.

The bread consists of huge leathern aprons of dough, which
I have already mentioned in describing the extraordinary pro-
ductions that result from a combination of Persian wheat and
old Iranian ovens.   The loaves are not loaves in our sense, but
enormous flat pancakes, two feet long, a foot or more wide, and
of the thickness of a griddle-cake.   In baking they are deftly
slapped against the side of an earthen jar or oven sunk in the
floor of some dingy living-room or of a real Persian bakery in

the bazaar. For travelling they are the most convenient article of food imaginable, for they serve not only to be eaten, but also as a wrapper to fold up the knife and fork, a chicken, sweetmeats, or what not, just as one would use heavy brown paper. This Persian bread, called *nān* or *nūn*, according to the dialect, is generally moist when served and often a bit soggy; but when allowed to grow dry and crisp, it is excellent to the taste, though sometimes fatal to the digestion.

But all this talk or description of breakfast is after all only a digression; for if one is in haste, the breakfast often consists only of a raw egg, some bread, and a good cup of tea, drunk from a glass crammed half full of sugar. When time allows, fortune may add a bit of roast meat (*kabāb*) or chicken, and two or three ginger-snaps as a special treat. The latter are the cherished remains of the parting box, or present for the road, given instead of a stirrup cup by the good housewife of the missionary whose hospitality it has been a privilege to enjoy.

Time has all the while been elapsing. The stray horses have at last been captured, we do not know how far away. Their thin-shod hoofs have a cheery ring as they approach the *manzil*, or halting-place of the caravansarai. The pack must therefore be made ready to load upon the draught-horse. This is the signal for commanding the *mafarashband* to be prepared. This piece of baggage consists of two huge oblong carpet pockets shaped like chests and bound round with stout goat-hair ropes. All the utensils, including the folding camp-bed, must be tumbled into these receptacles, with an eye, however, to equal balance. When both are firmly lashed, the sturdy *chārvādār*, or caravan-leader, skilfully lifts the first and afterward the second on his back and staggers beneath the burden down the unequal mud steps or lowers it from the roof to the court below, and deposits his load on either side of the pack-horse or mule. With signals, hoists, grunts, pulls, tugs, shoves, and punches, the loads are finally lifted on the animal's back

LOWERING LUGGAGE FROM THE
HOUSE-TOP AT DAWN

and properly adjusted. Then comes the tying. A Persian can give points to a jack tar in the matter of knotting a rope ; but despite all the skill the load sometimes does slip, and it is well to add or subtract a tip at the end of the day according to the way in which the pack was fastened.

Saddling likewise takes time, for everything except money goes slowly in Persia. All the native members of the caval-cade, man-servant, muleteer, guide, and armed guards, have their horses' girths passed through iron rings and cinched. Only the foreign *Ṣāḥib*, or Master, with his European saddle has recourse to buckles. Delays are still the order of the hour, and nothing but an oft-repeated *zūd*, *zūd*, *tēz*, *tēz*, 'quick, quick, hurry up,' followed by a threat and then a promise of silver, furnishes the means of securing even the slowest haste.

Among the animals of the cavalcade the Sahib's horse is supposed to be the best, which is not always saying a great deal; but usually better still is the horse of the head guard, who owns his own steed, which he proudly claims to be an Arab. The pack-horse generally has no rider. The servant takes the next best horse, and the *shāgird*, or postilion (if one may dignify this individual by so high a title), takes what is left. But the last shall be first, as experience will prove, for the postboy usually manages to reserve for himself one of the better horses out of the poor lot, and if he does not, there is little gain for the traveller. No train goes faster than its last car, and the caravan-leader is a bad man to leave behind.

At last we are ready to start. Nearly two hours of time have been used up, largely with unnecessary delays. 'Quick, hurry up!' is again the command. But payment for the night's lodging must not be forgotten. It is paid to the overseer of the *manzil*. A gratuity given to him generally means the same as a tip to all — as to the head waiter in the Vienna café system. If the gift be large enough to meet the general approval, a combined good wish, *khudā ḥāfiz*, 'God be mindful of you,' greets the departing company, and a word of praise, *khailī khūb*, 'very good,' is bestowed upon the best horse and serves as an omen of promise for the journey.

As we ride out through the low door of the courtyard, darkness is just beginning to vanish. For safe travelling it is always well to have the light of day. We find ourselves a moment later in the midst of a passing caravan. We join the motley assembly of camels, horses, mules, donkeys, muleteers on foot, pilgrims, and merchants, that make up this heterogeneous company. The never ceasing dong, dong of the big copper bells, the rasping bray of the little donkeys that are wide awake, but staggering beneath crushing loads, the dull pace of the wag-eared mules prodded on by their drivers, the chatter of the men, and the peculiar odor of the scraggly-coated camels, make a deep impression on the senses. The gray streaks of dawn now lighten in the horizon. The sky takes on a more silvery hue. Night withdraws her star-

I

bespangled fan and reveals the blush of dawn.   The night-ingale's song is hushed before the carol of the lark.   And out of the cavern of the hills the sun rises in splendor to shed its glory as of old over the ancient land of Iran.[1]

Such is the composite picture left on my mind by many weeks of caravaning through Persia ; but few of my earlier journeys were started amid sunshine and the carol of birds. Winter still reigned during most of the time I was in Azarbai-jan, and persistently refused to give up his sway ; the calendar pointed to the end of March when I left Urumiah, but spring was a long way off, and snow and bad roads were a constant source of delay on the journey and were destined to be so for a fortnight and more to come.

For the first three days after leaving Urumiah I had the com-pany of a Nestorian friend, Rev. Yaroo M. Neesan, whom I had met in America a number of years before, when I began my Persian studies, and who is now a priest in the Anglican Mission at Van.   He knew the country round about as only a native can, and his fund of information and stock of anecdotes were inexhaustible.   I still can see the humorous twinkle in his eye as he put on his cartridge-belt and pistol, before we mounted, and said, patting it affectionately, 'It is more blessed to give than to receive (bullets) ! '

To beguile the time as we rode along, he told story after story in a manner that would have delighted Chaucer's heart. It was now an account of the old woman whose cleverness saved the citadel of Van in time of siege by bidding her beleaguered countrymen adopt the strategy of pouring down from the citadel showers of fine white ashes.   These the enemy took for flour and abandoned the siege, because it seemed useless to beleaguer a fortress so well supplied with food that its oc-cupants could thus lavishly throw away flour.   Next it was the tale of the witty vizir whose artful dodge made Shah Abbas pay for the dish of cherries which he himself had eaten ;

[1] See my letter in the *Evening Post*, New York, October 3, 1903.

or, once again, an exciting narrative of Yaroo's own experience
when attacked by bandits some years before, while returning
from Sauj Bulak — a reminiscence called forth by passing a
pile of stones heaped up by the roadside to mark the spot
where a native had been murdered a month before. The soft
piping of a Kurdish shepherd in the hills turned the conversation to pastoral life. Neesan had tended the flocks in his youth,
and he told how the shepherds, as in the Bible, knew every
sheep by name, how they would sometimes seek shelter from
the cold by sleeping in the mud enclosures built to protect
the sheep at night on the plain, and he described some of the
primitive shepherd customs handed down from the earliest
antiquity.   All the birds that hovered about, the long-tailed
magpie, thrush, and crested lark, seemed to be familiar friends,
while the eagles and kites soaring above our heads were old
acquaintances of his.   And so the journey proceeded.

Saatlu, near Diza-Takiah, was our resting-place for the first
night. Here the courtesy of our native host, who was a relative of Mr. Neesan, appeared to contrast strangely with the
fierce appearance given him by a huge dagger at his belt and
the gun which lay by his side at night to forestall a surprise or
raid.   The equipment of his arsenal seemed to be plentiful, but
no less abundant was the supply of provisions in his larder.
From these he gave us in profusion at supper that evening, and
it was then that I noticed for the first time the fondness of the
Persians for melted butter (*rōghan*).   A new significance was
thus imparted to the Avestan passage which describes how
zaremaya raoghna, 'clarified butter of springtime,' is the first
food which the faithful who have died in Zoroaster's creed
receive when they enter into Paradise.[1]

Before daybreak I was awakened by a messenger who
entered my room armed with gun and pistol. He had
come from Urumiah and had ridden through the night to
deliver to me a cablegram which had reached the city after

[1] Yt. 22. 18.

sunset. The city gates were closed, and the guards, taking him for a horse-thief, had refused to let him pass until he presented his credentials, when he was allowed to hasten on his way to overtake my caravan. The cable had become much garbled in the course of transmission, but happily the cipher contained good news from my distant home.

A PERSIAN TELEGRAM

By this time day had broken and after a good breakfast in Persian style our pack was put in order by the servants, and we were ready for an early start. Neighing horses, barking dogs, and an oft-repeated *khudā ḥāfiz* from our host and his friends sped us onward upon our journey along the shores of the blue lake of Urumiah.

The village of Mahmadyar, a place of about one hundred houses, was our next night's lodging after ten hours on the road, and we again enjoyed native hospitality, this time in a large living-room filled with men, women, children, and smoke. Owing to the cold weather and the rain, all were huddled together around the urn-shaped hole in the mud floor contain-

A CARAVAN OF NOMADS

CHACHILI HILL, NEAR URUMIAH

ing some smoldering embers. A baby in its mother's arms was choking with the croup, and another small tot was gasping with whooping-cough. The rest of the children, however, looked healthy and kept constantly running in and out, chattering and playing, while the women were occupied with their work. The women, like the men, were dressed in a common blue cotton cloth, usually with their feet and limbs bare to the knees, and wore a red kerchief about the head. Their faces were not veiled, because the village women, especially among the Kurds, do not conceal their features, and as these women were Armenians and Nestorian Persians, they moved about with greater freedom from restraint in the presence of the men. The men, meanwhile, were holding a conference and drew nearer together to discuss a matter requiring important consideration. A band of Kurds had come down and carried off a young Armenian girl from the village, and had disappeared with the captive over the mountains. The deliberation of the council resulted in maturing a plan for restitution or revenge, and an appeal was also sent to the governor at Urumiah; but I never heard what the outcome of the affair was.

Early in the morning my caravan was on the march, and I had an opportunity of making what I believe to be an interesting identification in connection with Zoroaster's ministry — locating the district where he most probably made his first convert. This was near the village of Khor Khorah, between Mahmadyar, Daralak, and Miandoab. From tradition we know that the first adherent won by Zoroaster for his religion was his own cousin, named Maidhyoi-maonha in the Avesta, and Medhyo-mah in Pahlavi.[1] The scene of the conversion is located by the Pahlavi writings of Zatsparam 'in the forest of reedy hollows, which is the haunt of swine of the wild boar species.'[2] Now we know that Zoroaster passed much of the earlier part of his life in the region of Lake

---

[1] On the tradition of Zoroaster's first convert, see my *Zoroaster*, p. 54, and

cf. Rosenberg, *Livre de Zoroastre*, p. 24.

[2] Zatsparam **2**. 38.

Urumiah (Av. *Chaēchasta*), and that the southern shores of
this lake, from times of antiquity, have been covered with great
tracts of reeds. The map to-day shows a 'Forest of Reeds,'
some sixty miles in extent, and I had already heard accounts of
this when I was in Tabriz and Urumiah.   The 'forest of
reedy hollows' in the Zoroastrian tradition is evidently identical with this.   The highroad which leads around the lake
and toward Ragha (now Rei) near Teheran, where Zoroaster's
mother is said to have been born, passes along its very edge.
The region abounds in 'hollows' and 'reeds,' and I saw
immense masses of the slender stalks, some of them fifteen or
twenty feet high, cut from the 'forest,' and I heard a number
of stories from people who had been lost among them in the
marshes.   In this region, likewise, 'the swine of the wild boar
species abounds,' and the animals are hunted for sport by the
natives.   They are not eaten, however, by the Mohammedans,
to whom the flesh of the hog is forbidden by the Koran, but by
the Armenians, who have no such religious scruples in the
matter and derive actual benefit in the way of food from the
chase.[1] The surroundings of the place combine with what we
know of Zoroaster's life from traditional sources — the Avesta,
Zatsparam selections, Zartusht-Namah, and other works — to
make it reasonably probable that this 'Forest of Reeds,' south
of Lake Urumiah, is the region at least to which the passage
refers, even if we cannot identify the precise spot.[2]

At noon that same day, after luncheon at Daralak, I was
obliged to lose Mr. Neesan's good company, as his missionary
duties called him to Sauj Bulak. I parted from him with
regret, and the afternoon was lonely without him, despite the
novel experience of camel riding, which I tried as a change
from horseback. The dromedary which I mounted was one of

[1] Cf. Koran (tr. Sale), chap. 2, p. 18 ;
5, p. 73, etc.

[2] See my article in *JAOS*. 25. 183–
184 ; and, for a description of some
experiences in this 'forest of grass and
reeds,' compare Perkins, *Eight Years
in Persia*, pp. 193–194 ; consult also
Wilson, *Persian Life*, p. 105.

SARALAN, A VILLAGE OF MUD HOUSES

KHOR KHORAH, NEAR THE FOREST OF REEDS
(Probably the district where Zoroaster made his first convert)

the finest specimens of camel flesh that I saw in Persia, but I was glad to change back again to my horse, as the creature's gait was atrocious and one needs to be a good sailor to navigate with success the ship of the desert.

Sunset found my caravan entering Miandoab, a town of several thousand inhabitants, well named 'between two rivers' (*miān dō āb*) from its situation between the Jagati and the Tatavu.[1] Here I received a pleasant visit from an Armenian-Persian for whom I had brought letters from Urumiah.   As we chatted on various subjects I told him that I had been unable thus far to meet with any followers of Zoroaster's creed in Azarbaijan.   He replied that this was not surprising to him, for he knew of but one Fire-Worshipper (*Ātash-Parast*) in the district of Miandoab, and that man called himself a Babi, a follower of the religious reformer whom I have previously mentioned.   It may be possible that this 'Babi' may have actually turned from Zoroastrianism to Babism, but more likely that he had chosen to conceal his religion under the garb of that eclectic faith for fear of persecution from fanatical Mohammedans, at whose hands non-acknowledgment of the Moslem creed may mean cruel oppression, and apostasy from Islam, death.

Miandoab itself lies in the undulating region southeast of the lake, at a height of four thousand two hundred feet above sealevel ; and from this point the territory begins to be hilly and leads steadily upward through fine scenery in the high passes of the Mian Bulagh Mountains to Sanjud.   Before reaching these we had to cross the Jagati River, which we did next day

---

[1] I did not know until after my return to America that at Dashtapah, near the reed forest in the neighborhood of Miandoab, there is a cuneiform inscription on a rock, and there is said to be one also in the vicinity of Sauj Bulak; cf. Wilson, *Persian Life*, pp. 99, 105; Belck, *Inschr. Taschtepe*, in *Zt. f. Ethnol.* (*Verhandl. Berl. Anthrop. Gesellsch.*) 26 (1894), pp. 479 seq. (cf. Streck, *Zt. f. Assyr.* 14. 144). There is also a rock-hewn cave in the same region (Wilson, *Handbook of Asia Minor*, p. 324, and de Morgan, *Mission Scientifique en Perse*, 4. 294–296).

in a huge scow that was large enough to ferry our horses and all across. I expected to make an extra stage in that day's journey, as I had become thoroughly accustomed to early starts and long marches; but I only reached Kashavar, a village with an old fort, at which we arrived about three in the afternoon. Here I came into violent collision with my caravan-leader Shahbas, because of his negligence and laziness. Every one who travels in Persia is familiar with the struggle one usually has to go through with his *chārvādār* early in the journey, until it is settled once for all that the master is master and will tolerate no slackness, although ready promptly to reward good service. Shahbas had yet to learn this lesson and be cured of some of his shortcomings, and the first dose of the medicine, which varied from gentleness and coaxing, bribes and rewards, to sternness and chastisement, was administered at Kashavar. This needed to be repeated a few times afterward, and with excellent effect, so that by the end of a month, when I dismissed Shahbas to return to Urumiah, he had become quite a model, as far as a Persian muleteer can be, and was well rewarded for his improvement.

My man-servant Safar, on the other hand, who had been capable from the outset, showed himself more reliable and valuable every day. The effect of his training among the missionaries manifested itself in many ways, and his quickness and intelligence were a delight to me. To improve his English and my Persian, we used sometimes at night to read and translate a simple story-book which had been given him, and with his English vocabulary his manners also seemed to improve. He learned how to be polite in his address, and his first blunt 'yes' soon gave place to a more courteous 'yes, sir,' and he knew what it meant to say 'thank you ' — a phrase not common among the Persians of the lower classes. His businesslike methods in looking after my interests came more and more to the front; he found ways I should never have thought of for saving me money, and was quite impatient at my readiness to pay rather than debate a price. His honesty, moreover, was unimpeachable, and he was likewise always helpful in arranging the details of the journey. The next stages of the march proceeded well, except when my horse Rakhsh was taken with a chill and cramps in the mountain pass after leaving Sain Kalah,[1] and I feared I should have to leave the animal dead on the road where he lay. Shahbas, however, worked over him, and we managed to pull Rakhsh through, so that we reached Sanjud all right, though late in the afternoon.

Sanjud, where I passed that night, April 2, is situated on the side of a steep ravine amid masses of rugged mountains. The approach to it from the north lies over high ridges, through deep defiles, and past precipices, beneath which there run streams transformed into torrents by the rains and melting snows.

The night was a cold one, but the panes of oiled paper in the windows shut out some of the wind, and the fire burned brightly. Around it were gathered a number of villagers, who made pretexts to come and interview the *farangi*, most often to beg remedies for various ailments. One old man, a Kurd, stayed all the evening. He seemed to be a worthy personage and offered me the company of his two sons to act as guides the next day, as Shahbas did not know the road to Ahmadabad and Takht-i Suleiman. The two appeared to be reliable fellows and of a sturdy type. I looked them over by the flickering light of a lamp made of an earthen bowl, filled with the oil of the castor plant, into which was stuck a piece of cotton twist to serve as a wick, for there was not even a tallow dip in the village. To be sure that they would come back in the morning, I took from the father a *bei'*, or pawn, which he deposited as a guarantee for their appearance, and they departed with the promise to return betimes — *inshāllah!* Before sunrise they both were on hand, ready to guide the way over the heavy passes.

[1] In the vicinity of Sain Kalah there is reported to be a mound of ashes, the site of an ancient fire-temple ; see Bishop, *Journeys in Persia*, 2. 197.

The snow lay two feet deep on the side of the hills and sometimes three or four in the gullies. Twice that day the horse
which I rode went down under me in its treacherous depths.
The glare from its white surface, when the sun came up, was
dazzling and set up a painful inflammation in my eyes, one of the
first stages of snow-blindness. In places where the snow had
melted, the mud was an obstacle to progress, so our advance
was slow during most of the morning and afternoon. As we
crossed the last ridge of hills the snow lessened, but the rough-
ness of the road increased, since the path led for some distance
along the rocky and precipitous bank of a river. The horses
insisted upon walking as near the edge of the cliff as possible,
and it was sometimes a marvel that they kept their footing.
Rocks now and then almost totally barred the way and we had
to descend to the river's brink or else surmount them. It was
no wonder that the load on the pack-horse often became loose,
causing a halt. I remember one jutting crag in particular,
which stood like a giant buttress directly in our path. It was
impossible to go around in front of it, and the only way was to
climb up back of it. The angle seemed almost perpendicular,
and to sit in the saddle was out of the question ; so we had to
dismount and scramble up past the crag as best we could,
tugging the struggling horses behind us. As darkness began
to fall, the mountain gorges became dangerous because of robbers, and at each turn in the road it interested me to watch
the two guards lower their guns to the saddle-bow, the one
riding a short distance ahead, the other dropping behind.
Thus we pushed on until after sundown, when we reached
Ahmadabad, our *manzil* for the night.

The place where we lodged adjoined a cow-stable, but it was
a well-constructed building, the only one with two stories in
the village. The master of the house was entertaining his
brother and some friends as guests for the night, but he offered
me a welcome if I was willing to share the room with the party,
to which I gladly consented. I found that I had really to con-

HOSHABAH, MY GUARD FROM URUMIAH TO MIANDOAB

A CARAVAN LEADER

tribute my share also toward the entertainment, however, by being constantly on exhibition before the company, who plied me with questions till past midnight, though I should have been glad to sleep and to rest my inflamed eyes. At last all were ready to retire; the Persians crept under the quilts that covered the *kursī*, or brazier, made like a low wooden table over the fire-hole in the middle of the room, while I took to the blankets of my camp-bed.

CHAPTER XI

TAKHT-I SULEIMAN, AN ANCIENT FORTIFIED TOWN IN RUINS

'We scrutinize the dates
Of long-past human things,
The bounds of effaced states,
The lines of deceased kings;
We search out dead men's words, and works of dead men's hands.'
— MATTHEW ARNOLD, *Empedocles on Etna.*

THE sun had not yet drawn his sword from the scabbard of night — to adopt an Oriental phrase — before I was again in the saddle and ready to start from Ahmadabad to Takht-i Suleiman, or 'Solomon's Throne,' a ruined fortified city which Rawlinson claimed to be the capital of Media. I obtained as guide a peasant who was more familiar with the site than my own guides, and we set off at a brisk canter as the sun began to show over the hills, disclosing to the view Mount Zindan, 'Solomon's Dungeon,' toward which we directed our course.

The path lay along the crest of a volcanic ridge. This elevation, formed partly of grayish-brown lava from the crater of Zindan, extends for two or three miles like the prostrate form of some huge giant whose head is Mount Zindan. There is no longer any life in the monstrous frame, but from the cavernous mouth of the hill there still arise blasts of fetid air, which lead one to wonder whether Mount Arezurahe Griva, 'Neck of the Demon Arezura,' the entrance to hell in the Avesta, may not have been an extinct crater like this prison of the *Dīvs.*

The hard basaltic conglomerate of the ridge echoed with a hollow sound as we galloped over it, and a score of tiny warm calcareous springs bubbled up from a row of miniature craters

A MOUNTED GUARD

A TYPICAL PERSIAN VILLAGE

and showed the igneous origin of the ridge. It took me perhaps half an hour to reach the base of Solomon's Prison Height,
which rises to an elevation of nearly four hundred and fifty
feet above the plain and is capped by a massive cone of conglomerate produced by the discharge from the interior of the
volcano.[1] The ascent to the summit of the rocky mass is very
steep. On reaching the top I found the rim of the crater to
be about three hundred feet in circumference, and as I peered
over into the dizzy abyss I could but think of Milton's lines : —

> ' And in that lowest deep a lower deep,
> Still threatening to devour, opens wide. '

The natives, in fact, regard the funnel-like shaft of Zindan
as a bottomless pit, and there is no question that its depth must
be several hundred feet, judging from the time required for a
stone to reach what seemed to be the bottom. Crawling as
near to the edge as I dared, and looking down, I could discern
near the bottom a patch of snow, which showed that that part
of the crater is not warm now, but there was perhaps a still
lower depth, invisible, from which issued the sulphurous fumes
that were exhaled to the air above.

The view from the peak of Zindan is a fine one. On all
sides rise lofty mountains. One of these to the north, called
Takht-i Bilḳis, ' Throne of the Queen of Sheba,' towers skyward to the height of ten thousand feet, and on its summit (so
legends say) King Solomon built a summer palace for his
beloved. The ridges to the east are less high, but they combine with the others to form a huge caldron and shut in the
plain, out of the midst of which rises a low hill of scarped rock
crowned with the ruins of Takht-i Suleiman. The real size of
the hill of the Takht is dwarfed by the height of the surrounding

---

[1] Throughout I have taken Zindan,
and the ridge formed from it, to be of
igneous origin. Rawlinson (*Journ.
Roy. Geog. Soc.* 10. 53–54), however,
describes the scarped, rocky crest of
the hill as a ' cinter ' cone and assigns
to the mountain an aqueous origin ; so
do also Wilson, *Persian Life*, p. 162,
and Gordon, *Persia Revisited*, p. 62,
following Rawlinson.

mountains, but its appearance and the shape of the enclosure on its summit recalled to my mind the description of the Vara of Yima Khshaeta (Jamshid) in the Avesta, although tradition does not locate the Vara in this particular region.[1]

Leaving the horses at the base of Mount Zindan I started on foot with my guides over the snow toward the deserted ruin, half a mile or more distant. The sun was now some degrees above the horizon, and the glare from the crystal plain became excruciating to my inflamed eyes. I held my black hat before my face for relief, but it availed little against the blaze of light, and I hurried forward as fast as I could to reach my goal. As I approached them, the huge ramparts and colossal bastions of the massive pile, between thirty and forty feet high, came out in their true proportions. The entrance to the stronghold was once made by four great gateways, roughly facing the cardinal points. Not all the details of these were clear, since the snow was much drifted against them and the western rampart is falling into ruins. On scaling the battlements at this point I could make out, more or less distinctly, the general outline of the entire oblong enclosure, which is about three quarters of a mile in circuit; yet it seemed to me hardly possible to reconstruct, even in imagination, any walls within the great stronghold itself, unless we should convert into such structures what I regarded as the outlines of a drive or causeway. I mention this fact now because of its relation to the problem of the identification of the site of Ecbatana, which I shall touch on later, pointing out how important a part is played by the battlements.[2]

Within the enclosure the first feature that strikes the eye is the remains of two walls of stone and brick that once formed

---

[1] Cf. Bd. 29. 14 ; 29. 5 ; 32. 5.

[2] See pp. 151–156, below. I have since found that Canon George Rawlinson, following his brother, Sir Henry, in the belief that Takht-i Suleiman represents the ancient Median Ecbatana, says, 'Of the seven walls, one alone is to be traced ; and even here the Median structure has perished and been replaced by masonry of a far later age' (*Five Great Monarchies*, 3. 27).

part of a rather high structure facing eastward. The side walls of this building, though shattered and crumbling, are still standing, and they show that the edifice could not have been less than a hundred feet long and forty feet wide. To me, even in the distance, they did not give the impression of great antiquity, certainly not of antedating the Mohammedan conquest, and this fact was proved by the fragments of Arabic letters inscribed upon what had once been the portal.[1]

Some thirty yards to the north-northeast are the remains of a second structure, an arched and vaulted building partly sunk below the ground and now largely a mass of rubbish and débris. Its domelike outline rising amid the snowy surroundings may be seen in my photograph, and its general position with reference to the other remains in a rough sketch I made of the general elevation at this point. Conspicuous are the two arched portals through which one descends to the vaulted chamber of brick below, and also a small tower projecting above the northern elevation. The bricks which were used in the construction of the edifice are nearly a foot square,[2] while the walls themselves are four or five feet thick and convey the impression that the vaulted chamber and its arched recesses once served as a place for preserving a precious treasure.[3] The natives call the building the *hamām*, 'bath';[4] but its true identification, as a great fire-temple of most ancient date, was first made clear by Rawlinson, as will be explained hereafter.

The other remains of buildings within the citadel of Takht-i

---

[1] I have since found my observations borne out by Rawlinson (*JRGS.* 10. 51, 66), who cites a statement of Mustaufi to show that the Mongol king Abaka Khan (d. 1282), son of Hulagu Khan, restored this edifice. Compare also Wilson, *Persian Life*, p. 162. The site of the structures, however, was probably occupied originally by much older buildings, perhaps the ancient palace of the Keianian, Arsacian, and Sasanian kings.

[2] Resembling the bricks I afterward saw at the Fire-Temple near Isfahan and also in the walls of Rei; cf. pp. 253, 255, 435, below.

[3] Rawlinson, *JRGS.* 10. 51, describes the walls as fifteen feet thick, and he adds some details regarding the condition of the dome and the central chamber when he saw it; his description should be consulted.

[4] So also Ker Porter was informed; see his *Travels,* 2. 560.

Suleiman are a group to the extreme north, which the natives call the 'bazaar,' and two others near the rampart on the southern and southwestern side. One of these latter the guide called the 'market'; the other, somewhat to the southwest, which still has a towerlike shaft of its wall standing, he termed the 'kitchen.' But neither of these structures gave me the impression of being very old, although it was difficult to examine them because of the depth of the snow.[1]

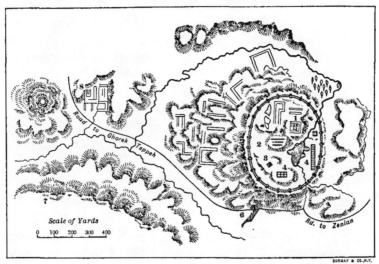

RAWLINSON'S PLAN OF TAKHT-I SULEIMAN

One of the most interesting features of the enclosure of Takht-i Suleiman is natural and not the work of human hands. It is a deep pond, some three hundred yards in circumference, situated south of the central part of the Takht and plainly owing its existence to some action of a volcanic character. The depth of this reservoir is evidently great, for its rich emerald hue shades into an azure that resembles the color of the deep sea.[2] The water is exquisitely clear, but somewhat saline or

---

[1] For some description of them see Ker Porter, *Travels*, 2. 560, and Rawlinson, *JRGS*. 10. 51.

[2] Rawlinson, *JRGS*. 10. 50, gives the depth as twenty-six fathoms.

calcareous to the taste, and it possesses a peculiar petrifying quality, imparted to it by the strong impregnation of calcium, so that its banks are encircled by a stony rim formed by the incrustation from the water wherever it overflows. In the plain a serpentine dike, called Azh Dahak by the natives, after the name of the mythical dragon, has also been built up by the deposit left as the stream flows down in a sinuous course from the height. When I saw the lake, the chief outlet seemed to be over the road leading out of the southeastern gateway, and the water was pouring through this in large quantities. Despite the outflow, which is constant, the volume of water, like the Avestan stream of Ardvi Sura, appears never to diminish, being constantly replenished from some unknown source.[1]

The great gateway at this point of the battlements is in an excellent state of preservation, and I even saw, if my memory serve me, the masons' signs marked on the bastions to the right and left of it, such as I saw on the wall of the terrace built by Cyrus near Murghab. The height of the rampart is here no less than forty feet, and its structure gives a good idea of the masonry of the rest of the wall. The large oblong blocks of which it is composed measure more than two and a half feet by one and a half, and are laid in a horizontal line with narrow upright stones fitted carefully between them, somewhat in this fashion.[2] I did not see elsewhere in Persia, either at Kangavar,

Murghab, or Persepolis, stones so peculiarly set, although in the latter cases the blocks were more massive than those of Takht-i Suleiman.

---

[1] I have since found that Rawlinson (*JRGS*. 10.48) conjectures that the pond is connected by an underground syphon with some obscure mountain source.

[2] My notes may be supplemented by Rawlinson (*op. cit.* p. 47), who also refers to the extreme nicety with which the stones are fitted.

Wishing to have a full view of the Takht from the eastern side as well, I walked along the citadel height, through the deep snow, to a point about the middle of the rampart, facing the rising sun. The descent from the battlement was here extremely steep, but with the aid of my guides I found a place by one of the bastions where the snow was drifted almost to the level of the wall, and, as the crust was hard, I slid down and tramped off to a considerable distance in the direction of the eastern hills, so as to view the Takht in its full extent, including the northern end. The light at the time was unfavorable for photographing, so that two of my pictures failed; but the third, which takes in a part of the middle section, especially the domed roof of the famous fire-temple, came out fairly well, and, when supplemented by my rough sketch of the side elevation, will convey some idea at least of Takht-i Suleiman as I saw it. The noble contour of the walls was clear to me, but the impression which I received from this side of the Takht, as from the others, was not favorable to the theory of identifying it with Herodotus' description of the walls of Ecbatana.

Up to this point I have given my own observations and memoranda without alluding to any historic accounts of Takht-i Suleiman and without any detailed references in the text to Sir Henry Rawlinson's claim that Takht-i Suleiman represents the Atropatenian Ecbatana and the site of the ancient capital of northern Media.[1] Although I knew in a general way of his theory, I purposely refrained from reading his monograph until I had studied the locality myself and had also visited Hamadan. In fact, I wrote out my notes for this chapter when on the steamer returning to America, and did not consult the famous essay until I reached home. Nor did I see Canon George Rawlinson's arguments, summing up his brother's treatise, until I had visited Hamadan and had already formed my own judgment in favor of the traditional

---

[1] Rawlinson, *Notes on a Journey to Takhti-Soleïmán and on the Site of the Atropatenian Ecbatana*, in *JRGS.* 10. 1–158, London, 1841.

view that Hamadan, and not Takht-i Suleiman, really occupies the site of ancient Ecbatana.[1] Although I do not accept Sir Henry's view that the Takht is the site of Ecbatana (and I am not alone in my dissent),[2] I fully accept his unquestionable identification of Takht-i Suleiman with the Shiz of the Arab writers, and probably also with the Gazna and Ganzah of the Persians, the Gazaka or Canzaca of the classical writers and, I may now add, the Ganjak of the Pahlavi texts.[3]

In dealing with the subject, I shall first present the grounds for Rawlinson's identification of the ruins with the ancient Shiz and the fire-temple of Adhargushnasp. Afterward I shall touch on their probable identity with Gazna, Ganzaca, Ganjak, etc., as Rawlinson believed. Some of the citations which he uses to prove his point will be found also in my book on Zoroaster, where I had independently given them for another purpose; but I reproduce the more important of them here because of their value in this connection and because they give an excellent idea of Takht-i Suleiman.[4]

The first statement which I cite, and which was used also by Rawlinson, is taken from an account of the stronghold written by Yakut (about A.D. 1220). Yakut speaks of Shiz as located among mountains that abound in ore and mineral wealth, and describes the lake, whose petrifying qualities I have mentioned, and speaks of the buildings, especially the ancient fire-temple, within the circuit of the city's walls. Yakut's account reads as follows : —

[1] See George Rawlinson, *Five Great Monarchies*, 3. 24–28, London, 1865.

[2] George Rawlinson mentions the fact that his brother's view was combatted by Quatremère in the *Mémoires de l'Académie des Inscriptions et Belles Lettres*, 19. 419 seq.

[3] The name *Shīz*, as stated above (p. 73), is derived through an Arabic corruption of *Cīz* from *Čaēčasta*, the Avestan name of Lake Urumiah. This title designates the district as well as

the city, and the same is true of *Gazn*, *Jazn*, *Ganjah*, *Ganzah* (Lat. *Canzaca* or *Ganzaca*), which is generally believed to be another designation for the same place.

[4] See my *Zoroaster*, pp. 195, 197, 201, 202, 204 ; and compare Gottheil, *References to Zoroaster*, in *Classical Studies in Honour of Henry Drisler*, pp. 40–45. Most important is the monograph by Rawlinson, *JRGS*. 10. 65–158.

'Shiz, a district of Azarbaijan. Its name is a form of Chis,[1] out of which the Arabs have made Shiz. It is said that Zaradusht, the prophet of the Fire-Worshippers, came from there. The chief place of the district is Urumiah. . . . Here is what Mis'ar ibn Muhalhal (A.H. 330 = A.D. 940) says about Shiz : " . . . This town is situated between Maraghah, Zanjan, Shahrzur, and Dinavar, in the midst of mountains containing mines of gold, quicksilver, lead, silver, orpiment, and amethysts. . . . A wall encloses the city, and within its circuit is a pool whose bottom cannot be sounded. I dropped a line in it more than fourteen thousand cubits, but the lead did not find any resting-place and remain steady.[2] The area of the lake is about one quarter of an acre. Earth soaked with water from it immediately becomes hard stone. Seven streams of water flow from the lake, each of which turns a mill before flowing out under the wall. At Shiz there is also a large fire-temple, which is held in great veneration. From it are lighted the fires of the Magians from the east to the west. On the top of the dome there is a silver crescent which is a talisman. Many rulers [3] have tried to remove it, but have not succeeded. One of the extraordinary things connected with the temple is, that a fire has been kept burning in it for seven hundred years without any ashes having been found;[4] nor has the fire gone out for a single hour. Hurmuz ibn Khusrushir ibn Bahram built the city of plaster (*kils*) and stone. Near (*'ind*) the fire-temple stand lofty palaces and large and magnificent buildings. Whenever an enemy advances to take the city and plants his ballista against its walls, the stone from the machines falls into the pool which we have mentioned; and if he move the ballista back [from the wall], even as far as one cubit, the stone falls outside the wall. . . ."[5] So far Abu Dulaf Mis'ar ibn Muhalhal, the poet; but I cannot vouch

[1] Variant readings are *Jis*, *Cis*, *His*, and *Jins*. In reality *Shiz* is a corruption of *Ciz*, Avestan *Čaēčasta;* see p. 73, above, and my *Zoroaster,* p. 197.

[2] This extravagant number in the Arabic text is reduced in the Persian version to 4000, which in itself is exaggerated enough. See Rawlinson, *JRGS.* 10. 68, n. 4 ; Barbier de Meynard, *Dict. géog.* p. 368, n. 1. The true depth is not more than 156 feet, as given by Rawlinson, *op. cit.* p. 50.

[3] Lit. *Amirs;* Kazvini has 'conquerors.'

[4] This is evidently the 'imposture of the coals' (πλάνη ἀνθράκων) alluded to by the Church Father Georgius Cedrenus ; see p. 141 below.

[5] I omit here a legend which recounts how the city was built by Hurmuz on the spot where a fire had appeared at the grave of a messenger whom he had sent to worship Christ and who had died on his return.

THE RUINED FIRE-TEMPLE AT TAKHT-I SULEIMAN, BURIED IN THE SNOW

TAKHT-I SULEIMAN FROM THE EAST
(After a sketch by the author)

for the truth of his statement, for things are told on his authority which are inaccurate and untrue. I have incorporated it here as I found it; but Allah knows best. Some one else has related that in Shiz there is the fire of *Ādharakhsh,* a temple honored of the Magians.[1] It was customary for their kings, when they ascended the throne, to make a pilgrimage thither on foot. The people of Maraghah and of this neighborhood call this place *Gaznā;* but Allah knows best.'[2]

Yakut has furthermore a separate short article on *Gazn* (*Kazn*) and its fire-temple, which, if taken in connection with his previous assertion that *Gazn, Gaznā (Gaznah)* is the Persian form and *Shiz* the Arabic form, shows that he regards the two places as one, and their identity is generally accepted.[3] Thus, in his brief note on *Gaznā,* he says : —

'Gazna is a small town about six farsakhs from Maraghah. In it there is a place of worship of the Magians and an old fire-temple, and also a great and very old palace built by Kei Khosru.'[4]

And again, in his statement under *Jaznak,* Yakut says : —

'Jaznak is a small but very flourishing town in the vicinity of Maraghah, and one may see there the ruins of edifices erected by the ancient kings of Persia, and also a temple of fire.'[5]

The Persian geographer Kazvini (about A.D. 1263) repeats almost word for word the same statement regarding the lake, the walls, and the fire-temple at Shiz, and adds that Zoroaster came from this city of Azarbaijan.

---

[1] Spelled *Ādhrkhsh,* without vocalization, but vocalized as *Ādhar-khush,* ('good fire') in the edition of Masudi, *Kitab at-Tanbīh,* ed. De Goeje, in *Bibliotheca Geographorum Arabicorum,* 8. 95. For other readings of the name (all of which are evident corruptions of Adhar-guš[nasp]), see Rawlinson, *JRGS.* 10. 104.

[2] See Yakut, ed. *Wüstenfeld,* 3. 354, and the translation by Barbier de Meynard, *Dict. géog.* p. 367 seq.; also the version by Gottheil, *References to Zoroaster,* in *Classical*

Studies in Honour of Henry Drisler, p. 42, cited in my *Zoroaster,* p. 200. For aid in translating the passage from the Arabic, I am indebted to my friend and former pupil, Dr. William Popper.

[3] See especially Nöldeke, *Geschichte der Perser und Araber,* p. 100, n. 1, accepting Rawlinson's view, which is maintained also by Marquart, *Ērānšahr,* p. 108, and others.

[4] Yakut, p. 488; cf. also Gottheil, *References to Zoroaster,* p. 44.

[5] Yakut, p. 161.

'Zaradusht, the prophet of the Magians, takes his origin from there (*i.e.* Azarbaijan). It is said that he came from Shiz. He went to the mountain Sabalan, living apart from men. He brought forth a book the name of which was *Basta* (i.e. *Avesta*).'[1]

Still earlier Arab and Persian writers mention Shiz and its renowned fire-temple, as I have shown in my *Zoroaster* (p. 198), to which work I may refer, and I therefore give only the main points here.   Thus Ibn Khordadhbah, who wrote about A.D. 816, and whose father is said to have been a Magian, enumerates the important cities of Azarbaijan and includes : —

'J a n z a h (*i.e.* Ganjah), the city of Abarwiz (*i.e.* Parviz), Jabrawan, Nariz, Urmiah, the city of Zaradusht, Salmas, and S h i z, in which there is a fire-temple Adharjushnas[f], which was venerated by the Magians; and it was customary when one of their monarchs ascended the throne, for him to make a pilgrimage [thither] on foot from Madain (*i.e.* the Sasanian capital Ctesiphon).'[2]

Al-Hamadhani (about A.D. 910) repeats the same statement elsewhere : —

'J a n j a h, Jabrawan, and Urumiah, the city of Zaradusht, and S h i z, i n   w h i c h   t h e r e   i s   t h e   f i r e - t e m p l e   o f   A d h a r j u s h - n a s [f], which is held in high veneration by the Magians.'[3]

In still another passage the same author says that the fire of Adhargushnasp belonging to Kei Khosru (and originally located elsewhere in Azarbaijan) was removed to Shiz.

'Adharjushnasf, the fire of Kei Khosru, was in Adharbaijan; but Anushirvan removed it to Shiz.'[4]

Masudi (died A.D. 951), in his account of the various fire-temples, in *Meadows of Gold*, chapter 68, says : —

---

[1] See Gottheil, *References to Zoroaster*, pp. 40, 42, n. 2 ; Rawlinson, *JRGS.* 10. 68 ; and my *Zoroaster*, p. 201.

[2] See Ibn Khordadhbah, ed. De Goeje, *Bibl. Geog. Arab.* 6. 119 ; and transl. p. 91. It is to be observed that Ibn Khordadhbah distinguished between Ganjah and Shiz, as will be noted below, p. 136.

[3] Al-Hamadhani, *Kitāb al-Buldān*, ed. De Goeje, *Bibl. Geog. Arab.* 5. 286 ; see also my *Zoroaster*, p. 198.

[4] Al-Hamadhani, p. 246 ; see also Gottheil, *References to Zoroaster*, p. 45.

'A fourth fire-temple is found in the country of Shiz and Arran; it was originally consecrated to those idols which Anushirvan destroyed. Others say that Anushirvan, having found in this temple an altar on which the sacred fire was burning, transported it to a place called al-Birkah ("the basin," near Shiraz). The [ancient Keianian] king Kei Khosru built a temple which was known under the name of *Kusujah.*' [1]

The still earlier writer, Asmaï (died A.D. 831), a scholar at the court of Harun al-Rashid, mentions Shiz and its fire-temple in his account of the campaign of the Sasanian king Khosru Parviz against the Byzantine emperor Heraclius (623–627).

'The king [Khosru] went on till he arrived at the city of Shiz, where there is a very great fire-temple which remains to this day. Khosru remained constantly at prayer in this temple, while he ordered his army to form an entrenched camp; and he abode for a month at Shiz to refresh himself and his troops, and employed himself in collecting provisions and establishing bazaars.' [2]

Tabari, the historian (840–923), speaks of the rich gifts made to the fire-temple (of Adhargushnasp) at Shiz in Azarbaijan by the Sasanian king Bahram Gor, after his victory over the Turkmans, about A.D. 420.

'Bahram's route, on returning from that campaign, lay through Azarbaijan. Accordingly he sent to the fire-temple in Shiz the rubies and other jewels which were in the crown of the [vanquished] Khakan, and also his own sword, inlaid with pearls and jewels, as well as many other ornaments. The Khatun, or wife of the Khakan, he made an attendant in the temple.' [3]

The native Persian lexicon, *Farhang-i Anjuman-i Arāi Naṣarī*, a modern but valuable compilation, cites an older work which

[1] See Masudi, *Les Prairies d'Or*, tr. Barbier de Meynard, 4. 74, Paris, 1865. The name *Kusujah* is evidently a scribal error for *Ganzah*. Shiz is mentioned by Masudi also at 2. 235.
[2] Asmaï, cited by Rawlinson, *JRGS.*
10. 76, from whom the passage is quoted.
[3] Tabari, translated in Nöldeke, *Gesch. der Perser und Araber*, pp. 100, 102, 104; also Rawlinson, *JRGS.* 10. 77, and compare Justi, *Grundr. iran. Philol.* 2. 527.

likewise speaks of the fire of Adhargushnasp at Shiz and the association of Zoroaster's name with the place.   Thus : —

'The author of the *Haft Iklīm* says that Shiz is the name of a city between Maraghah and Zangan, and there was a great fire-temple there, called Adharjus[nasf], which was held in great esteem by the Persian kings, who used to come to the mountain on foot.   The origin (*aṣl*) of Zaradusht was from there, and he went to the mountain Sabalan and composed there the book Abasta and brought it to King Gushtasp.'[1]

Taking all these quotations together, especially Yakut's statement about the mountains that contain ore, the lake whose waters produce petrifaction, and the famous temple of fire, it is clear that Takht-i Suleiman, or 'Solomon's Throne,' is actually the site of the ancient city of Shiz, and that when standing on its terrace we have the ruins of the historic pyræum of Adhargushnasp before us.   We may therefore accept Rawlinson's identification of the site of the so-called 'Throne of Solomon' (*Takht-i Suleimān*) as complete and convincing, just as we now know that the ruins in Southern Persia which the natives call 'Throne of Jamshid' (*Takht-i Jamshīd*) are really the historic Persepolis of the Achæmenians.

I shall now turn to the second part of the discussion, the arguments of the same scholar to show that the city referred to in the classics as Gazaka or Ganzaca, and in Armenian as Gandzag, is likewise identical with Shiz and consequently with the present Takht-i Suleiman.   We have already seen that Yakut regarded *Gazn* and *Shīz* as identical places, even if the earlier Ibn Khordadhbah differentiated them.[2]   To prove the correctness of the identification, Rawlinson makes use of data connected with the campaign of Khosru Parviz against Bahram

---

[1] This new allusion, which I add to Rawlinson's material, has recently been made accessible by Von Stackelberg, *Persische Sagengeschichte*, in *WZKM*. 12. 233.

[2] See quotation from Ibn Khordadhbah given on p. 134, above, and compare also the remarks by Nöldeke, *Geschichte der Perser und Araber*, p. 100, n. 1.

Chobin (A.D. 589), and the wars of the Byzantine emperor
Heraclius against Khosru (A.D. 624), and draws deductions
also from the movements of Mark Antony against the Parthians
six centuries earlier. I shall not attempt to reproduce Rawlinson's arguments in detail, but shall simply state that most
scholars accept his identification, together with the view that
the ruins represent the site of what was also called Phraaspa,
and the fortress of Vera in Media.[1] It may be taken as practically certain that if Ganzaca and Shiz in antiquity were not
absolutely one and the same city, the former cannot have been
located far distant from the latter, and we may perhaps distinguish between the city in the plain and the fortress on the
height, following the statement quoted by Rawlinson from
Strabo, who says, 'The summer residence of the kings is at
Gazaca, situated in a plain and in a strong fort named Vera,
which was besieged by Mark Antony in his expedition against
the Parthians.'[2] As a matter of conjecture, in that event, I
might refer to the modern place named Ganjabad, a short distance to the northeast of Takht-i Suleiman (about lat. 37° 15',
long. 47° 45') — see the map at the end of this volume — or to
a place marked Ganja between Sanjud and Tikantapah on the
map in Curzon's *Persia*.[3]

By way of supplement, however, to Rawlinson's monograph,
I present one or two new matters of evidence on the subject of
Ganzak, Shiz, and the fire-temple Adhargushnasp. The testimony is in the form of Zoroastrian traditions, relating especially to the earlier king Kei Khosru (Av. *Kavi Haosravah*),
who is supposed to have lived about B.C. 800, and his enemy,
Afrasiab the Turanian (Av. *Tūirya Frañrasyan*).

[1] Rawlinson, *JRGS.* 10. 71–111,
113–115; Nöldeke, *Geschichte der
Perser und Araber*, p. 100, n. 1;
Marquart, *Ērānšahr*, p. 108; Justi,
Grundr. iran. Philol. 2. 527, 542, 544;
Darmesteter, *Le ZA.* 1. 155, n. 12.

[2] Strabo, *Geog.* 11. 13. 3; cf. Rawlinson, *JRGS.* 10. 113. Some critics

read 'and [the winter palace] is in
a strong fort,' contrasting the residences according to the seasons, but
this is less good.

[3] Streck, *Zt. f. Assyr.* 15. 332, compares Ganzaka or Gazaka with *Gizin-
(i)kissi* and notices the forms of the
name *Jiz, Shiz*.

A Pahlavi treatise written early in the ninth century A.D. and entitled *Shatrōīhā-ī Airān*, from the account which it gives of the cities of Iran, says that the town of ' Ganjak ' or ' Ganzak ' in Azarbaijan was founded by Afrasiab of Turan.

'Frasiak of Tur (Afrasiab) founded the town of Ganjak in the region of Ataropatakan (Azarbaijan).' [1]

There is further evidence to associate Afrasiab, for a time at least, with this region, since Firdausi narrates that after his defeat in Turan by Kei Khosru, Afrasiab fled to Azarbaijan and took refuge in a cave on a high mountain near Bardah, a place located east or northeast of Lake Urumiah, somewhere between Ardabil and Maraghah, and frequently mentioned by the mediæval Persian and Arabic writers, including Yakut, who says it is ' nine farsakhs from Ganjah.' [2] The fugitive, according to the legend, was discovered by a hermit, whom Firdausi calls Hom (and the Avesta calls Haoma), and then sought to escape into the waters of Lake Urumiah (miswritten in the manuscripts of the Shah Namah as *Khanjast* for *Chēchast*, Av. *Chaēchasta*). [3] Afrasiab's place of concealment, however, was revealed, and he was captured and slain by Kei Khosru, who thereupon proceeded to the fire-temple Adhargushnasp, to give thanks for his success. [4]

Somewhat earlier in his narrative Firdausi had given an

---

[1] See Jamaspji Minocheherji, *Pahlavi Texts* 1, *Shatrōīhā*, 58, Bombay, 1897, and the translation of Modi, *Shatrōīhā-ī Airān*, p. 117, Bombay, 1899; also Blochet, *Villes de l'Iran*, in *Recueil de Travaux relatifs à la Philologie*, 17. 176, Paris, 1895. It is possible also in MKh. **27**. 44 to read instead of *Dūjako*, in the Pahlavi characters, *Ganjako* (*i.e.* Canzaca), but it would not give so good an interpretation of that particular passage; see West, *SBE*. 24. 62, n. 2.

[2] Yakut, p. 92. For the caves in the vicinity of Maraghah, see p. 104,

above, and cf. Ker Porter, *Travels*, 2. 495–496 ; Rawlinson, *JRGS*. 10. 45 ; Wilson, *Persian Life*, pp. 73–74.

[3] See the earlier form of the legend in the Avesta, Ys. 11. 7, and for the struggle between Franrasyan (Afrasiab) and Haosrava (Kei Khosru), seconded by Haoma, compare Yt. **9**. 17–23 : **17**. 37–43. See also next page and note that there is a ' cave ' at the ruined city of Shahr-i Afrasiab near Samarkand.

[4] See *Shāh Nāmah*, ed. Vullers-Landauer, 3. 1386–1398 ; tr. Mohl, 4. 155–169.

account of the founding, by Kei Khosru, of the fire-temple of Adhargushnasp, which he locates in the 'Castle of Bahman' (*Dizh-i Bahman*). The context would imply that this was on the 'frontier' of Ardabil,[1] where it is located also by Yakut,[2] but Rawlinson urges that the description answers to Takht-i Suleiman.[3] The lines about the founding of the pyræum after the castle was stormed run as follows : —

'Within the vast rampart the king found a city with gardens, public squares, mansions, and a palace. At the spot where the light had flashed out and the darkness had been utterly dispelled, Khosru gave orders that a domed temple should be erected to a height towering to the sky. It was ten noose-lengths square and was surrounded by high vaulted chambers, covering a circuit of half a horse-course. There he brought and installed the fire Adhargush-[n]asp, around which sat Mobeds, astrologers, and wise men.'[4]

In keeping with Firdausi's account of Afrasiab's temporary escape from Hom and Kei Khosru by concealing himself in Lake Urumiah, and in harmony also with the Avesta, which locates the struggle of Afrasiab and Kavi Haosravah 'behind (*or* in the sight of*) Lake Chaechasta (Urumiah),' we have still other Zoroastrian traditions preserved in the Pahlavi writings. These books associate the name of Kei Khosru with the fire of the warriors, Adhargushnasp, and locate this pyræum in the neighborhood of Lake Urumiah or on Mount Asnavand.[5] Thus

---

[1] Pers. *tā dar-i Ardabīl ba-marzī kih ānjā Dizh-i Bahman ast*, see *Shāh Nāmah*, ed. Vullers-Landauer, 2. 756, and compare tr. Mohl, *Livre des Rois*, 2. 435, 'à Ardebil ... sur la frontière'; compare also Pizzi, *Il Libro dei Re*, 3. 72, 'al confin d'Ardebil.'

[2] Yakut, p. 125. So also Sadik Isfahani, p. 14.

[3] Rawlinson (*JRGS*. 10. 82, n. 3) was mistaken in saying that Ardabil is not mentioned; it occurs in the text (Vullers-Landauer, 2. 756) a few pages before the fire-temple is described.

[4] *Shāh Nāmah*, ed. Vullers-Landauer, 2. 761; tr. Mohl, *Livre des Rois*, 2. 441; and Pizzi, *Il Libro dei Re*, 3. 78.

[5] See my *Zoroaster*, pp. 100, 48; and consult also p. 70, n. 1, above. On the Avestan phrase 'behind (*or* in the sight of*) Lake Chaēchasta,' see Bartholomae, *Air. Wb.* s.v. *pašne* (for *pasne*). Darmesteter, *Le ZA.* 2. 631, n. 92, locates the scene of the conflict to the north or northwest of Lake Urumiah, calling attention to both Lake Sevan and Lake Van as

the Pahlavi Bahman Yasht (about the seventh century A.D.) states: —

'The fire Ataro-gushnasp, near (*or* by) the deep Lake Chechast, which has warm water that drives away the demons.'[1]

Similar is the statement found in the Selections of Zat-sparam (about A.D. 881): —

'Two fountains of the sea were opened out for the earth : Chechast, a lake which has no cold wind and near (*or* on) whose shore rests the triumphant fire Gushnasp, and the other, Sovar (near Tus).'[2]

The Bundahishn, one of the oldest Pahlavi works extant, describes how the fire Ataro-gushnasp aided Kei Khosru when he was engaged in putting down idol-worship about Lake Chechast, and its shrine was in the same locality near Mount Asnavand.

'When Kai-Khusrob was engaged in extirpating the idol-temples of Lake Chechast, it (*i.e.* the fire Ataro-gushnasp) settled upon the mane of his horse and drove away the darkness and gloom, and made

possibly representing Av. *Vairi Hao-sravah* (Sir. **2.** 9; Yt. **19**. 56; Ny. **5.** 5) in contrast to *Vairi Čaečasta* (Lake Urumiah), noticing also the village of Khosrova near Dilman, to which I have referred above, p. 70, n. 1. See also West's note on Bd. **22.** 8, in *SBE.* **5.** 86, n. 7. Spiegel, *Érānische Alterthumskunde*, 1. 653–654, suggests Lake Sevan for *Vairi Hao-sravah*, but notices also that Masudi (2. 131) assigns some of the scenes of the Hom-Khosru-Afrasiab conflict to the town of Serav, between Ardabil and Tabriz (see Yakut, p. 306). It would be tempting to regard *Vairi Haosravah*, 'Lake of Khosru,' as our present lake at Takht-i Suleiman adjoining Khosru's fire-temple, and Mount Asnavand (Sir. **2.** 9, etc.) as Mount Zindan; the Iranian Bunda-hishn locates the Lake of Khosru at four parasangs from Lake Urumiah instead of fifty, which is the number given in the other text.

[1] BYt. **3.** 10. The Pahlavi word which I have rendered 'near (*or* by)' is *pavan* (*pa*), which West renders 'on,' *SBE.* **5.** 218. For the Pahlavi text see Noshervan, *Pahlavi Zand-i Vohuman Yasht*, p. 14, l. 12 (= p. 17, l. 1, translit.), Bombay, 1900. On the reading *garm*, 'warm' (for 'medicinal,' West, *SBE.* **5.** 218), consult Rosenberg, *Livre de Zoroastre*, p. 74.

[2] Zsp. **6.** 22, transl. West, *SBE.* **5.** 173. Again the Pahlavi for 'near (*or* on) whose shore' has *mūnaš pavan* (*pa*) *bār*, see text, ed. West, in *Avesta, Pahlavi, etc., Studies in Honour of D. P. B. Sanjana*, first series, p. lxxi, Strassburg, 1904.

AFRASIAB TAKEN CAPTIVE BY HOM

(From the Columbia University Manuscript of the Shah Namah)

BATTLE BETWEEN THE IRANIANS AND TURANIANS

(From the Columbia University Manuscript of the Shah Namah)

it quite light, so that they might extirpate the idol-temples; in the same locality the fire Gushnasp was established at the " appointed place " (*i.e.* shrine) on the Asnavand mountain.' [1]

The location of Takht-i Suleiman is some ninety miles distant from Lake Urumiah (Chechast), it is true, but near enough, perhaps, to answer to the general description given in the Pahlavi works, when compared with the other evidence in the case, even if we be not tempted to the extent of conjecturing that the lake adjoining Khosru's ancient fire, Adhargushnasp, in the Takht, is also the Lake of Khosru, Vairi Haosravah, referred to in the Avesta and Pahlavi texts, or go so far as to surmise that the extinct volcano of Mount Zindan, so near at hand, might possibly be Mount Asnavant (Asnavand), which is invoked together with Chaechasta in the Zoroastrian prayers. [2]

I shall cite a single other passage relating to Takht-i Suleiman, or Ganzaca, and its palace and fire-temple; but it is one of special interest because of its connection both with Zoroastrianism and Christianity. [3] Georgius Cedrenus, the Church Father, in narrating the progress of the war of the Byzantine emperor Heraclius against the later Sasanian king Khosru Parviz, or Chosroes, describes how Khosru had his own image enthroned amid emblems of the celestial bodies to which he did homage — a sight which so outraged the Roman emperor and his Christian soldiers that he burned the fire-temple and reduced the entire city to ashes.

---

[1] Bd. **16**. 7, translated by West, *SBE*. 5. 64. Here the Pahlavi text reads *pavan (pa) Asnavand kōf . . . barā (bē) val (ō) dād-gāh,* cf. Justi, *Bundehesh,* p. 41, Leipzig, 1868, lithogr.; Westergaard, *Bundehesh,* p. 41, Copenhagen, 1851; Unwalla, *The Pahlavi Bundehesh,* p. 48, Bombay, 1897. The Pahlavi treatise Mainog-i Khirad, **2**. 96, also alludes to the achievement of Kei Khosru in exterminating temples for idol-worship around Lake Chechast; see West, *SBE*. 24. 15.

[2] See Sir. **2**. 9; Ny. **5**. 5. The sanctity, not the size of the lake, would entitle it to consideration. But all this would be merely an attractive hypothesis upon which a theory might be built.

[3] Cited by Rawlinson, *JRGS.* 10. 52, 78.

'The Emperor Heraclius took possession of the city of Gazaca,[1] in which was the temple and the treasures of Crœsus, king of Lydia, and the imposture of the burning coals.[2] On entering the city he found the abominable image of Khosru, an effigy of the king seated under the vaulted roof of the palace[3] as though in the heavens, and around it the sun, moon, and stars, to which he did homage with superstitious awe, as if to gods, and he had represented angels bearing sceptres and ministering unto him.[4] And the impious man had arranged by cunning devices to have drops falling from above, like rain, and sounds resembling roaring thunder to peal forth. All these things Heraclius consumed with fire, and burned both the Temple of Fire and the entire city.'[5]

Viewed in the light of all this testimony from the historic past, the desolate scenes within the walls of Takht-i Suleiman take on new life. The so-called 'bath' resumes once more its ancient glory as the great fire-temple of Adhargushnasp, whose dome, once crowned with a silver crescent, has crumbled into decay. The deep-sunk vaulted arch beneath appears as the shrine where, eight hundred years before Christ, the Keianian king Khosru, robed in white,[6] prayed for victory over Afrasiab, and, on his triumphant return from battle, offered thank-offerings worthy of a king. The same example of thanksgiving was followed by the Sasanian king Bahram Gor, nearly five centuries after Christ, when he deposited in this shrine the treasures won in his victory over the Turanians and made the vanquished queen a priestess in the shrine. Here, likewise, two centuries later, the Christian emperor Heraclius destroyed the idolatrous images of Khosru Parviz. Some day the archæologist's spade may bring to light evidences even more tangible, if greater proof be needed, of the identity of this famous ancient shrine. As I retraced my steps from the ruins of Takht-i

---

[1] Gk. τὴν Γαζακὸν πόλιν.

[2] See p. 132, n. 4, above.

[3] Gk. παλατίον.

[4] For the sceptred angels, compare the carving over Khosru's arch at Tak-i Bostan ; see p. 221, below.

[5] Georgius Cedrenus (c. A.D. 1100), 1. 721–722, ed. Migne, *Patrolog. Graec.* 121. 789–790, Paris, 1864.

[6] Firdausi, *Shāh Nāmah,* tr. Mohl, 4. 155 ; compare also Yt. **9**. 21 ; **17**. 41.

Suleiman, I felt certain that I had visited the historic site of Shiz, designated also by other names, but I reserved my judgment regarding the claim that the walled enclosure might represent the Atropatenian Ecbatana, until I should have visited Hamadan.

CHAPTER XII

HAMADAN, THE ANCIENT ECBATANA

'Orchards stretch their bloomy span
Round the walls of Hamadan;
Purples deepen on the grape,
Lyric brooks make blithe escape,
Yet are all the glories gone
That the Lord of Macedon
Saw, ere drew the revel on
And the Bacchic orgy ran
Round the walls of Hamadan.'
— CLINTON SCOLLARD, *Round the Walls of Hamadan.*

THE four days' riding from Takht-i Suleiman were fatiguing ones, with forced marches of twelve hours a day in the saddle. The first night was spent at the small hamlet of Nasarabad in a mud hovel whose roof was adorned by the skull of a horse, which served apparently as a talisman to induce sleep, for I rested well. Toward evening on the second day we halted at Bab-i Roshani, ' Gateway of Light,' which looked its name as we entered the village at sunset, flooded with golden light from the closing portals of day. The third halt was at Kultapah, where I passed an uncomfortable night, but was ready at daybreak for an early start toward Hamadan.

Of the many hard stages that made up the journey of one hundred and fifty miles from Urumiah, over high, snow-covered mountains, this last was one of the most difficult, for, although April had advanced a week, the drifts in the passes were particularly deep, and the streams in the plains at the foot of the hills swollen and extremely hard to ford. My men and horses had stood the strain for twelve days well, but I had trouble with a guide,

144

DISTANT VIEW OF HAMADAN AND MOUNT ALVAND

THE MUSALLAH, HAMADAN

Lutfullah, whom I hired at Bijar a couple of days previously, to serve also as a guard, because the Muharram festival was at its height and a Christian's life is not altogether safe in some of the fanatical villages at this time, when the Shiite Mohammedans work themselves up to a religious frenzy in their lamentations at the martyrdom of Husein, lacerating themselves with swords, knives, and sharp stones and throwing themselves into a state of pious mania. As a guide Lutfullah proved very unsatisfactory and on the last day was so cruel to his horse and so disobedient to me that I was obliged to resort to force and eject him from the courtyard of the caravansarai. He took up a position outside the gateway, crouched half sulkily, half threateningly in a corner with his rifle, and awaited my coming out. I knew it was no time for hesitation, so I leaped on my horse and rode through the gate. For a moment he wavered, casting a sullen, menacing glance, then suddenly his face changed, he dismissed his anger, came quietly to my side, and from that time forward was absolutely obedient and devoted to me, and proved so useful a servant that I kept him a number of days longer than I really needed him.

The plain through which the road approaches Hamadan from the north was beginning to put forth signs of spring ; the dark, moist earth showed a tinge of green; the gardens and orchard leas were taking on a trace of color ; and the purple-stalked willows — such as I have seen only in the shading of the French impressionist school — told that days of sunshine were at hand. A hazy light spread a soft glow over the landscape and lent an air of enchantment to all around, when far in the distance I caught my first glimpse of Hamadan, that city of bygone glory.

Although the city was in sight at noon, it took nearly five hours to reach it, and this gave me a good opportunity to study its situation and the surrounding country. Nature has given Hamadan a location that is in many ways remarkable. A level plain spreads like a garden before the feet of the city for a

L

distance of fifteen miles in length and ten in breadth, and presents a smooth expanse of territory which is well watered and
responds readily to cultivation, yielding barley, wheat, fruit,
vegetables, and the poppy plant.   Mountains and hills form a
palisade on either side to enclose the plain.   On the southern
and western side the mass of peaks called Alvand towers six
thousand feet above it, or twelve thousand feet above sea-level,
and stretches for miles away, guarding the approach in that
direction and keeping watch by night over the sleeping town
like some giant sentry.   Night after night, during my stay at
Hamadan, I used to watch for the moon to light up the figure
of this silent sentinel muffled in ice and snow.[1]   On either side
back of the city are lofty hills, so that the town looked from
the distance, as I rode toward it, as if it were set on the side
of a height.   Directly adjoining the city is the elevation called
Musallah, the acropolis in ancient times, but the true proportions of this citadel height did not come out till I drew near
and saw from its outline how much more probable it is that
this, rather than Takht-i Suleiman, is the hill to which Herodotus alludes in his description of the walled city of Ecbatana,
the capital of ancient Media.[2]

About five o'clock in the afternoon my train of tired animals
slowly entered Hamadan, weary from almost a fortnight of
uninterrupted marching from Urumiah.

Not a sign of the ancient glory of Ecbatana, that was once
the home of kings, struck my eye, nor was there a trace of that
solemn grandeur which is noble in its decay at Persepolis and
Pasargadæ.   I saw instead only crooked streets, alleys where

---

[1] The name Alvand or Elvend is as
old as the Avesta, where it is found as
Aurvant; see Yt. 19. 3, *asta aurvantō
fánkavō*, 'the eight spurs (?) of Aurvant.'   In the Pahlavi Bundahishn it
is Alvand (Bd. 19. 3, *alvant*).   The
Greeks called it Mount Orontes
('Ορόντης).   The Mohammedans make

pilgrimages to the grave of one of the
followers of the Prophet, named Sahib
Zaman, who is buried on the top of
Alvand, and near the grave is a spring
known as Chashmah-i Malik, 'Fountain of the King.'

[2] See the description of Herodotus,
p. 152, below.

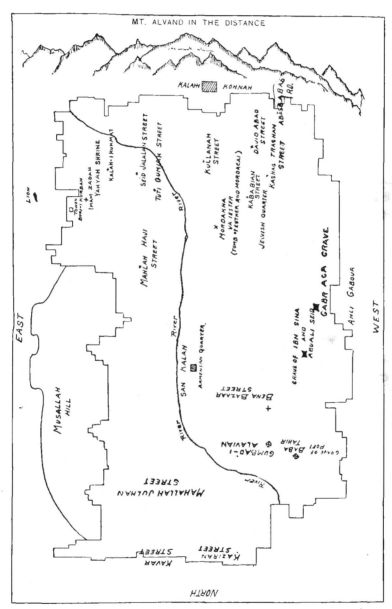

MT. ALVAND IN THE DISTANCE

KALAH KOHNAH

EAST

NORTH

WEST

LION

Tower
BURJ-I-AUBAN

IMAM ZADAN
YAHYAH SHRINE

KALAH-I-HUKMAT

SEID JALALH STREET

TUTI OUMJAH STREET

MAHLAH HAJI STREET

KULLANAH STREET

MORDAKHA
WA IESTER
(TOMB OF ESTHER AND MORDACAI)

DAVID ABAD STREET

KABABJAN STREET

JEWISH QUARTER

KASHAG TRASHAN STREET

ABÁS ABÁD RD.

River

River

SAN KALAH

River

ARMENIAN QUARTER.

MUSALLAH HILL

GRAVE OF IBN SINA
AND ABUALI SEID

GABR AGA GRAVE

AMLI GABOUR

BENA BAZAAR STREET

GRAVE OF BABA TAHIR

GUMBAD-I-ALAVIAN

River

MAHALLAH JULHAN STREET

KAZIRAN STREET

KAVAR STREET

ROUGH PLAN OF HAMADAN, DRAWN BY A NATIVE

ran channels of dirty water, rows of shabby houses with flat
mud roofs, and not a vestige of beauty anywhere. The winding street which I followed led past a Mohammedan burying-
ground located in the heart of the town. I shall never forget
the stench from the shallow graves. Nothing but the severity
of the winters and the healthy position of the town itself saves
Hamadan from pest. Street-cleaning ordinances appear not to
exist, and nature's scavengers, the birds of prey, seem sadly to
neglect their duty, for the carcass of a dead dog was lying in
one of the frequented lanes during the entire time of my two
visits at Hamadan.

The outline of the city is roughly that of a parallelogram,
running from north to south.[1] Mount Alvand lies at a distance of about three miles on the southern side; the Musallah,
or acropolis hill, is adjacent to the eastern section of the town,
of which it forms a part.[2] The town itself is divided into four
quarters, or wards, for administrative purposes, each under a
separate magistrate (*kadkhudā*), who is accountable to the governor, but whose office is practically hereditary. Through
the middle of the city runs the insignificant river Alusjird,
spanned by several single-arch stone bridges and some wooden
ones. In the spring it is swollen by the melting snows from
Alvand, but in summer it is nearly dry, although it suffices to
turn the Persian water-mills on its banks. This is evidently
the stream to which Ctesias refers when he says that Semiramis, queen of Assyria, on visiting this place, where she built a
palace, found the city poorly supplied with water, and caused

[1] For much information regarding
the localities of the city, and for a
sketch map of the town, I am indebted
to Aram Zohrabian, a native of Hamadan. For several notes I have also to
thank the courtesy of Mr. H. L. Rabino,
British Consular Agent at Kermanshah.

[2] Musallah, 'citadel,' is the name
by which the people generally know
the hill; but it is said to be called also
the Hill of Ahasuerus (Wilson, *Persian
Life*, p. 157), and I once heard it called
Fortress of Dara (Darius). But this
term was given by Mirza Sahak, a Persian of considerable education, who
may have had some knowledge of the
story of Darius Codomannus and his
overthrow by Alexander the Great.

a channel to be dug at vast expense to conduct the water from a lake on the other side of Mount Orontes into the town.[1]

The population of Hamadan is estimated conservatively at twenty-five thousand, which is probably less than in ancient times, when the city was a great metropolis.[2] The majority of the inhabitants are Iranian in blood, of the old Median stock, with some slight infusion of the Arab strain, and there are many Turks, both in the city and in the neighboring villages. The Turkish characteristics, however, are by no means so noticeable as at Urumiah, and my servant Safar, who spoke Persian fluently, now began to make jokes at the expense of Shahbas, the caravan-leader, because his speech was confined to the Turkish dialect of Azarbaijan and he could not converse freely with all the people. Among the inhabitants are also a considerable number of Armenians, about three hundred of whom occupy a special section of the town, and there is likewise a Jewish quarter, in the southern section, the community being estimated at five thousand souls, a figure not unlikely, since there have been Jews in Hamadan from the earliest times. The Europeans in the city are few in number. They are engaged chiefly in the work of the American Presbyterian Mission, which established two schools here for boys and girls in 1880, and of the Alliance Israélite, which began work among the Jews of Hamadan in 1900.

A tour of the bazaars will give the best idea of the Oriental population and of the city's commercial status. For the most part the bazaars are of the familiar type, vaulted over, and they contain more than five hundred busy shops. As a matter of course they are interesting, although only of secondary importance when compared with those in some of the large Persian towns, because the line of caravan trade turned for a time somewhat

---

[1] See the fragments of Ctesias preserved in Diodorus Siculus, 2. 13. 5, ed. Gilmore, pp. 51–52, London, 1888, and transl. Booth, *Diodorus the Sicilian*, 1. 110–111, London, 1814.

[2] The population is put at forty thousand in the *Sixty-seventh Annual Report of the Board of Foreign Missions of the Presbyterian Church in the U.S.A.* p. 233, New York, 1904.

aside from Hamadan, and cholera and famine decimated its
inhabitants. Nevertheless the commerce has been restored in
recent years, and the merchants speak of the town as 'the store
(*ambār*) of Persia.' Among the chief articles of trade are the
leather goods, as Hamadan is a city of tanneries and the Hama-
danis are renowned for their skill in dressing, tanning, and working hides and skins, and in manufacturing from them useful and
ornamental goods and articles. Saddles, straps, trunk-covers,
and pointed shoes are on sale at the various booths, while the
soft white felts (*namad*) used for mats, saddle-cloths, shepherd
coats, and helmet-shaped caps, can hardly be excelled in
Persia.[1] I still have as a memento of Hamadan's industrial
work a white felt saddle-cloth (*ghāsīah*) and two carpet saddle-
bags (*khurjīn*) purchased for me by Safar in the bazaar. The
caravansarais, which adjoin the bazaars or are located in the
vicinity, number more than fifty and do a flourishing business
in providing accommodation for the throngs of merchants and
pilgrims that pass through the city. There are likewise fully
sixty public baths which derive an added income from the same
source.

During my stay in Hamadan I was a guest of the American
missionaries and thus enjoyed a taste of home life again after
the wearisome days of halting at caravansarais. At the mission
house I made also my first acquaintance with the true Persian
cat of higher breed. Persia is sometimes called the land of
cats, but the best specimens come from the mountains of
Kurdistan and are a great contrast to the ordinary village cat,
which skulks about the caravansarai and is often a nuisance to
the traveller because of its thievish propensities, leading me
sometimes to say to Safar that I should prefer the mice if I
had my choice. The two Hamadan tabbies to which I refer
were superb creatures, larger than the largest Angora cats.

[1] Additional and detailed information regarding the trade of Hamadan
may be obtained from Rabino, *British*
Diplomatic and Consular Reports,
Persia, no. 3189, annual series, pp.
41–46, London, 1904.

One of them was pure white, the other was partly black, but in temperament both were exactly alike, and their tricks and gambols together were an endless source of amusement to me.

The most modern features of Hamadan are a telegraph office and a bank. The banking establishment is a branch of the Imperial Bank at Teheran and has for its director an Armenian Persian. The residence of this gentleman, to whose courtesy I was also indebted, was partly furnished in European style, adapted to Oriental needs, and it gave a good example of how ready the Iranian is, under certain conditions, to combine Western civilization with Eastern life. But it is not the modern phase of Hamadan that is interesting ; the chief interest in the place centres in its antiquity, and I shall devote the rest of the chapter to the historic associations of the city.

In the first place, the name Hamadan can be traced back to the earliest times. During the Sasanian era it was known as *Hamatān*,[1] and in the ancient Persian inscriptions as *Hagmatāna*,[2] which means literally 'a place of meeting or convening, concourse of many ways,' and Hamadan to-day is a meeting-place of as many highways from various parts of the kingdom as when it was the Median capital.[3] In the Babylonian inscriptions it appears as *Agamatanu*.[4] The Greek writer Ctesias, who knew Persian well, renders the name correctly as *Agbatana* (Ἀγβάτανα), although most of the Greeks called it *Ekbátăna* (Ἐκβάτăνα), with initial *E*, not *A*, and giving to the penultimate vowel the wrong quantity (*ă* for *ā*).

[1] Pahlavi *Hamaṭān*, Bd. **12**. 12 ; **22**. 6.

[2] OP. *Haᵑgᵃmᵃtᵃanᵃ*, Bh. **2**. 76, 77, from *ham*, 'together,' and *gam*, 'to go,' *i.e.* 'Co-ventry' (?). Bartholomae, *Air. Wb.* p. 1744, regards the etymology as uncertain.

[3] From the top of the Musallah, for example, it is possible to count roadways leading to twelve more or less important places, including Tabriz, Urumiah, Kazvin, Teheran, Isfahan, Kermanshah, and other cities known in antiquity.

[4] Babylonian *A-ga-ma-ta-nu*, Bh. 60, and Nabonid, *Annaleninschr. Av.* 2. 3, 4. Cf. also Bang, *Mélanges Charles de Harlez*, p. 8, Leiden, 1896 ; and Streck, *Armenien und Westpersien*, in *Zt. f. Assyr.* 15. 367.

Persian Cats at the Mission House, Hamadan

The antiquity of these allusions to the name shows how ancient the history of the city really is. Its existence as early as the twelfth century before Christ is believed to be vouched for by the mention of *Amadana* in an Assyrian inscription of Tiglath-Pileser I (c. B.C. 1100),[1] and we certainly have inscriptional evidence to prove that it must have existed in the time of Ramman-nirari, husband of Semiramis (Sammuramat),[2] or, according to some authorities, before the end of the ninth century B.C. Ctesias, who was court physician to Artaxerxes Mnemon for seventeen years (B.C. 416–399), and well acquainted with Persian traditions, says that 'when Semiramis came to Ecbatana, which is situated in a low, level plain, she built a palace and bestowed more care and attention upon it than she had done at any other place'; and Ctesias describes the watercourses which she caused to be constructed from Mount Alvand to Hamadan.[3] According to the same author, moreover, when Sardanapalus, the last Assyrian king, was overthrown by Arbaces, and the Median kingdom established, Arbaces conveyed to Ecbatana all the gold and silver treasure which was taken from Nineveh after its capture; but the historic accuracy of this report is, perhaps, open to question.[4]

The more generally accepted account of the founding of Ecbatana is that given by Herodotus, who ascribes its origin to Deioces, the first great ruler of the Median Empire, about B.C. 700. The description of the place is not only picturesque, but important for the purpose of identification, because of the allusion to the walls.

---

[1] Spiegel, *Ērānische Alterthumskunde*, 2. 246, and Browne, *Literary History of Persia*, p. 20.

[2] See Justi, *Geschichte Irans*, in *Grundr. iran. Philol.* 2. 404.

[3] These statements of Ctesias are preserved in Diodorus Siculus, 2. 13. 5. See p. 148, n. 1, above, for references.

[4] For the text of Ctesias, see Gilmore, *Fragments of Ktesias*, 29, p. 90, and the translation by Booth, *Diodorus the Sicilian*, 1. 124. Compare also Rawlinson, *JRGS.* 10. 125, and consult, for Arbaces, Justi, *Geschichte Irans*, in *Grundr. iran. Philol.* 2. 407–408. For other traditions regarding the founding of Hamadan, see Modi, *Shatrōīhā-ī Aīrān, or Cities of Iran*, p. 151, Bombay, 1899.

'Deioces built the massive and strong-walled city now called Ecbatana ('Αγβάτανα), the walls being arranged in circles one within the other. The rampart is planned in such a manner that each circle rises higher than the one preceding it by the height merely of the battlements. The nature of the ground, which is a gentle hill (κολωνός), is favorable for carrying out such a design; and, as there are seven circles in all, particular care was taken to have the royal palace and the treasury within the innermost circle. The circuit of the outer wall is nearly as large as that of the city of Athens. Of this first circle the battlements are white; the second, black; the third, red; the fourth, blue; and the fifth, orange. The battlements of all the circles are decorated in this manner with colors, but those of the two last are incrusted, the one with silver, the other with gold. Such were the palace and the surrounding fortifications which Deioces built for himself; but the rest of the people he ordered to build their houses round about outside the wall.' [1]

The Old Testament apocryphal book of Judith attributes the founding of Ecbatana (called Achmetha in Aramaic, Ezra 6. 2) to a king named Arphaxad, whose historic identity has not been satisfactorily proved, and gives an elaborate description of the city's walls, towers, and gates. I quote the account in full, although in the eyes of most critics it has no greater value than that which we should attach to an Oriental romance.

'1. In the twelfth year of the reign of Nabuchodonosor, who reigned in Nineveh, the great city; in the days of Arphaxad, which reigned over the Medes in Ecbatane, 2. And built in Ecbatane walls round about of stones hewn three cubits broad and six cubits long, and made the height of the wall seventy cubits, and the breadth thereof fifty cubits: 3. And set the towers thereof upon the gates of it, a hundred cubits high, and the breadth thereof in the foundation threescore cubits: 4. And he made the gates thereof, even gates that were raised to the height of seventy cubits, and the breadth of them was forty cubits, for the going forth of his mighty armies, and for the setting in array of his footmen: 5. Even in those days King Nabuchodonosor made war with King Arphaxad in the great plain, which is the plain in the borders of Ragau. . . .

[1] Herodotus, *History*, 1. 98, 99. Cf. also G. Rawlinson, *Herodotus*, 1. 191– 194, London, 1862; H. C. Rawlinson, *JRGS*. 10. 126–127.

13. Then he marched in battle-array with his power against King Arphaxad in the seventeenth year, and he prevailed in his battle : for he overthrew all the power of Arphaxad, and all his horsemen, and all his chariots, 14. And became lord of his cities, and came unto Ecbatane, and took the towers, and spoiled the streets thereof, and turned the beauty thereof into shame.' [1]

According to Polybius, the Greek historian, who wrote in the second century B.C., the magnificence of Ecbatana was such as to call for special notice, especially regarding the splendor of its palace and the temple of Aena or Anaias. This name is none other than a disguised form of Anahita or Anaïtis, the Zoroastrian goddess of the waters, who is celebrated in the Avesta and whose worship was especially popular among the Persians after the time of King Artaxerxes II (fourth century B.C.). [2] From other classic sources we know that this goddess had a famous temple at Ecbatana. [3] The description in full is as follows : —

' It was originally the royal city of the Medes, and vastly superior to the other cities in wealth and in the splendour of its buildings. It is situated on the skirts of Mount Orontes, and is without walls, though containing an artificially formed citadel fortified to an astonishing strength. Beneath this stands the palace, which it is in some degree difficult to describe in detail, or to pass over in complete

[1] Judith, 1. 1-14. Yakut, p. 597, asserts that Hamadan was founded by one of the great-grandsons of Noah, and some of the older Occidental scholars used likewise to point to the name of Arphaxad, grandson of Noah, in Genesis 10. 22 ; 11. 10-14, and associate with it the tradition that Media was so called from Madai, son of Japhet (Gen. 10. 2); see Ker Porter, *Travels*, 2. 94. Some attempts have likewise been made to identify Arphaxad, as founder of Ecbatana, with Deioces or with his son Phraortes ; but the trend of modern scholarship is to regard the name Arphaxad as hav-

ing no real historic importance, but as inserted to lend an air of antiquity to the Apocryphal story ; see Cheyne, *Encyclopædia Biblica*, s.v. Arphaxad, Judith. The value of the description is open to the same attack.

[2] See Windischmann, *Die persische Anahita oder Anaïtis*, p. 5, in *Abhandl. kgl. bayr. Akad. Wiss.* Bd. 8, Abthl. 1, Munich, 1856 ; compare also pp. 237–242, below.

[3] See Isidorus Characenus, *Mansiones Parthicae*, 6, and Plutarch, *Artaxerxes*, 27. 3 ; cf. Windischmann, *Die persische Anahita*, pp. 6, 13.

silence. To those authors whose aim is to produce astonishment, and who are accustomed to deal in exaggeration and picturesque writing, this city offers the best possible subject; but to those who, like myself, are cautious when approaching descriptions which go beyond ordinary notions, it presents much difficulty and embarrassment. However, as regards size, the palace covers ground the circuit of which is nearly seven stades;[1] and by the costliness of the structure in its several parts it testifies to the wealth of its original builders : for, all its woodwork being cedar or cypress, not a single plank was left uncovered ; beams and fretwork in the ceilings and columns in the arcades and peristyle were overlaid with plates of silver or gold, while all the tiles were of silver. Most of these had been stripped off during the invasion of Alexander and the Macedonians (B.C. 335), and the rest in the reigns of Antigonus (B.C. 325–301) and Seleucus Nicator (B.C. 312–280). However, even at the time of Antiochus's arrival (*i.e.* Antiochus the Great, B.C. 210), the temple of Aena still had its columns covered with gold, and a considerable number of silver tiles had been piled up in it, and some few gold bricks and a good many silver ones were still remaining. It was from these that the coinage bearing the king's impress was collected and struck, amounting to little less than four thousand talents ($4,730,000).'[2]

It is important to note that Polybius says that the city was ' without walls, though it contained a strongly fortified citadel beneath which the palace stood,' and that he says that the palace was built of wood, because this would render it peculiarly liable to destruction as contrasted with the stone used at Persepolis.

If we now ascend the hill known as the Musallah, or citadel, adjoining the city of Hamadan, which is built partly upon its western and northwestern slope, we can understand how it might be possible for the town itself to be without walls, as Polybius asserts, and for the fortified ramparts and battlements to be confined, in his own words, to the ' artificially formed citadel fortified to an astounding strength, beneath which the

---

[1] Four fifths of a mile in circumference.

[2] Polybius, *Hist.* 10. 27 ; see Shuckburgh, *The Histories of Polybius Translated*, 2. 26–27, London, 1889. See also p. 158, below.

The Mu͑sallah Hill, Hamadan

palace stood.'[1] The ascent of the Musallah, I may observe, is steep enough for the Persian horses to start up it at a sharp gallop, as they always do when approaching a marked incline. The height, in my judgment, would answer far better than Takht-i Suleiman to Herodotus' description of the place as a κολωνός and would fulfil all the requirements of his sketch.[2] There is room for the seven circles of walls, and the Median people could have 'built their houses round about outside the wall,' as Deioces bade them (Herodotus, 1. 99), on the very site still occupied by the city. Even at the present time the ridge of the Musallah is crowned by the remains of massive walls, some fifteen feet thick and twenty high, composed of clay, slate, brick, and small stones, and forming a parallelogram running northeast and southwest, in the midst of which the bed rock is here and there visible. Although no one would ascribe a great antiquity to these redoubts (in fact Agha Mohammed Shah, at the close of the eighteenth century, is said to have destroyed all remnants of antiquity at Hamadan),[3] nevertheless they may occupy the same position as those which crowned the κολωνός in Median days and be similar to them in structure, for things change slowly in Persia.[4]

Herodotus, moreover, does not say that the walls of Ecbatana were of stone, though this might be inferred, and it is almost certain that the color decorations were confined to the battlements raised upon them. It is true that the passage in Judith speaks of 'hewn stone'; but even if we are to press the phrasing of that historical romance, it may be possible that the

[1] Canon George Rawlinson, *Five Great Monarchies*, 3. 23, expresses doubt 'whether the Median capital was at any time surrounded by walls.'

[2] It is not clear to me how Sir Henry Rawlinson could have taken exception on this score, as my careful examination of the site on two occasions convinced me; see Rawlinson, *JRGS*. 10.

127, and George Rawlinson, *Herodotus*, 1. 191–192, note, London, 1862.

[3] See Ker Porter, *Travels*, 2. 102; Wilson, *Persian Life*, p. 157.

[4] Such is also the view of de Morgan, *Mission Scientifique en Perse*, 4. 248–249; it is worth noting that he refers also (p. 249) to the ruins of two Gabar towers.

blocks have been carried off in later times for building purposes, for one sees in the city a number of large hewn stones
built into the foundations of houses and possibly taken from
such a wall, if stone, rather than the earthen breastworks, be
insisted upon.[1] It must also be said that Canon George Rawlinson, when summing up his brother's claim that Takht-i
Suleiman represents the so-called northern capital of Media,
acknowledges that ' of the seven walls, one alone is to be traced
at Takht-i Suleiman ; and even here the Median structure has
perished and been replaced by masonry of a far later age.'[2]

The other claims advanced by Sir Henry, such as the statement of Herodotus (1. 110) that the country north of Ecbatana
is mountainous and covered with forests, seem to me equally
applicable to Hamadan as to Takht-i Suleiman, and a comparison of the two sites in detail convinced me that Hamadan has
the right and title to being the sole heir of Ecbatana, that the
Musallah was its citadel, and that the ruins of Takht-i Suleiman, although occupying a site that may be equally old, but
not so important as a metropolis, have a different history from
Ecbatana.[3]

In view of all these facts I felt convinced, when standing
upon the height of the Musallah and overlooking Hamadan,

[1] I am informed by Aram Zohrabian, of Hamadan, that about a year
after the time when I was in Persia, the
remains of a so-called *Ganj*, ' treasury,'
were discovered in the Armenian quarter of Hamadan and some magnificent
hewn stones were laid bare.

[2] George Rawlinson, *Five Great
Monarchies*, 3. 27, and n. 11. Consult
also de Morgan, *Mission Scientifique
en Perse*, 4. 248–249.

[3] My view has been anticipated, I
find, by de Morgan, *Mission*, 4. 238–
249, whose chapter on Hamadan should
be consulted. It is possible that excavations for archæological purposes may
show that the position of Hamadan

has changed in some slight degree, as
there are evidences of ruins around the
northeast side of the Musallah, where
old bricks are dug up and gold coins
are found. In notes sent me by Mr.
Rabino it is claimed that the site of
the city has been changed several times
and the present site of the town cannot be more than five hundred and fifty
years old, but this seems to me doubtful, and archæological researches alone
can settle the question. In the Musallah itself, however, there is little or no
chance for excavation, as the earth is
almost entirely washed away, so that
the bed rock is visible.

that I was surveying the site of the capital of ancient Media. Here within the fortress there once stood the royal treasury mentioned by Herodotus,[1] and here the stronghold where Arbaces deposited the silver and gold found in the king's coffers at Nineveh.[2] Hither also the untold riches of Crœsus were conveyed by the conqueror Cyrus;[3] and to this strong-hold Alexander, following the example of his victorious prede-cessors, transported the wealth he had plundered from Susa, Persepolis, and Pasargadæ.[4] Here likewise 'at Achmetha, in the palace that is in the province of the Medes,' was found the decree of Cyrus giving orders for the rebuilding of the temple at Jerusalem, a command which was carried into effect by Darius and his successor Artaxerxes.[5] The height served also as a Persian Bastille in ancient days, and here in a dungeon the Achæmenian kings caused offenders against the state to be confined and executed. Within its walls, for example, Darius put to death the Median leader Fravarti, who, like several others, had set up a claim to the throne while the king was engaged at Babylon, and had headed an army to support his claim. The pretender was defeated in battle at Raga, the modern Rei near Teheran, was taken prisoner, and met with a fate that is told in the Great King's own words in the rock inscription at Behistan : 'Fravarti was seized and brought to me. I cut off his nose and his ears, and cut out his tongue, and put out his eyes. He was kept in chains at my door; all the people saw him. Afterward I caused him to be crucified;[6]

---

[1] Herodotus, *History*, **1**. 98.

[2] Ctesias, *Fragments*, 29 (cited by Diodorus Siculus), ed. Gilmore, p. 90 ; tr. Booth, *Diodorus the Sicilian*, 1. 124.

[3] Herodotus, *History*, 1. 153.

[4] Arrian, *Anabasis*, **3**. 19. 7, and cf. **3**. 18. 10 ; **3**. 19. 2 ; also Quintus Curtius Rufus, *Alexander*, **5**. 6. 1–10 ; Diodorus Siculus, *Hist.* **17**. 71 ; Plu-tarch, *Alexander*, 36–37 ; Strabo, *Geog.* **15**. 3. 9, cf. also **15**. 3. 23. Compare

furthermore McCrindle, *Invasion of India by Alexander the Great*, pp. 34, 126, n. 1, London, 1896.

[5] Ezra **5**. 17 ; **6**. 1–3.

[6] Or 'impaled' (OP. *uzmayāpatiy*). All these mutilations as punishments are still practised in Persia, except that the barbarous mode of execution has given place to others. So also Hüsing, *Elamische Studien*, in *Mitteil. Vorderasiat. Gesellsch.* 3. 315.

and the men who were his principal followers I imprisoned in the fortress (*didā*) at Ecbatana.'[1]

Here on the citadel height, in addition to the dungeon, the treasure-house, and the temples of the ancient divinities of Iran,[2] there once stood the palace of the ancient Median kings. Deioces, the founder of the empire of Media, sought seclusion within its fortified walls, which he himself had built, when he assumed the crown and withdrew himself from the ordinary presence of the people.[3]   Probably within the same walls Astyages, according to legend, received the youthful Cyrus, who was destined later to wrest from him his crown and transfer the supremacy of Media to Persia.[4]   The Persian kings of the Achæmenian line kept up the old-time prestige of the Median city and its citadel by making Ecbatana their summer capital.   Here in their royal abode overlooking the plains and surrounded by high mountains they must have found a delightful change from Susa, whose warm climate was suited only for a winter residence, or from Persepolis, their spring and summer home.[5]   To Ecbatana likewise Alexander returned toward the end of his short career, in order to celebrate the glories of his campaigns in eastern Iran and India.[6]   The Parthian dynasty (B.C. 250–A.D. 226) still made the city a favored place,[7] and Antiochus found in the palace and temple an enormous amount of gold and silver bullion to turn into coin to pay his soldiers.[8] The Sasanian rulers (A.D. 226–651) were perhaps less partial to Hamadan, but the place was still so important when the Arabs captured the city (645) that they regarded this event as second

---

[1] Bh. **2**. 73–78. Foy, *Kuhn's Zeitschrift*, 35. 39–42, understands this latter to mean, 'I h a n g e d his principal followers b e f o r e the fortress.'

[2] The temple of Anaitis referred to above, p. 153, and probably here likewise the shrine of the Persian 'Æsculapius' alluded to by Arrian, *Anab.* **7**. 14. 5.

[3] Herodotus, *History*, 1. 99.

[4] Herodotus, *History*, **1**. 121–130; Xenophon, *Cyropaedia*, **1**. 3. 1–18.

[5] Xenophon, *Anabasis*, **3**. 5. 15, and *Cyropaedia*, **8**. 6. 22 ; Strabo, *Geog.* 11. 323 ; Quintus Curtius Rufus, *Alexander*, **5**. 8. 1.

[6] See pp. 163–165, below.

[7] Quintus Curtius Rufus, *Alexander*, **5**. 8. 1.

[8] See p. 154, above.

only to the triumph at Nahavand over the army of the house
of Sasan.[1] Early in the tenth century Hamadan was stormed
by Mardavij ibn Ziar of Gilan;[2] in the thirteenth century by
Tamerlane; and once again, five centuries later, sacked and
pillaged by Agha Mohammed Shah. It is no marvel that this
ancient home of kings and scene of great events is but a shadow
of by-gone glory. Its fate is best told in the verses of the
short poem from which I quoted at the beginning of the
chapter.

'Gone the great sun-temple where
Golden stair rose over stair;
Gone the gilded galleries,
Porticoes and palaces;
And the plaintive nightwinds plead
For the memory of the Mede,
Sob for alien ears to heed,
Pilgrim train and caravan,
Round the walls of Hamadan.

Nought of all the radiant past,
Nought of all the varied, vast
Life that throbbed and thrilled, remains
With its pleasures and its pains,
Save a couchant lion lone,
Mute memorial in stone
Of three empires overthrown —
Median, Persian, Parthian —
Round the walls of Hamadan.'

The famous but battered stone lion referred to in the verses
as the only monument that has lasted through the long ages of
Hamadan now lies near the foot of the Musallah not far from
the road leading to Isfahan. It is one of the landmarks of
Hamadan and is regarded as a guardian genius of the town.
Even a thousand years ago it was spoken of by Masudi as very
ancient, and he describes it as standing by the 'Lion Gate'

[1] See Yakut, p. 598, and Justi, *Geschichte Irans*, in *Grundr. iran. Philol.* 2. 546.

[2] See Masudi, *Les Prairies d'Or*, chap. 130, ed. Barbier de Meynard, 9. 21-22, Paris, 1877; and compare Horn, *Gesch. Irans in Islam. Zeit*, in *Grundr. iran. Philol.* 2. 564.

(*Bāb al-Asad*) on a low hill overlooking the road to Rei and Khorasan.[1] He speaks of its lifelike appearance and compares it in size to some great bull or a crouching camel, adding that it was carved after Alexander's return from Khorasan (as native tradition ascribes the founding of Hamadan to Alexander) and set up as a talisman to protect the walls of the city and its inhabitants, which were destined to be safe as long as the lion was not thrown down or broken. The overthrow of the lion was accomplished, he tells us, about his own time, when the army of Mardavij stormed Hamadan, as stated above,[2] and this event was accompanied by utter disaster, which fulfilled the prophecy. A legend almost as old, recorded by Yakut (about A.D. 1220), says that the image was set up by Belinas as a talisman against the severe winters of Hamadan.[3] If efficacious, we can hardly imagine what would be the rigor of the climate without its influence, for Hamadan is one of the coldest places in Persia. In the absence of authentic history we can only resort to legend and tradition regarding this lion monument and its origin, but popular belief has certainly surrounded the sculptured stone with a deep veneration in the eyes of the people. Dozens of superstitions are attached to it. Mothers hold up their babes to pat the huge beast or kiss its face, barren women touch its brow to remove the curse of sterility, and pilgrims lay offerings of stones, some of them carved, upon its head as a coronet or on the block below its mouth.

From the standpoint of art the lion is rather effective in the distance, as the mutilation of the stone does not then show, and I was impressed by the lifelike appearance of the image as I first rode toward it, an effect which is enhanced by the

---

[1] Masudi (died 951) devotes a paragraph to this monument in his *Meadows of Gold*, chap. 130, see *Les Prairies d'Or*, ed. Barbier de Meynard, 9. 21-22.

[2] See p. 159, above.

[3] Yakut, p. 606, who adds that Belinas also placed other talismans, no longer in existence, to the right of the statue to protect the people of Hamadan against snakes, scorpions, insects, and floods. Belinas is commonly explained as a corrupt Oriental form for Plinius, Pliny.

THE LION OF HAMADAN

THE LION'S FACE
(Votive stone offerings under the mouth)

yellowish sandstone out of which the figure is carved. The head is massive, and the heavy waves of the mane are realistic in appearance, but it is difficult to catch the exact expression of the face in its present prone position, although the chin is well marked and the jaws are partly open. A deep hole in the forehead mars the expanse of the brow, and the face is smeared by dirty hands and is greasy from the oil which pilgrims pour upon it. Between the shoulders and in the back there are eight or more holes, due to erosion, and the rain settling in these cavities has tended to enlarge them, so that several are big enough for the fist to be inserted. Although the legs of the creature are broken off at the shoulders and thighs, the body is entire and not split by a crack as the reproductions in some books, since the time of Flandin, would lead one to suppose.[1] A careful examination of the sculpture shows that the lion originally sat in an upright posture with the forelegs straight and without any curve from the shoulders except the natural rounding at the haunches. In other words, it was a lion *sejant*, not *couchant*. The right hip is lower than the left, and the tail, though missing, curved around the left flank, as is shown by a perceptible groove in the stone at that point. From head to tail the image measures between eleven and twelve feet (3.40 m.), the head itself being nearly forty inches in diameter (1 m.).

The present position of the lion, about an eighth of a mile from the foot of the Musallah, and facing south, is probably due to chance. Both Masudi and Yakut speak of the sculpture as being near a gate of the city, and, judging from a modern mud tower which guards the road at this point, it is possible that there once was a gate near by, or that the lion possibly guarded an entrance to the citadel height at this spot.

Concerning the age of the statue we can only make guesses, reckoning back from the time when Masudi spoke of it a

[1] See, for example, Flandin and Coste, *Voyage en Perse, Ancienne*, 1. pl. 25; *Texte*, p. 17; George Rawlinson, *Five Great Monarchies*, 3. 92; Justi, *Geschichte des Alten Persiens*, p. 5, Berlin, 1879.

M

thousand years ago. On the whole I agree with those who attribute a great antiquity to the sculpture, assigning it even to the times of the ancient Median kingdom, when it may have anticipated the lion of the royal Persian emblem.

Not far from the lion and in the southeastern section of the city, there is a towerlike structure which is generally called by the people *Burj-i Gurbān*, or *Kurbān*, ' Tower of Sacrifice,' but was pointed out to me as the *Zardushtīān*, or Zoroastrian fire-temple, by Mirza Sahak, an intelligent Persian. One morning, after coming down from the mound of the citadel, I paid a visit to this partly ruined turret. I found a structure decagonal in shape and built of ordinary Persian bricks, not the large sun-dried bricks as at Rei and in the fire-temple near Isfahan. It reminded me, in appearance, of another towerlike building which I had visited in the northern part of the city, the Gumbad-i Alavian, and like the latter it gave me the impression of being no older than the thirteenth century, the time of the Mongol sway. I could not see anything particularly Zoroastrian about it, nor was there anything in its interior to support such a view. The ten wall-spaces on the inside were set off by pointed niches, and there were four small window openings high up, which gave a good light. The woodwork around these openings had been partially burned away, evidently by some accidental fire. There were also one or two charred pieces of beams here and there in the walls. Otherwise the interior was empty, and the only opening in the floor was an irregular descent into what was probably once a tomb. Within the walls of the building the natives on certain occasions sacrifice a camel, which accounts for the name, ' Tower of Sacrifice,' by which the structure is known.[1]

[1] This rite may be a survival of some ancient rite, like the animal sacrifices in the Avesta, Yt. 5. 21, 25, 33, etc., and the festival '*īd-i kurbān*, '*īd-i azhā*, in which sheep are sacrificed even by Zoroastrians as well as Moslems on the tenth day of the twelfth Mohammedan month of *Zī-hijja*, in commemoration of Abraham's offering up his son Isaac (or, according to the Mohammedans, Ishmael), as I am informed by Khodabakhsh Bahram Raïs, of Yezd, in a

The Gumbad-i Alavian, to which I have alluded as being in the northwestern part of the town, is a shrine perhaps five or six centuries old, belonging to the Seljuk era, and sacred as a tomb; but its only interest for us consists in the stucco work of the interior. This is artistic alike in design and in execution, and there are also some scrolls of fine workmanship and Kufic inscriptions from the Koran, which are very ornamental.

Probably older, as far as concerns the site which it occupies, is the Kalah-i Kohnah, 'Ancient Citadel,' on the southern side of Hamadan, lying in the direction of Mount Alvand (see sketch map). If archæological researches should be undertaken in the neighborhood of this structure they might possibly yield interesting relics, as Hamadan is rich in antiquities, and the soil of the plain, when systematically dug, washed, and examined, as is done by some enterprising natives, yields a considerable harvest of old coins, seals, jewels, and other valuables, which repays the labor involved.[1] Gold-washing, in fact, is a regular occupation at Hamadan, and systematic washing of the fields has been carried on for the past twenty years. The yield in coins and nuggets has decreased, but the amount of gold-dust that is found gives a fairly good profit.

I have spoken of Alexander the Great in connection with Hamadan, and we know from history that he twice visited this ancient capital of Media, once when pursuing the vanquished Darius Codomannus, and afterward when returning from Bactria and India. His name is still well known among the people as *Iskandar* and various legends about him are preserved to the present time. A building, for example, near the bridge leading over the stream to the Musallah, is said to occupy the site of the 'Governor's Palace,' where he is supposed to have

letter dated May 14, 1905. See p. 371, below, and cf. also Pietro della Valle (1617), *Viaggi*, 1. 536; *Travels*, ed. Pinkerton, 9. 36; Tavernier, *Travels*, p. 143.

[1] See also the remarks by Wilson, *Persian Life*, p. 157; and compare the reproductions of the finds in the collection of de Morgan, *Mission Scientifique*, 4. 250-251.

stayed, and evil tales regarding his habits of excessive drinking still linger among the people.   They repeat a story that
one night in his cups he boasted how rapidly he was conquer-
ing the world. 'Sire,' said one of his generals, 'it is through
your father's soldiers that you win such successes.'   Angered
at the rebuke and inflamed with wine, he caused his remonstra-
tor to be put to death forthwith.   On the following day, not
knowing what he had done, he called for the general and then
learned of the crime he himself had committed.   The site of
the supposed tomb of his victim is pointed out on the street
overlooking the stream and is called *Gabr-i Iskandar,* 'Grave
of Alexander,' for the common people more generally believe
that the World-Conqueror himself is buried there, rather than
that it is the grave of Alexander's officer.   The so-called
sepulchre is nothing more than a recess in a rounded bastion of
clay, mortar, and stone, that now forms part of the foundation
of a mud house which is occupied as a dwelling and is entered
by a small door, a foot and a half wide and two feet high.
I made no attempt to inspect the supposed crypt more closely.[1]

The story as it is told in Hamadan seems to contain a reminiscence of the death of the general Clitus, whom Alexander
slew with his own hand in a fit of drunken madness because he
ventured to rebuke the conqueror — an event generally said to
have taken place at Samarkand — combined with a tradition
of the loss of his favorite, Hephæstion, who died at Hamadan
and whose death Alexander mourned in a wild despair.[2]
Plutarch describes the circumstances attending upon this

---

[1] Those natives of Hamadan who
maintain that Alexander is really
buried in their city narrate a legend to
the effect that he gave orders that after
his death his body should be carried
with outstretched arms, holding earth
in the hand, about the kingdoms which
he had conquered. His corpse should
be buried wherever he withdrew his
hand.   This happened at Hamadan

and the body was accordingly interred.
This note I have on the authority of
Mr. H. L. Rabino of Kermanshah. The
symbolism in the legend can easily be
recognized.

[2] See Plutarch, *Alexander*, 50, 51,
72, ed. Bekker, Leipzig, 1858 ; transl.
Langhorne, 5. 256–259, 282–283 ; cf.
McCrindle, *Invasion of India*, p. 43,
London, 1896.

BRIDGE OVER THE RIVER AT HAMADAN — MOUNT ALVAND IN
THE BACKGROUND

latter event. Alexander had returned to Ecbatana from
India, and on reaching the ancient capital, of which he was
now the victorious lord, he gave himself up to celebrating his
successes with all the wanton luxuriousness of the East, for
his habits had been growing more and more Asiatic, much to
the distress of his hardier Macedonian leaders. The rejoicings
were accompanied by games and public festivities conducted in
regal fashion. In the midst of these celebrations, which Plutarch pictures as little better than drunken orgies, Hephæstion
died. 'Alexander's grief knew no bounds,' he says. 'He
immediately ordered the manes of the horses and mules to
be shorn as a sign of mourning, and tore down the battlements
of the towns in the vicinity;[1] he caused the unfortunate physician who had attended Hephæstion to be impaled, and forbade
the flute and all other music in the camp for a long time.'[2]
Plutarch then describes how Alexander ravaged the country
round about, taking vengeance on the people for the death of
his minion, putting to the sword all those that were of youthful age and calling this 'a sacrifice to Hephæstion.' He
designed a superb tomb for the dead favorite, which was to
cost ten thousand talents and be executed by the celebrated
Greek architect Stasicrates ; but whether the mausoleum was
ever built or whether the body was less magnificently interred
at Ecbatana or perhaps even embalmed and carried with Alexander to Babylon, is not known. Nor is it at all certain that
the so-called sarcophagus of Alexander preserved in Constantinople was really the coffin of the great conqueror.[3]

Another tomb, which is less known, but in reality more interesting, is that which contains the body of the great physician
and philosopher, Ibn Sina, or Abu Ali ibn Sina, better known

[1] This is the statement of Plutarch, 72, τῶν πέριξ πόλεων, but generally understood to refer to the walls of Ec- batana ; see Ælian, *Hist.* 7. 8; cf. Lang- horne, *Plutarch's Lives,* 5. 283, n. 190.

[2] Plutarch, *Alexander,* 72. For other traditions about Alexander, compare Ker Porter, *Travels,* 2. 99–101.

[3] For a picture of the so-called Alexander sarcophagus at Constanti- nople, see Skrine and Ross, *Heart of Asia,* p. 9, London, 1899.

to the West as Avicenna. This remarkable man flourished about A.D. 1000 and was one of the finest intellectual forces that the Orient ever produced. He was a native of Bokhara in Turkistan, but lived long in Persia, spending his last days at Hamadan. His famous work on medicine, written in Arabic, but based on Greek authorities, ranks as a standard in the East and, through the medium of translations, enjoyed such distinction in Europe, some hundreds of years ago, that Chaucer refers to it in the *Pardoner's Tale* as a work familiarly known to his readers.[1] Avicenna's metaphysical writings, which were likewise affected by Greece, being influenced by Aristotle and Neo-Platonism, also found their way indirectly into Europe through the so-called Arabian philosophy of the Moors in Spain and thus affected scholastic philosophy.[2] In addition to his renown as a physician and philosopher Ibn Sina had some repute as an occasional writer of verse ; some of his quatrains anticipate *Omar Khayyam* by a century. I paraphrase a stanza which is particularly Khayyamesque in tone and looks almost as if 'that large infidel' might have written it.

> 'From Earth's dark Centre unto Saturn's Gate
> I've solved all Problems of this World's Estate,
>   From every Snare of Plot and Guile set free,
>   Each Bond resolved — saving alone Death's Fate.'[3]

[1] Chaucer, *Pardoner's Tale*, 889–891.

[2] See Browne, *Literary History of Persia*, p. 381.

[3] To show I am not over-influenced by FitzGerald (quatrain 31) I append the Persian text of the quatrain and translate it literally : —

*az ḳa'r-i gil-i sīāh tā auj-i zuḥal
kardam hamah mushkilāt-i gītī rā ḥal
bīrūn jastam zi-ḳaid-i har makr u ḥīl
har band kushādah shud magar band-i
      ajal*

'From the abysm of the dark earth to the height of Saturn,
I have made all mysteries of the world resolved ;
I have leaped free from the fetters of all machinations and guile ;
Every bond has been resolved, except the bond of Death.'

Instead of *gil* there is a reading *gul*, 'from the root of the dark rose,' and *'ālam*, 'world,' as a synonym for *gītī* in the second line. The text of this quatrain is given by Ethé, *Nachrichten*

TOMB OF AVICENNA (IBN SINA)

TOMB O... ...

The tomb itself is a simple brickwork building, rectangular in shape, and surrounded by an unpretentious walled court-yard which is haunted by dervishes, pilgrims, and loiterers. A carved and inscribed slab covers the dust of the great thinker, and by his side rest the remains of his contemporary, Sheikh Abu Saïd, the Persian mystic poet and author of quatrain verses in allegorical and symbolic style, who is said to have been acquainted with Ibn Sina.[1] A modern inscription written inside the tomb records the fact that this final resting-place of 'His Holiness Sheikh Abu Saïd and the Prince of Sages, Bu Ali Sina (Avicenna),' had fallen into ruins and had been restored by the Princess Nigar Khanum of the royal line of the Kajar family in the year 1877 (A.H. 1294).[2]

Still another poetical shrine, situated not far from the Gum-bad-i Alavian in the northwestern section of the city, is the tomb of another pre-Khayyamite, the dervish poet Baba Tahir Uryan (d. 1019), a native of Hamadan, whose verses are in especial favor with the Persians because of their sweetness and their moral tone, even though tinged with the tender melan-choly which marks the dervish character.[3]

Among the various tombs in the city by far the most inter-esting, because of its traditional claims upon the student of the

von der *Kgl. Ges. d. Wiss. zu Göttingen*, p. 558, Göttingen, 1875, and by Pizzi, *Chrestomathie Persane*, p. 89, Turin, 1889; for a German version of the stanza consult Horn, *Geschichte der Persischen Litteratur*, p. 150, Leipzig, 1901. For the phraseology of Omar's quatrain (no. 303) which resembles Ibn Sina's in many respects, see Whin-field, *Quatrains of Omar Khayyam*, pp. 204-205, London, 1883, who renders Khayyam's stanza : —

'I solved all problems, down from Saturn's wreath
Unto this lowly sphere of earth be-neath,

And leapt out free from bonds of fraud and lies,
'Yea, every knot was loosed, save that of death.'

[1] See Ethé, *Neupersische Litteratur*, in *Grundr. iran. Philol.* 2. 275.

[2] A verse from Hafiz on springtime and the Divine Love is added, and thanks are given to God for the resto-ration of the shrine. I am indebted to Mr. Rabino for a copy of the Persian inscription.

[3] See Heron-Allen and Brenton, *Lament of Bābā Tāhir*, London, 1902 ; and Ethé, *Neupersische Litteratur*, in *Grundr. iran. Philol.* 2. 223.

Bible, is the sepulchre alleged to be the burial-place of Esther and Mordecai. This is situated in an old Jewish cemetery south of the centre of the city and is said to occupy the same site as the original tomb, which was demolished when Tamerlane sacked Hamadan.[1] The building is a small brick structure with a high pointed cupola that has lost most of its stucco and tiles. The entrance is an unpretentious arch pierced by a very low door, which is made of a single stone turning heavily on rough-hewn pivots carved from the stone itself and set in deep sockets.[2] I had to crouch to pass through, and then found myself in a low winding passage leading into the crypt. The dingy walls of this vaulted room are so discolored by the smoke from tapers and ill-fed lamps used to light the hundreds of pilgrims who visit the shrine (Mohammedans as well as Jews) that the texts and graffiti in various languages are hardly noticed. Side by side in the middle of the chamber are the two graves, each covered by an ark-shaped sarcophagus made of ebony, one slightly smaller than the other, and inscribed with Hebrew letters. These and the inscriptions on the walls contain texts from Esther and eulogies of the Jewish heroine and of Mordecai, together with various other records.[3] Fragments of parchment scrolls of the Scriptures, crumbling, but too sacred to destroy, are scattered about, placed here for safe-keeping as in the Jewish *Genizahs*. Regarding the authenticity of the graves scholarly criticism is of the opinion that the Jews of Hamadan are the victims of a pious delusion and that the tradition that the tomb represents the sepulchre of Esther and Mordecai (whose names are inscribed on the cenotaphs) has no historic foundation. The Hebrews themselves in the city

---

[1] Cf. Ker Porter, *Travels*, 2. 108.

[2] There are socket-holes of similar pivots in the square building opposite the tombs at Naksh-i Rustam, which is described at p. 302, below.

[3] Ker Porter, *Travels*, 2. 107, described them nearly a century ago,

but the latest scholarly treatment of these inscriptions is by Israel Lévi, *Revue des Études Juives*, 36. 237–255, Paris, 1898, and by Kaufmann, *op. cit.* 37. 303–304. A picture of the two sarcophagi may be seen in Flandin, *Voyage en Perse, Moderne*, pl. 69.

never question the authenticity, however, and firmly believe
that miracles are wrought at the sepulchre, especially at the
time of the Purim festival.[1] To them the Biblical account of
Esther is not a work of fiction, but a record of fact, of scenes
enacted in this city where Xerxes, with whom King Ahasuerus
has been historically identified, had his summer residence and
carved an inscription on Mount Alvand. Haman, his minister,
is a living reality in their eyes, and they are capable of measuring the persecutions which he inflicted on their people by
their own sufferings endured from time to time in Persia.
Under these circumstances we can imagine what must have
been the rejoicings of their ancestors at Susa, if not at Hamadan,
in Bible times when the appeal of their beautiful heroine
touched the heart of King Ahasuerus (Xerxes) and caused
him to spare their people and to hang their enemy on the
very gallows that had been prepared for Mordecai.[2]

Other stories from the Scriptures, besides these, haunt our
memory when in Hamadan. Here at Ecbatana, as described
in the apocryphal book of Tobit,[3] lived Sara, daughter of
Raguel, who was under the fatal ban of the demon Asmodeus
until freed by Tobias.[4] If this story be dismissed as too
legendary, we still may advert to another Scriptural fact,
known from later history, namely, that Antiochus Epiphanes
(about B.C. 164) came to Ecbatana after the outrages he committed at Persepolis, and was here smitten by the disease that
brought about his death as a direct visitation of the curse of

---

[1] See the article by Sidi of Hamadan,
in *Revue des Ecoles de l'Alliance Israélite*, no. 8, pp. 64–68, Paris, 1903.
Sidi endeavors to refute the claims
against the authenticity made by Israel
Lévi (see reference in preceding note)
and points to the miraculous manner
in which women are freed from barren-
ness by performing certain rites in the
monument.

[2] Esther **7**. 10 seq.

[3] Tobit **3**. 7 ; **6**. 5 ; **7**. 1 ; **14**. 12, 14.
See also Moulton, *The Iranian Back-
ground of Tobit*, in the *Expository
Times*, 11. 257–260. Again Sir Henry
Rawlinson, *JRAS*. 10. 136–137, pleads
that Takht-i Suleiman, not Hamadan,
fulfils the conditions described in Tobit.

[4] The demon Asmodeus is generally
regarded as identical with Aeshma the
Daeva, in the Avesta, but this is doubted
by some.

God, alluded to in 2 Maccabees 9. 1–3.   In addition to this
I may again recall the Biblical statement to which I have
already referred, describing how the edict of Cyrus the Great
in favor of the Jews was found at Hamadan.   In connection
with the Bible, likewise, although not confined to Hamadan,
I observed a parallel to the custom of cities of refuge ; for, as
I walked through the streets of the town, I saw several precincts marked off by chains over the entrances and gateways
to indicate that the places were asylums of refuge, like those
recognized in the Pentateuch.[1]   One of these *bast khānah*, as
they are called, is the Imam Zadah Yahya, not far from the
Musallah Hill.

A visit to Hamadan would be incomplete without a sight of
the Ganj Namah inscriptions carved by Darius and his son
Xerxes on one of the rocky peaks of Mount Alvand, southwest
of the city, on the summer route to Tuisirkan.   The distance
is about an hour's easy ride on horseback, but owing to the
snow and muddy roads it took me double the time to reach the
place.   The inscriptions are carved in two niches in the face of
a granite rock, about a hundred feet above a small stream
which flows past the base of the hill.   The situation is a picturesque one, and the approach, under ordinary circumstances,
is not difficult, but I had to clamber up the hillside through
knee-deep snow which extended almost to the base of the inscriptions and formed an artificial terrace under the lower edge.

The position of the rock is such that the tablets face directly
east.   The niches are rectangular in shape, measuring about five
feet by eight and a half, and sunk about a foot deep in the rock.
The inscription of Darius is in the niche to the left and is
slightly higher than the Xerxes tablet.   Both are about of the
same size and proportions and both show signs of weathering in
places, for the rain and melting snow have proved destructive
to the stone, despite the fact that the framework of the recess
serves somewhat to protect it.   The Darius inscription has

---

[1] See, for example, Numbers **35**. 6, 11–15 ; Deuteronomy **4**. 41–43.

THE GANJ NAMAH INSCRIPTIONS IN WINTER

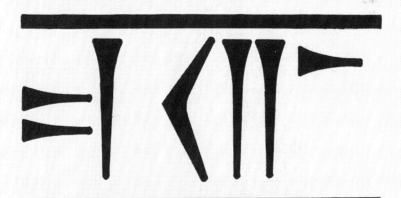

THE WORD 'GOD' (BAGA) IN ANCIENT PERSIAN CUNEIFORM LETTERS

suffered most. A crack runs through it from top to bottom on the left, or southern, side and broadens out as it nears the lower ledge till it becomes a fissure almost five inches wide and thus destroys several letters. Moss was growing in this cleft when I saw it and water was trickling through the groove, tending to expand the crack still more. A small crack also mars the upper part of the third column of this tablet, and there is a defacement in the lower part of the middle column. The socket holes noticeable about the framework of both recesses are apparently ancient and were probably intended to hold the supports for the scaffold while the sculptor was at work.

The Darius inscription, like its companion-piece, is arranged in three columns, written respectively in Old Persian, Susian (Neo-Elamitic), and Babylonian. The columns are clearly separated from each other by a narrow space that looks like a perpendicular band, and the lines of the inscription are sharply marked off by narrow grooves about four inches (10 cm.) apart. Each column contains twenty lines of text. The height of the cuneiform letters themselves is between $2\frac{3}{8}$ in. and $2\frac{3}{4}$ in. (between 6 cm. and 7 cm.). The width of the first column is $44\frac{1}{2}$ in. (113 cm.), of the second, 29 in. (77.5 cm.), and of the third $26\frac{3}{4}$ in. (68 cm.).[1] The letters of the inscription may perhaps best be likened in shape to horseshoe nails; the carving is in general clear and bold, and the words are perfectly legible, with the few exceptions caused by the cracks to which allusion has been made. The first word in the Persian column, *baga*, the word for ' God,' looks nearly as in my drawing reproduced on the accompanying page.

More interesting than such technical details and measurements is a statement regarding the contents of this inscription, which begins *Baga vazraka Auramazda, hya imām bumim adā, hya avam asmānam adā*, etc., and may be translated as follows : —

[1] For assistance in making the measurements while I was examining the inscription, I am indebted to Rev. N. L. Euwer of Hamadan.

'A great god is Auramazda, who created this earth, who created yonder heaven, who created man, who made Peace for man, who made Darius king, the one king of many, the one ruler of many. I am Darius, the Great King, the King of Kings, King of the countries which have many peoples, King of the great earth even to afar, the son of Hystaspes, the Achæmenian.'[1]

The inscription of Xerxes by the side of this is precisely identical with it in contents except that the name of Xerxes is substituted for that of Darius throughout the tablet. The first, or Persian, column in this table is slightly marred near the top, and a crack, beginning in the eighth line of the second column and running nearly to the eighteenth line of the third, slightly damages several words. In width the first column is 46 in. (116.5 cm.), the second, $27\frac{1}{2}$ in. (70 cm.), the third, 25 in. (65.5 cm.), and, as in the other inscription, each column has twenty lines of text, the letters being nearly of the same size as in the Darius inscription.

In addition to their historic value there is a special interest attached to these two tablets of Darius and Xerxes, from the standpoint of importance in deciphering cuneiform records. They are the two tablets that gave the key to the English decipherer, Sir Henry Rawlinson, whose work contributed most to placing cuneiform studies in general on a firm foundation. In the modern Persian tongue *Ganj Nāmah* means 'Treasure-Story,' and the natives call the sculptured tablets so because they imagine that a secret of some hidden treasure is concealed in them and that this will be revealed to the one who shall be able to decipher them. This fiction has proved to be a fact, though in a different way. The stone has been forced to tell its story of hidden riches in the realm of history and has handed over the key which the great decipherer used when

[1] Dar. Alv. 1–20. For transliteration of the Persian text of this, see Weissbach and Bang, *Die Altpersischen Keilinschriften*, pp. 36, 42, Leipzig, 1893 (containing also a bibliography, p. 6) ; Spiegel, *Die Altpersischen Keilinschriften*, pp. 46, 64, Leipzig, 1881. See also pp. 175–185, below.

THE GANJ NAMAH CUNEIFORM INSCRIPTIONS OF DARIUS AND XERXES NEAR HAMADAN.

he translated the rock records of King Darius at Behistan and thus unlocked many treasures of the past.

Scarcely a hundred paces distant from the tablets of Darius and Xerxes, but around the spur to the right of the mountain, and overlooking the gully through which the stream flows, are two small niches. They are blank, without the trace of a single letter, but they appear to have been prepared to receive short inscriptions. One of these recesses is cut at a considerable slant, shaped like a rhomboid, the other is a narrow parallelogram carved vertically so that it looks almost like a small window in the rock. How these panels were to have been filled fancy alone can surmise.[1]

On the road homeward from the Ganj Namah I stopped to examine the site of some ruins on a high ridge called that of the *Naḳārah Khānah*, or 'Band Tower,' about two miles distant from the city. The outlines of a structure which the people name the *Burj*, 'Tower,' can be clearly made out in spite of its razed condition. Fragments of bricks mark the walls of a building which the guide termed the 'Governor's House,' a title commonly given by the Persians to the ruins of any large edifice that looks as if it might have been used officially. The remnants of a circular tank or reservoir (*hōz*), whose thick walls of red brick were set in a very durable mortar, could also be traced, and there were evidences, besides, of a terraced approach to the brow of the hill, and no doubt the pick and spade, if used, would reveal more and tell something perhaps of the history of these crumbled remains.

The view of Hamadan from this height, overlooking the plain of many colors, repaid me for the ascent, if nothing else did, for it presented the distant city to me in still another light. The Musallah, once crowned with walls, stood out clear to the

---

[1] There is also a cave in the mountains in this same vicinity, about two miles south of Hamadan, and likewise a 'windstone,' which, when shaken, is believed to create wind for threshing grain (this information I owe to Mr. H. L. Rabino of Kermanshah), but I did not see either of these.

view, but looked barren and desolate. Fine gardens, which
afford a delightful resort for an afternoon in the suburbs,
especially in the vicinity of the Armenian village of Sheverin,
border the town. The domes of the shrines of the *Imāmzadahs*,
or Moslem saints, tell how the newer religion has supplanted
the old religion of Zoroastrianism, and the minaret of the
'Friday Mosque,' *Masjid-i Jum'ah*, points to the fact that
the older worship has given place to a newer. As I
rode back through the busy streets, all astir with life and
activity, and fully alert to the interests of the present, I could
not help thinking that, despite its three thousand years, Hamadan is still youthful in spirit as in appearance, even though
reft of the magnificence which once made the city the boasted
pride of Media.

> ' Where's the wisdom-hoary sage
> Shall unriddle us this page?
> Temples toppled from their base,
> Victor race o'errunning race,
> Yet, within the ancient place,
> Mirth, and love of maid and man,
> Round the walls of Hamadan.'

CHAPTER XIII

THE ROCK INSCRIPTIONS OF THE GREAT PERSIAN KINGS

'Sermons in stones.'
— Shakspere, *As You Like It*, 2. 1. 17.

THE Bible refers to 'the book of chronicles of the kings of Media and Persia,' [1] but those documents written on perishable parchment were not the only records which the Persian monarchs, Cyrus, Darius, Xerxes, and Artaxerxes caused to be made of their deeds and of memorable events in their reigns. I refer to the cuneiform records, covering a period of nearly two centuries (B.C. 541–340), which the Achæmenian kings inscribed upon the living rocks. These documents in stone have defied the ravages of time, in part at least, and preserved for the present and the future an account of events long past, many of which would otherwise have been buried in oblivion.

By far the most important of these inscriptions is the great inscription of Darius, carved far up on the mountain side of the Behistan rock. Next in interest and value are those which the same monarch caused to be chiselled on the palace walls and platform at Persepolis, as well as around his tomb at Naksh-i Rustam. The portals and pillared halls of Xerxes and Artaxerxes at Persepolis, though in ruins, contain also short inscriptions left by these kings, and a sculptured monolith near the tomb of Cyrus the Great at Pasargadæ was inscribed with four words from the lips of the great king himself. Besides these, there are tablets of Darius and Xerxes on Mount Alvand near Hamadan, which I have already described, and additional inscriptions of the Achæmenians are found at Susa

---

[1] Esther 10. 2, cf. 6. 1.

in southwestern Persia, at Kerman in the southeast, at Van in Armenia, and even at Suez in Egypt.[1]

We owe to travellers our earliest direct knowledge of the Achæmenian inscriptions and of the places where they are found. The list begins with the Venetian envoy Josafa Barbaro in the fifteenth century and ends with the scholarly Niebuhr in the eighteenth, whose more accurate copies of some of the inscriptions at Persepolis gave a basis for students to work upon.[2] But up to the year 1802 no Daniel had been found to interpret the mysterious handwriting on the wall, although scholars were generally agreed that the inscriptions owed their origin to the Achæmenian kings. It was the German schoolmaster and philologist Grotefend who first solved the mystery of the cuneiform writing, and to him belongs the honor of being the first to decipher the Old Persian inscriptions. Attracted to the subject by reason of his classical interests, he devoted himself to the cuneiform problem with the enthusiasm that marks a scholar, and the story of how he deciphered the characters, letter by letter, reads like a chapter in a novel. Placing side by side two of the shorter Persepolitan tablets, which he assumed to be Achæmenian records, he made the shrewd conjecture that one of the words which was most often repeated was the name for king and that the king's name preceded it. In this manner, by means of a number of careful comparisons and scholarly deductions, he was able to spell out the name of Darius, of his father Hystaspes, and of his son Xerxes. The results of these investigations he laid

---

[1] With regard to the location of the inscriptions, the history of their decipherment, editions of texts and translations, see Rogers, *History of Babylonia and Assyria*, 1. 1–83, New York, 1901; Booth, *Discovery and Decipherment of the Trilingual Inscriptions*, London, 1902; Weissbach, *Die altpersischen Keilinschriften*, in *Grundr. iran. Philol.* 2. 54–74; Weiss- bach and Bang, *Die altpers. Keilinschr.*, Leipzig, 1893; Spiegel, *Die altpers. Keilinschr.*, 2d ed., Leipzig, 1881; Tolman, *Old Persian Inscriptions*, New York, 1893.

[2] For a detailed account of the earlier travellers and investigators of the cuneiform inscriptions see the books by Rogers and by Booth referred to in the preceding note.

THE ROCK OF BEHISTAN FROM THE SOUTH
(From Rawlinson)

VIEW OF THE BEHISTAN ROCK FROM THE UPPER END
(Sketched from a photograph by the author)

before the Academy of Sciences at Göttingen, September 4, 1802, and thus founded the science of cuneiform decipherment. The key to the riddle having at last been discovered, other scholars continued the work begun by Grotefend, so that we are able to-day to read all the Persian inscriptions and also to translate the parallel versions of them in Elamitic and Babylonian.[1] But foremost among the contributors to the science of cuneiform interpretation, whether German, French, or Danish, was the noted Englishman Rawlinson, who was a soldier as well as a scholar. To Major Henry Creswicke Rawlinson, afterwards Sir Henry Rawlinson, Privy Councillor, belongs the honor of deciphering the Ganj Namah tablets at Hamadan, and the glory of being the first to ascend the Behistan rock and copy the inscription of Darius.[2]

The Behistan Mountain, Βαγίστανον "Ορος, or Bisitun, as the natives call it, had been known from times of antiquity, but no one understood the meaning of the inscribed tablets or could identify the dozen or more human figures sculptured above them on the inaccessible side of the rock. Diodorus Siculus in the first century B.C. attributed them to Semiramis.[3] Yakut, twelve centuries later, has little to say about Behistan, except to allude to the equestrian statue at the base, which is now known, even in its mutilated condition, to be of Parthian origin[4] (about A.D. 50). The first European to call attention to Bisitun seems to have been the French traveller Otter, about the year 1734; Olivier noticed it also some sixty years

[1] It is appropriate to mention the names of the earlier workers in cuneiform philology, such as de Sacy, Saint-Martin, Rask, Burnouf, Lassen, Beer, Jacquet, Rich, Westergaard, Holtzmann, Oppert, Ménant, and Spiegel, without including names of the present time.

[2] Consult the interesting biography by his brother, Canon George Rawlinson, *Memoir of Sir Henry Rawlinson*, London, 1898, and compare the account of his work in Rogers, *History*, pp. 63–73, and Booth, *Discovery*, pp. 102–114.

[3] See p. 189, below.

[4] See p. 209, below. Yakut, pp. 124–125, speaks of the finely carved horse, which shows that he gave his attention only to the Gotarzes sculpture below, which is now destroyed. He calls the horse 'Shabdiz,' another statue of which he describes at Tak-i Bostan, cf. p. 224, below.

N

later ; Jaubert visited it ; and Gardanne fancied that the sculptures might represent the twelve apostles.[1] Ker Porter, in 1818, conjectured that the bas-reliefs were portraits of King Shalmaneser and two of his generals, together with the ten captive tribes of Israel.[2] But no one had examined the carvings in detail or copied the inscriptions below and beside them. The danger of climbing the rock proved too great a barrier. Kinneir, in 1810, did not attempt the task ; Ker Porter climbed halfway up and sketched the sculptures, but did not reach the ledge to copy the inscriptions, and in speaking of the danger of the ascent he says that 'at no time can it be attempted without great personal risk.'[3] It remained for Rawlinson to accomplish the feat, in the year 1835.

Rawlinson was at that time a young military officer, twenty-five years old, and employed in training native recruits for the army of the Shah.   While stationed at Hamadan he had learned to decipher the cuneiform characters,[4] and he was now given an excellent opportunity to examine the Behistan rock by receiving an appointment from the Shah, in 1835, which transferred him to Kermanshah, some twenty miles distant from the inscription.   He made the best of his opportunity, and at risk of life and limb made several ascents of the rock in the next two years, 1835–1837, and was able to transcribe the first column of the Persian text with remarkable exactness and prepare it for publication.   Nearly ten years later, in 1844, after active service in the Afghan war, he transcribed the rest and took a copy also of the Elamitic version (variously called Median, Scythian, Neo-Susian).   He supplemented this, in 1847, by a revision of the entire text and a reproduction of the Babylonian

---

[1] See Ker Porter, *Travels*, 2. 154, and Booth, *Discovery*, pp. 82, 105.

[2] Ker Porter, *Travels*, 2. 159–162.

[3] Ker Porter, *Travels*, 2. 158.

[4] See p. 172, above. While working on the Ganj Namah inscription Rawlinson knew that the key to the cuneiform had been discovered long before his time and that scholars were at work on the texts, but it is clear from his later correspondence with European savants how much he had been able to accomplish independently. See his account in *The Athenæum*, no. 2976, p. 593, Nov. 8, 1884.

version, which he secured through the help of a wild Kurdish lad, who performed the perilous feat of taking a paper squeeze of that almost inaccessible inscription.[1]

This is not the place to discuss the great importance of Rawlinson's work and the value of later contributions based upon it, as they are well known to scholars ;[2] but Rawlinson's copy was made more than half a century ago, and there had been no opportunity to test its accuracy, as he was the only one

---

[1] Rawlinson's account of the lad's dangerous climb may be found in *Archæologia*, 34 (1850), pp. 73–75, reprinted in George Rawlinson, *Memoir*, p. 156, n. 1. Rawlinson's own devotion to the work on the Behistan rock may be judged from what he wrote more than forty years later in *The Athenæum*, no. 2976, p. 593, Nov. 8, 1884, from which I make a selection: 'During my service as a military officer in Persia, from 1833 to 1839, my visits to the rock of Behistun were few and hurried. On these occasions I worked hard, but the difficulties were so great that I had only succeeded in copying one half of the Persian text of the inscription (the Median and Babylonian texts being entirely untouched) when I was compelled to leave the country in order to take part in the first Afghan war. At the close of that war in 1843 I was offered, as a reward for my services, the highest political employment and an assured career in India ; but I had not forgotten Behistun. It had become the ambition of my life to carry on my cuneiform researches, and especially to work out the Babylonian puzzle ; and accordingly, to the astonishment of my friends, I deliberately declined the brilliant prospect opened out to me in India, and elected to return to what was called "exile" at Baghdad, where for twelve weary years — broken by only one brief visit to England — I resided, in an exhausting climate, cut off from all society, sparingly supplied with the comforts of civilization, and, in fact, doing penance in order to attain a great literary object. During this period of probation, on two occasions — in 1844 and 1847 — I again visited the rock of Behistun, riding 1000 miles for the purpose and disbursing above 1000 *l*. from my own funds for the expenses of the expeditions. I will not say much as to the danger or difficulty of ascending the rock and reaching the upper part of the sculptures, which are some 500 feet above the plain. I did not think much at the time of the risk to life and limb, but it must be remembered that Messrs. Coste and Flandin, having been deputed to the spot by the French Government with express instructions to copy the inscriptions, returned *re infectâ*, declaring the sculptures to be absolutely inaccessible ; and I may further add that although there is still something to be copied and much to be verified, I have never heard but of one traveller accomplishing the ascent since the period of my last visit.'

[2] Rawlinson's epoch-making work was published in the *Journal of the Royal Asiatic Society*, 10. 1–349, London, 1847.

who had studied the rock itself.   Accordingly, one purpose of my journey was to make the ascent, if possible, and examine some of the mooted passages in the cuneiform text.   How far I was able to accomplish this, in the limited time at my disposal, will be recorded in the next chapter.

Before giving an account of the contents of the inscriptions, it may be well to give some idea of the bas-reliefs that are carved above them on a surface over twenty feet in length and more than ten feet in height, and to tell whom the sculptures are intended to represent.

The king, who is the principal figure in the group, is Darius himself, and the image is majestic in its bearing and carved in bold relief.   In his left hand Darius holds a bow, and he raises his right hand as he pronounces sentence of doom upon nine captives standing before him, each with the hands tied behind the back and a rope about the neck.   Above the head of each of the captives, but below the prostrate figure and on the skirt of the tunic of the third prisoner, is the name of the rebel king whose effigy is given, and in each case the nature of the rebellion and the place where it started is recorded in a short tablet and a word is added to the effect that the pretender ' lied' in making his claims to the throne.[1]

The names of some of these rebels, like Nadintabaira, or Nadintu-Bel of Babylon, we know also from other sources, and the last in the line is ' Skunka the Scythian,' who is marked by his high pointed cap.   Beneath the feet of the king lies a tenth foe, imploring mercy with upstretched hands, but trampled upon by the stern monarch.   This fallen enemy is Gaumata the Magian, otherwise known as the False Smerdis, who usurped the crown upon the death of Cambyses, under pretense of being the king's brother, but was unmasked and slain by Darius and his six trusty followers, as described in the inscription itself and narrated also by Herodotus.

---

[1] In the main body of the inscription below the bas-reliefs an account of each revolt, and the battles which followed, is given.

THE KERMAN INSCRIPTION OF KING DARIUS

1. The Persian Text

Directly back of the king stands his quiver-bearer and chamberlain, Aspachanah, and behind the latter is the king's spear-bearer, Gaubruva, if we may assign to these the names attached to the similar figures at Naksh-i Rustam — names known also from the Greek sources as Gobryas and Aspathines.[1] Above the head of the king there floats a winged figure of the god Auramazda, who presents to him a ring, the symbol of sovereignty, and adds his blessing in sanction of the king's deeds.[2] This figure, like the rest of the sculptures, shows the influence of Assyro-Babylonian art, and all the figures are very robust and stocky in build, like some of those at Persepolis. The king is represented as heroic in size in contrast to the captives, who appear dwarfed beside him.

The position of the inscriptions with reference to the bas-reliefs may next be noted. The Persian tablets are directly below the sculptured group ; the Elamitic version is carved around the ledge on the lower left-hand side and is very difficult to reach ; the Babylonian projects over this, on the face of the scarped rock ; and supplementary inscriptions and translations are carved around the bas-reliefs and on tablets to the right. After giving these details we may turn to the inscriptions themselves and their contents.

The five columns of the Old Persian give a brief history of the main events that occurred in the early part of the reign of Darius. They are carved in about four hundred lines of beautiful cuneiform writing, on polished tablets, and are supplemented by versions in Elamitic and Babylonian, which comprise together as many lines more. Darius tells in brief form how he became king 'by the grace of Auramazda' — vashnā Auramazdāha — and by his own prowess, and he recounts the battles he fought and the victories he won and how many revolts he had to crush in organizing and adminis-

---

[1] For references, see Justi, *Iranisches Namenbuch*, pp. 46, 111 ; Bartholomae, *Air. Wb.* pp. 217, 482. Cf. also Andreas, in *Verhandl. 13. Internat. Orientalisten-Kongr.* p. 97, Leiden, 1904.

[2] See *Grundr. iran. Philol.* 2. 631.

tering his great empire. The language is nearly allied to that of the Avesta, and the style, which shows the influence of the Assyro-Babylonian inscriptions,[1] is marked by a dignity and simplicity that is suited to such a record, despite the inevitable baldness of an official document and the tendency to repetition which characterizes an Oriental communication. 'I am Darayavaush (Darius), the Great King, the King of Kings, the King of Nations, the son of Vishtaspa, the Achæmenian'—such are the opening words; and after tracing his right to the throne through a double line of descent and enumerating his tributary countries, he gives a notable account of the usurpation and overthrow of Gaumata the Magian, already referred to. Throughout the entire five columns each paragraph that deals with a new subject is introduced by 'Thus saith Darius the King'— *thâtiy Dârayavaush khshâyathiya* — which lends a certain formal dignity to the style ; and a religious tone is imparted to the edict by the fervor with which Darius again and again attributes his successes to Auramazda. This is particularly noticeable in the fourth column, where the style rises to some degree of literary merit. To illustrate what I mean I shall translate a portion of that column, as I devoted especial attention to it during the time which I spent upon the rock. I shall follow the original closely in my rendering, so as to convey an idea of the inscriptional style, making only trifling modifications for the sake of greater intelligibility, and one or two slight omissions for the sake of brevity.

Bh. **4.** 33–36. 'Thus saith Darius the King: Those countries which became rebellious, the Lie made them rebellious, so that they deceived the people.[2] Auramazda delivered them into my hand.'

---

[1] See Gray, *Stylistic Parallels between the Assyro-Bab. and O.P. Inscr.* in *Am. Journ. Semit. Lang.* 17. 151–159, and compare my article, *Persian Literature*, in *Progress*, 2. 35–55, Chicago, 1896.

[2] The word *drauga*, 'Lie, Falsehood, Deceit,' is personified in the inscriptions and used almost as an equivalent of Satan, Fiend ; see my article in *JAOS.* 21. 170.

THE KERMAN INSCRIPTION OF KING DARIUS

2. The Elamitic Text

36–40. 'Thus saith Darius the King: Thou who shalt be king hereafter, be constantly on thy guard against the Lie. The man who is a liar, punish him well with punishment, if thou thinkest "my country must be firmly established."'

40–45. 'Thus saith Darius the King: That which I have done I have done altogether by the grace of Auramazda. Thou who shalt hereafter read this inscription, let that which hath been done by me appear to thee true; hold it not for a lie. Thus saith Darius the King: May Auramazda be witness that it is true, not false; I did it altogether.'

45–50. 'Thus saith Darius the King: By the grace of Auramazda there is much else, besides, done by me, which is not written in this inscription; on this account is it not written, lest that which I have done may seem exaggerated to him who shall hereafter read this inscription, and may not appear to him true and may seem to be a lie. . . .'[1]

52–59. 'Thus saith Darius the King: Let that which I have done appear unto thee true, as it is; therefore conceal it not. If thou shalt not conceal this edict, but shalt publish it to the people, may Auramazda be a friend unto thee, and may thy seed be multiplied, and mayest thou live long. Thus saith Darius the King: If thou shalt conceal this edict and shalt not publish it to the people, may Auramazda be thy slayer, and may thy seed be cut off.'

59–64. 'Thus saith Darius the King: That which I have done I have done altogether by the grace of Auramazda. Auramazda, and the other gods that be, brought aid unto me. For this reason did Auramazda, and the other gods that be, bring aid unto me, because I was not hostile, nor a liar, nor a wrong-doer, neither I nor my family, but according to Rectitude have I ruled.'[2]

The inscriptions of Xerxes and of the later Artaxerxes are hardly more than reproductions of the minor tablets of Darius, formulaic in their contents and mechanical in their structure; but they have a historical and philological value, and are interesting also from the standpoint of religion, because the inscriptions of Artaxerxes II and III recognize Mithra and Anahita as divinities by the side of Auramazda, whereas they are not men-

---

[1] The frank simplicity of this statement is delightful.

[2] For the difficulties in the last two lines, see pp. 203–207, below.

tioned in the inscriptions of Darius, although perhaps included in 'the other gods that be' (*aniyā bagāha tyaiy hantiy*). Auramazda, however, is still the supreme head of the world according to all the tablets: 'A great god is Auramazda, the greatest of the gods, he who created this earth, who created yonder heaven, who created man, who created Peace for man, who made Xerxes (or Artaxerxes) king.'[1] But in general the ring of the metal seems less true, and in these later inscriptions the language, like the style, shows signs of decadence.

Before I close this chapter I wish to call attention to one small inscription of Darius, previously known but not easily accessible in the cuneiform characters. It is preserved at the village of Maghan, near Kerman, in the shrine of Nimat-ullah Vali, founder of the order of Nimat-ullah dervishes, but its previous history is unknown. The characters are carved on three faces of a small tetragonal pyramid of dark stone, which is about 4 inches high and 3½ inches square at the base,[2] and therefore a little larger than the photographs that I reproduce. The photographs were kindly sent me by the late J. C. Van Roosbroeck, Director of Persian Customs and Post, and forwarded to him by the courtesy of Mr. A. Miller, Russian Consul at Kerman. The contents of the eight lines are familiar from other inscriptions of Darius, and they read: 'I (am) Darius, the Great King, the King of Kings, the King of Nations, King of this Earth, son of Vishtaspa, the Achæmenian.' The same lines are repeated in an Elamitic and a Babylonian version.[3]

It may be said in conclusion that, viewed as a whole, the story of the deciphering of the cuneiform records is one of the most instructive chapters in the history of philological research, and the achievements of Grotefend and his successors are to be

[1] With regard to the expression Peace (*šiyāti*) cf. Isaiah 45. 7, and see *JAOS.* 21. 166.

[2] Approximately 10 cm. by 9 cm.

[3] For the text of this inscription in transliteration, see Weissbach and Bang, *Altpers. Keilinschr.* pp. 7, 38, and Gobineau, *Traité*, 1. 323 seq.; also Bartold, *Historico-geographical Account of Iran*, pp. 94–95 (in Russian), St. Petersburg, 1903.

The Kerman Inscription of King Darius

3. The Babylonian Text

reckoned among the memorable accomplishments of the nineteenth century. Let us hope that those blessings may always
come true which Darius invokes in the inscription itself upon
those who preserve the inscription and make it known to the
people, for Auramazda shall be their friend.

CHAPTER XIV

THE GREAT BEHISTAN ROCK AND AN ASCENT TO READ THE CUNEIFORM RECORDS OF DARIUS[1]

> ' I wol yow all thys shap devyse
> — and site, and all the wyse
> How I gan to this place aproche
> That stood upon so high a roche
> Hyer stant there noon in Spayne,
> But up I clomb with allè payne.'
>
> —CHAUCER, *House of Fame*, 3. 23–28.

EASTER MONDAY, April 13, 1903, will remain for me a memorable date in the calendar, for on that morning, after four days on horseback from Hamadan, I caught my first glimpse of the mountain of Behistan and the great inscription of Darius. For miles before one reaches it the huge mass of rock is constantly in sight, lifting its giant head seventeen hundred feet above the plain; and several times in the distance my eager eyes were mistaken in fancying I could see from afar the smoothed surface where the Great King's edict is inscribed. This was an error, for in approaching by the Hamadan road one must round the northeast corner of the mountain before the inscription can be seen. It was shortly before noon, or, to be more accurate, 11.25 A.M., when my caravan halted at the base of Bisitun, as the Persians call it, and far above I could see the inscription and the sculptured figures which the natives term 'the Nine Dervishes.'

---

[1] Reprinted with some additions and minor corrections from my report in *JAOS.* 24. 77–95. The additions are : 1. 51, *patiyāvahyaiy*; 2. 61, Θauravā- *harahya*; the notice of the Gotarzes sculpture; and the account of the monolith at the close of the chapter.

REAR VIEW OF THE ROCK OF BEHISTAN

With all I had read about Behistan, with all I had heard about
it, and with all I had thought about it beforehand, I had not
the faintest conception of the Gibraltar-like impressiveness of
this rugged crag until I came into its Titan presence and felt
the grandeur of its sombre shadow and towering frame. Snow
and clouds capped its peaks at the time, and birds innumerable
were soaring around it aloft or hovering near the place where
the inscriptions are hewn into the rock. There as I looked
upward, I could see, more than three hundred feet above the
ground, the bas-relief of the great king, Darius. Prone at
his feet lay Gaumata, the Magian usurper, who had seized the
throne on the death of Cambyses. In front of Darius stood
the row of captive kings, and above the head of each I could
discern a faint trace of the tablet with the 'lie' which each
had uttered in his false claims to the throne, although the
letters were not legible at such a distance. My memory
recalled the story of each of these rebel lords, and I could
picture the torture and agonized death that each suffered at
the hands of the king.

From the descriptions I had read, or perhaps from the mental
picture I had previously formed of the scene, I had always
fancied that the inscriptions and the sculptures were carved
nearer the middle of the mountain, whose general contour on
this side runs from northeast to southwest. Not so. They
are cut high up in the side of a steep gorge or craggy gully
that makes a deep gash in the face of the rock and extends
three hundred feet downward to the plain beneath. But
before proceeding further with the description, it may be well
to turn to the middle part of the mountain front itself and
examine its appearance.

As one faces the great Behistan rock, the striking feature
that catches the eye is a huge space carved near the middle
of the base, but left entirely bare of an inscription. Even Ker
Porter in his description seems to have given less attention
than it deserves to this magnificent *tabula rasa*, the more

conspicuous because of its vacant, wall-like stare.[1] It must have been prepared with an especial design of recording some historic event, as I felt certain after devoting part of an afternoon to a study of it. A space of nearly five hundred feet in length — I paced it off — and over a hundred feet in height has been cut out of the mountain front to form a rocky canvas for commemorating some record of importance. The idea that it is due to mere quarrying vanishes at once when one studies the appearance of it and observes the evident design. Two rocky ledges, one somewhat higher than the other, are cut on either side to furnish a means of nearer access to the mammoth screen, while the overhanging canopy of rock forms a framework above, and a terrace of earth and stones offers an approach to the place from below. Such is the general scheme of arrangement.[2]

The question naturally arises, and is always asked by those who have seen the great blank space: ' When and by whom was it cut, what was its purpose, and why is it without a trace of the cuneiform chronicler's chisel ? ' To this inquiry the natives respond by saying ' it is the work of Farhad.' The sentiment of such an explanation will appeal to every reader of Nizami's romantic epopée ; he will recall the tragic story of the enamored sculptor and the lovely Shirin, and he will trace in fancy the marks of the ambitious wooer's steel or hear the ring of the mallet as the rock yielded to his herculean blows.[3] But the

[1] See Ker Porter, *Travels*, 2. 149–162.

[2] When I gained access to my library I found that M. de Morgan (*Mission Scientifique*, 4. 286–289) has given an elaborate description of the probable manner in which the vast surface was prepared by the stone-cutters, and he shows how the markings on the stones which have been thrown down may have been made. He is of the opinion that the surface was prepared to receive an inscription, ' qui, peut-être, devait relater tous les faits de l'histoire perse ' (*op.* *cit.* p. 287). Mr. E. L. Mitford (*From England to Ceylon Forty Years Ago*, London, 1884) believed that it was designed ' apparently for the back wall of some extensive building,' and he adds that ' the only sculpture on the scarp was a single female mask.' If this still exists, I failed to see it, and I am inclined to think that the signs in the fallen stones which are scattered about are mason's marks rather than characters of an alphabet. But I may be wrong.

[3] See p. 226, below.

THE UNFINISHED ROCK-SCREEN AT BEHISTAN

UP ON THE LEDGE

(The white bands in the photograph show how the inscription
has been damaged by the water)

classicist at the same moment will remember a passage in Diodorus Siculus, which tells how Semiramis visited 'Bagistanon,'
encamped near by, built a 'paradise' on the spot, and commemorated the occasion by an inscription on the mountain.
The quotation from this Greek author, who lived in the first
century before the Christian era, is worth repeating for the
sake of comparison : —

'When Semiramis had brought to an end the works upon which
she was engaged, she set out for Media with a large military force
and, halting near the mountain called Bagistan, pitched her camp
there. She made a park, twelve furlongs in circumference, in the
plain, which has a great fountain that waters all the cultivated area
round about. The mountain of Bagistan is sacred to Zeus, and on
the side toward the garden it has steep rocks extending upward to
the height of seventeen furlongs. On the lower part of this she
caused her own image to be carved, with a hundred lance-bearers
standing round about her. She inscribed likewise in Syriac characters (Συρίοις γράμμασι) on the rock, that " Semiramis had ascended
from the plain to the top of the height by laying, one upon the other,
the packs of the beasts of burden that followed her." ' [1]

That we have in this passage a direct allusion to our rock is
undoubted. The only question is whether the story which
Diodorus gives is to be applied to the unlettered space or to the
familiar sculptures and inscriptions of Darius. The difficulty
with the former application is the fact that a careful examination of the huge central table does not reveal the slightest trace
of its ever having been inscribed. I studied it with great attention, having in mind the Diodorus passage, and I asked also the
judgment of my native servant, who was very intelligent in
such matters ; but I could not convince myself that this portion
of the rock had ever been engraved, or that an inscription had

[1] Diodorus Siculus, *Hist. Lib.* 2. 13,
tr. Booth, 1. 110. The statement
'seventeen furlongs, or stadia,' *i.e.*
above 10,000 feet, is greatly exaggerated, as is noticed also by G. Rawlinson,
Five Great Monarchies, 3. 31, n. 18.
Yakut, p. 125, says that Behistan is
so high that 'its summit cannot be
reached,' which is also exaggerated,
although the peak is very lofty.

been obliterated.   If one were inclined to theorize and to build
up a fanciful hypothesis on flimsy foundations, it would be easy
to suggest that King Darius, after completing the well-known
record and sculptures, had directed the present vacant space to
be prepared for a memorial of his later deeds, especially the
campaign against Greece.   The misfortunes at Athos and Marathon, the uprising in Egypt, and the hand of death, frustrated
his plan, changed the course of history, and left the blank page
on the rock to bear witness *e silentio* to the triumph of Hellas
and the beginning of the downfall of Iran.   But this is mere
guesswork, idle fantasy, especially when one asks why Darius
should have reserved the central and best position on the mountain for the last.   All that we can say is that the general appearance of the place and the nature of its surroundings gives the
impression of great antiquity.   So much for the blank and
unfinished wall-space.   We may now turn to the well-known
tablet and sculptures that form the special subject of discussion.

As stated before, the great record of Darius is situated farther to the northeast, some four or five hundred paces removed
from the central point.   As one stands beneath and looks
three hundred feet upward within the rocky ravine, the general
outline of the inscription and the figures of Darius, the two
viziers, and the ten captive kings, come clearly into view.   It is
easy to understand why the natives regard the latter as ' the
Nine Dervishes,' because the prostrate figure of Gaumata, with
his upstretched hands, is not so easy to distinguish in the distance.   As to Skunka with his high Scythian cap, I am inclined
to agree with the view that his figure was added some time
after the others were carved.   On viewing the smoothed spaces
where the inscriptions are cut, I could make out, as I knew it
beforehand, the general arrangement of the Old Persian in the
centre below the sculptures, the Neo-Elamitic to the left of the
ledge, and the Babylonian above this and also above on the right.
The familiar broad bands that indicated by their peculiar
grayish color where the water had streamed down and washed

away portions of the inscription, were all too plain. Even at the moment, water was oozing out from the upper part of one of the tablets and trickling over its face. It was evident at a glance that a telescope would be of no service in copying the lower part of the Old Persian text, because the projecting ledge cut off a portion of the inscription from below. It was necessary to get nearer. Climbing past huge boulders and fragments of fallen crags, which make the ascent of the gorge not easy, it was possible to get closer to where the tablets and sculptures are. The precipitous sides of the gorge form an angle; the Darius record is on the side that faces almost directly toward the east. The opposite wall or other face of the shaft-like ravine is so steep and rugged as to defy the climber's attempts to ascend it for the purpose of photographing the inscriptions from their own level. The natives assert that it is practically impossible to mount that side of the rocky couloir. The question now arose, how best to ascend to the inscriptions.

Having heard from a Persian friend that it would probably be best to be let down from above, I had previously studied some of the methods employed by the bird-nesters in the Hebrides in being lowered by ropes over craggy cliffs. A brief examination of the situation, however, showed that the only feasible approach was by climbing and being drawn up by cords. In less than an hour the preparations for the task were begun. Meshad Ali, the owner of the caravansarai nearest to the rock, found five men who were ready to undertake the ascent. A sixth, Kuli, the guide and best of them all, was added later; and the procession with ropes and a ladder was soon under way toward the beetling precipice. Whatever may be said against the ladder, which proved of little use, nothing can be maintained against the Persian goat-hair ropes, for their quality is excellent. The cords that bound the luggage on the caravan pack-horse, supplemented by ropes furnished by the Bisitun guides, and firmly fastened about my chest with knots that only a Persian knows how to tie, were a precaution against the danger of slipping and gave confidence for the climb. The stout protest of the guides against my riding-boots was well founded, as the risks of the first day proved ; but a happy substitute for these was later found in the native *gīvahs*, resembling rough tennis shoes, which were loaned by one of the Persian bystanders and firmly sewed upon the feet with a heavy pack-thread needle. All was then ready. The exciting task began.

The ascent of the first huge fissure in the side of the couloir, the clamber with torn hands and clothes along the brink of a precipitous crag, the tugging ropes that helped up the steep incline of the second rock, the scramble past the thorn bush that barred the way farther up, and the final tug and spring that brought to the edge of the ledge, together with *khailī khūb*, ' very good,' and the encouraging word of the guides, 'no fear now, the danger is over '— will not readily be forgotten. Only when one has stood on the narrow ledge by the side of the inscriptions and looked out over the magnificent plain far beneath, and listened to the dull murmur of the stream below, as it bursts from the mountain's base, does one know how to appreciate Rawlinson's work. It may interest others, as it did me, to learn that he has carved his name in the stone, a few inches below the very inscriptions which he first made known to the modern world. This he was entitled to do, and one is almost inclined to append after his simple ' H. C. Rawlinson, 1844 ' the words of ancient India's homage — *namo namah*.

In the words of Rawlinson, ' the climbing of the rock to arrive at the inscriptions, if not positively dangerous, is a feat at any rate which an antiquary alone could be expected to undertake.' On the first day it took a while to get somewhat used to the giddy height, so I devoted my attention to examining the general condition of the rock, making notes, observing the sculptures, which one can study better, however, from below than from the ledge, and to getting the size of the cuneiform letters and of the tablets themselves. The four columns of the Old Persian

THE BEHISTAN SCULPTURES AND INSCRIPTIONS
(From Rawlinson)

KULI, THE HEAD GUIDE IN THE ASCENT

record are each about six feet broad. The exact measurements in meters, if one cares to have them, are: 1st col. = 1.90 ; 2d col. = 1.94; 3d col. = 1.95 (approx.) ; 4th col. = 1.94 (approx.). The 5th column I did not measure, owing to the difficulty of access to it. The place occupied by the Neo-Elamitic (Scythian or Median) inscription is around a crag to the left of the Old Persian, as one faces the inscription, and for taking me there my most reliable guide wished to quintuple his price, while the Babylonian tablet on the overhanging ledge above to the left and to the right is the most inaccessible of all, as Rawlinson himself discovered, when his guides failed him and he found only one Kurdish shepherd lad who would venture to undertake to reach it and accomplished with difficulty the risky task of taking the squeezes of that inscription.[1]

On looking at the mass of scarped rock one wonders how the daring boy ever accomplished the perilous feat. Perhaps he still lives and can tell, but, as regards Rawlinson, I could not find the slightest recollection of him among the inhabitants of whom I inquired ; although I learned afterwards that his special Persian guide died a few years ago at Hamadan.

A study of the Old Persian tablets soon revealed the fact that the inscription has suffered much since the days of Rawlinson. Mention has already been made of the water that was oozing from the upper part of the inscription when first I saw it, so that it was wet in places for the space of several feet. Some photographs, which I succeeded in taking on the second day upon the ledge, make clearer what we have lost and are losing, and I fear that other and fresher proofs of this will be found when the rock is examined with more detail than was possible in my short week's stay. But I wish to call attention to one point. I found that after the eye had become accustomed and had some practice, it was possible to restore lost letters and words by a careful examination of the indentures

[1] See p. 179, above, and cf. H. C. Rawlinson, *Archæologia*, 34. 73–75, and G.   Rawlinson, *Memoir of Sir Henry Rawlinson*, pp. 156–157, London, 1898.

which the heavy stroke of the engraver's chisel had left in carving the character.   The head of the nail-shaped letters (for the
Behistan letters look perhaps more like horse-shoe nails than like
wedges) can still be discerned as a dot or hole in the washed-away
stone; and a knowledge of the cuneiform writing enables one to
combine these indentures into skeleton letters that often remove
all doubt as to the true reading.   I understood how Rawlinson
must sometimes have done this, and more easily, because the
stone had suffered less in his time, I believe, than to-day.

In contrast to the disintegrated parts stand those portions
of the inscribed tablets where the flow of the water has not
mutilated and defaced the rock.   Here, instead of the peculiar
dull steel-gray bands, we have the beautiful brown color of
the inscription as perfect as when the stone-cutter of Darius
laid his mallet aside.   No granite tablet in Central Park or
Trafalgar Square could be more perfect.   It was interesting,
moreover, to compare the style of the Behistan characters with
the somewhat larger letters of the Ganj Namah inscriptions
(Dar. Alv. and Xerx. Alv.), which I had been examining at
Hamadan the week before.   On Alvand the space between
the lines is 4 inches and each letter averages nearly 3 inches
in height.   At Behistan, where economy of space was necessary owing to the length of the inscription, the sharply drawn
lines are about $1\frac{5}{8}$ inches (42 mm.) apart, and the clear-cut letters
each approximately $1\frac{1}{4}$ inches (32 mm.) high.   The brown
shellac or varnish makes them stand out in bolder relief and
gives a fine finish to the whole, although I could see no traces
of the 'flakes' of the cement, which Rawlinson speaks of as
having sifted down upon the narrow ledge ; nor, again, did I
observe any evidence to show that letters had been preserved
by reason of this shellac withstanding the water when the rock
itself had disintegrated beneath its surface.[1]   But this may be
still another proof that the rock has suffered since Rawlinson's
time, and it is to be hoped that M. de Morgan will make casts

[1] So Rawlinson in *JRAS*. 10. 193.

of the entire inscription, as I learned in Persia it is the intention of his Mission to do.

My attempt to take squeezes of certain words was a failure; this was due partly, among other causes, to the wind that prevailed during the four days when I was up on the ledge, and was the stronger owing to the height and the peculiar formation of the rocky cut. This made me wish for more time, in order to wait for better conditions. Owing to the physical strain of the ascent, for it requires some athletic prowess, and owing to the exciting interest of the work, which is somewhat of a tax on the nerves, the element of time is necessary for accomplishing what one would wish to do. To this I may add that money is likewise an indispensable factor in the equation. But above all one must not be hurried. On the last day of my stay, for example, after I had finished all I could reach or clearly see, I begged the guides to let me use the ladder in order to examine some of the less certain readings in the upper part of the inscription. This they stoutly refused to do on account of the extreme danger from the high wind blowing at the time. And that afternoon I was obliged to start back to Hamadan. But although some points like these had to be left, I was glad to find I had been able to examine most of the doubtful passages and to prove in general the wonderful accuracy of Rawlinson's transcript. To this I shall revert also below when I speak of the two or three photographs I took, the first, I believe, ever taken on the ledge; they were 'snapped' as I leaned out over the precipice, held by the guides, while focusing the camera and hastily taking the picture. Most of my time, however, was spent in copying, collating, or verifying the readings on the rock itself without resorting to my photographic apparatus. I may add, regarding the means of ascent in ancient times, that there is not the slightest trace of anything of the kind to-day. If ever there was any, it cannot have been of a permanent material.

Regarding the descent I may say that after I had been for

hours on the cramped and narrow ledge, the going down seemed much more difficult than the ascent, and it was a joy each time to hear my faithful Persian servant, Safar, who had remained below, call out, 'Now you are safe,' when I passed the last dangerous place and could jump to the ground. The unloosening of the tight-bound ropes quickly followed with his aid. All had gone well.

So much for the incidental side. I now turn to the far more interesting and important matter of what I was able to note, verify, or restore.

Bh. **1**. 47, $\bar{a}y^a s^a t\bar{a}$: the reading of each letter is quite clear.

Bh. **1**. 51, *paranam* : reading absolutely certain.

Bh. **1**. 55, *patiyāvahyaiy* : so my photograph (*hy*), cf. also Skt. *avasya*, 'flee for refuge.'

Bh. **1**. 65, $v^i\theta^a b^a i\check{s}^a$. $\bar{a}$: barring this troublesome word, the entire line from *-čariš gaiθāmčā māniyamča* to *tyādiš gaumāta hya* is quite as given in Spiegel and in Weissbach and Bang, except that the *g* and *u* of Gaumata's name are defaced, and the *y* of *hya* is illegible, owing to the weathering of the rock. The question arises with regard to the much-discussed word beginning with v^i in the middle of the line. The latter part of the word is mutilated, but my memoranda show that we must accept two letters after *-biš*. The latter I have marked as 'apparently $\bar{a}$,' the former I noted at first as 'illegible,' but added afterwards, 'probably right as *č*.' This shows the bearing of Rawlinson's 'extremely doubtful' as regards the *č* at least. A photograph which I took of the first part of the word $v^i\theta^a b^a i\check{s}^a$. $\bar{a}$ is interesting as showing that there is no *i* inserted either before or after the θ. This is a matter of importance for future reference. I am not unmindful of the various discussions of this word in the journals — the most recent being that of Gray, *JAOS.* 23. 56–60. Regarding *abi-* or *abā-* of *abičariš*, I unfortunately find on returning to America that I had made no special memorandum, but my inference from the absence of a note is that the text stands as first given by Raw-

PHOTOGRAPH OF A SECTION OF THE INSCRIPTION OF DARIUS, BEHISTAN 1. 61–71
(Taken up on the ledge)

u š | x ̆ ā y

| a v a | a d a m | p a t

ā | p a r u v a m č i

m a g u š | v i y a k a |

n i y a m č ā | v i . . b

ā r a m | g ā θ (v) ā

v a | y a θ ā | p a r u v

r a m a z d ā h a | i m a |

ā x a m | g ā θ v ā

| v a š n ā | a u r a

n a i y | p a r ā b a r a | .

linson (*abi-*) and also by Weissbach and Bang, because I had
the latter volume with me on the rock and should probably
have recorded a variation if there had been one.

Bh. 1. 66: my memoranda and 'snapshot' photographs of
portions of l. 66 show that this line stands as given in the
accepted text, excepting the *č* in *pārsaměā* and the final *měā*
of *māda[měā]*. But this is a matter of minor importance.
My 'snapshots' also help to assure the accuracy of several
other words in ll. 65–70 ; I only wish I had taken more photographs, despite the great difficulty in using a camera on the
ledge.

Bh. 1. 86, *mᵃ-yᵃkāuvā* (?) etc. : the first letter of this word is
very uncertain, but the notes which I made upon it on two
different days seem to confirm the accuracy of the initial *m*.
My notes on the last occasion remark that the first part of the
word looks more like *mᵃyᵃ*, and I twice sketched the remnants
of the cuneiform characters, with a special comment on the very
scanty space between the *m* (?) and the *y*. My second drawing
in pencil indicates more especially the illegibility of the *m*,
which can be inferred, however, from the dots that are faintly
visible, but can be made out only with difficulty. The same
sketch seems to emphasize again the small space between it
and the *y*. On returning to America and gaining access to
my books, I find that whereas in *JRAS*. 10. p. xlv, Rawlinson
first said, ' There would appear to be a sufficient space for two
letters between *m* and *k*,' he afterwards corrects this statement
(*JRAS*. 12. p. ii, appendix ; cf. Bartholomae, *IF*. 12. 132
note) by noting ' there is only one character wanting in the
word *ma-kᵃˊuvᵃ*.' This later remark would agree precisely
with my own independent observations. As to the correctness
of *y*, which is not given in any of the editions except in that
of Weissbach and Bang and is marked as doubtful by them, I
have no hesitation. Both my pencil sketches of the cuneiform
characters present a *y*, and so do my memoranda. The last
part, -*kāuvā*, of the word under consideration is perfectly clear,

as my notes on each letter show.   The only Avestan word that I can recall that is at all like this dubious $m^a y^a k^a auv^a a$ is Av. *maēkaintīš*, Ys. **38**. 3 ; or is it 'beasts of burden,' cf. Skt. 2 *máya?*[1] As to the reading of the two words *adam kāram*, which stand before this provoking word, there is no uncertainty.

Bh. **1.** 86, *aniyam ušabārim* : an examination and re-examination of the rock proves the certainty of this reading.   The word-divider precedes the *u* and is all right.   The *u* itself, while not clear, can be made out sufficiently well, for I examined it on two different occasions in order to be perfectly sure. The *š* I found to be beyond question, and that without noticing the loss of any sign after it in the margin, as Foy, *KZ*. 35. 36, would assume.   The chiselling of *-bārim* in the following line shows that portion of the compound to be perfectly clear. Oppert's original conjecture *ušabārim* would therefore be substantiated.[2] I refrain here from entering into a discussion of the derivation of this much mooted word.

Bh. **1.** 87, *aniyahyā asam* (sic) [..] *ānayam* : the form *aniyahyā*, as given, is accurate, though the word is damaged.   The reading *ašm*.. of Spiegel and Kossowicz, or *tašma[kam]* of Friedrich Müller, *WZKM*. 1. 222; 11. 253, and *as[pā]* of Weissbach and Bang, though the latter were on the right track (cf. Gray, *AJP*. 21. 21), must be abandoned.   The word is simply *asam*, 'horse' (acc. sg.).   The *m* at the end is very distinct ; the *s* is very plain ; and the initial *a* is quite clear.   To these comments my note-book further adds, 'the word-divider after it is quite clear.'   Further conjecture is therefore unnecessary, and I find that my observation as to the *m* receives additional corroboration

---

[1] [I should now be inclined to read *maškāʰuva*, accepting the suggestion made to me by Professor Ferdinand Justi, in a letter dated Nov. 25, 1903, and in his published notes in *IF. Anzeiger*, 17. 125.   Similarly also Foy, *KZ*. 37. 553, and Hüsing, as mentioned by Justi, *IF. Anzeiger*, 17. 125.]

[2] Foy writes me, however, (Dec. 20, 1903) that he still believes that *uš[tr]a* should be read and that the stone-cutter made a mistake as the word stands at the end of a line — 'ein steinmetzversehen (*uša* statt *uštra*).' I should feel considerable hesitation about accepting such a view.

from Rawlinson, who read '*asm . . . ánayam*,' but he did not notice the word-divider after *asam* and consequently vocalized the word erroneously. The old difficulty, however, with regard to the obliterated prefix of [..]*ānayam*, still remains. Over each of the cuneiform letters of the legible part, -*a n^a y^a m^a*, I have written 'O.K.,' *i.e.* 'all right,' in my note-book. But on examining the conjectural *pati* as prefix in Weissbach and Bang I have added a memorandum '*pati* extremely questionable; the initial letter can hardly be *p* at all.' In fact, as my notes continue, ' it is hardly possible to read the prefix,' because the rock is so damaged. I appended a further note that the appearance of the word suggested rather [*up*]*ānayam* or [*uz*]*ānayam*. As to form and composition neither of these prefixes would be impossible, as I have since found on being able to consult my Sanskrit dictionary on the verbal prefixes under √*nī*. But such a restoration is quite uncertain, though I tried my best to assure it by examining the weathered stone again and again. Whatever the prefix may be, the sense seems clear when combined with the new reading *asam* (acc. sg. for plur., special for general), and the sentence *aniyahyā asam upānayam* may be rendered, ' I brought up horse(s) for the rest (of the army).' This interpretation is apparently also in accord with the Elamitic version, cf. Weissbach, *Achämeniden-inschriften Zweiter Art*, pp. 63, 64, and Foy, *KZ*. 37. 554.[1]

Bh. 1. 88, exit *avadā*, re-enter *avam*: the reading of Spiegel, Kossowicz, and Weissbach and Bang is wrong as far as *avadā* is concerned, and that too despite the fact that Spiegel, *Keilinschriften*, 2d ed., p. 11, n. 88, is following the authority of Rawlinson's revision in *JRAS*. 12. p. ii, appendix. The rock plainly gives *avam* at this particular point, even though *avadā* occurs often elsewhere in the inscriptions. The *m* of *avam* is clear, as is shown by my notes and my sketch of the

---

[1] [Messrs. King and Thompson, of the British Museum, now write me (June 13, 1905) that they also read *asam*, 'horse(s),' and they suggest *frānayam*, 'I led forward,' for the verb.]

cuneiform characters. The *v* is not quite plain, but can be made out. Regarding the initial *a* there is absolutely no doubt. In *JRAS.* 10. 211, etc., Rawlinson originally read quite correctly '*awam kâram,*' 'that army,' just as in Bh. **2.** 20, 25, 41, 46, etc. There was no occasion for his departing from that. It may be added by way of supplement that the letters -*āva* of the adjacent word [*pas*]*āva* are right, though the first part of the word is broken.

Bh. **1.** 92–96 : the *t* in *nadi^{n}tabaira* (**1.** 92) is legible, and may reasonably be removed from italics in our transcribed editions of the text. I made an incidental note also that *āiša hadā* (**1.** 93) is accurately recorded in our texts, and that *akumā* (**1.** 96), though defaced, is still legible. There were evidences also that the rock has suffered since the days of Rawlinson.

Bh. **2.** 59–61 : these three lines are precisely as given in Rawlinson and Spiegel. The lacuna indicated by Weissbach and Bang in '*nā* . . *avam kāram*' (**2.** 61) is wrong and is evidently due to a misprint (which misled Bartholomae, *IF.* 12. 135). In printing, the two points . . have accidentally slipped in by mistake from the fragmentary -*iyamanam* in the next line. The reading is therefore *manā avam kāram*, as in Spiegel. This note applies consequently to the Weissbach and Bang edition alone.

Bh. **2.** 61, [$\Theta^a u$]$r^a v^a a h^a r^n h^a y^a a$: the first two letters are much defaced, but the third letter (*r*) may be deduced from the three dots or holes left in the rock by the deeper cutting at the head of the wedge, although the less sharply chiselled parts of the letter have been marred by the disintegration of the rock. By practice on the rock the eye becomes accustomed to distinguishing such details, and the restoration can be made with comparative certainty.

Bh. **2.** 75 (cf. 2. 89), *utāšai*[*y*] [*čašma*] *avajam*, etc. : at the beginning of this line the *y* of *utāša|iy*, though faint, is nevertheless to be inferred from the indentures or dots that are still quite distinguishable. Recall what was said above on such dots as means of restoration. The obliterated word, read as *čašma* or *čaxšma*, yielded no new results and is equally illegible in both **2**. 75 and **2**. 89.[1] At **2**. 75 I have merely noted regarding the fragments of an internal letter that it 'looks more like an *h* than it does like an *š*,' but the likeness between the two letters in the cuneiform character leads easily to misapprehension, and certainly *čašma* suits the sense, for the loss of an eye or both eyes, inflicted as a punishment in addition to other mutilations, is precisely what one notices or hears of in remote parts of Persia to-day, as in the days of King Darius. The sight is destroyed by means of a red-hot iron brought near to the ball — as noted, for example, by Landor, *Across Coveted Lands*, 2. 191. This latter observation may throw some additional light on the meaning of *avaǰam* (2. 75). The reading of this word is beyond question. So also is *duvarayāmaiy* ; but the words *basta adāriy* are now illegible — still another proof of the damage done by the water since Rawlinson examined the rock some sixty years ago. Simply by way of record it may be worth adding that the last two words of this line (**2**. 75), *haruvašim k|āra*, are in perfect condition at present.

Bh. **3**. 87–91 : some time was spent in trying to see if anything new might possibly be got out of the closing lines of the third column, but the action of the water had so completely obliterated the words that even the last two at the bottom of the tablet were less clear than they were to Rawlinson. My notes show that *āp* of [*uzmay*]*āpatiy* may be inferred from the faint remnants of these two letters ; the last part of the word is all right. The *k* of *ākariya*ⁿ*tām* is apparently rightly read ; I have added '*k* is best,' but have repeated that it is much damaged.

Bh. **4**. 46 : so far as the first three words *xšāya|θiya vašnā*

---

[1] [Messrs. King and Thompson write me they read '*učšam avajam*, with *učša*, "eye," cf. Skt. *akṣa*.' There seem to be phonetic reasons against this, but I could understand *ašam* as a possibility, comparing Av. *aš*- in Bartholomae, *Air. Wb.* p. 229, although a dual would rather be expected. I have not overlooked the remarks by Foy, *KZ.* 37. 554–555.]

aura[*mazdāha*] are concerned, the reading is as in the texts
already cited; but I was able to make out the faint remnants of
$m^a z^a d^a$ in the divine name. In the fourth word, like Rawlinson, I could only read the latter portion, or -*maiy*, so there is
still an opportunity for conjecture, and the suggestion of Gray,
JAOS. 23. 62, to read *avāmaiy* for *avāt̲-maiy*, is as satisfactory
a way of filling the lacuna as any. The word *aniyašč̌iy*, furthermore, I have marked with an 'O.K.' ('all right') in my
memoranda.

Bh. **4**. 49, *avah|yā paruv θada* . . . : the first two words are
clear, but the verb is in bad condition. Its introductory part,
however, can be made out, and I have marked the *d* as 'O.K.,'
but with the latter part of the word I could do nothing.

Bh. **4**. 50, *maniy*[*ătaiy*]: despite the syntactical grounds
favoring a subjunctive, we must accept a short *ă*, judging
from the rock. On the margin of my text I have distinctly
recorded, 'no space for long *ā*; what remains of the *t* comes
directly after *y*.'[1]

Bh. **4**. 51, *paruvā xšāyaθ*[*iyā*] . *ātā āha*, etc.: the first two
words are quite clear on the rock; the remnants of the third
one I read as . *ātā* without looking at the printed text of Spiegel
or of Weissbach and Bang, which I had with me. Rawlinson,
followed by the later editors, gives only the final *ā*, whereas I
distinctly made out . *ātā* independently, as stated. Weissbach
and Bang conjecture [*yāt*]*ā*, and compare Elam. *kuš̆*. With
regard to the next word, I have noted: '*āha* can be made out
on the stone without question.' The reading, therefore, is
assured, and I have marked *avaišām* and *astiy* as all right; but
the *naiy* between them is no longer clear, although it may be
inferred from the appearance of the stone. Accordingly I have
marked it 'O.K., inferable.'

Bh. **4**. 53, *dāraya*[*vauš̆ xšāya*]*θiya nūram*: the name of
King Darius is apparently somewhat more damaged now than in
Rawlinson's time; but that is a minor matter. More important

[1] Cf. also Foy, *KZ*. 37. 488, note.

is a memorandum regarding the absence of any break before
nŭram. In my notes I have drawn a circle around the dots in
the Weissbach and Bang edition, to indicate that the lacuna is
to be struck out, and have added a definite memorandum, ' omit
the space ; the word *nŭram* comes after the word-divider that
followed [*xšāya*]*θiya*.' Foy's conjecture of *adā*, *KZ.* 35. 34, n. 1,
is therefore needless.

Bh. **4**. 64, *na⎮iy zūrakara āha*[*m*]: the last part of *naiy* is
much broken, but the reading appears to be all right. On
examining *zūrakara* I first noted ' not wholly clear, as the stone
is somewhat marred, but still *z*ᵃ *u rᵃ kᵃ r*ᵘ does seem all right.'
On re-examining it the following day in a better light, I added
that the reading is confirmed. On looking up Rawlinson I
find that he gives the cuneiform quite clearly, which again bears
out the idea that the rock has suffered since his time. As to
āha[*m*] I have marked ' all right ' over *āhᵃ* in my copy and
have added ' probably right ' with reference to what can be
made out of the final *m*. The printed editions have the same.

Bh. **4**. 64, [*naiy adam na*]*imaiy taumā* : I was not able to
make anything out of the missing letters that are indicated here
by being enclosed in brackets, and I wrote ' absolutely illegible
to me ' over [*adam*]. But on the last day in the strong sunlight I corrected this by a supplementary remark that ' I fancied I could discern the *a* quite clearly, and remnants of the
crossbar and upper parts of a *d*, together with a fragment of
the horizontal wedge and possible traces of the indenture caused
by the deep strokes in the nail-heads of an *m*.' This, therefore,
is something towards assuring the accuracy of [*adam*]. Regarding the first *i* in [*na*]*imaiy* I have noted that it is ' right,
but broken badly.' As to *taumā* there is no doubt. The reading is quite accurate, as in all our texts.

The next three words, and those following them, called for
much study, the results of which will now be given.

Bh. **4**. 64, *upariy āᵇᵃ⎮štām upariy* : I spent much of my last
two days in examining this passage, which was one of the

incentives for my going to Behistan, because of the bearing of the whole sentence on the question of the religion of Darius as a Zoroastrian and the faith of the Achæmenian kings, which I have discussed in *JAOS*. 21. 169, 172–175. I returned to the line again and again, studied each word under different lights, sketched it, and made rubbings, so far as I could without injuring the stone, which I was fearful might in some way become defaced. The first of the two *upariy*'s is much damaged and difficult to read; but on the last day I was fortunate in having bright sunlight, so that I could examine it well and compare it again and again with the similar word at the end of the line. I found distinctly that it is *upariy* (with *u*), not *apariy* as has been suggested, for example, by Foy, *KZ*. 35. 45, n. 1; 37. 502, where the Elamitic version is also discussed. This first *upariy* therefore remains unchanged, as in Rawlinson. I came to like results as to the second *upariy*, which is more distinct. Over its *u* in my text and over a part of *p* and over the *y* I have written 'all right.' Below the part *pari* I have marked 'much defaced.' But on the following day when the sun was bright the word came out quite clearly, and I appended the note, 'it is all right.' Therefore the second *upariy* must likewise stand, as in Rawlinson.

I was most anxious, however, to examine the word between these two and to find whether it is *abištām* (R_1), *abaštām* (R_2), or *ārštām* (Foy's conjecture) — see my remarks in the article already referred to, *JAOS*. 21. 169, 172–175. Great care and attention were given to the examination, and after working on the individual letters I made it a point to turn to something else and then to return again and again to verify my memoranda and my sketches. In the first place, there is no *i* in the word; any such reading as *abištām* must therefore be dropped. We have, accordingly, to do either with *abaštām* or with Foy's conjecture *ārštām*, the point being merely whether the text has a *b* or an *r*, because each of the other letters *a.štām* is perfectly clear, as my memoranda again and again show. The whole

question between the two mooted letters is whether we have
the slight horizontal mid-bar of the cuneiform ⟨⟩ *r* or simply
the two parallel wedges of the ⟨⟩ *b*. I must mention at once
that the shape of the cuneiform character for *r* on the Behistan
rock does not exaggerate the middle of the three horizontal
strokes so much as does the type in our printed editions. I
noticed this particularly, and my photographs taken on the ledge
also bring it out. Therefore the middle wedge is naturally
less prominent, and when defaced by the action of the water, as
this word has been, it becomes very faint. A feeling of uncertainty arises as to whether the mark be an intended indenture
or an accidental dot, because of the peculiar brownish mottled
appearance of the somewhat porous stone when it is exposed
to the disintegrating water. But each time I returned to the
word I became surer that Foy is right and that *r*, not *b*, is to
be read. I examined the letter in comparison with the other *r*'s
in the vicinity, when these had suffered from the water, and
always with the same result. I believe therefore that *ar^aš^at^am^a*,
i.e. *ārštām* for *ārštātam*, 'Arshtat, Uprightness, Rectitude,' is to
be read with Foy, and he is to be heartily congratulated on his
shrewd conjecture.[1] At the same time, I would suggest the
need of caution in making further conjectures. The days spent
up on the ledge at Behistan have made me more conservative
than ever, and in cases of doubt I should generally rely on the
faithful Rawlinson until the rock itself be examined.

As to the beginning of the next line, which is variously given
as *mām naiy*, as *āyam naiy*, etc., I confess that when I first read
the fragmentary second element I marked it as agreeing with
naiy in the transcribed text which I had with me. But on
re-examining the damaged fragment I recorded in my note-book
that 'instead of *āyam naiy*, it looks more like a long word
ending in *-h^aiy* or *-j^aiy* — the former, *-h^aiy*, is, however, better,
and it seems so to be clear.' Later I added again, 'it does

---

[1] On the grammatical formation of   [King and Thompson also read *arštām*
the word, see also Foy, *KZ*. 37. 503.   — letter dated June 15, 1905.]

not look like *naiy*.' This makes the question of the reading *naiy* for a moment uncertain. On returning to America and gaining access to Rawlinson's draft of the cuneiform characters, I was interested in finding that he also has -$h^a iy$, and he must likewise have had the impression of a longer word, as his y^a . . $t^a h^a iy^u$ seems to prove. Yet in his later revision (*JRAS.* 12. p. viii, appendix) his cuneiform text runs $up^a r^a iy^a$ $m^u am^u$ $n^a iy^a$, with the word-divider before *mām*, and with this reading Spiegel and the other editors have operated. Whatever we may say on that matter, the Elamitic version is certainly in favor of reading the second word as *naiy*, for it has the usual negative particle *inne*, 'not,' as I find on consulting the text.

Bh. **4**. 65, . . . *šakaurim*, etc.: the text in Spiegel and Kossowicz, partly following Rawlinson, gives *upariy|mām naiy šakaurim . . . . . huvatam zura akunavam*; Oppert, *Le Peuple et la Langue des Mèdes*, p. 183, writes '*upariyāyam naiy uvārim naiy druvaçtam zaura akunavam*'; Fr. Müller, *WZKM*. 1. 60, reads, '*aparijā|jāma naiȷ̈ šakaurim [naiȷ̈ a]huwātam zaura akunawam*'; Weissbach and Bang present *upariy āyam naiy šakaurim [naiy]* . . . . *huvatam zura akunavam*; Foy, *KZ*. 35. 45, first suggested a correction of the text, *i.e.* 'in *apari-yāyam* zu verbessern,' and 'he altered *šakaurim* into $^h ukārim$ and *huvatam* into $d^u uškaram$ (on which see Bang, *IF*. 8. 292); then Bartholomae, *IF*. 12. 130, made the radical conjecture *naiy ā^h urim naiy duruva^n tam*; finally Foy, *KZ*. 37. 557, shifted his ground and made a new guess, *dasurim . . . [ai]na^h uva^n tam*. I can only add that with regard to *šakaurim* suggestions for altering the text may be practically abandoned. The stone plainly gives $š^a$ k^a u r^a i (?) m^a. Regarding the first three letters, $š^a$ k^a u, there is no doubt, as a repeated examination of the word proved. The r^a, however, is very unclear, but the holes or dots of the defaced wedges would allow an *r*. The same is true of *i*, which looks somewhat like an *a*, but the dots favor an *i*. The final letter *m* is marked in my notes as 'even less clear, but the dots would not be against *m*'; and on a third examination I became still surer of the *m*. I added a remark to the effect that the passage must have suffered since Rawlinson's time.

Bh. **4**. 65, *n*[*aiy*]: regarding the word after *šakaurim*, I have noted 'the *n* of *naiy*(?) after *šakaurim* can be made out by the dots.' This reading is supported by the Elamitic, which again has *inne*, 'not,' just as it has before the word corresponding to *šakaurim*.

Bh. **4**. 65, [..]*uvatam*(?): for this much debated word, formerly read .. *huvatam*, etc., I have now some new material to offer. The text is indeed much mutilated, but each of the letters *u vᵃ tᵃ mᵃ* is legible, although the final *m* is in bad condition. On studying the first part of the word, I noticed that instead of an *h*, as is commonly supposed, we have another letter, a character that looks more like *š*. On looking closer, it became perfectly clear to me that the supposed *š* was not *š* at all, but apparently *nᵘ*, although this might possibly be a mistaken reading for *rᵘ*, the uncertainty being due to the resemblance between the characters in the original cuneiform if the horizontal bars are somewhat marred. The sketch made in my notes, however, looks precisely like *nᵘ*. A further examination of the damaged part revealed an apparent *m* standing before this, so that we may assume that the word began with *m*.[1]

Bh. **4**. 65, *zura akunavam*, etc.: each letter of these two words is legible, and the same is true with regard to each of the words that follow in this line.

Bh. **4**. 66, *vⁱ*[*i*]*θiyā*: this is rightly read, although the *vⁱ* is 'broken, but O.K.,' and it is 'hard to be sure of the final *ā*,' although it is 'probably correct,' as I have noted in my text.

Bh. **4**. 68, *hya aparam ahy*, etc.: these first three words of

---

[1] [Even if my reading be correct, I have no etymology to offer in explanation of the word, not even to compare Skt. *manuvat* — as I doubtfully suggested at a hazard in *JAOS*. 24. 24. I am not unmindful that the Elamitic version is read as ᵐ*ištukra* ; nor have I overlooked the various conjectures by the scholars I have mentioned in my paragraph on *šakaurim*, above.]

the line are weathered and defaced, but they are rightly given in the texts. The same may be said of 'italic' *martiya* of the editions, but the word is to be inferred from the stone. With regard to *draujana* I have recorded 'weathered, but O.K.' The subjunctive *ahatiy* stands as in the editions; so does *hyavā*, but it is weathered. Regarding [*ā*]*tar*[*tā*], the whole word, except the internal letters, is 'so weathered as to be practically illegible.'

Bh. **4.** 69, *ahat|iy avaiy mā dauštā avaiy*, etc.: the first and third words are all right; so also is the first *avaiy*, although it is hard to read. The last part of *dauštā* is scarcely legible, though it may be inferred from the appearance of the stone. The second *avaiy* is illegible. The long word *ahifraštādiy* is 'all right, but in part difficult to read.' The imperative *parsā* is 'almost illegible.'

Bh. **4.** 71, 73, *vikanāhy* : 'so best with the letter *k*, not *s*.'

Bh. **4.** 76, *avataiy auramazdā* : the first word is 'apparently all right, but almost illegible'; the second, or divine name, is 'inferable'; as to *mazānam(?)* of Weissbach and Bang, for which Oppert conjectured *vazrakam* (see Foy, *KZ.* 35. 47; 37. 558), I have written 'illegible' above it.

Bh. **4.** 77, *vikanāh*[*i*]*diš:* the *k* is 'fairly clear' and 'best read so.' The [*i*] is 'omitted on the stone.'

By this time the westering sun — for one learns in Persia to live by the sun — warned me that I must descend for the last time from the rocky height in order to start once again for Hamadan and begin my journey to Southern Persia. I was loath to leave, but leave I had to at last if I were to carry out my plans for seeing Isfahan, Persepolis, and Shiraz, and for visiting the Zoroastrians at Yezd before going to the capital and journeying thence to Merv, Bokhara, and Samarkand. On reaching the plain once more there was an opportunity to urge the inhabitants of Bisitun charily to guard their inscription and to tell them of the divine blessings which King Darius invoked upon all such as do so, and of the curses that were assured if it were injured.

I did not leave Behistan, however, without making an examination of the mutilated Parthian sculpture on the panel at the base of the hill, upon the right of the approach to the great inscription. The bas-relief has been nearly destroyed, but we know that it represents the triumph of the Parthian king Gotarzes (A.D. 46–51) over his rival Meherdates, who was likewise a Parthian, but was brought up at the court of the Roman emperor Claudius, and made an unsuccessful attempt to gain possession of the Persian crown. An inscription, written in Greek, after the manner of the Philhellenic Parthians, records, or once recorded, the names of ' Mithra[da]tes the Persian . . . Gotarzes, Satrap of Satraps (*i.e.* king of kings), the son of Gev'; but now the names are almost obliterated with the exception of ΓΩΤΑΡΖΗΟ, which can still be read distinctly. Most of the sculpture was destroyed about a hundred years ago by an act of vandalism of a curious kind. A Persian overlord, Sheikh Ali Khan Zanganah, cut an arch-shaped panel directly in the middle of the sculpture, in order to record, in an Arabic inscription, a gift of the income of two villages, which he donated for keeping up a caravansarai he had built at Bisitun. We can but regret that his act of generosity led him to mutilate a valuable historic sculpture.[1] The elements have likewise contributed much to the destruction of the bas-relief, which was but rudely carved at best, so that the carvings are greatly weathered, but it is still possible to distinguish two figures of heroic size on the left as one faces the panel, and vestiges of still another on the right. Above the latter there once were two small figures of mounted warriors, each armed with a spear, one pursuing the other; over the latter's head, however, floats an angel holding a garland of victory.[2] These effigies symbolized the struggle between

[1] The arched panel is seen already in the sketch by Ker Porter, *Travels*, 2. 151; for a note on Sheikh Ali of Zanganah, cf. also 2. 85–86.

[2] These figures are to be seen in the drawings of Flandin and Coste, *Voyage en Perse, Ancienne*, 1. plates 16, 19.

P

Meherdates and Gotarzes, but the figures are now nearly
obliterated, and I could make little out of the sculpture, although
much depends upon favorable light at the time when it is
examined.[1]

As we stand at the base of the panel and look out over the
plain in the direction of the village of Bisitun, the eye can
plainly see the site of what must have been an ancient building,
as indicated by the outlines of the walls. The natives call this
'Khosru's Place' (*Gāh-i Kei Khosru*), and possibly this Sasanian king once had a villa there, as the country round about
was a favorite territory of his and his name is preserved in the
locality in various ways.

There is still one more relic of antiquity at Bisitun, which
I shall describe, because it seems to have escaped detailed
notice in the books that I have consulted, although the monument is well known to the natives. My guides, when asked
whether there were any carvings or inscriptions besides those
which I had examined, told me that there was a sculpture on
a large boulder around the right flank of the mountain, not far
from the base of the cliff where the Gotarzes panel is cut.
Pointing out the direction, they led me around the spur and
then up a slight incline to a place where stood a huge boulder
of stone, some twenty feet in circumference and ten in height,
carved on three sides with life-size figures in low relief. As I
could not take a photograph, because it was too late in the
afternoon, I made careful notes of the sculptures and shall
describe them with more detail than might otherwise be
necessary.

The middle figure, facing the natural approach up the
mound, is a bearded personage, with mustache and hair
distinctly marked, and wearing upon the head a roundish cap.

[1] For the history of Gotarzes, and
for bibliographical references concerning the inscription, see Justi, *Grundr.
iran. Philol.* 2. 504–505 ; cf. also Rawlinson, *Sixth Oriental Monarchy*, pp.
249–261. Mr. Rabino kindly sent me
notes regarding the Greek inscription
to supplement my own memoranda.

FLANDIN'S SKETCH OF THE GOTARZES SCULPTURE

THE PARTHIAN SCULPTURE OF GOTARZES, MUTILATED BY A MODERN INSCRIPTION

The close-fitting upper garment and tunic have no decoration, but a girdle is worn about the waist and a necklace encircles the throat, as five rings of the band can be distinctly seen. The left hand holds a bowl; the right hand is extended over a low column that may be a fire-altar, and it holds some object which I could not make out, but which is apparently connected in some way with the oblation. The legs of the figure are very fat and are spread apart, as in walking, and they appear to be encased in greaves, or in coverings marked with grooved lines, which make them look like the buckskin leggings of a cricketer. In appearance the figure looks as if it might possibly be intended to represent a Magian priest, although it would be difficult to affirm this; there is certainly nothing either military or kingly in the bearing of the sculpture.

The second figure is carved on the right side of the boulder. The face is fat and round and apparently without a beard, so that the head looks almost like that of a woman or a youth. There is a necklace about the throat, and a bracelet on the left arm, which is clearly marked, although the right arm is not distinct. The body is so poised as to throw the weight on the right foot, which is close to the left, as if making a step, and the fatness of the legs is as noticeable as in the case of the other effigy.

The third figure occupies the left side of the boulder and appears to be approaching the central figure. Like that of the central figure, the face seems to have a scraggly beard, but this detail is not clear. The left arm is not visible, but the right is clearly carved and in the hand something is held, which again is indistinct. The legs look as if they were covered by a low boot or cothurnus, somewhat after the manner of the sculptures at Persepolis. In pose the figure is quite lifelike.

From the standpoint of art the figures are crude and heavy, although not wholly lacking in effectiveness. The plumpness of the legs in each case is striking, and it reminded me of the bas-reliefs over the inscriptions of Darius which I had been examining, and also of some of the Achæmenian sculptures at Persepolis. There was no evidence of the flowing trousers or the balloon-shaped hats that belong to the Sasanian period. On the whole I believe that the sculptures on this monolith near the Behistan rock are to be ascribed to the Achæmenian era rather than to any other.

Time was now up, and I left the scene of the great inscription on Friday afternoon, April 17, feeling painfully aware that I might have accomplished more if my time had been longer and my means greater, but happy in heart at the thought of having possibly contributed something toward our better knowledge of the Behistan text of the inscription of Darius, and inspired by the hope that an opportunity may in some way be offered me to go again and complete such parts as had to be left undone at the moment.

THE VAULTED STONE GROTTOS OF TAK-I BOSTAN

CHAPTER XV

TAK–I BOSTAN AND KERMANSHAH

THE crags of Mount Bisitun looked black and gloomy through a mass of fog in the early dawn as I rode out of the *manzil*, after my first two days at the scene of the inscription, and directed my way toward the city of Kermanshah and the beautiful villa of Tak-i Bostan in its environs. This latter place was a famous park in Sasanian times, thirteen centuries ago, and it is still renowned for its ancient sculptures. As it was necessary to make only a slight detour on my way to reach it, I decided to go to Tak-i Bostan before proceeding to Kermanshah.[1]

My road lay through a rolling plain bounded on the north by the mountain ridge of Kuh Paro, which runs from Bisitun to Tak-i Bostan, and on the south by spurs of the great range of hills that extend past Kermanshah into Luristan. This tract of country is one of the richest pasture-lands in Persia and is renowned for the good horses which it produces and for which Persia has ever been famous.[2] It is well watered by the Gamasiab River, which runs past Bisitun, and the river Karasu, which joins with the latter not far from Kermanshah and converts the region into a succession of meadows. The nomad tribes of the Iliats pitch their black tents for a longer stay with

[1] In point of time this chapter falls between my two different sojourns at Bisitun, which I have combined in the preceding chapter.

[2] Darius calls Persia the land ' of good horses ' (*uvaspa*) in his inscription, Dar. Pers. d. 8.

their flocks when they reach this fertile belt, and they dot the green plains for miles with their portable villages. My own small caravan quickened its pace as the sun burned the mist away, and we traversed the twenty miles quickly, reaching Tak-i Bostan before ten, having passed in that time to scenes associated with events a thousand years later than Achæmenian Bisitun. The sculptures of Darius and the carvings of the Parthian Gotarzes gave place to bas-reliefs cut by Sasanian kings, and the cuneiform characters of the Achæmenian inscriptions were transformed into the cursive ligatures of the Pahlavi script of the Middle Persian period.

Tak-i Bostan lies about four miles northeast of Kermanshah and now forms part of the estate of a wealthy Persian landowner, the late Haji Agha Hasan, *Vakīl ad-Daulah*, 'Deputy of State,' and British agent at Kermanshah. The people look upon the enclosure as a pleasure ground, and many of them have forgotten that it was once a chosen seat of the Sasanian kings. Its situation is certainly a delightful one. Couched at the base of the mountain ridge that runs from Bisitun, and richly supplied with water that springs from the mountain's feet and converts the enclosure into a garden, the place when I saw it showed traces of the veritable paradise that it must have been in the palmy days of the Sasanidæ.

The name *Ṭāḳ-i Bostān*, which often sounds like *Ṭāgh-i Bostān*, or is even turned into ' *Taw-ou-stān* ' by a slovenly labial pronunciation among the peasants, means 'Arch of the Garden' and is given to the enclosure because of the arched recesses carved in the rocky base of the mountain. The place is often called also *Takht-i Bostān*, ' T h r o n e of the Garden,' apparently from a stone ledge cut high in the rock above the arches and approached by a hundred or more steps in the face of the cliff.[1] In earlier times it was sometimes popularly known as

---

[1] The Arab geographer Ibn Rostah (about A.D. 950) speaks of these steps as numbering 'about 250,' in his *Kitāb al-Aʻlāk an-Nafīsah*, ed. De Goeje, *Bibl. Geog. Arab.* 7. 166. See p. 224, below.

THE SCULPTURED PANEL AT TAK-I BOSTAN
(From de Morgan, *Mission Scientifique en Perse*)

Shabdīz, from the statue of Khosru's horse, and sometimes spoken of as *Ḳaṣr-i Shīrīn,* ' Castle of Shirin,' from the beautiful favorite of Khosru Parviz. The former name we know from Ibn Rostah and Al-Hamadhani, a thousand years ago,[1] and the latter, ' Shirin's Castle,' from Yakut, two centuries later, who mentions it as a place containing the remains of ' many porticoes, halls, pavilions, great vaulted arches, lofty terraces, gardens, and a park, which surpassed in magnificence even the splendor of its royal founder.'[2] The name Kasr-i Shirin, however, belongs more strictly to the great mass of ruins known by that title some eighty miles westward from Kermanshah, near the Turkish border.

A wall surrounds the park of Tak-i Bostan, and as we pass through the crumbling gateway we find ourselves directly on the edge of a miniature lake, a reservoir about one hundred and twenty yards square, fed by the waters which burst from beneath the massive rock that overlooks its crystal surface, and find outlet in the reservoir below, whence they stream through a number of channels used for irrigation. A pathway shaded by willows leads around the pond, and by the water's edge and near its channels there are to be seen several fragments of white marble columns, capitals of pillars, and some broken pieces of statuary dating from Sasanian times.[3] A comparatively modern two-story building belonging to the Vakil ad-Daulah stands as a pavilion on the edge of the pond at the point where the water rushes into it.[4] The whole scene when I saw it, clothed in the rich green of springtime and set off by a background of blue sky

[1] Ibn Rostah, ed. De Goeje, 7. 166 (see preceding note), and Al-Hamadhani, ed. De Goeje, 5. 214–215 (*Shabdīz*) and 5. 211 (*Ḳaṣr-i Shīrīn*).

[2] Yakut, p. 448 ; cf. also pp. 438, 345.

[3] Drawings of these may be seen in Flandin and Coste, *Voyage en Perse, Ancienne,* 1. plates 1–14, 17, 17².

[4] This villa does not appear in the sketch made nearly a century ago by Ker Porter, *Travels,* 2. 169, pl. 61, nor were the reservoirs full, judging from his drawing and description of the place, but the water is to be seen in Flandin's plate (*Voyage en Perse, Ancienne,* 1. pl. 3), which I have reproduced below.

that brought the rugged outline of the bare hills into bolder
relief, was picturesque in the extreme and reminded me of
some Italian villa ; but I can imagine that much of its beauty
may be lost when the water of the reservoirs dries up or is
reduced to a running stream, which happens in the drought
of summer.

To the visitor at Tak-i Bostan the most interesting feature is
the collection of Sasanian bas-reliefs sculptured in two large
grottos that are hewn in the bosom of the rock and carved
upon a panel on its lower surface.   These sculptures are perhaps the best extant examples of Sasanian art, and they show
Roman influence of the Byzantine period, with a possible trace
of Greek art due to Alexander's conquest.[1]   There are three
separate groups of bas-reliefs, and I shall discuss them in
the order of their arrangement, and probable sequence of
time.   I shall begin with the one on the panel at the base
of the rock, then proceed to the two statues in the smaller
grotto, and conclude with the elaborate sculptures in the
larger vaulted recess.

The first set of bas-reliefs and presumably the oldest, although
this is not certain, consists of four figures carved on a smoothed
surface of the rock next to the villa and covering an expanse of
about eighteen feet by ten.   A special interest attaches to the
group, as I have stated in my *Zoroaster*, because it has been
thought that the figure to the extreme left may represent the
Prophet of ancient Iran.[2]   For that reason I devoted particular attention to it on the occasion of my visit to Tak-i
Bostan.   I shall briefly describe the composition of the sculptured group.[3]

The two figures to the right represent personages of royal
rank ; the central one is a king who stands with a triumphant
air, his left hand on his sword and his right hand grasping a rib-

---

[1] See Justi, *Empire of the Persians*,
p. 258; de Morgan, *Mission Scientifique*, 4. 309, 333, and cf. p. 221, below.

[2] See my *Zoroaster*, pp. 288–294.

[3] Consult in this connection the accompanying photograph.

THE NIMBUS-CROWNED FIGURE

bon-decked coronet, which he receives from or bestows upon a second personage of lofty bearing. The latter stands before him with the right hand on the chaplet and the left resting gracefully upon the hip. Both figures wear crowns, the central one a helmet-shaped cap surmounted by the globular adornment commonly seen in the sculptures of the Sasanian kings, but conventionalized here into a bulb, the other wearing a mural crown, beneath which thick, flowing hair is seen. Both figures have the characteristic Sasanian head-decoration (*sarpūsh*) of streamers and veil hanging down behind, and the remainder of their ornaments and dress belong also to that period. So much for the two royal personages.

Directly behind the central figure stands a third, differing from the other two in that he has his head encircled by a halo of rays and his feet resting upon a heavily carved sunflower, while he raises before him in both hands a long fluted staff. This image the Parsis of India, as well as the Gabars of Persia, have taken to represent Zoroaster, and they have made it the basis of all the pictures of their Prophet, a matter which I discussed with them in Bombay and likewise at Yezd. For this reason I shall give further details regarding the sculpture, making use largely of my memoranda as I jotted them down on the spot, and then I shall briefly touch upon the question of the identification of the image.

The outlines of the figure are good, and in general the pose is excellent, the weight being thrown slightly upon the left foot. The body is clothed in a tunic-like robe, belted at the waist and richly set off at the neck by an embroidered border with tassels. The elaborateness of this decoration makes it difficult to decide whether a necklace is worn (as appears in the case of the central figure) or whether the band at the throat is a part of the decorative edging of the garment. The tunic itself falls into natural folds, the effect of which is particularly good in respect to the wrinkles at the elbow; and the tunic is decorated quite as much as those of the other two figures, although the belt is simpler than the ornate girdle of the central figure and is more like the belt of the figure to the right. The nimbus about the head is sharply cut, and a cap of some sort, though not surmounted by the globular ornament, covers rich hair which can still be seen despite the damaged condition of the statue. It looks as if earrings might have been worn, but this is uncertain because we have no evidence of such a decoration in the case of the other figures. The upper lip is covered with a short straight mustache, and the chin is bearded with a curly beard. The expression of the face is hard to catch because the eyes, nose, and forehead have been destroyed, probably at the time of the Mohammedan conquest, by some iconoclast that carried out the commandment of the Koran against graven images. The staff in the hand has not been broken, however, and the grooved lines which run parallel with its entire length are plainly visible and resemble the flutings on the scabbard of the middle figure. As in the case of the others, the peculiar head-dress with crinkled streamers, and the wavy scarf flowing down from the shoulders to a point below the waist are particularly noticeable.[1] The trousers are flowing and heavily fringed, as in the case of the other two figures, and the footgear, which appears to include spurs, is quite the same as theirs. The sunflower beneath the feet of the image, an early symbol of sun-worship, is a triple flower, and the stem from which it rises is clearly marked. The size of the entire statue is more than that of an ordinary man, being seven feet from crown to foot.[2]

[1] A crack in the rock has cut the sar-pūsh in two, and in this fissure a plant had taken root, but I had it dug out so that it should not enlarge the split and damage the sculpture any more than it has done.

[2] I add here the more important measurements of this figure, which I took with the assistance of the Rev. N. L. Euwer, of Hamadan, who accompanied me on my visit to Tak-i Bostan : Height of the image, 7 ft. (213 cm.) ; breadth across the shoulders, 2 ft. (62 cm.) ; height of head, including cap, 1 ft. 7 in. (48 cm.) ; length from waist to top of head, 3 ft. ⅞ in. (93 cm.) ; length from waist to sole of foot, 3 ft. 11¼ in. (120 cm.) ; diameter of sunflower, 2 ft. 4⅜ in. (72 cm.) ; length of staff, nearly 4 ft. (119 c.m).

THE SCULPTURED FIGURE OF THE FALLEN FOE AT TAK-I BOSTAN

A fourth figure completes the group. It is that of a prostrate warrior who is trampled beneath the feet of the two victorious kings, the one of whom to the right tramples upon his head, the other upon his feet. The head of the fallen foeman rests limply upon the left arm in a manner intended, apparently, to portray death. The helmet, which differs from the others, is decorated by a band that seems to be jewelled and is set off by large bosses, which might be thought to be pearls in a massive setting, but are more probably the studding of the iron-nailed crown of the Parthian kings.[1] The face is bearded, although the whiskers are not curly like the others. In the case of this figure also iconoclasts have perpetrated their vandalistic work. The entire trunk of the body has been shattered to such a degree that much of the effect of the sculpture is lost; but the remains of the sword, although much damaged, can be traced beneath the body, and the scabbard is marked with sharp grooves, which show up sufficiently to be noticed and compared with the furrows on the sheath of the central figure, which they resemble. The folds of the mantle, moreover, can be clearly seen at the arms, neck, and shoulders, and there is a jewelled collar or necklace worn about the throat. The legs of the fallen enemy have a different sort of buskin from the others, but in size the image is not less heroic than they, since it measures 7 ft. $2\frac{5}{8}$ in. (220 cm.) in length from head to foot.

The question of the identity of this and the other three figures of the group, as I have stated in the book already referred to, is still open to discussion.[2] The trend of present opinion is against identifying the nimbus-crowned figure with Zoroaster, even though opinions may vary as to the other three effigies. The latest and best authority on the subject, Professor Ferdinand Justi of Marburg, maintains the view which he formerly expressed to the effect that it represents the sun-

---

[1] For the nail-studded helmet of the Parthian kings Vologases and Artaban at Naksh-i Rustam, see Justi, *Grundr. iran. Philol.* 2. 515–516.

[2] See my *Zoroaster*, pp. 289–293.

god Mithra, that the central figure is Ardashir I, and that the
figure to the right is Ormazd, who is bestowing upon him a chaplet of victory on the occasion of his overthrow of the Parthian
dynasty represented by Artaban V, the fallen foe.[1] I must confess that, although the radiated figure may not portray Zoroaster
personally, it represents to me an embodiment of the religion, the
authority of church and state combined in some Magian vizir,
or priestly chancellor, who blesses the occasion by his presence,
while the other figures seem to me to represent Ardashir and
his son Sapor (Shahpur), triumphing over the fallen fortunes
of the Parthian dynasty represented by Artaban at their feet.[2]

The second group of bas-reliefs is carved in the smaller of the
vaulted chambers, a few yards beyond the sculptures just
described, and the identity of the personages is fortunately
given by inscriptions adjoining the images. The two effigies
are carved in the tympanum of the vaulted recess, and the
vault itself is nearly twenty feet wide by seventeen high and
twelve deep. The sculptures represent two kings, larger than
life size, standing side by side. Each monarch holds perpen-
dicularly before him a sword, blade downward, the point of
which rests upon the ground, while the hilt is clasped in both
hands which rest over it. The style of dress, including the
balloon-shaped headgear, is characteristically Sasanian and the
identity of each king is made known by the inscription beside
it. Sapor II, son of Hormizd, stands to the right, and his son
Sapor III to the left. The former reigned for seventy years
(A.D. 309–379) during a period which was one of the brightest
in Sasanian history, though stained by cruel persecution of the

[1] See Justi, *Life and Legend of
Zarathushtra* in *Avesta Studies, etc.,
in Honour of Peshotanji Sanjana*,
p. 157, Strassburg, 1904. The Zoroastrians of Yezd gave me a metaphysical explanation of the sculpture,
interpreting the prostrate figure as
representing one's evil nature over-

come and trodden under foot. They
regard the figure with the halo as probably Zoroaster, and seem to associate
it in some way with a sculpture at
Balkh, but they did not appear to be
quite positive on the subject.

[2] See also my *Zoroaster*, p. 291.

THE LARGER AND THE SMALLER ARCH

TAK-I BOSTAN, OR THE ARCHED GARDEN

Christians in Persia ; the latter, Sapor III, ruled only five years (A.D. 383–388) and was then assassinated in an uprising of the soldiers and succeeded by his brother, Bahram IV, the founder of Kermanshah.[1]

The larger arch directly adjoins the smaller recess and is nearly double its size, measuring twenty-four feet in width, twenty-two in depth, and more than thirty in height. It is far more elaborate in its arrangement and more ornate in its decoration, and contains several sets of carvings instead of a single group. Around the outer edge of the arch there is carved in alto-relievo a border that resembles a heavy cording faced with a notched beadwork of a lotus pattern, which lends a graceful finish to the sweep. The base of the arch is balanced on either side by heavily carved panels filled with conventional floral designs in scroll-form. The framework above the vault is cut in such a manner as to resemble miniature battlements, and a streamered crescent in high relief crowns the point which would correspond to a keystone in mason-work. On either side of this emblem hover two winged Victories, like angels,[2] bearing coronets and cups, and they are sculptured in Roman style. The design throughout shows the influence of Byzantine art and is thought to have been executed by Grecian artists from Constantinople — an inference which would be borne out by the statement of Al-Hamadhani, that 'the sculptor was Fatus (or Katus) ibn Sinimmar Rumi (*i.e.* of Rum, the Byzantine Empire), who was the architect also of Khvarnak in Kufah.'[3]

---

[1] See Justi, *Grundr. iran. Philol.* 2. 525, and for reproductions of the sculptures and inscriptions, consult Flandin, *Voyage en Perse, Ancienne,* 1. pl. 3 (from which my photograph is taken) ; Ker Porter, *Travels,* 2. 188; Dieulafoy, *L'Art Antique,* 5. 115, 120, 122 ; and (especially for the inscription) consult de Morgan, *Mission Scientifique,* 2. 104–105, pl. xxxi ; 4. 310–318, pl. xxxvi, and fig. 185.

[2] See p. 142, above.

[3] Al-Hamadhani, ed. De Goeje, *Bibl. Geog. Arab.* 5. 214. For a more detailed description of this arch and the other, see Ker Porter, *Travels,* 2. 169–195 ; Curzon, *Persia,* 1. 560–563 : de Morgan, *Mission Scientifique,* 4. 304–335. See also Justi, *Grundr. iran. Philol.* 2. 527. For the name Fatus or Katus (perhaps a disguised form of Farhad), see p. 226, n. 2, below.

On the outer wall, adjoining the steps to the right, there has been cut in recent times a panel, which looks like a church window, and in it is carved a modern Persian inscription commemorating a visit of the late Shah Nasr ad-Din. This, however, has nothing to do with the grotto or its sculptures, which antedate it by thirteen centuries. These carvings (although two centuries later than the bas-reliefs which have previously been described, and showing a corresponding advance beyond them in the matter of artistic design and execution) are to be assigned to the time of the Sasanian king Khosru Parviz.

Khosru Parviz, with whom we have already become acquainted as Chosroes II in the chapter on Takht-i Suleiman, had a reign of nearly forty years (A.D. 590–628) and enjoyed great prosperity during a part of it, although his later years were marred with misfortune and darkened by defeat. The present sculptures were made when he was at the zenith of his fortune, and they portray happy scenes in his life. As we enter the vaulted chamber we see carved on the right a hunting-scene in which the king is engaged in pursuit of the deer — a favorite sport with the Persian kings from the time of Cyrus the Great — and on the left is chiselled a panel showing Khosru hunting the wild boar. Each of the groups is spirited in conception, although imperfect in execution, especially in the manner of representing perspective ; the panel of the boar hunt, moreover, appears not to have been completely finished and polished. Nevertheless, both bas-reliefs have a historic interest and an archæological value. Still more important are the two great bas-reliefs on the rear wall, and I shall describe these with some detail.

The wall is divided by a carved ledge into two parts, an upper and a lower. The lower portion is devoted to a huge equestrian statue of Khosru, representing him as mounted upon a war-horse of gigantic size. This is Khosru's favorite charger Shabdiz, ' Black as Night,' a steed praised by Oriental writers as the nonpareil of horses. He is caparisoned in heavy war-

BAS-RELIEFS OF KHOSRU II

VIEW OF THE LARGER ARCH

trappings, the poitrel, or metal flounce which protects his chest, being richly ornamented with tassels artistically chiselled, but here again iconoclasts have marred the effect of the figure by mutilating the animal's head and legs. The royal rider is of superhuman size and is clad in massive armor. A coat of mail covers his body, a casque with chain hangings protects his head, and a round shield held in the left hand guards his breast, while the right hand poises an enormous spear. All the details of the king's accoutrements, including the quiver at his side, are executed with great care and will bear the closest scrutiny of the archæologist.

The upper part of the rear wall is occupied by a threefold group resting upon the carved ledge directly above the equestrian statue. In the middle of the group stands the king in full regalia, holding his sword before him, with the point resting upon the ground. With his right hand he receives a chaplet decked with streamers, which is presented by a bearded figure clad in a long mantle belted at the waist, a tunic, and heavy trousers that do not reach quite to the ankle. The third figure, directly at the king's right, is that of a woman, who presents to the king a garland of victory and pours upon the ground at the same time a libation from a vessel held in her left hand.[1] There is no doubt that in this threefold group, as in the case of the equestrian statue, the king is Khosru, but before I discuss the interpretation of the scene that is represented I shall quote from some of the Oriental writers who described this bas-relief and the equestrian statue a thousand years ago.

The earliest notice of the sculptures that I have been able to find is the one quoted above from Al-Hamadhani (A.D. 903) who devotes to 'Shabdiz and its wonders' a section in his geographical work written about three centuries after Khosru's time.

[1] The photograph which I have of the group no longer leaves any doubt that the figure is that of a woman, as stated also by the Oriental writers a thousand years ago, although some later writers have been in doubt on the subject.

'It is one of the wonders of the world, and its sculptor was Fatus
(or Katus) ibn Sinimmar Rumi, who was the builder of Khvarnak in
Kufah.' (He then devotes a paragraph to the praises of the horse
Shabdiz, and says that if two men came from the farthest ends of
Iran, Ferghana, and Susa, to see the sculpture they would not have
any occasion to regret the journey.)[1]

To the same period belongs the more detailed notice by Abu
Dulaf Misar (A.D. 940), quoted by Yakut.

'The monument of Shabdiz is one farsakh from the town of
Kirmasin (Kermanshah). Carved there in the rock is the figure of
a warrior whose head is surmounted by a helmet and whose body is
protected by a coat of mail. The workmanship of the armor is so
perfect that you would declare that the joints of the mail-coat were
movable and twisted as you examined them. The statue is that of
[Khosru] Parviz mounted upon his horse Shabdiz, and as a sculpture
there is nothing comparable with it in the world. In the same arch
there are also several carved figures of men, women, footsoldiers, and
horsemen. Before the king[2] there stands a man who looks like a
workman. Upon his head he wears a round cap and about his waist
a girdle. In his hand he holds a cup, out of which he pours water
upon the earth, and it seems to run under his feet. . . .[3] [The third
figure] is the image of Shirin, the favorite slave of Parviz.'[4]

A third writer belonging to the same epoch, Ibn Rostah
(about A.D. 900–950), gives a similar account.

'It is a distance of three farsakhs from Kirmasin to Shabdiz.
The latter is an arched recess hewn in the mountain, and in it there
are pictures of various birds and other representations. In the bosom
of the vault there is a sculpture of a man wearing a coat of mail, and
in front of him the effigy of a woman, who, they say, is Shirin; and
on the side of the arch is a figure of a man, from under whose feet

[1] Al-Hamadhani, ed. De Goeje, *Bibl.
Geog. Arab.* 5. 214–215.

[2] Here begins the description of the
threefold group above the equestrian
statue.

[3] Here a digression is made by the
author, who quotes at considerable
length Al-Hamadhani's account of
Shabdiz.

[4] Abu Dulaf Misar, cited by Yakut,
pp. 345–347. The attribute of the
vessel of water would seem to refer
to the figure at the king's right rather
than to the one at his left, as seen in
the photograph of the sculpture and
in the published drawings of the bas-
relief.

there flows a stream of water large enough to turn the two stones of a mill. On the other side there are about two hundred and fifty steps, which are hewn in the rock from below to above the arch.'[1]

Contemporaneous with these accounts is the allusion by a fourth writer, the well-known Masudi (A.D. 944), who speaks of these sculptures of Khosru and Shabdiz.

' He (*i.e.* the horse Shabdiz) is carved in the mountain in the district of Kirmasin in the region of Dinavar and Mah al-Kufah. In these sculptures Khosru and the horse are represented beside others. Because of the marvellous pictures sculptured in the rock, this place is one of the curiosities and wonders of the world.'[2]

Scholarly opinion is unanimous in agreeing that the central figure of the group represents Khosru, although the views differ with regard to the interpretation of the other two figures, some authorities maintaining that the feminine figure to the right of the king is Anahita, goddess of the streams, and that the effigy to the left is the god Ormazd.[3] The most probable identification, in part at least, was given more than a thousand years ago by the anonymous poet from whom Yakut quotes a verse which gives the names of the figures as ' Khosru, Shirin, and the High Priest of the Magi.' The natives to-day, as of old, all regard the feminine figure as Shirin. According to some accounts she was the daughter of the Byzantine Emperor Mauricius, and a Christian, and Khosru fell in love with her at the time when he was an exile from Persia at her father's court.[4] The scene,

[1] Ibn Rostah, ed. De Goeje, *Bibl. Geog. Arab.* 7. 166. I am indebted to Dr. A. Yohannan for this version from the Arabic.

[2] Masudi, *Les Prairies d' Or*, ch. 24, ed. Barbier de Meynard, 2. 215. For help with the Arabic I am again indebted to Dr. Yohannan.

[3] Such a view is held by Justi, *Empire of the Persians*, p. 275 (although the central figure is there called Sapor II) and *Grundr. iran. Philol.* 2. 540, where the origin of the sculpture is

attributed, by implication, to Khosru Parviz. G. Rawlinson, *Seventh Oriental Monarchy*, pl. facing p. 613, calls the two figures by the side of the king ' emblematic.'

[4] For the view that Shirin, or Sira, was a Christian, see Rawlinson, *Seventh Oriental Monarchy*, p. 497. According to Justi, *Iranisches Namenbuch*, p. 302, she was an Aramæan from Khozistan and is said to have been the daughter of Mahin-Banu, although the latter point has been questioned.

Q

it has been thought, represents Khosru receiving back his crown at the hands of Mauricius, who had espoused his cause, and obtaining at the same time in marriage the Princess Shirin, who bestows upon him as a dower a share in her crown.[1]

Popular tradition repeats many legends of Shirin and Khosru, and of her admirer Farhad, the royal sculptor, who was attracted by her beauty and is said to have executed the group at the king's command.[2] The story of the enamored artist's passion was a favorite theme with the older Persian poets, but Nizami has carried off the palm by his romantic treatment of it in his poem entitled *Khosru and Shirin*.[3] According to this version of the story, Khosru discovered the admiration of Farhad for Shirin and took advantage of it to evoke new miracles in marble from the inspired sculptor's chisel under promise of receiving Shirin's favors as a reward, and to this fact we owe the sculptures at Tak-i Bostan, like many others in Persia, according to the popular view. Farhad's *chef d'œuvre*, however, was to be the accomplishment of the herculean task of cutting a channel through Bisitun and leading a stream from the other side of the valley, after which the longed-for boon was to be bestowed. Nizami's verses immortalize the achievement of the task and its fatal consequences; I quote them from a free poetic version in English.[4]

> ' On lofty Beysitoun the lingering sun
> Looks down on ceaseless labours, long begun :
> The mountain trembles to the echoing sound
> Of falling rocks, that from her sides rebound.
> Each day — all respite, all repose denied,
> No truce, no pause — the thundering strokes are plied ;
> The mist of night around her summit coils,
> But still Ferhad, the lover-artist, toils,

---

[1] Thus Ker Porter, *Travels*, 2. 186, and after him Curzon, *Persia*, 1. 561–562 ; Kiash, *Ancient Persian Inscriptions*, p. 198, Bombay, 1889.

[2] It might possibly be suggested that the name of *Farhād* is preserved in a disguised form as *Faṭūs* or *Ḳaṭūs* in Al-Hamadhani, quoted above, p. 224.

[3] See also pp. 5, 84, 188, above.

[4] Quoted by Costello, *Rose Garden of Persia*, pp. 84–92, London, 1845, 1887; new ed., pp. 91–97, London, 1899.

And still — the flashes of his axe between —
He sighs to ev'ry wind, "Alas! Shireen!
Alas! Shireen! — my task is well-nigh done,
The goal in view for which I strive alone.
Love grants me powers that Nature might deny;
And, whatsoe'er my doom, the world shall tell,
Thy lover gave to immortality
Her name he loved — so fatally — so well!"

   The piles give way, the rocky peaks divide,
The stream comes gushing on — a foaming tide!
A mighty work, for ages to remain,
The token of his passion and his pain.
   As flows the milky flood from Allah's throne,
Rushes the torrent from the yielding stone;
And sculptured there, amazed, stern Khosru stands,
And sees, with frowns, obeyed his harsh commands:
While she, the fair beloved, with being rife,
Awakes the glowing marble into life. . . .
   Around the pair, lo! groups of courtiers wait,
And slaves and pages crowd in solemn state;
From columns imaged wreaths their garlands throw,
And fretted roofs with stars appear to glow;
Fresh leaves and blossoms seem around to spring,
And feathered songs their loves are murmuring;
The hands of Peris might have wrought those stems,
Where dewdrops hang their fragile diadems;
And springs of pearl and sharp-cut diamonds shine,
New from the wave, or recent from the mine.
   "Alas, Shireen!" at every stroke he cries;
At every stroke fresh miracles arise.
"For thee these glories and these wonders all,
For thee I triumph, or for thee I fall;
For thee my life one ceaseless toil has been,
Inspire my soul anew — Alas, Shireen!"'

The sequel of this rapturous devotion is a tragic one; the
keynote is struck in two lines: —

   'Ah, hapless youth! Ah, toil repaid with woe!
   A king thy rival, and the world thy foe.'

Khosru, in his anxiety to be relieved from fulfilling his promise
to the sculptor, resorted to the counsel of an old hag, who
engaged, for a rich reward, to free the monarch from the necessity of redeeming his pledge.   Intrusted with the task, this
messenger of evil portent proceeds to the lofty rock where
Farhad is employed, and hoarsely whispers her fatal falsehood.

> ' " Cease, idle youth, to waste thy days," she said,
> " By empty hopes a visionary made ;
> Why in vain toil thy fleeting life consume
> To frame a palace ? — Rather hew a tomb.
> Even like sere leaves that autumn winds have shed,
> Perish thy labours, for — Shireen is dead ! "
>   He heard the fatal news — no word, no groan ;
> He spoke not, moved not, — stood transfixed to stone.
> Then, with a frenzied start, he raised on high
> His arms, and wildly tossed them towards the sky ;
> Far in the wide expanse his axe he flung,
> And from the precipice at once he sprung.
> The rocks, the sculptured caves, the valleys green,
> Sent back his dying cry — " Alas ! Shireen." '

Even when robbed of its poetic garb the story seems to have
an element of truth as its basis, and the legend lends a romantic
interest to the ' Villa of Shirin ' and its sculptured halls.

Another monument of Khosru, a platform on which royal
assemblies were held, was located in the vicinity of Kermanshah, according to Yakut, and probably not far from Tak-i
Bostan.   I shall quote Yakut's own words describing it : —

'Near Kermanshah is situated the famous platform where Khosru
Parviz received homage in royal assembly from the kings of China,
Turan, India, and Byzantium.   It is a quadrilateral, a hundred
cubits long and a hundred cubits broad, built of dressed blocks
of stone, skilfully matched and joined together by iron clamps so
closely that they look like a single piece.'[1]

This description should be sufficient to allow an identification
of the location of the platform to be made, as some remains of

[1] Yakut, p. 438.

the structure must exist, but I am unable to give any precise information on the subject myself, although there are ruins near Tak-i Bostan,[1] and the natives point out some mounds as the site of Khosru's palace.[2] I noticed also some marble walls and columns on the road between Kermanshah and Bisitun.[3]

I have made my description of Tak-i Bostan somewhat more detailed than otherwise might be expected, because of the historic associations connected with the place, and we may now resume our journey to Kermanshah, which lies about four miles to the south-southwest on rising ground that commands a considerable view over the plain.

To reach the city I found it was necessary to take a somewhat circuitous route, as the Karasu River, though ordinarily narrow, was now swollen by floods and could be forded only at a particular point. Leaving the miniature lake and its associations with the name of Shirin, our cavalcade proceeded on its way, and we soon were approaching a modern three-story building, near the river, which looked in the distance like a European apartment house suddenly transported to Persia, where three-story houses are a rarity. I found it was a ducal palace belonging to the family of one of the former governors of Kermanshah, Imam Guli Mirza, known as Imad ad-Daulah, and hence the building was called the Imadiah. It is now going to rack and ruin, because the heirs of the original owner have failed to keep up this villa and its grounds, in order to avoid the expense it would entail to entertain in it with lavish hospitality each new governor that assumes the administration of Kermanshah.

Hardly had we crossed the Karasu and ridden a mile farther toward the city than we were completely enveloped in a snow

[1] See the plan of Tak-i Bostan in Flandin and Coste, *Voyage en Perse, Ancienne*, 1. pl. 1.

[2] Information from Mr. H. L. Rabino.

[3] See likewise Wilson, *Handbook of Asia Minor*, p. 327. A 'Takht-i Khosru' was pointed out to me near Bisitun, but this was too far from Kermanshah to answer to Yakut's description. I am not unmindful that there are ruins at Kasr-i Shirin, Sar-i Pul, and Takht-i Girrah, cf. de Morgan, *Mission Scientifique*, 4. 335–357.

squall which was severe enough to blot out the recollection that we had been lunching only a short time before in a garden of springtime, and to leave only a memory of the snowstorms produced by the black art of the sorcerers in the Shah Namah. But it soon passed over, and in another half hour the tin-covered minarets of the mosques of Kermanshah and the lofty towers of the Governor's Palace shone out in the afternoon sun.

Kermanshah, or Kermanshahan, as it was more generally called in former times, is a place of considerable antiquity as well as the modern capital of the district of the same name.[1]   Tradition ascribes the founding or the re-establishing of the town to the Sasanian king Bahram IV (A.D. 388–399), who had been ruler of Kerman (*Karmān-shāh*) before he came to the throne, and for this reason gave that name to Kermanshah, although Yakut assigns the founding of the city to a date a century later, ascribing it to Kobad I, son of Piruz (A.D. 488–531).[2]   It is probable that the city is much older than either of these dates and that it may occupy the site of the ancient Kambadene, mentioned in the itinerary of Isidor of Charax.[3]   Little is known in detail regarding the history of the city for a long time after the Sasanian period.   Although mentioned by the Arab geographers Al-Hamadhani, Ibn Rostah, and Yakut, already referred to, no allusion is made to it by Pietro della Valle, who must have passed near it on his journey through this plain three hundred years ago (1617).[4]   There are native records, however, including poetical accounts in Kurdish, which give the history of some of its wars in the eighteenth century, and since the nineteenth century the town has become better

[1] The Arab pronunciation of the name of the town varies between *Karmāsīn* and *Kirmīsīn*.

[2] Yakut, p. 438.   For the tradition about Bahram IV, see Justi, *Grundr. iran. Philol.* 2. 525–526, and for the reign of Kobad (Kavadh), 2. 531.

[3] Gk. Καμβαδηνή, see Isidorus Characenus, *Mansiones Parthicae*, 5, ed. Müller, Paris, 1855, 1882 ; and cf. de Morgan, *Mission Scientifique*, 2. 100.

[4] For the itinerary of Pietro della Valle's journey in this region, see the edition of Pinkerton, 9. 16 seq.

KERMANSHAH: THE PARADE-GROUND AND THE GOVERNOR'S PALACE

known to the West through trade and travel, although as regards familiarity its name can bear no comparison with Teheran and Isfahan. Many persons, in fact, know of Kermanshah only through the rugs for which the city and its vicinity once were famous, even if the rug manufacture is almost a lost industry now in Kermanshah itself and the carpets which are exported through its customs to-day come mostly from other parts of Persia and are merely shipped by way of this distributing-centre.[1]

Commercially the city of Kermanshah is favorably situated, as it lies on the main caravan route between Persia and Mesopotamia, being nearly equidistant from Teheran and Baghdad, two hundred and twenty miles from the latter and two hundred and fifty miles from the former. The town enjoys the advantages of a busy trade, especially on commission, and its population is now reported at fully sixty thousand, the inhabitants being largely of Kurdish blood, besides Persians, Turks, some Jews, and a few Christians.[2] The municipal administration is in the hands of three magistrates (*kadkhudā*), each of whom presides over one of the three wards into which the city is divided, and is accountable, through a number of higher officials, to the Governor of Kermanshah appointed by the Shah.

In area the extent of the town is considerable, as it measures about four miles in circumference, and its circuit was formerly enclosed by walls, although these have now disappeared, except that one or two of the towers have been built into the walls of dwellings, and traces of the moat are visible where it has not been completely filled up. The five city gates have been preserved in name at least, as their names are still employed to designate the several quarters where the main roads enter the town.

[1] Just as 'Hamburg' grapes and 'Astrakhan' furs are so named from the place of shipment.

[2] For valuable information regarding Kermanshah I am indebted to the kindness of Mr. H. L. Rabino, Agent of the Imperial Bank at Kermanshah, and to the *British Consular Reports, Persia*, no. 590, miscell. ser.; no. 3189, annual ser., London, 1903, 1904.

Architecturally the city has little of interest to attract the traveller, and most of its buildings are of comparatively recent date. There are a number of public squares and buildings, but they are of minor importance. Among them may be mentioned the Governor's Palace, whose high towers overlook the *Tōp Meidān*, or 'Artillery Square.' In the midst of this square is a reservoir, and around the plaza are shops adjoining the bazaars. The arsenal itself is behind the palace, and to the south is another square called *Meidān-i Sarbāz Khānah*, or 'Barrack Square,' because the soldiers' quarters are built around it and it serves as a parade-ground. There are several mosques in different parts of the city, but none of them are ancient or especially renowned. A bank, custom-house, post and telegraph office, and about thirty baths make up the rest of the quota of public buildings; there are some private houses of the finer sort and a number of handsome gardens and villas in the environs, the property of wealthy owners.

The city is well supplied with caravansarais, and they are usually crowded with merchants or with pilgrims on their way to and from Kerbela. The principal hostelry was full on the afternoon when I arrived, so that I had to seek elsewhere for lodgings. I met with the same experience at the next, and again at the next, riding for more than an hour through crowded streets and bazaars, jostling against camels and pack-mules, whose load nearly tore one of my riding-leggings to pieces, stopping only long enough to repair damages and sample a baker's supply of sugar cakes, which were really excellent, then proceeding once more. At last I found shelter in an unpretentious *manzil*, the owner of which was an obliging person, and he succeeded in making me fairly comfortable. My enforced peregrination had at least this in its favor, that it gave me an opportunity to gain some idea of the commercial activity of Kermanshah. The bazaars seemed to be carrying on a prosperous trade in the products of the district, grain, wheat, barley, fruit, gum, and also opium, besides doing a fair business in goods which are transported through the city, a traffic which includes also numerous imports from abroad, so that I was able to stock up again with several articles of foreign manufacture which I found I needed on the journey.

I had expected to remain an extra day at Kermanshah, especially as I had met with kind hospitality at the Imperial Bank, but I changed my plans when I learned that the two other scholars whom I thought I might meet and have join in the work upon the Behistan rock had been prevented from coming. I felt, therefore, that I must return to the rock at once and accomplish as much more as I could in the limited time at my disposal before leaving for the south of Persia. Accordingly I started shortly after sunrise the next morning and galloped my horse, Rakhsh, most of the twenty-one miles back again to Bisitun. After taking a hasty meal I proceeded immediately to the height, and within an hour after noon I had again ascended the cliff and was busy at the work, which I continued that day and the next with all the intensity of application of which I was capable, and with the results that I have already described.

CHAPTER XVI

THE GREAT RUINED TEMPLE OF THE PERSIAN DIANA AT KANGAVAR

'I shall offer unto the holy Ardvi Sura Anahita, goddess of the heavenly streams, pure and undefiled, a goodly sacrifice accompanied by an oblation.
— AVESTA, *Yasht* 5. 9.

KANGAVAR is a small town of great antiquity, lying directly on the route between Bisitun and Hamadan, and it is the site of some important ruins which I shall describe, as they are those of a temple of the Ancient Persian Diana. On my journey outward to Bisitun I knew that there were some ancient remains to be seen at the place, but in my anxiety to reach the inscription of Darius I had no time to visit them, and I waited till I should be able to inspect them on my return journey to Hamadan. Accordingly, I mounted my horse and started with Safar, Shahbas, and the rest of my caravan on the road to Hamadan by way of Kangavar, the same route I had traversed eight days before.

As I rode along, my attention was attracted by a large land-tortoise, the first I had seen in Persia; it had been tempted out of its winter quarters by the warm spring sun and was slowly crawling along by the side of the trail. The Persians call the tortoise 'stony-back' (*sangī-pusht*), but the ancient Zoroastrians named it *zairimyaṅura* or nicknamed it *zairi-myāka* (a word of uncertain meaning) and looked upon the tortoise as one of Ahriman's creatures and therefore to be destroyed.[1] Happily in this respect the harmless creature is

---

[1] Avesta, Vd. **13**. 6 ; see also (*kasy-apa*) Vd. **14**. 5. Darmesteter, *Le ZA.* 2. 195, n. 8, gives the meaning of *zairimyaṅura* as 'qui dévore la ver-dure'; Bartholomae, *Air. Wb.* p. 1682, as 'des Glieder (oder Zehen) in einem festen Gehäus stecken.'

234

A PERSIAN SHEPHERD
(Near Sahnah)

A TYPICAL CARAVANSARAI

no longer under a ban, and my Mohammedan attendants allowed it to pass unmolested. Sunset found me entering the hamlet of Sahnah, riding through lanes lined with rows of plum and apple trees in full blossom. I directed my caravan to proceed to the same *manzil* at which we had stayed on the outward journey, and hardly an hour had passed before I was asleep in the *bālā-khānah*, or upper room above the entrance. If I had known at the time that a tomb, fabled to be that of the legendary king of Iran, Kei Kaus, is located in a gorge back of Sahnah, I should have engaged some of the natives to take me, with torches, to visit the chamber and draw me up to inspect it, or should have waited an extra day to examine it.[1] But Sahnah meant for me, on my two visits, only a halting-place, as it does for the Kerbela pilgrims whose passing to and fro is a source of revenue to its thousand or more inhabitants, so I arranged to continue my march early next morning.[2]

The hands of my watch indicated precisely 6.00 A.M. when I gave the signal to start, and our slow-moving procession filed out beneath the mud portal of the caravansarai and headed eastward again toward Hamadan.

In an hour and a half we reached a pretty village which I remembered noticing particularly, on the outward journey, because of its green groves and orchards, its rich grass, and abundant water. The frogs in the pools were croaking lustily, no longer in fear of the old Zoroastrian law (long since passed into oblivion) which accounted them noxious animals and regarded it as a meritorious act to kill thousands of this brood of Ahriman.[3] The merry chorus of their voices reminded me of the Frog Hymn in the Rig Veda,[4] as each tried to out-croak the other, but the inharmonious music was soon lost

---

[1] Sahnah is mentioned by Ibn Haukal, p. 167, Yakut, p. 305, and Pietro della Valle, *Viaggi*, 1. 440; *Travels*, ed. Pinkerton, 9. 17; but none of them allude to the tomb of Kaus.

[2] For a sketch of the 'Tomb of Kaus,'

see Flandin and Coste, *Voyage en Perse, Moderne*, pl. 75 b, and *Texte*, p. 11.

[3] Vd. **14**. 5; **18**. 65, 73.

[4] See Rig Veda, 7. 103. 1–10.

in the distance, and before long we were ascending a ridge of rolling hills and after that descending into a plain flooded with sunlight.

I halted for a few minutes here to speak to a Persian shepherd who was grazing his flocks along the rich plain. His short-sleeved sheepskin coat, shoes of rough hide, heavily rolled turban, and shepherd's staff gave me an impression of what the pastoral life must have been in early Media. It was, perhaps, to such a shepherd, in these very mountains, that King Astyages committed the infant Cyrus with orders that the child should be exposed to die, if we are to believe the ancient legend, and possibly this very shepherd's wife resembled the fictitious Spaka who reared the foundling to become a shepherd lad and king.[1]

We rode forward through a fertile plain and reached Kangavar before noon. The town is about thirty-two miles distant from Bisitun, or four farsakhs from Sahnah, and is now a settlement of about eighteen hundred houses,[2] the lodging of some eight thousand inhabitants. The main street, which winds up and down the elevation on which the town lies, is lined with shops and booths of merchants trading especially in wheat, barley, cotton, and pears, and is bordered on either side with halting-places to offer a *manzil* to the heavily laden trains of camels and asses on their way to Kermanshah and Baghdad.

Kangavar is a place of genuine antiquity; it was known, under the name of Konkobar, to the Greek geographer Isidor of Charax in the first century of our era;[3] and my attention

[1] Herodotus, *History*, 1. 107–114.

[2] Information from Mr. H. L. Rabino. The Italian traveller Pietro della Valle, who stayed in the town Jan. 20, 1617, described Kangavar as a large place ('grossa terra chiamata Chienghieuer,' *Viaggi*, 1. 440 ; *Travels*, ed. Pinkerton, 9. 17).

[3] The first scholar to identify Kangavar with 'Concobar,' I believe, was D'Anville, *Compendium of Ancient Geography*, pt. 2, p. 460, London, 1791. Since that time much has been written about the site ; see Rawlinson, *JRGS.* 9. 112 ; Buckingham, *Travels in Assyria, Media, and Persia*, pp. 150–154, London, 1829 ; Masson, *Illustrations of Isidorus of Charax*, in *JRAS.* 12 (1850), pp. 97–124 ; Ker Porter, *Travels*, 2. 139–144 ; Texier,

was at once attracted by certain peculiarities of its site. The low hills and mounds which surround it, some of them capped with buildings erected on the foundations of older structures, immediately suggested to me an etymology for Kangavar. The name *Kangavar*, or *Kankivar*, Gk. Κογκοβάρ, may be derived from a hypothetical Avestan form *Kaṅha-vara, 'enclosure of Kanha,' the first element of the compound being probably a proper name, *Kaṅha*, as in Avestan *Kaṅha-daēza* and Firdausi's *Kang-diz*, and the second element, *vara*, 'enclosure,' being cognate with the designation of the Vara of Jamshid.[1] The mounds and elevations which surround the acclivity on which Kangavar is built, make the attribute a fitting one and the suggested etymology probable.

Among the buildings which attract notice at Kangavar are one or two mosques and a brick citadel, but they are of minor importance when compared with the ruins of what must once have been a magnificent edifice in the heart of the town. Here, on the principal thoroughfare and near a large caravansarai, are the remains of a wall of white marble blocks of mammoth size, hewn with precision, and crowned with broken columns and pilasters which show the outline of a grand enclosure of buildings. The style of the architecture is noticeably Greek, and I made a series of memoranda concerning the ruins, although I did not know at the time that they had been subjected to a detailed examination by others. I shall give my notes as I took them down, and supplement or correct them from other sources when occasion demands.

So far as my observations allowed me to judge, the ruins seemed to represent the remains of two large buildings, the one to the northwest, lying directly on the main street, and

Description de l'Arménie, la Perse, etc., 1. 160 seq., pls. 62–64; Flandin and Coste, *Voyage en Perse, Ancienne*, 1. pls. 20–23, *Moderne*, pls. 72–74, *Texte*, pp. 11–14; Dieulafoy, *L'Art Antique de la Perse*, pt. 5, pp. 7–8, 11, 207; Curzon, *Persia*, 1. 51, n. 1; Marquart, *Ērānšahr*, p. 24; and E. A. Floyer, *Unexplored Baluchistan*, pp. 424–425, London, 1882.

[1] See p. 126, above. *Kaṅha* was located somewhere in eastern Iran.

the other at some distance to the southeast, situated on the edge of a declivity. I find that authorities such as Ker Porter, Texier, Flandin and Coste, and Dieulafoy, to whose judgment I should defer in such a matter, see in the granite blocks which compose the structure the remains of a single great platform with a peristyle, in the midst of which stood the chief edifice.[1] Ker Porter, for example, who visited the ruins in 1818, regarded the whole enclosure as a temple precinct whose walls formed a huge rectangular terrace, three hundred yards square and crowned with a colonnade.[2] Flandin's drawings and Texier's sketches, which apparently served as the chief source of Dieulafoy's information, give a plan of the possible arrangement of the platform and the temple precinct. To speak with positive certainty as to details, however, would only be possible after a careful re-examination of the ground, and it would also be necessary to make clearings and excavations, since a mass of modern buildings and dilapidated structures has been built over the ruins, or crowded in among them, in order to take advantage of some of the ancient material still standing.

The supposition that the original structure was an extensive platform, on which various superstructures were raised, is borne out by an allusion to Kangavar in Yakut, about A.D. 1220. This Arab writer says that the place was called also *Ḳaṣr-i Shīrīn,* 'Castle of Shirin,' after Khosru's favorite,[3] but more often *Ḳaṣr al-Laṣūs,* 'the Robber Castle,' because the Arab army which invaded Persia after the battle of Nahavand lost some pack-animals here, which were stolen by robbers; it is

---

[1] Compare Ker Porter, *Travels* (1822), 1. 141; Texier, *Description de l'Arménie, la Perse, etc.* (1842), 1. 160–162, and pls. 62–68; Flandin and Coste, *Voyage en Perse, Ancienne,* 1. pl. 21 (reproduced below), *Texte,* p. 13, *Moderne,* pls. 72–73; Dieulafoy, *L'Art Antique,* pt. 5, pp. 8, 207. For measurements of the platform, compare Flandin and Coste, *Texte,* p. 13, who give 217.93 m. by 229 m.; Texier, *op. cit.* 1. 161, gives 202 m. by 172 m.

[2] The Arab geographer Al-Hamadhani (ed. De Goeje, 5. 267) says that ' in all the world there are no columns more wonderful than those at Ḳaṣr al-Lasus (*i.e.* Kangavar).'

[3] See p. 225, n. 4, pp. 226–228, above.

more likely, however, as Mustaufi says, that the name was given it because the place was later infested by bandits, a reputation which it long retained.[1] Yakut describes the place as follows:

'The Robber Castle is a very remarkable monument, and there is a platform some twenty cubits above the ground and on it there are vast portals, palaces, and pavilions, remarkable for their solidity and their beauty.'[2]

The part of the foundation which is best preserved stands at the northwest corner. A solid retaining-wall can there be seen, twelve or fifteen feet high, running north and south for more than seventy feet and forming what I took to be the base of a single building. The northern wall, which extends at right angles eastward from this point, is equally massive, being composed of granite blocks, some of them more than seven feet long and four feet high,[3] and broad in proportion, although it was not easy to measure the stones, as the wall is partly buried beneath earth and débris. The rampart is capped with a heavy coping which forms a stylobate to sustain what once must have been an imposing colonnade.[4] Three of these columns, each nearly six feet in diameter, were still standing on the cornice of the northwestern wall when I saw it, having been preserved by being built into the side wall of a modern building, as shown also in Flandin's picture (which I have reproduced), while a fourth truncated shaft at the extreme upper angle of the stylobate, where the wall turns eastward, was standing and could be easily measured because it was quite detached.[5] Several of the pillars have fallen since the time

[1] Yakut, p. 451; cf. also pp. 450, 495; for the robbers cf. Mustaufi, cited by Barbier de Meynard, *Dict. géog.* p. 451, n. 1, and Le Strange, *JRAS.* 1902, p. 511; furthermore, Ibn Haukal, p. 166 (*Ḳaṣr-i Duzdān* ' Robber Castle '), and Masson, *JRAS.* 12 (1850), p. 116, which bears out the idea that the place was infested by freebooters.

[2] Yakut, p. 451.

[3] 210 cm. by 130 cm.

[4] For a sketch of a section of this cornice, see de Morgan, *Mission Scientifique,* 2. 139.

[5] The height of this drum was over six feet, and its diameter nearly six feet also, or, more exactly, 170 cm. by 160 cm.

of Ker Porter (1818), who speaks of pedestals of eight columns as still surmounted by the chief part of their shafts in good preservation, thus evidently not including the base of the rectangular shaft adjoining the column at the upper end, which is shown in the drawings and plans of the Frenchmen Texier (1839–1840) and Flandin and Coste (1839–1841), and of the Englishman Masson (1845).[1]

Following my guide eastward along the elevation and then turning southward among the hovels and rubbish, I found a large collection of massive stones near the southeast corner. A mass of huge blocks was tossed about in confusion, as if a building had collapsed, but I was able to trace the general outline of a wall running for about a hundred feet north and south, as shown in my photograph. The stones were of the same large size as at the northwest corner, and one granite drum, which had fallen down the slope, measured nearly five feet by eight.[2] The base of another column was still to be seen in its place in the line of the wall, and near it a third pedestal rising two feet above the ground.[3] Within the enclosure where the main edifice must have stood was a part of a column (shown in the middle of my photograph), which had apparently been set partly on a foundation of stone and mortar, so that it looked like an altar for libations, as it was slightly hollowed out, but it may have been simply an overturned capital. I was inclined to the former view because I believed, when examining the ruins, that they were the remains of a temple of Anahita, the great Persian goddess of the heavenly streams, whom the Greeks identified with Artemis, or Diana,

[1] Compare Ker Porter, *Travels*, 2. 141 ('pedestals of eight'); Flandin and Coste, *Voyage en Perse, Ancienne*, 1. pls. 21, 22, *Moderne*, pls. 72, 73 (8+1 columns, including the pilaster); Texier, *Description de l'Arménie, la Perse*, etc. 1. pls. 64, 65, [66] (8+1 columns); Masson, *JRAS*. 12. pl. p.117 (8+1 pillars, with most of the wall of the modern building between them still intact). Dieulafoy's plans (*L'Art Antique de la Perse*, 5. 8–9) are after Flandin.

[2] More exactly, 230 cm. by 144 cm.

[3] For a sketch of the mass of columns as they lay about half a century ago, see Flandin and Coste, *Voyage en Perse, Moderne*, pl. 74 b, and Texier, *Description*, 1. pl. 68.

and whose worship was widespread throughout Iran in the time of Artaxerxes Mnemon, in the fourth century before Christ.

On gaining access to my books I was able, by positive evidence from the classics, to substantiate the view that I held regarding the identity of the temple, but I find that I have been partly anticipated by others.[1] The Greek geographer Isidor of Charax, who entered Media by this route in the first century A.D. and kept detailed notes of his itinerary, which he published under the name of 'Parthian Stations,' mentions Kangavar as Konkobar, and alludes to its temple, sacred to Artemis. His laconic note reads : —

'Three *schoeni* (eight or nine miles) from the frontier of Upper Media is the city of Konkobar, where there is a temple of Artemis. Three *schoeni* beyond this is Bazigraban, which is the place of receipt of customs. Four *schoeni* thence to Adrapanan, a palace in the territory of Batana (*i.e.* Ecbatana),[2] destroyed by Tigranes the Armenian. Twelve *schoeni* thence is Batana (Ecbatana) the capital of Media, the treasury, and the temple where they sacrifice constantly to Anaïtis. Then after that there are three villages, in each of which is a station.'[3]

---

[1] See the names referred to above, p. 236, n. 3.

[2] Lit. 'of those in Batana' (*i.e.* Ecbatana).

[3] Isidor of Charax, *Mansiones Parthicae*, 6. For convenience I add the Greek text of Isidor's entire itinerary from Cambadene (Kermanshah ?) and Behistan (miswritten as *Baptana* for *Bagistana* — Greek ππ for πcτ) to Konkobar and Ecbatana, thence to Rhaga (mod. Rei) and the Caspian Gates. The passage reads : 5. Ἐντεῦθεν Καμβαδηνὴ, ἥτις κατέχει σχοίνους λα΄, ἐν ᾗ κῶμαι ε΄, ἐν αἷς σταθμὸς, πόλις δὲ Βάπτανα ἐπ' ὄρους κειμένη· ἔνθα Σεμιράμιδος ἄγαλμα καὶ στήλη. 6. Ἐντεῦθεν ἡ Μηδία ἡ ἄνω, σχοῖνοι λη΄· καὶ ἄρχεται εὐθὺς πόλις Κογκοβάρ· ἔνθα Ἀρτέμιδος

ἱερὸν, σχοῖνοι γ΄. Εἶτα Βαζιγράβαν, ὃ ἐστι τελώνιον, σχοῖνοι γ΄. Εἶτα εἰς Ἀδραπάναν τὰ βασίλεια τῶν ἐν Βατάνοις, ἃ Τιγράνης ὁ Ἀρμένιος καθεῖλε, σχοῖνοι δ΄. Εἶτα Βάτανα, μητρόπολις Μηδίας καὶ θησαυροφυλάκιον καὶ ἱερὸν, ὅπερ Ἀναΐτιδος ἀεὶ θύουσιν· σχοῖνοι ιβ΄. Εἶτα ἐξῆς τρεῖς κῶμαι, ἐν αἷς σταθμός. 7. Ἐντεῦθεν [Ῥαγιανὴ] Μηδία, σχοῖνοι [νη΄]. Ἐν ᾗ κῶμαι ι΄, πόλεις δὲ ε΄. Ἀπὸ σχοίνων ζ΄ Ῥάγα καὶ Χάραξ, ὧν μεγίστη τῶν κατὰ τὴν Μηδίαν ἡ Ῥάγα. Εἰς δὲ τὴν χάρακα πρῶτος βασιλεὺς Φραάτης τοὺς Μάρδους ᾤκισεν· ἐστιν ὑπὸ τὸ ὄρος, ὃ καλεῖται Κάσπιος, ἀφ' οὗ Κάσπιαι πύλαι. (See Isidorus Characenus, *Mansiones Parthicae*, in *Geographi Graeci Minores*, ed. C. Müller, Paris, 1855, 1882.)

R

The ruined temple, therefore, was one dedicated to Ardvi Sura Anahita, as goddess of the streams. The situation at Kangavar must have been a suitable one for a sanctuary devoted to her worship, for within the town itself is a cascade which pours its waters down into the plain to be lost ultimately in the Gamasiab, and may therefore be described in the words of the Avesta itself as 'a holy stream enriching life, enriching the herds, enriching property, enriching wealth, enriching the whole country.'[1]

My idea that the temple was erected in Achæmenian times and may have been founded by Artaxerxes II, is not in agreement with Dieulafoy, I find, who argues that the remains show a confused Greek style, that the columns are bastard Doric,[2] that the architecture has nothing in common with the Persepolitan, which shows Egyptian characteristics, and that we must conclude to assign the temple to the Parthian period, ascribing it to some one of the Arsacid kings, all of whom were strongly under Hellenic influence.[3] If this assumption be correct, I should regard it as an addition to our knowledge of the Zoroastrian religion during the Parthian period, regarding which our information is in many respects scanty. In any event Kangavar offers a good field for archæological research, and I believe that scientific excavations in the vicinity, as at Tak-i Bostan and throughout the valley, would yield important results.

Continuing the journey toward Hamadan, I stayed over night, for the second time, at the small walled village of Asadabad, or Saïdabad, four and a half farsakhs (about twenty miles) distant from Kangavar.[4] This settlement lies at the

---

[1] Yt. 5. 1.

[2] For specimens of the bases and capitals of the columns, see Ker Porter, *Travels*, 1. pl. 43 c ; and compare also the drawings of Flandin and Coste, *Voyage en Perse, Texte*, p. 13, and the allusions to the Doric order.

[3] Dieulafoy, *L'Art Antique de la Perse*, pt. 5, pp. 7, 8, 207.

[4] The distance is given by Masson, *JRAS*. 12. 99 (after Webb) as twenty-two miles ; Curzon, *Persia*, 1. 57, says (approximately) twenty-three miles.

THE RUINED TEMPLE AT KANGAVAR
(Flandin's drawing of the northwest wall. The modern buildings to the left of the
picture have disappeared)

RUINS OF THE TEMPLE AT KANGAVAR
(Part of the southwestern wall with a modern building in the background)

base of the great mountain ridge whose steep and rugged heights make a formidable barrier to surmount before reaching the city of Hamadan. Asadabad is the regular halting-place for all caravans that go by this ancient route, and I believe that this not inconsiderable village represents, in location at least, the Bazigraban, or Custom House, mentioned by Isidorus in the passage already quoted. The etymology of the name *Bazi-grabān* (Gk. Bαζιγράβαν) immediately becomes clear when we restore the word to its probable form in Ancient Persian, **Bāji-grabanā*, 'tribute-taking, toll-collecting,' indicating the place where the customs dues were levied, somewhat like the Modern Persian *bāj-gāh*, 'toll place.'[1]

Asadabad, being situated in a plain at the base of the spurs of Mount Alvand and watered by the streams that descend from the great ridge, has a fertile soil and a temperate climate, and it was once a place of some renown. Yakut, writing seven hundred years ago, says that it was formerly the residence of the son of the Sasanian king Khosru Parviz (A.D. 590–628), although the monarch himself resided for the most part at Kangavar. The Arab geographer narrates an amusing legend, which he characterizes, however, as poetic fiction and a 'lie,' to the effect that 'Khosru's Kitchen' was located midway between Asadabad and Kangavar; and whenever the king dined, a long line of pages 'passed the dishes from hand to hand' over the entire distance. His son observed the same custom when living at Asadabad. The viands, Yakut says, must have been cold when they reached the king, even if borne on eagle's wings, but he adds that we are, perhaps, to understand that 'Khosru's Kitchen' (*matbakh*) was merely the place which served as headquarters from which the royal cuisine was stocked.[2]

My journey over the desolate pass from Asadabad was made

---

[1] Cf. also Spiegel, *Altpers. Keilinschriften*, 2d ed., p. 233. Cf. likewise OP. *Pati]grabanā*, Bh. **3**. 4.

[2] See Yakut, pp. 34, 536, whose description and comments are worth consulting.

on the following day, April 20, through fierce storms of sleet and snow that swept pitilessly from the north during most of the day; and it was not until after five o'clock in the afternoon that I again reached Hamadan, having taken twelve hours to accomplish a distance of less than thirty miles.

CHAPTER XVII

FROM HAMADAN TO THE RUINED FIRE-TEMPLE NEAR ISFAHAN

'Unto Fire, the son of the God Ormazd! Unto thee, O Fire, thou son of Ormazd, be grace, for thy worship, praise, propitiation, and glorification.'
— AVESTA, *Introduction*, 2.

AFTER remaining two nights at Hamadan upon the occasion of my second visit, I started late on the morning of the third day to continue my journey southward toward Isfahan, especially to visit the ruined fire-temple near that city. Weather and road alike were favorable, and we reached Nanaj at sunset, having travelled some thirty miles, which, owing to the late start, was less than my usual march, for I sometimes accomplished fifty miles, and occasionally even seventy. But I felt fatigued enough to be glad when my camp-bed was stretched for the night on the floor of the *chāpār-khānah*, after the servant of the post-house had swept the room a little more clean. There was much talk about bandits, as the post had been robbed on the previous night, but I paid little attention to the stories, fell asleep soon, and after a good night's rest was ready before daylight to mount Rakhsh and sit thirteen hours in the saddle.

Our cavalcade halted for the second night at the small village of Hassar, and we rose with the lark again next morning and proceeded along a well-watered plain that was fed by streams from the rocky hills on the right. The pace of our animals was good, and we easily overtook several caravans that had started an hour ahead of us, and all that day the conditions were favorable for rapid progress. It was Shakspere's birthday, a day memorable to me even in Persia, and the season of spring was well advanced, so that I had an opportunity to watch the progress made by the peasants as they tilled their farms, and to compare their way of working with the agricultural methods employed in Zoroaster's day, when the occupation of the husbandman was synonymous with a religious pursuit.[1]

The Avesta alludes to farms, fields, and husbandry; it praises the work of the laborer who tills the earth 'with his right arm and his left, with his left arm and his right,' and lauds the irrigation of arid land and the production and harvesting of crops. All kinds of work connected with the soil were equivalent to acts of 'righteousness,' and the agriculturist ranked next to the priest and the warrior in the constitution of the Zoroastrian community. Farming is not a lost industry in Persia to-day, but it has made little progress since the days of the Avesta, more than two thousand years ago.

The Persian farm is not fenced off, like ours, but has its boundaries marked by trenches and watercourses, which the Avesta describes as being 'the depth and breadth of a dog,'[2] or has its limits indicated by a row of trees, which it well repays the laborer to plant, because of the scarcity of wood for fuel and timber in many parts of Persia. The government to-day would do well to encourage arboriculture, as it apparently did in the time of Darius.[3]

The implements of the husbandman are still of the most primitive kind, and my notes regarding them will serve as a commentary upon a passage in the Avesta which describes the equipment of the peasant.[4] The first to be mentioned is the plow (Avestan *aēsha*, Mod. Pers. *khīsh*) which I have already described as a rude affair,[5] consisting generally of the crotch of a tree cut so that one of the branches may serve as a plowshare

[1] See Vd. **3**. 23–33.
[2] Vd. **14**. 12–14.
[3] For general references see Darmesteter, *Le ZA.* 2. 32; Jackson, *JAOS.* 21. 183; and Geiger, *Ostirā-*

nische Kultur, pp. 373–387, Erlangen, 1882.
[4] See Vd. **14**. 10–11.
[5] See pp. 85–86, above.

PERSIAN SHOVELS

(Compare Avesta, Vd. 14. 11)

PLOWING WITH COWS

when shod with iron (cf. Av. *ayazhāna paiti-darezāna*).[1] Such a plow, as contrasted with the heavy plow for deep furrowing, to which several yokes of oxen are hitched,[2] is drawn only by two cows or heifers (cf. Av. *gavā azī*)[3] and only loosens the surface of the ground, as shown in my photograph, which gives an idea also of the kind of ox-goad (Av. *gavāza*) and yoke (Av. *yuyō-semi*) that are still in use in Persia.[4] Another stock article in the peasant's outfit, which has remained practically unchanged, I believe, since ancient times, if we may judge from an allusion in the Avesta, is the handmill. An essential part of this machine is the round hopper, or funnel, into which the grain is poured when about to be ground; and with this I would compare *zgeresnō-vaghdhana*, one of the obscure Avestan terms applied to the handmill.[5]

A third article used by the Avestan husbandman was the spade (Av. *kāstra*). The Persian spade has a long handle, to which is generally attached a wooden foot-rest to serve as a support for the foot when driving the spade into the ground, as shown in my photograph.[6] Instead of the wooden footpiece the upper part of the blade is sometimes bent over on either side so as to form a metal flange on which the foot can rest.[7] When digging, two or three laborers, either barefoot or wearing the Persian *gīvahs*, work side by side, striking the shovel into the earth at the same time and lifting it again at a given signal, working in unison as they cut the trench.

[1] This is at least a suggestion which I offer in explanation of the difficult Avestan words, Vd. **14**. 10.

[2] See the illustration in the chapter on Urumiah, above.

[3] Ys. **46**. 19; cf. Ys. **29**. 5, etc.

[4] For the technical terms in the Avesta, see Vd. **14**. 10. The photograph which I took was snapped between Hassar and Leilhahan, on the third day after leaving Hamadan. For illustrations and descriptions of plows and plowing, see Knanishu, *Persia and its People*, pp. 109–112, Rock Island, Illinois, 1899; Adams, *Persia*, pp. 153–155; and Ker Porter, *Travels*, 2. 533.

[5] So I explain Vd. **14**. 10, *asmana hāvana, yāvarᵊnᵊm zgᵊrᵊsnō-vaɣδanᵊm*; cf. also Knanishu, *Persia*, pp. 107–109. Query: cf. Nir. 94.

[6] This photograph I took between Hamadan and Asadabad.

[7] This I noted particularly at Kurd Balah, near Isfahan, and then more generally as I passed southward.

In tilling the fields an ordinary large rake and harrow are employed, and sometimes a flat scraper, with spikes around the lower edge and with handles above to guide it, is drawn over the field by oxen. A mallet is likewise employed to break up the clods after plowing. The hoe, as far as my observations served me, has cords attached to it, which are pulled by one of the workmen while another guides the implement.[1] The sickle which is used in cutting the grain at harvest time I shall describe in a later chapter. The manner of threshing it is as primitive as in early Bible times. The wheat or barley is commonly trodden under the feet of muzzled oxen or mules, who drag over it a sort of sled ; but sometimes it is crushed beneath a spiked roller or flailed with a peculiar flail, after which the chaff is separated from the wheat by the winnowing process when a good wind is blowing. The threshing-floor itself is usually situated on the outskirts of the village, and lumbering carts (*'arabah*) carry the grain to the barn of the peasant, or more often to the granary of the landlord.

Our halt on the night of the third day was at Leilhahan, a settlement of a thousand families, I should judge, the majority of them being Armenians. Here I was visited by a native preacher, Rev. Rabin Joseph, who was doing evangelistic work among the people of the place. He spoke English quite well, having acquired it at the Urumiah Mission, and was Europeanized to the extent of collecting souvenir post-cards from foreign countries, and he asked me to add one from America to his album, a request which I fulfilled before the year was past. He gave me useful information regarding my route for the following day, and advised me to take the longer road to Khomain because the shorter route was at the time infested by brigands, who had pillaged several caravans.

An early start next morning brought me before eight o'clock to Khomain, and I was directed to the house of the chief man of the place. His courtyard was filled with servants, though

---

[1] For illustrations, see Knanishu, *Persia*, p. 110 ; Adams, *Persia*, p. 154.

he himself had not risen, but he sent a message that he would be ready in a few minutes to receive me, which he did with a gracious welcome. In manners he was Eastern, but in costume more European than Persian, and the watch which he wore was carried so as to be appropriately conspicuous. His black wool hat was wholly Iranian in appearance, however, being a replica of the balloon-shaped head-covering worn in Sasanian days, and I noticed that this style of headgear was peculiarly characteristic of the people in this vicinity. He served tea as an act of hospitality and asked various questions, until it was time for me to take my leave, whereupon he sent two armed horsemen to accompany me over a part of the road, which was dangerous because of freebooters. The guards proved to be of little use beyond raising clouds of dust as they made their horses curvet in circles around our party and fired shots at imaginary robbers supposed to be lurking in the hills. By the time we crossed the last mountain pass I was glad to dispense with these attendants, and we descended without accompaniment into the great plain in which lies the town of Gulpaigan.

Gulpaigan is a town that was visited by the famous Italian traveller Pietro della Valle on his way to Isfahan three hundred years ago. He says that 'it resembles Hamadan, but is smaller,' and that its name is composed of the three words *gul*, *pāi*, and *gān* — which is merely a popular etymology.[1] As a matter of fact, the older name of Gulpaigan was *Garbādakān* in Persian, or *Jarbādakān* in the Arab geographers, and in still earlier times it is said to have been called *Samrah*, after a daughter of the Keianian queen Humai who is alleged to have founded it.[2]

[1] Pietro della Valle, *Viaggi*, 1. 449; *Travels*, ed. Pinkerton, 9. 21.

[2] See Yakut, p. 152, for the former statement, and compare Barbier de Meynard, *Dict. géog. de la Perse*, p. 152, note, for the latter. Yakut (p. 153) speaks of '*Jarapādakān*' (Gulpaigan) as 'a large and celebrated place.' For other allusions to the town see likewise Sadik Isfahani, *Geographical Works*, p. 86; Mokaddasi, ed. De Goeje, *Bibl. Geog. Arab.* 3. 257, 402 (mere mention); and Ibn Khordadhbah, ed. De Goeje, 6. 20, 155. Consult furthermore Tomaschek, *Zur histor. Topog. von Persien*, in *Sb. Akad. Wiss. zu Wien*, 102 (1883), pp. 168, 171.

Two roads approach it from this direction across the wide plain. Since we had no guide to direct our choice I selected the one to the right, which was longer, but had the advantage of conducting us through the entire length of the town, as it led to the lower end of the main street. We were thus able to see something of the town, which I judged to be a place of considerable activity. In the way of antiquities I noticed a number of large carved stones that looked as if they were ancient, and I observed several sculptured rams, with horns curved into a tight spiral, resembling the granite figures I had seen elsewhere in old Armenian settlements, especially in the burying-ground near Dilman.[1] From the impression which I received (an impression borne out also by the passages I have cited) I believe that Gulpaigan would be an interesting place in which to make archæological researches, although Ker Porter was against attributing any great antiquity to the town.[2]

I did not halt to make inquiries regarding ancient relics, for it was nearly three in the afternoon and I was anxious to reach the next station, so I proceeded at once to the principal caravansarai, which I found so crowded that many of the muleteers were obliged to lie on the ground by the side of their beasts of burden, for lack of other quarters. After an hour's stay we started once more, allowing sufficient time for making our second station before nightfall.

Our route lay through a lonely plain girt on either side by barren hills which sometimes thrust their spurs almost across the track. Near the base of one of these jutting promontories the worthless guide whom I had hired at Gulpaigan to show us the way, fell into a violent altercation with the leader of my caravan and drew his carbine to shoot him. There was an uproar at once. Quickly wheeling my horse about, I struck at the good-for-nothing rascal, diverted his aim, and separated the angry combatants. I did not wait to argue the respective

---

[1] See p. 79, above, and compare Ker Porter, *Travels*, 2. 614 (illustration).

[2] Ker Porter, *Travels*, 2. 67–68.

merits of the claimants in the case, but immediately dismissed the fellow, with a threat to have him punished by the governor of the district if I saw his face again, and restored order once more in the excited caravan. We had no further trouble, but had to trust to luck in finding our way. This was not difficult, however, and we reached our destination before dark.

Our halt for the night was at Banishun, or Wanishun, called ' Oniscion ' by Pietro della Valle.[1] This garden spot gave us a foretaste of the still greater attractions of Khonsar, where we arrived on the following morning. Khonsar left on my mind the impression of terraced hills, abundant streams, green foliage, and blossoming fruit trees. The town is picturesquely situated in a long and narrow gorge between high hills and through this passage it winds its way for five or six miles, now at the base of the mountains and now climbing over their spurs. It is a settlement of some twelve thousand inhabitants and is believed to date back to the time of Alexander, who is thought to have marched through it on his way to Ecbatana.[2] In Persian the name is written as *Khuānsār*, and Yakut says that the town had the reputation of being the birthplace of several minor poets.[3] In addition to its romantic site and historic associations Khonsar is a place that does a thriving business in cotton goods, so that its taxes, combined with those of Gulpaigan, with which it forms a single district for administrative purposes, yield a considerable revenue to the government.[4] I could have wished that the town had a municipal ordinance to prevent butchering sheep in the public streets.

Directly after we left Khonsar and entered the mountain passes of the Ashnar Kuh we encountered one of those sudden changes of weather which are characteristic of Persia, for we had to struggle for two or three hours through snow, hail,

[1] Pietro della Valle, *Viaggi*, 1. 450; *Travels*, ed. Pinkerton, 9. 21.

[2] Ker Porter, *Travels*, 2. 70; Zolling, *Alexanders des Grossen Feldzug in Central-Asien*, p. 79, Leipzig, 1875.

[3] Yakut, p. 195; cf. Barbier de Meynard, *Dict. géog.* p. 195, note, and also Sadik Isfahani, p. 94 ; Tomaschek, *op. cit.* p. 170.

[4] See Curzon, *Persia*, 2. 480.

sleet, torrents of water, slush, and mud, which transferred us
from April 25 back into the heart of winter.   About four miles
this side of Dombanah I noticed the snow-covered outlines of a
rectangular structure which looked as if it might have been
one of those square-shaped dakhmahs, or Towers of Silence,
pictured in the old volume of travels by Olearius three centuries ago.[1]   I dismounted to examine the general contour and
arrangement of the place, but the snow prevented me from
making a careful investigation.   There were many fragments
of bricks and, in the middle of the enclosure, a depression which
might have corresponded to the central pit, or grave, generally
found in a dakhmah, but the ruin seemed to be too remote
from any present settlement to have been an ancient ground
for disposing of the dead.   I am not unmindful, however, that
in early times the entire region was occupied by Zoroastrians
and that I was not many stages distant from the famous fire-
temple near Isfahan, the ruined sanctuary which was my goal.
Halting only for a night at Kurd Balah, and another at
Hajiabad, I arrived early in the forenoon of the following day
within sight of this ancient shrine of the Fire-Worshippers,
which is commonly known as the *Ātash Kadah* or *Ātash Gāh*
near Isfahan.

The sky had all the peculiar clearness which belongs to a
true April morning in Persia, and a soft light quivered over
the plain beyond Najafabad.   The animals of my caravan
moved slowly along the well-worn trail; Shahbas, the muleteer,
was asleep in the saddle ; but my own eyes were busy watching to catch the first glimpse of the *Ātash Gāh*, or *Kuh-i Ātash
Kadah*, ' Hill of the Fire-Temple.'   Far in the distance over
the level horizon there arose unexpectedly before my view a
lake bordered with delicate green cypress trees, and I fancied
that the beautiful spot must be one of those Persian parks,
or ' paradises,' which were so enchanting in ancient Iran.
Instinctively I quickened my horse's pace ; but suddenly the

[1] Olearius (1600–1671), *Persianische Reise-beschreibung*, p. 296, Hamburg, 1696.

picture vanished. I then became aware that I had been deceived by a mirage. This was the first of many experiences with that magic phenomenon which transforms rocks into ruined castles, bushes into troops of horsemen, puddles into sheets of clear water, and molehills into mountains. So vivid was this first impression that it took me some time to recover from the surprise, and I felt almost inclined to question my eyes when I actually caught sight of the ruined fire-temple.

The deserted shrine stands on the top of a hill which rises about seven hundred feet sharply above the plain at a distance of three or four miles from Isfahan. The ascent is by a winding path which starts from the southeastern slope of the elevation and proceeds by a series of natural steps formed by ledges of the unhewn rock. Fragments of bricks and pottery of a yellowish clay strewed the rough pathway, and a few of these which I found were decorated by ornamental raised lines.

The ruined sanctuary stands on the very crest and is about fourteen feet high and fifteen feet in diameter, octagonal in form, and constructed of large unburnt bricks. The roof was originally a dome, but most of this vaulted covering has fallen. As shown in the accompanying photograph, which I took from the western side, eight doorways look out toward the different points of the compass.[1] The brick and stucco columns which form the sides of the doorways and support the roof are so arranged that they give a pillared effect to the temple. There was no artificial foundation beneath the structure ; the building was erected directly upon the natural rock, part of which thrusts itself into the middle of the floor.

On entering the crumbling fane I noticed over each doorway a sunken niche, the lines of which curved symmetrically to a point in such a manner as to give an arched finish to each entrance on the inside. Traces of a brownish plaster or stucco

---

[1] The dimensions of the shrine are nearly as follows: height, 14 ft. (4.00 m.) ; diameter, 15 ft. (4.50 m.) ; height of doorways, 7 ft. 3 in. (2.20 m.) ; width of doorways, 3 ft. 7 in. (1.10 m.).

were preserved in these panels, and portions of the dome and walls which were above ordinary reach were still intact. Imagination alone could restore the original finish of the walls, whether a layer of tiles, a wainscoting of marble, or panels of stone around the columns. There was not a trace of an inscription, tablet, or sculpture anywhere to be seen, except modern Persian names written by those who had scrambled up to scrawl their signatures in its niches. The Oriental does not differ much from some of his cousins in the West in the reprehensible fondness for inscribing his name in conspicuous places. The floor of the sanctuary was 13 feet 8 inches in diameter (4.16 m.); it was nearly circular in shape, and in the centre there was the curved outline of what was probably a mortar base on which the fire-altar rested. Beneath the débris I found ashes; who knows whether some of them may not have kindled the fire of the Magi?

In addition to the shrine, the summit of the hill is capped by the remains of a series of buildings which are gathered about the fane itself, but stand a little below it, and occupy the southeastern, eastern, and northeastern sides of the hill-crest. These form together a part of the general temple precinct, having probably served as an abode for the priests, a sanctum for the fire, and perhaps also as a temple treasury. The design and arrangement reminded me of the ruined sanctuary of fire which I noticed near Abarkuh on my journey to Yezd.

To examine the crumbling chambers I had to descend a few paces from the sacred building which I had been inspecting. Some walls of a ruined edifice on the southeastern side of the summit first attracted my attention. They were the remnants of a succession of halls and rooms built of clay and brick according to a definite plan of construction, but they were all in a hopeless state of dilapidation. I turned from these to the northeastern side of the crest. Here I found a still more elaborate structure, but even in a worse state of ruin than the preceding. One room, about twenty feet square, was still in a

PART OF THE TEMPLE-PRECINCT ADJOINING THE SHRINE OF FIRE

THE ANCIENT FIRE-TEMPLE NEAR ISFAHAN

sufficient state of preservation to allow me to make out its general outlines, but it was filled halfway up the sides with dirt and rubbish. The walls were made of clay and bricks covered over with plaster, and two of the side walls, which had no doorway or window, were marked by blind arches indicated by columns of unburnt brick and capped by burnt bricks set in the manner here shown, to lend a decorative effect.

There were also niches in the wall, resembling the familiar *ṭākchahs* seen in modern Persian houses. The other two sides of the room, as shown in my photograph, had archways looking out over the plain, and the view from these, comprising the silver thread of the Zendah Rud River and a rich succession of gardens about Isfahan, was a contrast to the ruin and decay which reigned within the walls. Besides the chamber which I have been describing, there was still another ruined apartment, the stuccoed walls and outlines of which could be seen ; but it was smaller than the one I have just mentioned and had nothing particular about it to require special notice.

After I had inspected the ruins I made some observations with regard to the general contour of the hill. The sides drop with a fairly steep declivity, except at one particular point, and there a defensive wall guards the approach to the shrine. No one knows how often it may have been of service in ages past. As I descended from the hill I noticed several arched recesses on the side of the crest. They looked like cells and were partly constructed of large sun-dried bricks, like those at Rei. Some of these recesses were small, others fairly large. One of them, which showed careful construction, was about twelve feet deep, three feet wide, and less than four feet high. I have no opinion to express regarding the original purpose of these cells. They were in too exposed a position to allow one to conjecture that they may have been used as places of deposit for the temple treasure, and it would be hazardous to surmise that they were intended to be hermit cells, or that they were employed as shrines for consecrated lamps, or as repositories in which the wood for the sacred fire was prepared.

This is but one of a number of interesting problems connected with the fire-temple and its history. For the very reason that the subject has been little dealt with, I have gone into more detail in describing the appearance of the ruined shrine, and I shall continue this by giving such an account of its historic past as I am able to present. I have not been able to find anything on the subject in five of the earliest European travellers : Josafa Barbaro, Pietro della Valle, Herbert, Olearius, and Mandelslo. So far as I can see, Tavernier, in the seventeenth century, is the first Occidental to mention it. I shall give his statement and those of his successors, and after that I shall cite three or four Oriental authorities, which are centuries older than the early French traveller and will give considerable help toward identifying the temple historically.

Tavernier, who made several journeys to Persia between the years 1638 and 1663, alludes incidentally to the ruins in question as a 'fortress,' but he does not associate them with the ancient religion of Persia. His statement is this : —

'Upon the south (southwest?), about two leagues from Isfahan, lies a very high mountain, on the top whereof toward the west are to be seen the remains of a very strong fortress, where Darius kept himself when Alexander gave battle to him in that plain. In the side of the rock is a grotto, either natural or artificial or both, out of which issues a natural spring of excellent water, where a *Dervis* usually inhabits.' [1]

Daulier-Deslandes (1665) merely mentions the mountain in connection with Gabarabad, the Gabar suburb of Isfahan.[2]

Chardin (1666, 1677) confines his remarks to a few words about 'le Bourg des Guebres' when he is describing the section known as the Gabar settlement near Isfahan, which was cleared

---

[1] Tavernier, *Travels*, p. 149, London, 1684.

[2] Daulier-Deslandes, *Les Beautez de* *la Perse*, p. 51 (cited from Hyde, *Historia Religionis Veterum Persarum*, p. 359).

by Shah Abbas in order to make room for a part of the royal residence in the environs.[1]

Bell (1715) repeats the story which speaks of Darius and Alexander. The Englishman's statement reads as follows: 'About three or four miles to the southward of the city are to be seen the ruins of a tower on the top of a mountain, where it is said Darius sat when Alexander the Great fought the second battle with the Persians.'[2]

Ker Porter (1821) devotes a paragraph to the description of the hill and concludes his observations with these words : 'But as this *Attush Kou* is an artificial mount and stands close to the quarter of the city where the Guebres, and particularly those who followed the arms of Mahmoud, dwelt, no doubt they reseated themselves in a spot that had been inhabited by their ancestors from the first peopling of the banks of the Zeinderood ; and they found it thus marked by the High Place of their worship.'[3] Ker Porter's last statement is right in so far as he emphasizes the antiquity of the place ; but he is wrong in calling the mount 'artificial,' as an examination of the living rock which composes it would have shown him.

Sir William Ouseley (1823) has a mere mention of the hill: 'In the view [from Julfa] is seen, above the bridge, a mountain distant five or six miles, on which are some remains of an edifice not very ancient but occupying, as tradition states, the site of a ruined Fire-Temple. Hence the mountain has been denominated *Kûh átesh Kadah* or *áteshgáh.*'[4]

Ussher (1865) gives a brief description of the mount and alludes to the large size of the bricks seen in the ruins; he adds that the fire-temple was 'erected, it is said, by Ardeshir, or Artaxerxes.'[5]

Lord Curzon (1892) has but a couple of sentences on the

---

[1] See Chardin, *Voyages*, 2. 105, Amsterdam, 1735. Compare also Curzon, *Persia*, 2. 47.

[2] Bell, *Travels in Asia*, ed. Pinkerton, 7. 308, London, 1811.

[3] Ker Porter, *Travels*, 1. 437.

[4] Ouseley, *Travels*, 3. 49, and pls. lvi, c, London, 1823.

[5] Ussher, *Journey from London to Persepolis*, p. 595, London, 1865.

subject of this 'isolated rocky hill, the summit of which is crowned by some ruins of mud-brick.   This is called the Atash Gah, from a tradition that a fire-altar was here erected by Ardeshir (Artaxerxes) Longimanus.   The tradition may be true, but the present ruins are not old.'[1]

To these meagre statements I am now in a position to add more material which will throw fresh light on the subject and carry the history of the fire-temple more than a thousand years back of the present.   This material is to be found in the Arab geographers of the ninth and tenth centuries, who call this pyræum the fire-temple of *Mārabīn*, or *Māras* (according as we are to read the name and its variants),[2] the name of a village or district in the vicinity of Isfahan.

The first of these Oriental witnesses is Ibn Khordadhbah (A.D. 816) whom I have already quoted on several other occasions.   In describing the district of Isfahan he mentions 'the village of Marabin (v.l. Maras) in which there is a citadel built by Tahmurath, and in it a temple of fire.'[3]   This statement shows that even in Ibn Khordadhbah's time the temple was regarded as very ancient.

The second author is the well-known writer Masudi, who died in the year 957.   In his *Meadows of Gold*, written in 943–944, Masudi refers to the fire-temple near Isfahan as the second of seven sanctuaries, which were originally idol-temples devoted to the worship of the sun, moon, and the five principal stars.   His statement is as follows : 'The second of these

---

[1] Curzon, *Persia*, 2. 58.

[2] The reading of مارس in an un-pointed text will easily account for these differences in spelling, the forms *Māras*, *Māraš*, being in fact the variant, and *Mārabīn* the more original. It is true that Ptolemy, *Geog.* 6. 4. 4, mentions a place, Μαρράσιον, near Aspadana (*i.e.* Isfahan), but we cannot be sure that this was the ancient Maras, cf. Tomaschek, *Zur historischen Topographie von Persien*, p. 171.

[3] Ibn Khordadhbah, ed. De Goeje, *Bibl. Geog. Arab.* 6. 20, transl. p. 16. In the same manner Hamadhani (ed. De Goeje, 5. 265) says, 'When Tahmurath reigned he built the villages of Mārabīn (v. l. Māras) and Ruvandast in the district of Isfahan'; and again (5. 263) he associates 'Jei (*i.e.* Julfa) and Marabin.'

temples is situated on the summit of a mountain called *Māras* (*Mārabīn*), near Isfahan. There were idols in this until they were removed by King Yustasf (*i.e.* Vishtaspa, the patron of Zoroaster) when he adopted the religion of the Magi and converted the shrine into a temple of fire. It is three *farsakhs* from Isfahan and is still held in great veneration by the Magi.' [1]

This important statement by Masudi proves conclusively that the temple was not in ruins in the early part of the tenth century of our era, and that tradition (like the previous allusion to Tahmurath) ascribed to it an antiquity even prior to Zoroaster's day, since it is said to have existed as a shrine of idols before Vishtaspa converted it into a fire-temple. I feel positive that the present ruins go back at least to Sasanian times, and there may be reasons for assigning them to a still earlier period. The site was certainly an ancient one, as is shown by the statements of both the Oriental authorities whom I have quoted, and there may be grounds for laying more stress on the tradition, cited above, which connects the temple with the name of Ardashir Dirazdast, known to us through the classics as the Achæmenian king Artaxerxes Longimanus. This monarch reigned B.C. 465–425, a century and a half after the date assigned by tradition to Vishtaspa, and it is said in the Bahman Yasht that he made the religion of Zoroaster current in the whole world.[2]

In corroboration of such a suggestion regarding Bahman's connection with this particular fire-temple I may cite the authority of a third Oriental writer, Ibn Rostah (about A.D. 950) who says: 'Marabin borders upon the town of Jei. It was one of the pleasure-grounds of the early Khosrus. Kei

[1] For the original text of Masudi and a French translation, see *Les Prairies d'Or*, ed. Barbier de Meynard, 4. 47, Paris, 1865. I may add that Muhammad Hasan Burhan (1651), in his Persian dictionary *Burhān Kāta'*, repeats practically the same statement as that which I have quoted, see Vullers, *Lexicon Persico-Latinum*, s. v. *Māraš*.

[2] BYt. **2.** 17 ; see my *Zoroaster*, p. 160.

Kaus is said to have resided there and to have beautified the place. At his command a lofty and magnificent citadel was erected on the mountain peak there. It towered aloft so as to overlook the valley of the Zendah Rud ; [1] and from its summit there was a commanding view of the entire country. But King Bahman, son of Isfendiar (*i.e.* Vohuman Ardashir Dirazdast),[2] took possession of it and burned it ; and he built below it a stronghold and established in it a shrine of fire which stands till this day, and even the fire remains in it.'[3]

A similar tradition connecting the temple with the name of Ardashir Bahman Dirazdast (Artaxerxes Longimanus) is preserved in the annals written by Hamzah of Isfahan (A.D. eleventh century), who, as a native, was well acquainted with the traditions of Isfahan. He writes as follows regarding Ardashir Bahman : ' He founded in one day three fire-temples in the Province of Isfahan. The first was in the east, the second in the west, and the third in the middle. The first of these is situated near the citadel of Marin (*i.e. Mār*[*ab*]*īn*, or *Māras*) and is the Fire of Shahr Ardashir, the word *Shahr* signifying district, and *Ardashīr* being a name of Bahman; the second is the Fire of Zervan Ardashir, located in the territory of Darak called Barkah ; and the third is the Fire of Mihr Ardashir, located in the territory of Ardistan of the same name.' [4]

One other Oriental passage is to be mentioned. It is found in a Persian history of Isfahan based on an Arabic original composed in the year A.D. 1030 by Mufaddal b. Seid b. Al-Husein Al-Mafarrukhi and entitled *Risālatu Maḥāsini Iṣfahān*. But it must be noticed that this source attributes the temple

---

[1] The text has *Zarrīnrūdh.*

[2] See my *Zoroaster*, pp. 157–163.

[3] Ibn Rostah, ed. De Goeje, *Bibl. Geog. Arab.* 7. 152–153.

[4] See Hamzah of Isfahan, *Annalium Libri X*, ed. Gollwaldt, 2. p. 27, Leipzig, 1848. For the names *Darak* and *Barkah* compare Yakut, pp. 99, 222. Yakut (p. 509) has a brief mention only of a place which he calls *Mār-bānān*, situated ' one half farsakh ' from Isfahan, but he makes no mention of the fire-temple.

rather to Sasanian times, assigning it to the reign of Piruz, son of Yazdagard (A.D. 459–484), and ascribing its erection to Adhar-Shapur, the head man of the village of Muristan in the district of Marabin.[1]

Whether we ultimately decide to assign the origin of the temple to Achæmenian times or to assign the present ruins to Sasanian times, something has been added to our knowledge of the shrine and its site by carrying its history back for at least fifteen centuries. It is sufficient for the present to know that the sacred fire burned for ages upon its altar and we may leave it to the future to decide to which particular Zoroastrian divinity the temple may have been dedicated.

[1] For this reference, see the article by Browne, *A Rare Manuscript History of Isfahan*, in *JRAS.* 1901, pp. 417–418.

CHAPTER XVIII

ISFAHAN, THE FORMER CAPITAL

'Following on o͏ͬ io͏ͬney we came to a towne called SPAHAM, which hath been a notable town till of late.'
— JOSAFA BARBARO (1474), *Travels in Persia*, p. 71.

GARDENS, palaces and pavilions, mosques and madrasahs, bazaars, splendid bridges, and above all a magnificent Royal Square — these are the impressions which the traveller carries away from Isfahan, and so vivid are they that time dulls them but slowly. The city has a special claim to attention, as it was ranked as the metropolis of Persia from the sixteenth to the eighteenth century, before Teheran usurped its place as capital of the Shah's dominion. Isfahan, nevertheless, retains its traditional title *Niṣf-i Jahān*, 'Half the World,' even though the rest of the world to-day may know it only as a centre of trade in rugs, or possibly as the scene of the Persian novel, *Hajji Baba of Isfahan*.

The city lies in a level tract of country which extends around it for miles. Entrance to the town is made through a maze of walled vineyards and orchards, whose variety of color resembles a Persian carpet. Mosques pierce the sky-line with their slender minarets, or rival the blue of heaven with their turquoise domes; poplars and plane trees lend grace and color to the scene; and distant hills form a serrated background for the picture. A peculiar feature of the landscape is the large number of pigeon-towers which line the sides of the road and dot the plain beyond. These turreted columbaries, which are built of clay and brick and look like windmills that have lost their arms and sails, provide shelter for myriads of pigeons and

262

FLANDIN'S SKETCH OF THE HILL OF THE ISFAHAN FIRE-TEMPLE, WITH A
PIGEON-TOWER IN THE FOREGROUND

ISFAHAN AND THE BRIDGE OF ALI VERDI KHAN

form a lucrative source of revenue to those who sell the droppings of the birds to be used as a fertilizer on the neighboring fields.

In some respects Isfahan offers to the traveller who is attracted by the modern phases of Persia more objects of interest than any city of Iran. It may be true that the city has lost much of the splendor that distinguished it three hundred years ago as the capital of Shah Abbas the Great, whose lavish hospitality to the foreigners that visited his court is described by the early European travellers, Tavernier, Chardin, Sanson, Fryer, and Kaempfer. It is equally true that the city never fully recovered from the blow that it suffered in the eighteenth century from the Afghan invasion, which lost for it its prestige as capital and resulted in the transfer of the imperial seat to Teheran. Nevertheless, enough of the old lustre remains (even though the effect is sometimes produced by tinsel) to make Isfahan a Persian Delhi and a worthy rival to its modern successor on the Caspian littoral. I cannot quite agree, therefore, with some of the recent writers in their tendency to bemoan the decadence of Isfahan and lament over its vanished glory. I acknowledge that it has been dimmed, but I should be far from accepting that pessimistic view which would interpret the title *Zil as-Sultān,* 'Shadow of the Sultan,' held by its governor, a brother of the Shah, as symbolizing the shade into which Isfahan has been thrown by Teheran. From what I could learn about the vigorous possessor of this umbrageous attribute, I should judge that he and the city resemble each other in being very substantial shadows and important factors in Persian affairs. The general condition of the people, the evidences of commercial activity, and the apparent signs of a growing trade, seemed to me to be indications of promise again for the future.

I have called Isfahan a modern city; it is so in its present form, for it owes its surviving traces of beauty to Shah Abbas I, the contemporary of Queen Elizabeth, and to his successors in the seventeenth century. Historically, however, Ispahan, or Isfahan, as the natives more generally call it, can lay claim to great antiquity. The Greek geographer Ptolemy, in the second century after Christ, mentions it as *Aspadāna*, which would be the equivalent of an Old Persian word signifying 'having horses as a gift.'[1] The Pahlavi texts designate the city as *Spahān*, in one case mentioning it in a comment on an Avesta passage,[2] in another stating that the original governor was Sparnak, who was apparently a brother of the hero Rustam,[3] and in still another adding that Rustam and King Kaus defeated Afrasiab, the great enemy of Iran, in a battle near the borders of Isfahan.[4]

The most ancient section of the city (corresponding in part to the modern suburb Julfa) was called *Jei* by the Arabs, a name which answers to the Pahlavi *Gaī* and the classical *Gabae*, and is associated in some way with the name of Kavi the blacksmith, of legendary fame in Iran.[5] Tradition makes him a native of Isfahan and tells how he headed a rebellion against the tyrant Zohak, or Azhi Dahaka, of Babylon. Zohak is represented as a monster from whose shoulder grew two serpents that had to be fed each day with the brains of children. When the tyrant caused Kavi's two sons to be killed for this purpose, the blacksmith raised an insurrection, hoisted his leather apron upon a spear as a standard, marched with the hero Feridun to Babylon, and overthrew and slew the

[1] Ptolemy, *Geographia*, 6. 4. 4 ('Ασ-πάδανα).

[2] Phl. Vd. 2. 23 (52) *čigūn Spāhān*.

[3] See Bd. 31. 10, tr. West. *SBE*. 5. 140 ; and regarding the uncertain reading of the governor's name as 'Sparnak,' see Justi, *Iranisches Namenbuch*, p. 307 b.

[4] See Great Iranian Bundahishn, 41. 7, tr. Darmesteter, *Le ZA*. 2. 402 ; cf. also West, *Grundr. iran. Philol.* 2. 102. Another incidental allusion to the city is found in Shikand-

Gumanik Vijar, **2**. 2 (West, *SBE*. 24. 123, ed. Hoshangji and West, pp. 11, 188).

[5] For the names, cf. Shatroiha-i Airan, 53 (Gaī or Gaē), Strabo, *Geog.* 728 (ed. Meineke, 1015. 2), and Ptolemy, *Geog.* 6. 4. 7 (Γάβαι). See also Marquart, *Ērānšahr*, p. 29. The hero is called 'Gavah of Ispahan' in the Persian Sad Dar, **63**. 5 (cf. West, *SBE*. 24. 323). On Jei-Julfa, see also Justi, *Grundr. iran. Philol.* 2. 485, with references.

monster. The leather apron mounted upon a spear became the national ensign of Iran, and the keeping of this treasured emblem was entrusted to Isfahan and remained its cherished privilege for ages.[1]

Another quarter of Isfahan in early times was called *Yahū-diah*, ' Jewry,' having received its name, according to Persian tradition, from a colony of Jews who came to Isfahan as exiles from Jerusalem in the reign of Nebuchadnezzar.[2] The Sasanian king Yazdagard I had as his queen a Jewish princess of Gae, or Isfahan, descended from these exiles,[3] and there is still quite an extensive settlement of Persian Jews, numbering some five thousand, in Isfahan.

The history of Isfahan from the time of the Mohammedan invasion differed little from that of other Persian cities which were conquered successively by Mahmud of Ghazni, Jenghiz Khan, and Tamerlane, down to the end of the sixteenth century, when Shah Abbas lifted the town to the rank of capital of the empire, a dignity which it had already enjoyed, though only over a limited province. Its central position is such as to qualify it well for a metropolis, even if Teheran has now an advantage in being more accessible to Europe, and it is certain that during the two centuries of its ascendancy Isfahan merited the renown for beauty to which the great Shah Abbas believed his capital was entitled.[4]

The topography of Isfahan is easy to grasp, if we bear in mind that the city lies on the north side of the Zendah Rud, and that Julfa, its Armenian suburb, lies on the south side of

---

[1] See Yakut, p. 43.

[2] Al-Hamadhani, ed. De Goeje, *Bibl. Geog. Arab.* 5. 261-262, and Yakut, p. 613. On Nebuchadnezzar cf. also Gray, *Kai Lohrasp and Nebuchadrezzar*, in *WZKM.* 18. 291-298.

[3] See Shatroiha-i Airan, 53 (ed. Modi, pp. 111-113), and compare Darmesteter, *Textes Pehlvis relativs au Judaisme*, 2. 41, in *Rev. Études*

Juives, 19. 41; idem, *La Reine Shasyān Dōkht*, in *Actes du Huitième Congrès International des Orientalistes*, sec. 2. 193-198, Leiden, 1892.

[4] For additional material in a rare Persian manuscript relating to Isfahan and its history, see Browne, *JRAS.* 1901, pp. 411-446, 661-704. Cf. also Houtum-Schindler, *Eastern Persian Irak*, pp. 119-129, London, 1897.

the river and is connected with the main part of the town by
several fine bridges.

The heart of the city, and central point of interest, is the
magnificent *Meidān-i Shāh*, 'Imperial Square,' which is mentioned even in the Shah Namah [1] and is one of the most imposing plazas I have ever seen.   Its length from north to south is
more than a quarter of a mile, and its breadth from east to
west is nearly an eighth of a mile.   It is as level as a parade-
ground, and as we canter over its smooth surface we are reminded of the days, three hundred years ago, when the rulers
of the capital used to have exhibitions of the traditional horse-
manship of the Persians given here.   A prize, sometimes a
golden goblet, was set on the top of a pole in the midst of the
vast arena and shot at as the marksmen galloped by ; or sides
were taken by the princes and nobles in the ancient game of
polo, *gui u chugān*, and a large marble goal-post is still
standing at each end of the Meidan to mark the terminus
toward which they drove the ball that, in the words of Omar
Khayyam,

> ' no question makes of Ayes and Noes,
> But Here and There as strikes the Player goes.

But polo is no longer played here ; only occasional parades and
processions are held, and the caravans wend their slow way
across it to unload their burdens in the bazaars.

The four sides of the Meidan are bordered by low-galleried
buildings, the uniform outline of whose roofs is broken at various points by stately edifices that have real architectural merit.
These I shall describe only briefly, for it would be impossible
for me to add anything to the many excellent and full descriptions which have been given from the days of Tavernier and
Chardin to Curzon and Browne.[2]

---

[1] See Firdausi, *Shāh Nāmah*, ed.
Vullers-Landauer,   2. 746, and tr.
Mohl, 2. 423.

[2] In general I should refer the

reader to Lord Curzon's admirable
account of Isfahan (*Persia*, 2. 18–59),
which summarizes all that is best in
the authorities that preceded him.

MASJID-I SHAH, THE KING'S MOSQUE

PALACE OF THE ZIL AS-SULTAN, PRINCE GOVERNOR OF ISFAHAN

On the north side, at a point leading into the bazaars, is the *Nakārah Khānah*, 'Music Hall,' 'Band Tower,' where, as at Urumiah and other places, a noisily beaten signal and a blast of horns accompanies the rising and setting of the sun.[1] Conspicuous on the east side of the plaza is the blue enamelled dome of the mosque of Sheikh Lutfullah, which dates back several centuries. On the southern side of the square, near the middle, is a grand arched portal leading to the handsome *Masjid-i Shāh*, 'Mosque of the King,' which stands somewhat back of it, to the southwest. This fine specimen of a Mohammedan sanctuary was founded in 1612 by Shah Abbas, but it is now unfortunately beginning to fall into decay. On the west of the great quadrangle, but nearer the southern end, rises the Royal Palace with its grand entrance Ali Kapi, a sort of 'Sublime Porte.' The Ali Kapi, with its open porch above, and columns noticeable in the picture, served formerly as an audience-hall in which the Safavid kings received ambassadors. It was used also as an asylum of refuge for fugitive debtors and manslayers. But its importance has long since vanished. The Royal Palace itself, which stands back of this entrance, is now occupied by the Zil as-Sultan, the Prince Governor of Isfahan. This princely residence covers a considerable area with its gardens, courts, and pavilions, one of which, the *Chahal Sitūn*, 'Hall of Forty Pillars,' was famous as the veranda and throne-room of Shah Abbas.

The bazaars in Isfahan lie behind the rows of buildings on the northern and eastern sides of the Meidan. It is possible to walk for two or three miles under their covered shade, or rather to push one's way through the crowded mass of camels, donkeys, packs, porters, buyers, sellers, and money-changers. The bazaars have all the characteristic features which I have already described as belonging to an Asiatic mart. Their trade has preserved for the city some at least of the prestige which once belonged to Isfahan as the emporium of Persia. Brocaded

[1] See p. 104, above.

cloths, felt goods, saddles, native weapons and armor, lacquered ware, articles of silver filigree-work, and objects made of metal are among the wares exposed for sale. I still can hear the deafening rattle and beat of the coppersmith's mallet and the brass-worker's hammer, busily engaged in the manufacture of useful culinary utensils and of vessels that were often artistic specimens of Persian metal-work.

To the west of the Meidan, and beyond the precincts of the Royal Palace, is the parklike section of the city with its grand avenue that leads to the river. In the extreme western portion of this quarter, and beginning at the grand promenade, is the section of gardens known as the *Hasht Bahisht*, ' Eight Paradises.' In the midst of this 'paradise' region there stands a pavilion built by Shah Suleiman, about 1670, and once a masterpiece of the creative art of the Safavid dynasty, but, like its surroundings, it has been allowed to run down, so that its beauty and sumptuousness are a thing of the past.[1]

The grand avenue itself is called the *Chahār Bāgh*, ' Four Gardens,' from the vineyards which Shah Abbas devoted to this purpose when he embellished his capital, and it is sometimes referred to as the ' Champs Élysées of Isfahan.' It is a long boulevard, nearly three quarters of a mile from end to end, and two hundred feet broad, laid out with watercourses and fountains through its centre and with promenades shaded by alleys of poplar and sycamore trees on each side. Little is left to tell the story of its former beauty ; neglect and decay are all too evident.

On the eastern side of this shaded avenue, between it and the Meidan as we ride toward the river, an impressive building attracts the attention. It is the Madrasah-i Shah Husein, an educational institution, built about the beginning of the eighteenth century by Shah Husein, whose name it bears, and designed as a college for the training of mullahs and dervishes.

[1] For a description of this ' Garden of Nightingales,' see Curzon, *Persia*, 2. 36–38 ; Brugsch, *Im Lande der Sonne*, pp. 317–319 (after Chardin).

MADRASAH OF SHAH HUSEIN, FROM THE CHAHAR BAGH

WITHIN THE COURT OF THE MADRASAH

The handsome portal, with its doors encrusted with brass and chased with silver, calls forth admiration, and its turquoise dome, girdled with arabesques in rich yellow, is as beautiful as it is graceful. But much of the exquisite tiling on the dome has dropped off, and some of the marble panels on the outer wall of the building itself have disappeared, while parts of the framework and lattice of the windows are broken. But within the walls of the Madrasah, in its arched cells, Mohammedan students continue to learn the Koran, or find leisure, in their recreation hours, to smoke their *kaliāns* around the shady tank in its courtyard.

At the end of the avenue of Chahar Bagh is a great bridge, which is one of the five that lead over the Zendah Rud to Julfa. This bridge is called Pul-i Ali Verdi Khan, after the name of the distinguished general of Shah Abbas, and it is one of the finest bridges of its kind in the world. It is about twelve yards broad and three hundred and eighty-eight yards long and it spans the river with a succession of thirty-four arches solidly built of brick and stone masonry. The design and construction of the bridge is such that it offers at least three viaducts for traffic at the same time. The main causeway is for mounted passengers and for the occasional vehicles that traverse it. The galleried arcades on each side of this are for the use of those on foot. A vaulted passage, in addition to these, pierces the stone arches on which the bridge is built and may be employed as an extra means of transit, if needed. All day long, till nightfall is signalled by the curfew horn of the Nakarah Khanah, this great bridge is thronged by an unceasing crowd, and the other bridges are almost equally frequented in the daytime.

It was toward evening when I first crossed the Zendah Rud and had a view of the picturesque surroundings. The sun sent long slanting rays across the river, whose water was then high from the melting snow and whose shimmering surface was stirred by the breeze into a thousand sparkling ripples. The shores of the river were decked in the rich verdure of spring, and the banks were spread with bright cloths which the dyers had laid out in the air to dry after their day's work, and these heightened the color-effect of the picture. In less than half an hour I reached Julfa, the Armenian suburb of Isfahan and residence of most of the Europeans, but once a sort of Persian Versailles, the royal pleasure-grounds of the Safavid kings.

Although Julfa occupies an older site, which possibly even corresponds in part to the ancient Gabæ and Jei, it is nevertheless, in its present form, hardly older than three centuries, and owes its name and Armenian population alike to the fortunes of war and the wisdom of Shah Abbas the Great. About the year 1603 that memorable monarch gained some successes in battle over the Turks on the northwestern frontier of his realm, whereupon, for political and other reasons, he transplanted several thousand families of Christian Armenians from Julfa on the Araxes, which I mentioned in the third chapter,[1] and settled them in a new Julfa on the outskirts of his capital. Here they flourished under his liberal treatment, but not so under his successors. The latter were less generous in their policy toward these colonists, whose number consequently decreased considerably and has continued to fall off down to the present time, when the settlement is estimated at not more than three thousand souls. They are still Christians, have a cathedral (built under the auspices of Shah Abbas), and one or two places of worship besides, and among them the Mission of the Church of England is doing earnest work.

I had with me letters of introduction to the Mission House, and I chanced to overtake my prospective host and hostess on the way to their home. They had returned only the day before from a fortnight's journey to Shiraz and were so sunburnt that I almost mistook them for Eurasians — an experience which I myself met with later in the journey, when my own face had

[1] Cf. pp. 22-23, above.

THE MEIDAN OF ISFAHAN
The Royal Mosque and the Porch of the Palace

PAVILION OF MIRRORS

become almost as dark as a Persian's from weeks of exposure under the tropical sun of Southern Iran. These English cousins received me hospitably at the Mission, and we soon felt like old friends. I had an opportunity to learn something about their evangelical labors and also about the philanthropic work in medical and surgical lines. The sick and suffering come sometimes from a distance of several hundred miles for treatment and relief; some, alas, come suffering from the effects of barbarous mutilations, inflicted as punishments, an instance of which I saw during my short stay in Isfahan.

I had almost forgotten the rumor I had heard on the road some days before, to the effect that the mail had been robbed. On reaching Isfahan, I was told that the presumable culprits had been captured, but I thought nothing more about the matter. Next morning, as my host and I were riding into town, we met a small company of excited people following a man who was seated upon a donkey and looked deathly pale. He held up his right arm, which was covered with a cloth, and from beneath this a purple stream of blood was flowing. We took little heed of the fact until, a short distance beyond, we met another, whose ashen pallor contrasted with the ruddy drops that trickled into the dust. He was on foot and alone. A hundred yards behind him followed a third man seated upon a small white donkey, which was stained with a similar crimson stream that poured from a rag-swathed arm. Some women followed behind him and were beating their breasts and tearing their cheeks with their nails. The men that marched behind the sufferer gesticulated and gave vent to imprecations. Seeing that we were foreigners, the bleeding man cried out in Persian, ' Masters, let the sword of your Government be sharpened to avenge the outrage of this unjust punishment! ' In an instant it dawned upon us that these were three of the men who had been convicted of the robbery. Their right hands had been cut off.

The manner in which the punishment is inflicted is as brutal as it is summary. The public swordsman, emboldened to his task by a dose of *hashīsh*, seizes the prisoner by the arm and with his scimitar slashes the hand from the wrist. No care is taken, as in a surgical operation, to draw back the skin before amputating the member, and no attention is paid to the offender after the hand is severed, except to thrust the bleeding stump of the arm into melted butter and let the victim go. The three men whom we had just passed were on their way to the surgeon of the Christian Mission for treatment. In each case he had first to saw off enough of the bone to allow the skin to cover the lopped-off member, before he could begin treatment for the injury.

This was not all of the incident. When we reached the Meidan, there was a crowd gathered. A fourth prisoner had been punished, but his sentence was death. In such cases the execution is swift, but inhuman. Steel hooks are thrust into the doomed man's nostrils and his head is quickly drawn back by these; a hasty gash then cuts the throat, and the bleeding victim is tossed upon the ground to go through the death-agony before the eyes of the gaping crowd. I was told that the sisters of the dead man were weeping over his lifeless body, but I turned away to be spared the sight. It is true that the majesty of the law had been upheld and justice administered by the sword, and that, too, in the public square near the doors of the very bank whose post these highwaymen had robbed. The road was now safe — *rāh ṣalāmat būd* — but what a way of making it safe!

Capital punishment of this kind may be a necessary measure in Persia, but its barbarousness is none the less revolting. Nor does it effectually eradicate crime, for it was not long after this incident that eight men were punished in a similar manner in the same public square. Four of these had their throats cut, two had their hands cut off, and the remaining two were hamstrung. One of these latter had previously suffered mutilation, some eighteen years before, by losing a hand. I did not hear whether eventually he died from being hamstrung, but this cruel punishment frequently results fatally. In much the same fashion, as I learned later, three bakers at Shiraz had their tongues cut out for selling their bread at too high a price. But, as my correspondent concluded, *Īrān hamīn ast* — 'Persia is always the same !'

While on the subject of Persian punishments, I may mention one of the death penalties, inflicted by torture, which is still in use. This is the method called 'gatching' (from *gach*, 'gypsum, mortar'). The malefactor is plastered up in gypsum, so as to form a pillar by the roadside, but with his face exposed to the public gaze, and there left to die. At the time when the late Shah was assassinated, five persons who had been accused of treacherous designs were thus put to death on the main road near Shiraz. At Taft near Yezd, moreover, I passed a place where a convict had thus been dealt with a month before; but, more mercifully for the victim, he was immured in the mortar with his head downward, so that his sufferings were less prolonged.[1] Instances of other barbarous methods of execution might easily be multiplied.

During my short stay in Isfahan I found time to inquire whether there were any Zoroastrians engaged in business there, as I thought this would be probable in so large a place. It seemed the more likely also because there once was a suburb of Isfahan called *Gabarabād*, 'Settlement of the Gabars,' to which the German traveller Olearius alluded, three centuries ago, giving a picture likewise of the Tower of Silence (*dakhmah*) in the vicinity.[2] Thus far on my journey through Persia I had not met with a single Zoroastrian, but had only heard of the one at Miandoab, who called himself a 'Babi,'[3] and had learned that there were two or three Gabars at Sultanabad, a town largely devoted to the weaving of Persian rugs, but I had not

---

[1] It is not improbable that some of the pyramids of human skulls left as monuments by Jenghiz Khan and Timur Lang may owe their origin to this ghastly practice.

[2] See Olearius, *Persianische Reisebeschreibung*, Hamburg, 1696, p. 293 ('Kebrabath'), p. 296 ('Dakhmah').

[3] See p. 119, above.

T

been able to visit them on my way to Isfahan.[1] This, therefore, was my first opportunity to see some of the Persian followers of the Prophet of Ancient Iran.

I found that, although there were some six of them doing business in the bazaar, only three resided regularly in Isfahan; the rest were Gabars from Yezd. I have designated them as *Gabars*, after the native fashion, but this term is derogatory, being equivalent to 'unbelievers,' and is never employed by the Zoroastrians themselves. They designate themselves as *Zardushtiān*, 'Zoroastrians,' sometimes as *Bah-Dīnān*, 'those of the Good Religion,'[2] or again *Fārsīs*, *i.e.* 'Parsis,' from Fars, or Pars, the old province of Persia Proper. As for the name 'Fire-Worshipper' (*Ātash-Parast*), the Zoroastrians in Persia as well as in India object to that title. They claim that they regard fire as a symbol or manifestation of Ormazd, as an emblem of purity and power, and not as a divinity. It would be equally logical, they urge (and I was prepared to hear this argument), for Christians to be called 'Cross-Worshippers' after the symbol of their faith.

Through the ever ready kindness of the English Director of the Imperial Bank at Isfahan, I obtained the address of the principal Gabar merchant, who bore the old Zoroastrian name Bahman Jamset, that is, Vohuman Jamshid, and I proceeded to call upon him at his shop, as he happened to be in the city at the time. He was a man over six feet in height, and large in proportion, and he was dressed in a snuff-colored garment peculiar to the Gabars. His face, which was smooth-shaven, except for the black mustache, was round and full, and his features showed a marked contrast to the Mohammedan physiognomy, in which an admixture of foreign blood is often noticeable. His appearance reminded me somewhat of the types in the Old Persian and Sasanian sculptures at Behistan

---

[1] See also my article, *The Modern Zoroastrians of Persia*, in *Homiletic Review*, 48. 14–19, New York, 1904.

[2] The name *Bah-Dīnān* is generally used by the Parsis in India to denote the laity in the Zoroastrian community.

and Tak-i Bostan, especially the rough bas-relief figures carved
on the boulder near the famous inscription of Darius, as I have
already described.[1] His manners were polite and dignified,
but I did not understand at the moment a certain reserve in his
demeanor, nor did I appreciate his almost concerned look when
I began to question him regarding the subject of religion. I
afterwards discovered the cause : there were a number of
Mohammedans present, and he hesitated to speak freely in
their presence about his faith. A meeting, however, was planned
for the next day, but I was then unfortunately prevented from
keeping the appointment, so he sent word forward to his
brother, Rustam Shah Jahan, at Shiraz, asking him to extend
hospitality to me in case I should call, and telling him about my
interest in Zoroastrianism and in its present followers.

At Isfahan there were a number of other matters which I
should have liked to investigate, for I felt interested in the
city in spite of the signs of decay and notwithstanding the fact
that the Isfahanis have always borne a reputation for untrust-
worthiness and superficiality, like the tinsel and veneer on some
of their buildings. I should likewise have been glad to have
an opportunity of learning more about the condition of the
people themselves, as contrasted with the past, but that may
well be left to others, better qualified than myself, to treat.
I neglected, moreover, to perform what would be regarded as
a ' Baedeker duty ' in European travel : this was to see the
Shaking Minarets of Abdallah's Shrine. These slender towers,
which rise from the roof of the tomb, oscillate back and forth,
describing an angle of several degrees, when simply pushed by
the hand. I felt privileged to forego this piece of sight-seeing
in order to hasten my departure again southward to visit the
historic sites of Pasargadæ and Persepolis.

I found that for this journey, and as far as Shiraz, I could
obtain the regular post-horses, as I was on the main route over
which the Persian mail is carried. I decided, therefore, to give

[1] See pp. 210–212, above.

up my caravan and allow Shahbas, who had been my *chārvādār*
and guide for a month, to return to Urumiah with his horses.
I was sorry to say good-by to Rakhsh, whom I had ridden so
long ; Safar parted also somewhat reluctantly with his mount,
which was known as the ' brown horse ' ; a farewell was taken
of the gray pack-horse who had carried his heavy load so well ;
and Shahbas made ready to ride his own stumbling jade,
accompanied by the others.   I then wrote a letter of recommendation for Shahbas, stating how he had served me on the
journey.   Owing to the broad smile which lighted up his
round face, as it had so often during the four weeks, I probably made the report somewhat more favorable than I might
otherwise have done.   I paid him in full for his month's work,
gave him a gratuity of from two to four *krans* (twenty to forty
cents) for each day that he had served me particularly well,
and added an extra *tōmān* (dollar) for every day that he
gained for me by reaching the several destinations earlier than
the time scheduled.   This concluded our regular business
transactions ; but I wished to have two of the pack-ropes
from the baggage because they had been used in drawing me
up the Behistan Rock.   Shahbas still had an eye to the main
chance, and he made me pay a stiff price for the ropes, but I
am glad now that I have them as a memento of the climb and
of the journey.

Having dismissed Shahbas, I completed my arrangements
with the head of the *chāpār-khānah* for my first relay of post-
horses ; but, as it was already late in the afternoon when we
started, we made only ten or twelve miles, covering the distance at a swift gallop, and spent the night at the hamlet of
Marg.   The second day was a record-breaker; we rode seventy-seven miles in the hours between 5.10 A.M. and 10.45 P.M.,
when we reached Yezdikhast, one of the most curiously situated places that can be imagined.   It is perched on top of a
rocky height that looks, as one approaches it, like some gigantic ship that has been turned to stone in the midst of a river-

bed that has been dry for ages.   Our third night was passed at
the walled village of Abadah, eleven farsakhs, or forty-two
miles, farther on ; and the fourth at the small settlement of
Deh-Bid, with poor quarters, but the convenience of a telegraph
office.   Finally, at noon on the fifth day, we reached Meshad-i
Murghab, the nearest halting-place to the Tomb of Cyrus and
the scenes of the past glory of the Achæmenians.

CHAPTER XIX

ANCIENT PASARGADÆ AND THE TOMB OF CYRUS THE GREAT

'The paths of glory lead but to the grave.'
— GRAY, *Elegy*, 36.

PASARGADÆ, the subject of this chapter, and Persepolis, the topic of the next, are sad themes, in a measure, for both are silent cities of a dead past, although each was in turn the capital of ancient Persia — Pasargadæ, the royal seat of Cyrus and Cambyses; Persepolis, that of Darius and his successors on the Achæmenian throne. Cyrus and Darius still remain in effigy of stone, and the vestiges of royal halls, untenanted for more than two thousand years, bear witness to the departed splendor of a period of grandeur ; but ruin reigns supreme, and even the tombs that housed the bodies of the dead kings have been crumbling for ages. Time's relentless touch has worn away the clear-cut features of these monuments and destroyed the beauty of their lineaments, yet they still endure to mark daily by their shadows the advance of centuries across the dial of eternity and to give tangible evidence of the ancient magnificence of the Persians, whose law, like that of the Medes, knew no change and whose sceptre once swayed the fortunes of the Eastern World.

The brilliant career of Cyrus, the founder of the Achæmenians, took Asia captive by its splendid triumphs, and his successes have thrown such a halo about his memory that it is sometimes difficult to view the events of his reign in their true light and separate facts from the legends gathered about his name. This is due in large measure to an early, and for the

278

THE TOMB OF CYRUS THE GREAT

THE PLATFORM OVERLOOKING PASARGADÆ

most part erroneous, identification of Cyrus with the shadowy figure of Kei Khosru — an identification which lingers still in the hearts of the Persian people. Whatever value we are to attach to the picturesque accounts of the youth of Cyrus as told by Herodotus, Xenophon, and other classical writers, his real elevation to power began with his defeating Astyages and then overthrowing the Median Kingdom, before the year B.C. 550.[1] This vanquisher of Media next conquered Crœsus and the realm of Lydia, subdued Ionia, Lycia, and Caria on the west, reduced a part of the Hindu Kush region in the east, and at last humbled the proud city of Babylon, thus rendering firm the foundations of his vast kingdom before death stayed his hand. He chose as the seat for his capital the spot where he had first gained his victory over the Medes. Here he built Pasargadæ, the royal city whose ruins still cover several miles,[2] and here he erected his tomb.

The location of the classic Pasargadæ is now acknowledged to have been on the Plain of Murghab, about six miles from a present small settlement called Meshad-i Murghab, which I reached on my fifth day from Isfahan and where I stayed over night on three different occasions. Pasargadæ is not visible from Meshad-i Murghab, as it lies beyond a low range of hills that encircle the plain around it. An hour's easy ride, crossing once or twice the intersecting channels of the Polvar, or ancient Medus, brought me to the foot of the ridge. The ascent was rough, but not at all difficult, and as the horses surmounted the rocky crest a sharp bend in the old caravan-road threw open to the view the historic Plain of Murghab in all its rich fertility, spreading its green expanse fully nine miles in one direction and fifteen in another, and surrounded on all sides by hilly barriers.[3] As a battlefield for the hosts of

---

[1] For details see my article *Cyrus the Great*, in *New Internat. Encyclop.* 5. 582–583.

[2] Strabo, *Geographia*, 15. 3. 8.

[3] For a topographical map of the vicinity, see Perrot and Chipiez, *Histoire de l'Art*, 5. 444.

Astyages and Cyrus it must have been superb, and I could imagine the women of Persia gathered on the hilltops to the south to watch in breathless anxiety the issue of the eventful fray.[1] And here in the plain I could see memorials of the victory still surviving in the granite remains of the capital which Cyrus had founded.

As the rider begins to descend from the northern ridge, the first object that catches the eye is a massive platform of stone, built on a terrace to the left of the way and overlooking the plain below. It is outlined in immense blocks of masonry and is believed to have been intended for the foundations of an audience-hall of Cyrus. If so, Mohammedan tradition has obliterated the historic truth by dubbing the structure *Takht-i Suleimān*, 'Solomon's Throne,' after the usual manner in which it has renamed most objects and places of Ancient Persian or Zoroastrian date. This solid piece of masonry is over two hundred feet long and fifty feet broad, and in many places the beautifully matched stone blocks of the facing are in perfect order and still show the mason's building-marks upon them, while in others they have been torn away in great rows, to furnish material for buildings in after ages. In every instance the great cramp-irons that secured the blocks have been gouged out, leaving holes that afford nesting-places for hundreds of pigeons and other birds.

Descending from the ridge, we come, in a few minutes' ride southward, to the first group of the ruins that are scattered over the plain.[2] They form the remains of a solid square building which must have been more than forty feet high, but only one of its shattered walls is standing. The natives conveniently call it 'Solomon's Prison' (*Zindān-i Suleimān*); Dieulafoy

---

[1] Compare the accounts of the battle given by Nicolaus Damascenus and Polyænus, cited by Gilmore, *Fragments of Ktesias*, pp. 115-128.

[2] For an outline map showing the position of the ruins, see Flandin and Coste, *Voyage en Perse, Ancienne*, 4. pl. 194 (reproduced in Perrot and Chipiez, *Histoire de l'Art*, 5. 596).

SCULPTURE OF CYRUS

A FIRE-TEMPLE OR A TOMB?

believes that it was the Tomb of Cambyses, the father of Cyrus ; Curzon agrees that it was a sepulchre, even if he does not go so far as to assign it definitely to the father of Cyrus. All scholars unite on one point, in comparing it with a similar edifice near the tombs of the kings at Naksh-i Rustam, and I believe that most of them are correct in supporting the view that the edifice was an Achæmenian shrine of fire, as I shall maintain in the next chapter.[1] But scarcely a stone of the only wall that survives is in its exact position to tell the story of the past. The present dilapidation of the building, the hard, cold whiteness of the stone, and the contrast which it showed to the soft green of April that freshly decked the plain, as it does ever anew, made a vivid impression upon me.

Several hundred yards farther southward is a solitary shaft, nearly twenty feet high and broken at the top. It is composed of three blocks, as shown by my photograph, and looks as if it might have formed part of a doorway. Near the summit of this column are carved in cuneiform script, in three languages, the simple but dignified words, 'I am Cyrus, the King, the Achæmenian — ADAM KURUSH KHSHĀYATHIYA HAKHĀMANISHIYA.' The same device is repeated on the angle-piers of a ruined edifice or court several hundred yards farther to the southeast, and it once decorated the top of a high round column within this enclosure, but in the latter case the inscription has disappeared, and the whole structure is in utter ruin. The like is true of a fourth collection of ruins still farther to the east-southeast on a raised flooring of white stone sustaining the pedestals of former columns and bases of ruined doorways.[2] But to these I paid less attention, because my

---

[1] See p. 302, below, and compare Justi, *Grundr. iran. Philol.* 2. 422. For the view that the edifice was a tomb, see Dieulafoy, *L'Art Antique de la Perse*, 1. 14–21, cf. also pl. 5; and for a summary of the opposing theories consult Curzon, *Persia*, 2. 73.

[2] All the ruins have been so well described by Curzon, *Persia*, 2. 71–75, with measurements and observations regarding their position and state of preservation, that I have contented myself with a brief outline without elaborating the notes I made on the

. thoughts were riveted upon a monolith standing alone in the plain some distance to the east of the circular column and paved court that I have mentioned. I had long known about it and had always looked forward to the time when I should see it.

This impressive monument is a huge slab, over twelve feet high, five feet broad, and about two feet in thickness. Upon its weathered front is carved in low relief the figure of a king. On his head there rests a curious crown which shows traces of the influence of Egyptian art; but the most striking feature of the image is a double set of immense vanlike wings that rise from the shoulders and droop almost to the feet.[1] The sculptured form is the very idealization of sovereignty. The top of the monolith, which once was inscribed, is broken off, but the missing device, as we know from the drawings of the earlier travellers, consisted of the simple words, 'I am Cyrus, the King, the Achæmenian' — in keeping with the dignity of the surroundings.[2]

spot, except where I could add something new.

[1] For a good description of the bas-relief as it appeared almost a hundred years ago, see Ker Porter, *Travels*, 1 492–496.

[2] The inscription is clearly drawn in the sketch made in the last century by Ker Porter, *Travels*, 1. 492, pl. 13, and is seen in other early pictures. (For references compare Justi, *Grundr. iran. Philol.* 2. 422.) I looked in vain for some trace of the broken piece that held it. There was a stone lying some fifty feet to the southeast, but, although it showed some chisel marks, it did not appear to match the capstone of the monument. The two photographs which I took (one of which is here reproduced) are interesting not alone because they show the present condition of the bas-relief, but also from the fact that they prove that the face of the king is slightly turned toward the spectator, as both eyes apparently are shown. The head is not therefore in profile as all the drawings (including those from Ker Porter, *op. cit.* pl. 13, to Dieulafoy, *L'Art Antique*, 1. pl. 17) represent it. In addition to this I do not believe that Dieulafoy is justified in representing the figure as holding some object in the hand; a careful study of enlargements of my best photograph convince me that Ker Porter was right in regarding the hand simply as raised (like the hand of Darius at Behistan and Naksh-i Rustam) and that Dieulafoy has mistaken the feather-tips of the smaller wing for an instrument grasped in the hand of the king.

I, CYRUS, THE KING, THE ACHÆMENIAN

I remounted my horse and, followed by Safar and the guides, turned his bridle in the direction of the lonely mausoleum that forms the principal object in the plain. To reach the road that leads to it, I had to ride nearly a mile west and southwest over fields freshly turned up by plows of the primitive Jamshid type.[1] In Persia one has little hesitation about riding over newly sown ground, for a drop of water from the irrigation trenches quickly restores each trampled blade. My thoughts were centred only upon the massive stone structure in the distance, which looked towerlike enough to merit the name *púrgos* applied to it by Strabo.[2]

I had long been interested in the accounts which the Greek and Latin authors have given of the death of Cyrus, and in their descriptions of his tomb. I had devoted considerable time some years before to investigating the mooted question whether this 'Grave of Solomon's Mother,' or 'Mosque of the Mother of Solomon,' as the natives call it, was actually the vault of the great king.[3] After a careful and unbiased study of the classical testimony on the subject and a thorough examination, on three different occasions, both of the site and the building itself, I became convinced that no doubt should be entertained on the subject, and that we should accept the generally current view that it is the authentic tomb of the founder of the Achæmenian dynasty. I shall briefly present the main facts that lead to this conclusion, and then describe the sepulchre itself.[4]

[1] Cf. pp. 85–86, 246, above.

[2] Strabo, *Geographia*, 15. 3–7: πύργον οὐ μέγαν.

[3] The Persian designations are *Ḳabr-i Mādar-i Suleimān* and *Masjid-i Mādar-i Suleimān*. For traditions referring to the tomb as the burial-place of a woman, see Curzon, *Persia*, 2. 78, 84.

[4] I made my studies of the classical writers on the subject wholly independently of Curzon, *Persia*, 2. 75–90. On completing my investigations I found that he had covered the field so thoroughly and come to the same results, that I could confine myself largely to the main points, adding comments wherever it seemed necessary. I may remark, for example, that Curzon, *op. cit.* p. 78, correctly assigns the first real identification of the tomb to Ker Porter (1818), *Travels*,

In the first place I may speak of the death of Cyrus. According to Herodotus, who wrote less than a century after the event, Cyrus met with defeat and death at the hands of the Scythian hordes led by Tomyris, queen of the Massagetæ, about the year B.C. 530, and the victress thrust his severed head into a wine-skin filled with human blood and bade him glut to the full his thirst for gore.[1] The Father of History adds that this is only one of several accounts of Cyrus's death, but the one which seemed to him nearest the truth. The same story in an abridged form, but drawn evidently from Herodotus, is repeated in the first century B.C. by Diodorus Siculus, who states, however, that the Amazon caused the vanquished king to be impaled.[2] The narrative, with the details as in Herodotus, is repeated by Justinus (c. A.D. 150) in his epitome of the history of Pompeius Trogus, and briefly sketched by Polyænus (c. A.D. 163).[3] The early historian Berosus (c. B.C. 280) says that Cyrus perished 'in the plain of the Dahæ.'[4] The still earlier authority Ctesias (c. B.C. 400), who knew Persian traditions well, states that Cyrus was mortally wounded in battle against the foreign hosts of the Derbicæ (apparently somewhere in the east of Iran), and died three days afterward, and his body was conveyed to Persia by his son Cambyses.[5] Less confidence may be placed in Xenophon's historical novel, the *Cyropaedia*, which depicts Cyrus as passing away at a good old age among sorrowing friends, to whom he imparts

---

1. 502–508, but Pietro della Valle (*Viaggi*, 2. 276 ; *Travels*, ed. Pinkerton, 9. 112) was on the right track when he wrote, under the date July 22, 1622, that he arrived at two o'clock in the morning at the site of the ancient 'Passargada, where, according to Pliny and Quintus Curtius, was the place of sepulture of Cyrus the Great.'

[1] Herodotus (B.C. 484–408), *History*, 1. 201–214.

[2] Diodorus Siculus, *Bibliotheca Historica*, 2. 44 (Tauchnitz edition).

[3] See Justinus, *Historiae Philippicae*, 1. 8. 11–13 ; Polyænus, *Stratagemata*, 8. 28.

[4] Berosus, quoted by Eusebius, ed. Schöne, 1. 30, cf. Müller, *Fragmenta Historicorum Graecorum*, 2. 505 a, Paris, 1848. See also Justi, *Grundr. iran. Philol.* 2. 421, and Gilmore, *Fragments of Ktesias*, p. 136, n.

[5] Ctesias, *Fragments*, 29 (38–40), ed. Gilmore, pp. 135–137.

the sagest counsels and whom he urges to commit his body to the ground in the simplest manner possible.[1] Cyrus was about seventy-one years old, and the year of his death is placed at B.C. 530. On the whole Ctesias's account of the event may be regarded as the most trustworthy, if compared also with the statements of Arrain, Strabo, Pliny, Quintus Curtius, and Plutarch regarding the tomb.[2] From the statements of these writers, which I shall next give, we may accept it as a fact that the body of Cyrus was laid to rest here at Pasargadæ, and it is not impossible that it was first coated with wax in the custom of the Persians, or perhaps embalmed after the manner of the Egyptians.[3]

Arrian, the Greek historian who lived early in the second century of the Christian era and drew material from the writings of Aristobulus, who accompanied Alexander the Great on his Eastern Campaign, gives an excellent description of the tomb of Cyrus and of the visit which Alexander paid to it.[4] He describes the mausoleum as standing in the midst of a park surrounded by a grove and rich meadows of grass. The tomb itself stood on a rectangular base of stone and the sepulchre is described as 'a stone house,'[5] roofed over, and having a door so small as to be difficult to enter even for a man of no large stature.' In this 'house' the body of Cyrus was laid in a

---

[1] Xenophon, *Cyropaedia*, **8**. 7. 1–28. There is a suggestion of a dying-speech also in Ctesias, *Fragments*, 29 (39).

[2] See also Katz, *Cyrus des Perser-königs Abstammung, Kriege und Tod*, pp. 36–42, Klagenfurt, 1895; and compare Justi, *Grundr. iran. Philol.* 2. 421, n. 3.

[3] I have referred elsewhere to the statement of Herodotus (**1.** 140) that the Persians coated the bodies of their dead with wax before interring them. The remarks upon the tombs of Darius and those of the later Achæmenians,

in the next chapter, may be consulted. For the suggestion regarding embalming, see Curzon, *Persia*, 2. 80, n. 1.

[4] Arrian, *Anabasis*, **6**. 29. 4–11. A version of the passage may be found in Curzon (*Persia*, 2. 79–80), and for that reason I merely paraphrase the contents, adding the original Greek wherever it seems necessary. For another rendering of the original, see *Anabasis of Alexander and Indica*, translated by E. J. Chinnock, pp. 340–341, London, 1893.

[5] Gk. οἴκημα λίθινον.

'golden coffin'[1] that rested 'upon (or beside) a couch, the
feet of which were of hammered gold.'[2] Under this catafalque
carpets of royal purple were spread, and over it was laid a
covering of Babylonian tapestry, while around it were lying
rich vestments of purple and other colors, costly jewels and
precious stones, placed doubtless on the 'table,' which is also
mentioned.[3] When Alexander visited the tomb, he found that
it had been rifled of its treasures, the body had been thrown
out of the coffin, which was broken and battered, for the
plunderers found it too heavy to drag with them, and only
the casket and catafalque remained.[4] On discovering the outrage Alexander gave orders that the body should be replaced
in the coffin and that everything should be restored to its
former condition. He obliterated the doorway, closed up the
entrance with a stone, cemented it with mortar, and sealed it
with his own signet.[5]

The account of Strabo (c. B.C. 30) is substantially the
same, but somewhat less detailed; he calls the building 'a
tower of no great size,' and adds, on the authority of Onesicritus, who was with Alexander, that this tower had 'ten
tiers, or stages,' and the body of Cyrus lay in the 'upper-
most stage,' an allusion evidently to the terraced courses and
plinth on which the mausoleum stands.[6] Plutarch (about A.D.
50), like his two predecessors, speaks of the inscription which

---

[1] Gk. πύελον χρυσῆν.

[2] The Greek words literally mean
that the couch stood ' beside the coffin'
(κλίνην παρὰ τῇ πυέλῳ), whereas a
statement that follows seems to imply
that the allusion is to a catafalque
' upon which (lit. ' in the midst of the
couch') rested the coffin that contained
the body of Cyrus' (ἐν μέσῳ δὲ τῆς
κλίνης ἡ πύελος ἔκειτο ἡ τὸ σῶμα τοῦ
Κύρου ἔχουσα).

[3] Gk. καὶ τράπεζα ἔκειτο.

[4] Lit. ' he found that everything had
been carried off except the coffin and

the couch ' (πλὴν τῆς πυέλου καὶ τῆς
κλίνης).

[5] Gk. τὸ σημεῖον τὸ βασιλικόν.

[6] Strabo, Geographia, 15. 3. 7, 8,
πύργος and τὸν μὲν πύργον δεκάστεγον
. . . τῇ ἀνωτάτω στέγῃ. Compare also
Falconer's translation of Strabo, 3.
133–134, Bohn's Classical Library,
London, 1857.   The idea of the
' tower' appears again in the Latin version of Callisthenes made in the third
century A.D. by Julius Valerius, who
uses the term turris in his Alexandri
Polemi, 2. 29. 18 (Teubner edition).

Cyrus had bidden to be placed on the tomb, and states that the name of the ghoul who had desecrated the vault was Polymachus.[1] The later and less trustworthy Quintus Curtius, on the other hand, says that Alexander was disappointed at finding Cyrus simply interred with his shield, two Scythian bows, and a sword, and not with silver and gold, as was reported; whereupon the Macedonian placed a golden crown upon the coffin and covered the sarcophagus with his own rich cloak.[2] The incidental statement of Pliny the Elder (d. A.D. 79) adds information that is important both for the identification of the tomb and its site, when he says: 'The Magi hold the fortress of Pasargadæ, in which is the tomb of Cyrus.'[3] The allusion is in harmony, moreover, with Arrian and Strabo, who say that the Magians were the hereditary guardians of the tomb, dwelling near it and offering a sheep every day and a horse each month as a sacrifice.[4]

As we ride nearer to the sepulchre the details of the classic descriptions become even more clear. The structure, which in the distance might be spoken of as a *púrgos*, now looks like 'a house of stone, roofed over,' as Arrian says, and the terraced steps (though seven, not ten, in number) answer to the statement of Onesicritus in Strabo's account.[5] The door, which faces west, or rather northwest, is strikingly small, and around the tomb there are the remains of what was once a colonnade that formed a rectangular enclosure around the tomb. With the exception of a few pillars which, though broken, show where the entrances must have been, most of the columns have disappeared or lie tumbled about in confusion upon the ground.[6] A score of Mohammedan graves have been crowded within the area next to the tomb so as to be as

---

[1] Plutarch, *Alexander*, **69**. 1–2.

[2] Quintus Curtius, *Hist. Alex.* **10**. 1. 30–32.

[3] Pliny, *Historia Naturalis*, **6**. 26. 29, 116.

[4] Arrian, *Anabasis*, **6**. 29. 7; Strabo, *Geographia*, **15**. 3. 7 (the latter says they 'received' these animals).

[5] On this subject, see also Curzon, *Persia*, 2. 82.

[6] Ker Porter, *Travels*, 1. 499, reported seventeen columns as 'still erect,

close as possible to this shrine of 'Solomon's Mother.' In further confirmation of Arrian's statement concerning 'a small house for the Magi who guarded the tomb of Cyrus,'[1] we find, about a hundred yards north of the mausoleum, the foundation of a building which may have been at the same time a sanctuary and a residence for the priests; but practically nothing remains of the structure except the base upon which it stood, and this is now partly buried by a mass of wretched hovels.[2]

From a distance the tomb of Cyrus looks dwarfed by the vastness of the surrounding plain, but when viewed near-by, its true size becomes apparent, and the nobility of its lines, the symmetry of its proportions, and the striking whiteness of the marblelike stone of which it is constructed, come out in full effect. It stands high upon a terraced base, seven steps of which are now visible, and the stones which compose both the substructure and the tomb are very massive. The lowest stage of the seven terraced steps is a plinth over two feet high, nearly fifty feet long, and more than forty feet broad.[3] Each of the other stages above this flooring is proportionately smaller in area, but not in height, and the combined elevation of the pedestal thus formed is more than sixteen feet. The mausoleum itself is about eighteen feet high, the point of its roof being nearly thirty-five feet from the ground; the length of the building is about twenty feet and its width seventeen feet. I give the more precise measurements in metres below, as I took them with considerable care.[4]

but heaped round with rubbish and barbarously connected with a wall of mud.' Each generation will find less to record. For a theoretical restoration of the colonnade, see Dieulafoy, *L'Art Antique*, 1. pl. 18, and compare Perrot and Chipiez, *Histoire de l'Art*, 5. 598.

[1] Arrian, *Anabasis*, 6. 29. 7.

[2] For a picture, see Stolze and Andreas, *Persepolis*, 2. pl. 130.

[3] In Ker Porter's time this was almost covered, so that he calls it a 'sort of skirting-stone' and counts only six steps (*Travels*, 1. 499; and cf. Curzon, *Persia*, 2. 77, n. 1). Excavation might perhaps reveal the 'ten steps' of Onesicritus.

[4] The plinth, as nearly as I could measure it, is 13.50 m. long, 12.20 m. broad, and .70 m. high. The next stage is also .70 m. high; the third,

The mammoth blocks which make up the tomb and base alike are set together with the utmost precision. There is no evidence of the use of mortar, but iron clamps were employed in uniting the masonry, as I afterward learned from Mr. J. R. Preece, British Consul at Isfahan, who informed me that some years ago a friend of his actually found *in situ*, on the east side of the tomb, one of these great clasps binding two blocks together. Nature has added to her destructive forces an extra one : several bushes of the evergreen type have taken root in the interstices worn between the great stones of the terraced steps, and a small tree has sprouted out from the roof; both of these agents, as time goes on, will take part in bringing about the general ruin of the monument.

It is natural to suppose that an inscription of some sort adorned this resting-place of the mighty dead, and we have the authority of the Greek writers for asserting that there was such an epitaph. Both Arrian and Strabo say that Aristobulus, who was appointed by Alexander to restore the tomb after it had been desecrated, mentions a Persian inscription, to this effect : [1] —

> O MAN, I AM CYRUS, THE SON OF CAMBYSES, WHO
> FOUNDED THE PERSIAN EMPIRE AND WAS KING OF
> ASIA.   GRUDGE ME NOT THEREFORE THIS MONU-
> MENT.

Strabo, after repeating this epitaph, which he says Aristobulus quoted from memory, adds that Onesicritus says 'the inscription was in Greek, engraved in Persian characters . . . and there was another in Persian of the same import' : [2] —

> I, CYRUS, KING OF KINGS, LIE HERE.

1.02 m.; the fourth, also 1.02 m. ; the fifth, .53 m. ; the sixth, .54 m. ; the seventh, .53 m. The sepulchre is 6.24 m. long on the outside ; 5.26 m. broad ; and about 6 m. high to the top of the pointed roof, which has a total height of about 11 m. above the level of the ground.

[1] Arrian, *Anabasis*, 6. 29. 8.

[2] The Greek words form a hexameter line : 'Ενθάδ' ἐγὼ κεῖμαι | Κῦρος βασιλεὺς βασιλήων — Strabo, *Geog*. 15. 3. 7.

U

Plutarch has a statement to the same effect, and relates that when Alexander found the tomb violated by Polymachus and read the epitaph, he ordered the inscription to be engraved in Greek letters underneath, and it read as follows : [1]—

> O MAN, WHOSOEVER THOU ART, AND WHENCE-
> SOEVER THOU COMEST (FOR I KNOW THOU WILT
> COME), I AM CYRUS, WHO FOUNDED THE EMPIRE
> OF THE PERSIANS.   GRUDGE ME NOT THEREFORE
> THIS LITTLE EARTH THAT COVERS MY BODY.

The tone of the inscriptions sounds genuine, especially in the combination of proud glory and deep humility, and the brief line given by Onesicritus — I, CYRUS, KING OF KINGS, LIE HERE — would answer admirably to a presumable Persian inscription ADAM KURUSH KHSHĀYATHIYA KHSHĀYATHIY-ĀNĀM, ' I, Cyrus, King of Kings, (lie here),' with the customary omission of the verb, which Onesicritus would naturally supply, even if the authenticity of the version be questioned because the Greek words form a hexameter.   A single glance at the façade of the tomb shows a large stone over the doorway, which looks as if designed for holding an epitaph, but I could not find a trace of a letter upon it, though I examined it with care, nor do any characters appear in the photographs which I took.   But the original letters may have been destroyed, or possibly they were carved on tablets attached to the wall, as seems likely if we notice the holes on each side of this slab over the entrance.   In fact I see no reason to doubt the existence of an inscription when Aristobulus and Onesicritus visited the tomb with Alexander, any more than we might now argue that the bas-relief of Cyrus never had an inscription, because one no longer exists, although there was one less than a hundred years ago.

The entrance to the tomb is low and narrow, as the Greek authorities state.   The height of the doorway is only 4 ft.

---

[1] Plutarch, *Alexander*, **69**. 2.

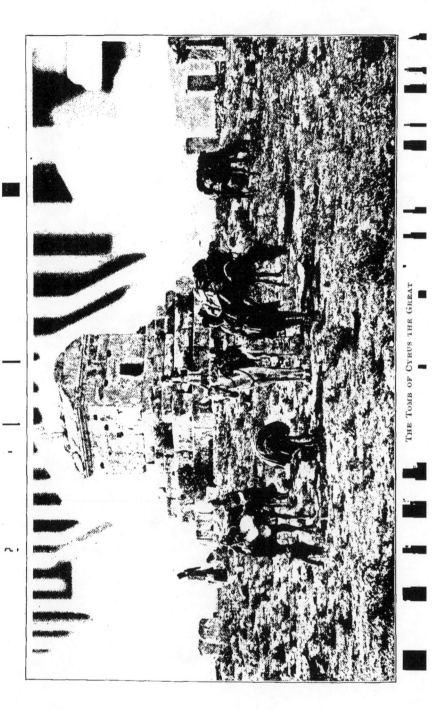

THE TOMB OF CYRUS THE GREAT

2 in. and its width 2 ft. 7½ in.,[1] and it is necessary to crouch in order to pass through, as Arrian affirmed. The original door to the vault was probably a heavy stone swinging on pivots, such as may be seen at the supposed tomb of Esther and Mordecai at Hamadan and also in the square monument at Naksh-i Rustam,[2] but I do not recall seeing the socket-holes, as in those cases. Dieulafoy's ingenious suggestion of two doors, an outer and an inner door, so arranged as to open upon each other, but not both at the same time, seems plausible[3]; and even if the original means of closure have long since disappeared, there are actually to be seen two rickety wooden doors which guard the ingress, as the thickness of the wall allows space for two. But the second of these wretched board structures was off its hinges, when I visited the tomb, and was lying in one corner of the vault.

Crawling through the low entrance, without having the slightest objection raised by the bystanders, who I thought might prevent me, I found myself within the chamber where death had held his court. The room is 10 ft. 5⅝ in. long, and 7 ft. 7 in. wide, and 7 ft. 11½ in. high.[4] Two enormous blocks that look like marble form the floor, and the side walls and flat ceiling are composed of stones equally large. In one part of the eastern wall, facing the doorway, there is a great gaping chink, and the block of the floor at the same end shows a rough sort of depression which suggests the idea that something had been scooped out or forcibly wrenched away, perhaps by robber hands. It may have been that the sarcophagus stood here.[5] I could picture its position and I lay down to measure my length

---

[1] The dimensions in centimeters as I took them are: height, 126 cm.; width, 80 cm. Curzon gives 4 ft. 3 in. by 2 ft. 3 in.; Ker Porter, 4 ft. by 2 ft. 10 in.

[2] See p. 168, and note 2, above.

[3] See Dieulafoy, *L'Art Antique*, 1. 48, fig. 54.

[4] The measurements as I took them in meters are: length, 3.18 m.; width, 2.30 m.; height, 2.12 m. They are practically the same as Curzon's, who gives: length, 10 ft. 5 in.; width, 7 ft. 6 in.; height, 6 ft. 10 in.

[5] See Arrian's description, p. 286, above.

near the depression in order to determine whether the space were in proportion to a human form. I found there would indeed have been room enough, and space besides for the table or couch holding the purple vestments, the sword, and the other regal insignia which Arrian and Strabo enumerate.

The condition of the royal chamber is not what it once was. The wall to the right, or on the south side, has been desecrated by a modern Persian inscription and verses from the Koran. They are handsomely carved, it is true, and are surrounded by an ornamental border shaped like a prayer-niche, but they are out of place in the tomb of Cyrus. Innumerable *graffiti*, scratched by Orientals with the scribbling craze, cover the walls. One of the names was in Pahlavi characters and interested me, as it was that of a Zoroastrian priest, Mobed Ormazdyar Bahram. As a lineal descendant of the race of the Magi he had more right perhaps than the others to carve his name in the tomb, for the Magi were the traditional guardians of the tomb of Cyrus. A worn copy of the Koran lay upon the floor, and the wind sweeping through the vault turned its pages. A manuscript of the Avesta would have been more appropriate in this chamber. But most inharmonious of all, for it hung over the place where the body must have lain, was a cord with an incongruous collection of worthless trash in the way of votive offerings. A piece of rag, a bit of brass, a fragment of a lamp, a bell, a copper ring, and what not, made up the motley string. They were the customary donations of pilgrims as mementos of the journey or as talismans for a safe return.

Happily the note so out of tune with the historic surroundings lasted only for a moment. An instant later the setting sun streamed through the doorway and flooded one corner of the dingy vault with a gorgeous splendor. The image of the *kāvaya hvarenah*, the 'Kingly Glory,' or symbol of sovereignty in the Avesta, flashed across my mind. In ancient times a reflection of this same divine light was believed to shed a halo about the person of the King of Kings. Its sacred majesty

was shining this instant from heaven around the tomb of
Cyrus and made it seem too hallowed to remain. As I slowly
descended the deep steps and mounted my horse, the sun sank
low behind the western hills. I turned for a last look at the
historic shrine. A vision seemed to rise before my view, and
I saw in fancy the scene of the last obsequies of the Great
King. From the classical writers we know with what pomp
and magnificence the processions of the Persian kings were
conducted during their lifetime; the richly caparisoned
horses, chariots of state, purple robes, heavy accoutrements,
and barbaric splendor were always present in gorgeous profusion. With no less pomp, but with greater solemnity, must
the sorrowing nation have borne their dead hero to the tomb.
His body, not left in Magian fashion to be torn by dogs
and birds, but covered with wax or perhaps embalmed, was
laid in a gold-adorned casket and carried to the sepulchre,
attended by the flower of the Persian army. I still could hear
the tramplings of the horses that led the funeral train; the
measured tread of the soldiers in clanking armor rang dully on
my ear; the smoke of imagined incense rose heavenward to
Auramazda from the huge urn holding the sacred fire; and
the chanting voice of the Magian priest intoning perchance
the Zoroastrian psalm *Kãm nemōi zãm* — 'to what land am I
going' — beat rhythmically through my brain. The Great
King Cyrus was no more! The shroud of darkness fell like a
pall upon the plain and the moon rose slowly over the distant
hills.

CHAPTER XX

PERSEPOLIS AND ITS MONUMENTS

'Among the ruined temples there,
Stupendous columns, and wild images
Of more than man, where marble demons watch
The Zodiac's brazen mystery, and dead men
Hang their mute thoughts on the mute walls around.'
— SHELLEY, *Alastor*, 116–120.

THE scene now shifts from Pasargadæ to Persepolis, the royal seat of Darius, Xerxes, Artaxerxes, and their successors, who bore in turn the title 'King of Kings,' having inherited the throne of Cyrus through a side line, as his son Cambyses had died childless.[1] These monarchs located their capital some forty miles south of Cyrus's city, at the site now marked by the great platform of Takht-i Jamshid and the ruins of the city of Stakhra, as well as perpetuated by their tombs at Naksh-i Rustam. The new capital may have been called *Pārsa-karta*, 'City of the Persians,' like the older Pasargadæ, for the Greeks appear simply to be paraphrasing the name when they refer to the city as *Perse-polis*.[2] It is not improbable, moreover, that the name *Stakhra*, 'Strong,' still preserved among the natives as Stakhr or Istakhr, and which we can

---

[1] See pp. 26, 180, above. The date of Cambyses's death was B.C. 522. Herodotus (*History*, **3**. 61–66) states that it occurred at the Syrian Ecbatana; Ctesias (*Fragments*, 43–44, ed. Gilmore, pp. 144–145) says that the event occurred at Babylon, and adds that the body was brought back to Persia. Yet to this day no man knows the place where Cambyses is buried.

[2] The earliest occurrence of Περσέπολις in Greek appears to be in the fifth century B.C., after the Persian War, as we then find the word used by Æschylus, *Persians*, 65, apparently with a punning allusion to 'destroying (πέρσις) cities (πόλις).' This I believe to be the best interpretation of the passage in question.

294

TOMBS OF THE ACHÆMENIAN KINGS AT NAKSH-I RUSTAM

(Tomb of Darius to the right)

trace back for centuries, if not to Achæmenian times, may have designated the city in the plain north and west of the platform, that is, the abode of the people in distinction from the residence of the kings on the grand terrace.[1] Be that as it may, the monuments in this vicinity are the most interesting and historic in all Persia; Susa alone can make any claim to comparison with them.

To reach Persepolis, we strike southward toward the Plain of Mervdasht.   The road runs at first through a mountain gorge, picturesque in wild scenery, but dangerous at night because of its rugged track and robbers.   The river Polvar, the classic Medus, pushes its way with turbulent stream through the craggy defile.   A part of the road above its rocky bed exhibits one of the most remarkable pieces of ancient engineering in the Orient.   For a considerable distance, through the solid limestone rock, a narrow causeway was hewn ages ago to afford, as it still does, a passage for caravans on their route from the south to the north of Iran, and an ingress more than once for great armed forces.   It is known as the *Sang-Bur*, ' Rock-Cutting,' or the *Tang-i Bulāghī*, ' Water-stream Pass,' and is thought by some to be identical with the mountain gorges of Vash-Shikuft, mentioned in the Bundahishn.[2]

[1] On the problem of the names Persepolis and Istakhr, compare Curzon, *Persia*, 2. 132, n. 2, 133, 148, 187; also Nöldeke's article on Persepolis in *Encyclopædia Britannica*, 9th ed., 18. 557–560.   The Greeks and Latins naturally did not observe this distinction, and we can understand how the Tabula Peutingeriana should in late Parthian times speak of ' Persepolis, the emporium of Persia,' although this could only refer to the city itself, because the place had lost its prestige as a capital under the Arsacids.   See Tomaschek, *Zur historischen Topographie von Persien*, pp. 166–175.

[2] Bd. **12**. 2, 21 ; so Justi, in *Indogermanische Forschungen, Anzeiger*, 17. 106.   For a picture of the pass, see Stolze and Andreas, *Persepolis*, 2. pl. 127 ; and for descriptions, cf. Curzon, *Persia*, 2. 90 ; Browne, *A Year Amongst the Persians*, p. 243. In the opinion of Justi (*IF. Anzeiger*, 17. 106, cf. *Grundr. iran. Philol.* 2. 425) it was on a mountain in this vicinity that the Median pretender Gaumata, the False Smerdis, first asserted his claim to the sovereignty of Persia, only to be overthrown by Darius.

From the ravine we emerge into a succession of valleys between hills and cliffs. At this point my cavalcade overtook a band of Cossacks in the employ of the Shah. These finely mounted horsemen had been sent down to clear up the road which was infested with highwaymen (*rāh-zan*), and they were not long in finding an opportunity to exercise their functions. A shepherd came past with tears in his eyes, complaining that he had been robbed of a sheep by a peasant who was acting as 'a guard of the road.' The Cossacks pursued the offender to the hills, quickly caught him, pinioned his arms behind him, and marched him at the rifle's muzzle to the nearest village, where punishment, I presume of the cruellest kind, was inflicted upon the culprit.

At Sivand, the station beyond, I found no occasion to wait for a longer time than to change horses, and then resumed the trail near the Polvar, though I regret that I missed seeing the famous Pahlavi inscription in the hills near the village of Hajiabad, some miles below Sivand. I have in my possession, however, a picture of the tablet taken by Mr. A. O. Wood, of the bank at Isfahan, and there is a large photograph of the inscription in Stolze's work on Persepolis, besides copies that have been made by others.[1] The writing on the stone is in Chaldæo-Pahlavi and Sasanian Pahlavi, and it appears to record a remarkable shot with an arrow by King Shahpur, or Sapor I, of the House of Sasan.[2]

The afternoon was considerably advanced when I reached Naksh-i Rustam and the tombs of the Achæmenian kings. Here in the face of a long high bluff are hewn four sepulchres belonging to the elder kings of the second line, Darius, Xerxes, Artaxerxes I, and Darius II. These rock-cut vaults lie five or six miles to the north of the great platform where once stood

[1] See Stolze and Andreas, *Persepolis*, 2. pl. 126; Ker Porter, *Travels*, 1. 513; Flandin and Coste, *Voyage en Perse, Ancienne*, 2. pl. 164; Westergaard, in the appendix to his *Bunde-* *hesh*, pp. 83–84, Copenhagen, 1851; cf. also Curzon, *Persia*, 2. 116.

[2] See West, *Grundr. iran. Philol.* 2. 77. (Hajiabad is not to be confused with the place mentioned on p. 252.)

the palaces of the kings and behind which are three other Achæmenian tombs of a somewhat later date.

The rocky cliff in which the sepulchre of Darius and those of his son, grandson, and great-grandson are carved, resembles a jagged wall, over five hundred feet long and between one and two hundred feet high. It extends in a generally easterly and westerly direction, but makes a rather sharp turn at the eastern end, so that we can understand how Ctesias came to speak of it as a 'double mountain' — δισσὸν ὄρος.[1] The natives call it *Husein Kūh*, 'Hill of Husein,' or more often *Naksh-i Rustam*, 'Rustam's Picture,' from a mistaken idea that the equestrian statues of the Sasanian kings at its base represent Rustam and his famous charger.

The four tombs which are hewn in the bosom of the rock are practically of the same size and dimensions and absolutely uniform in their exterior design. The shape of each façade is roughly that of a Greek cross, some seventy feet high and sixty feet wide,[2] and the arms are hewn deep into the stone. In the middle of each façade a door with decorative lintel is cut, but only the lower half is pierced so as to furnish a small aperture, the upper part being left solid as a screen. Two columns, cut in high relief, stand on each side of the doorway. They are capped with the heads of bulls after the characteristic manner of the Persepolitan architecture and they support an entablature, with ornamental architrave, frieze, and cornice, forming a base for the elaborately sculptured panel that fills the upper limb of the cross. Here, carved in two rows, one above the other, are bas-reliefs representing the vassal nations as supporting the staging upon which stands the king, who thus makes his enemies his footstool. The monarch is portrayed in the same manner as he is seen on the Behistan sculptures, bow in hand,[3] but his attitude is now that of worship

---

[1] Ctesias, *Fragments*, 46 (15), ed. Gilmore, p. 150.

[2] The disproportion between the height and the breadth was doubtless designed for the sake of effect.

[3] See p. 180, above.

before the sacred fire, over which floats the familiar winged effigy of Auramazda with the emblem of the sun shining in the background.

The identity of only one of the four tombs is positively known ; this is the tomb of Darius. It is the third sepulchre to the right, near the point where the cliff makes the sharp angle. The identification is made by means of two trilingual inscriptions, of like contents, carved near the figure of the king and around the doorway.[1] In some sixty lines the king glorifies Auramazda, enumerates the nations that acknowledge his sway, and exhorts the people not to depart from 'the Way which is Right.' All the bas-reliefs, including the sculpture of the king, the two figures behind him, which are known from inscriptions to be Gobryas and Aspathines,[2] as well as the effigies of the vassal nations, have suffered much from the elements and from lapse of ages, but the corresponding carvings on the other tombs give considerable aid in restoring them.[3] By comparing the national garb, the characteristic features, and the position of the figures with the names enumerated in the adjoining inscription, we may identify to-day almost every one of the nations represented on the bas-relief.[4] The entrance to the sepulchre is so high from the ground that it is impossible to reach it except by the aid of ropes or ladders. The interior of the vault has been several times examined and described by travellers.[5] It consists of a passagelike chamber into which

[1] These are the well-known inscriptions Naksh-i Rustam a and b (Weissbach, Die altpers. Keilinschr. pp. 34–36 ; Spiegel, Die altpers. Keilinschr. pp. 52–57). The lower one (b) of the two inscriptions is now almost illegible.

[2] See Weissbach, op. cit. p. 36 ; Spiegel, op. cit. p. 58, and compare p. 181, above.

[3] Photographs may be seen in the well-known works of Stolze and of Dieulafoy, and we may look before long for the publication of Dr. F. Sarre's admirable pictures, referred to by Andreas, in Verhandl. des 13. Internat. Orientalisten-Kongresses, p. 96, Leiden, 1904.

[4] See Andreas, op. cit. pp. 96–97, and cf. Justi, Grundr. iran. Philol. 2. 454–455. MM. Babin and Houssay, collaborators of M. Dieulafoy, in 1885, actually discovered names carved under seven of the figures; cf. Perrot and Chipiez, Histoire de l'Art, 5. 622.

[5] For a plan of the interior of the

INTERIOR OF THE TOMB OF DARIUS

ENTRANCE TO THE TOMB OF DARIUS

the low door opens, and opposite the entrance is a recess whose floor is higher than the level of the passageway. Into the stone flooring of this are hewn three deep troughs to serve as sarcophagi, probably for the king and whichever two persons he regarded as nearest to him, while in the extension of the passage to the left six more such *loculi* are chiselled. All the receptacles are entirely empty, and the sole tenants of this lofty catacomb are bats and birds.

Two interesting stories in connection with this sepulchre are told by Ctesias, who must have had them at first hand during his residence in Persia as Greek physician to Artaxerxes. In his brief notice regarding the tomb of Darius he says (and I translate fairly literally) : ' Darius ordered a tomb to be made for himself in the Double Mountain, and the work was brought to completion ; but when he wished to inspect it, he was dissuaded from so doing by the Chaldæans (the Magian soothsayers) and by his parents. His parents, however, were anxious to go up to see it. As they were being drawn up, the priests who had hold of the ropes saw some serpents and became so frightened that they let go the ropes, and the parents of the king fell and were killed. The grief of Darius was so great that he caused to be beheaded forty of those who had pulled on the ropes.'[1] The other story that is told by Ctesias is to the effect that Bagapates, the favorite eunuch of Darius, lived by his dead master's tomb for seven years until death released him from his devoted charge.[2]

The other tombs apparently belonged to Xerxes, Artaxerxes I, and Darius II ; but in the absence of inscriptions we can only surmise how they were occupied respectively.[3] It is natural to suppose that the tomb of Xerxes was next to that

tomb, see Flandin and Coste, *Voyage en Perse, Ancienne*, 4. pl. 170 ; cf. also Perrot and Chipiez, *op. cit.* 5. 626.

[1] Ctesias, *Fragments*, 46 (15), ed. Gilmore, p. 150.

[2] *Ibid.* 59 (19), ed. Gilmore, p. 152.

[3] See, for example, Nöldeke's article on Persepolis, *Encyclop. Brit.* 9th ed., 18. 558. A less likely assignment may be found in Dieulafoy, *L'Art Antique*, 3. 2, n. 1.

of his father, but its position, whether to the right or the left, would affect the assignment of the other two. If we assume, as I think we are entitled to assume, that the three sepulchres which are in the main face of the rock were cut one after the other in regular order,[1] and that the one in the bend to the extreme right (the so-called 'first tomb') was cut last, and partly for that reason is better preserved, then the vault of Xerxes would be on the left of that of Darius, as we face the hill, the vault of Artaxerxes Longimanus at the end, and the vault of Darius II, latest of them all, in the angle at the extreme right.[2]   On the other hand, if the so-called 'first tomb' at the extreme right be assigned to Xerxes, then Artaxerxes would have occupied the 'third tomb' and Darius II the last.[3]

Owing to the peculiar conformation of the cliff that has been already referred to, the 'first tomb' faces almost to the west, whereas the other three face nearly to the south. The more protected position of this tomb, and its greater inaccessibility, for it is the most difficult of the four to reach, may account for its being better preserved, even if one is not prepared to grant that it is more recent than the others. Passing by the tomb of Darius, already described, I may remark that the façade of the 'third tomb,' the one on its left, is comparatively well preserved, much better in fact than that of Darius, and we must regret that we cannot be sure whether we are looking at the sepulchre of Xerxes or not.[4] The fourth and last of the group is nearer the ground than the others and is the most damaged of them all. Like the others, moreover, it is empty.

Along the base of the rock below the tombs there is carved a series of seven panels which date from a later dynasty, as they

[1] It is worth noting that the Sasanian bas-reliefs are sculptured only in the base of this main wall, and not below the tomb in the cliff at the bend.

[2] So also Justi, *Empire of the Persians*, p. 203.

[3] Such seems to be the view of Andreas, *op. cit.* p. 96.

[4] For a good photograph of this and the other façades, see Dieulafoy, *L'Art Antique*, 3. pls. 1–3. A picture of the first tomb is also given below.

FIRST SASANIAN SCULPTURE AT NAKSH-I RUSTAM

FOURTH SASANIAN SCULPTURE AT NAKSH-I RUSTAM

bear Sasanian bas-reliefs of the third and fourth centuries of the
Christian era. If we adopt the same order of enumeration from
east to west as for the tombs, we may describe the first bas-
relief as located between the first and second sepulchre and
adjoining a large incised space that is vacant, except for three
rectangular holes and an unimportant modern Persian inscription dated early in the eighteenth century.[1] The bas-relief itself
represents a Sasanian royal group, one figure in which is a
woman. The scene portrayed has been variously interpreted
as representing Shahpur I (A.D. 241–272) and his queen, or as
Varahran II (A.D. 275–293) and his chief royal consort, or else
as figuring the marriage of Varahran V, Bahram Gor (A.D. 420–
438), with an Indian princess.[2] The second and third bas-reliefs
(the latter nearly buried by the sand blown against it)[3] are equestrian sculptures, carved one above the other in the space below
the tomb of Darius. They represent two stages of a combat on
horseback, in which the king on the left triumphs over his
enemy on the right, whose spear is broken and whose horse is
worsted in the fray. These panels may, perhaps, commemorate
victorious engagements of Varahran IV of Kermanshah (A.D.
388–399).[4] The fourth panel, or that in the lower space between the tomb of Darius and its neighbor on the left, has a
peculiar interest, as it portrays the surrender of the Roman
emperor Valerian (A.D. 260) to the Sasanian monarch Sapor,
Shahpur I. The victor, mounted upon a war-horse, triumphantly
receives the submission of the suppliant who kneels before him.
The fifth sculpture, like the second and third, represents in

[1] For a note on this modern Persian inscription, see Browne, *A Year
Amongst the Persians*, p. 248. The
blank space with the three holes, seen
in the photograph which I reproduce,
appears in the seventeenth-century
drawings of Chardin, *Voyages*, 2. pl.
74 and p. 175.

[2] For the various views, see Justi,
Grundr. iran. Philol. 2. 519 ; Curzon,

Persia, 2. 118–119; Modi, *JRAS.
Bombay Branch*, 19. 58–75, Bombay,
1895 = *Asiatic Papers*, pp. 67–84,
Bombay, 1905.

[3] This partially buried panel is
shown in a photograph by Stolze
and Andreas, *Persepolis*, 2. pl. 121,
and in the drawings of Flandin and
Coste, 4. pls. 174, 184.

[4] Compare also p. 221, above.

a spirited manner an engagement on horseback, but the personages in the combat have not yet been identified. The sixth, near the lower end of the crag, portrays Varahran II and his courtiers, and the seventh, or last of the group, represents in effigy King Ardashir (A.D. 226–241), the founder of the Sasanian line, mounted on horseback and receiving from the god Ormazd, who is similarly mounted, a ring that symbolizes the gift of sovereignty. Trampled beneath the feet of the horses lie the prostrate forms of Volagases and Artabanus, the last of the Parthian dynasty.[1]

Opposite the fourth tomb, and about twenty yards away, is a square building that evidently dates back to Achæmenian times and recalls the ruined structure at Pasargadæ to which I drew attention in the preceding chapter.[2] The natives call it *Ka'bah-i Zardusht,* 'Shrine of Zoroaster.' Lord Curzon, however, like Dieulafoy, has stoutly maintained that the structure served as a royal tomb and was, perhaps, the mausoleum of Hystaspes, the father of Darius.[3] The majority of Iranian scholars, including so distinguished a specialist as Justi, are agreed with Ker Porter in regarding the building as a fire-shrine, like the modern Parsi *sagri* that commonly adjoins a Tower of Silence. Any one who has visited Malabar Hill at Bombay, or crossed the harbor to inspect the dakhmah at Ooran, after studying the history of Persia's sacred fire in connection with the representations on the coins, will be inclined to agree with this Zoroastrian explanation. Without again mentioning the Pasargadæ building, it is sufficient to compare the kindred structures near Naubandajan[4] and at Firuzabad, and the representation of fire-shrines on coins of the Parthian dynasty, to become convinced of the sacred

[1] For a fuller description of all these sculptures, together with abundant material in the way of bibliography, consult Curzon, *Persia,* 2. 117–126.

[2] See p. 280, above.

[3] Curzon, *Persia,* 2. 144–147.

[4] Near Fasa below Fahliyan in western Farsistan. For a photograph of the fire-temple at Naubandajan, see Stolze and Andreas, *Persepolis,* 2. 147.

SIXTH AND SEVENTH SASANIAN SCULPTURES AT NAKSH-I RUSTAM

STONE EDIFICE NEAR THE TOMBS AT NAKSH-I RUSTAM

character of the building.[1] Although not strictly a temple, since the Persians had no true temples like the Greeks, it is precisely the sort of building that would have been adapted to the purpose of preserving the sacred fire which was kept burning in some hallowed urn. The absence of windows (for the window-spaces are blank) and of a smoke-vent is no convincing argument against this view, because smoke was regarded as a creation of the evil spirit and every effort was doubtless made to provide against its formation.[2]

Leaving this square building and riding around the lower end of the bluff we come to two *Ātash-Gāhs,* 'Fire-Altars,' carved out of the living stone and dating back to Achæmenian times, according to the generally accepted view, from which there is no occasion to dissent. They recalled to me the *dāitya gātu,* or fire-altar, of Avestan days, and I could fancy the Magian priest heaping high the incense and sandalwood upon the sacred flame on some solemn occasion when the Great King, mindful of death in the midst of all his earthly pomp, came to offer sacrifice at the royal tombs.

Ascending the hill so as to overlook the tombs, we see near the lower edge of the bluff a low pillar, about five feet high, hewn out of the solid rock.[3] This shaft may have commemorated some event no longer discoverable, as it is not recorded by an inscription, but I may refer to the fact that Darius set up inscribed pillars at Tell al-Maskhutah in Egypt and at Chaluf, and also, according to Herodotus, in Thrace.[4]

---

[1] See especially the points made by Justi, *Grundr. iran. Philol.* 2. 456, and *Empire of the Persians,* pp. 203–206.

[2] Cf. also Justi, *Empire of the Persians,* p. 205, and *Grundr. iran. Philol.* 2. 456. The peculiar pitted appearance of the exterior of the building is a puzzle to archæologists. Justi (*l. c.*) has suggested that it may be caused by spaces left for securing a stucco spread over the surface or as cavities for sheets of metal plates or for tiles.

[3] For a somewhat imperfect sketch of the cliff and the pillar, see Flandin and Coste, *Voyage en Perse, Ancienne,* 5. pl. 89.

[4] For the στήλη in Thrace, see Herodotus, *History,* 4. 91; and for the others compare Dr. L. H. Gray's appendix to my article in *JAOS.* 21. 183–184.

Still farther up on the bluff there are some level spaces, hewn out of the rock and peculiar in their character. They are presumed to be the tables on which the dead were exposed to be devoured by dogs and birds in accordance with the ordinances of the Avesta. Because of their possible connection with the question of the religion of the Achæmenians, I paid more attention to them than I might have done otherwise, and I visited the spot twice. I counted three of these repositories on my first visit and noticed two more on my second, and possibly there may be others that I overlooked. The one to which I paid most attention was finished with more care than the rest, and the rock had been cut in such a manner as almost to form a divan, with a level flooring in front of it, measuring perhaps eight feet by ten, but hewn in the roughest style and shape. By the side of this quasi-couch of stone and at the head as well as near the feet were holes, which suggested to me the idea that they might possibly have been intended for use in securing the body, as enjoined by the Vendidad, 'so that the corpse-eating dogs and birds might not carry away any of the bones of the dead and thus defile the water and the trees.'[1] The difficulty, however, is to determine precisely by whom and at what particular period this mortuary platform was used, if we regard it so and similarly construe the other spaces which are not so distinctly marked. The bodies of the kings themselves can hardly have been exposed here before being laid in the tomb, as those catacombs were evidently designed to hold large coffins, if we may judge from the size of the *loculi* and from the description of the tombs back of the platform as given by Diodorus, who says that the body was raised by 'machines' expressly devised for the purpose.[2] Nor does it seem likely that the bones were first denuded of the flesh any more than in the case of Cyrus, whose 'body' ($\sigma\hat{\omega}\mu\alpha$) is spoken of by Arrian and Strabo when describing the mausoleum at Pasargadæ.[3]

---

[1] Vd. **6**. 46.

[2] Diodorus Siculus, *History*, **17**. 71.

[3] See pp. 285-286, above.

First Tomb at Naksh-i Rustam
(Possibly that of Xerxes)

Rock-hewn Fire-Altars at Naksh-i Rustam

The Persians in Achæmenian times, moreover, had not generally adopted the Magian fashion of exposing the dead, but
rather buried the body, merely coating it with wax, as a con-
cession to the Magi, who followed the strict Zoroastrian law
for exposing corpses;[1] and it was not until the time of the
Sasanians that the custom of exposure became universal among
the orthodox throughout Iran. For that reason, if we are to
assign these presumable dakhmahs to Achæmenian times, we are
entitled, perhaps, to suggest the possibility that they may have
been first employed by the Magian priests themselves — perhaps to give currency to this tenet of the religion — and then
may have come into more general use later, especially when the
city of Stakhr was under Sasanian rule. But this is only a
conjecture, and the whole subject requires further consideration.

On the highest point of the bluff, and just above the sepulchres, is one other noticeable object. It is a sort of parapet
cut near the rocky ledge and ascended by five roughly hewn
steps. It appears to date from the same period as the other
cuttings and looks as if it might have been for use on some
occasion when sacrifice was offered to 'Auramazda and the
other divinities,'[2] or when the king was laid in the tomb, but
nothing is actually known of its real character.

After finishing my examination of the necropolis cliff, its
altars, and its presumably early dakhmahs, I proceeded downward and remounted my horse to ride toward the river Polvar,
which winds its way through the plain between Naksh-i Rustam and the great platform of Persepolis. My ultimate goal
was the small station of Puzah, on the other side of the Polvar,
but to reach it I had first to cross some deep irrigation-canals
and then ford the stream. To make the progress of our little
caravan slower, the horses persisted in stopping to nibble the
tempting tops of the barley which had grown high from the

---

[1] We may deduce this from the account given by Herodotus, *History*,
1. 140.

[2] Bh. **4**. 61, 63, etc. Cf. also Ker
Porter, *Travels*, 1. 570.

effect of the spring rains, but in this way I had a better opportunity to survey the plain.

The north side of the Plain of Mervdasht is dotted here and
there with ruins of the ancient city of Stakhra, the capital as opposed to the platform, or capitol.[1] Although the name Stakhra
has not been traced back beyond Sasanian times, it must be an
old Iranian word meaning 'strong,' as applicable to the strategic
character of the place in ancient times, and we have traditional
authority for even assigning the founding of the city to the
early dawn of the legendary Pishdadians, since Yakut says, 'Its
commencement is attributed to Istakhr, son of Tahumars
(Tahmuraf).'[2] Mustaufi (A.D. 1340) reports a twofold legend,
stating that, 'according to some, Istakhr was built by Keiomars;
but according to others, it was founded by his son Istakhr,
enlarged by Hoshang, and completed by Jamshid.'[3] The still
earlier writer Ibn Haukal, in the tenth century, acknowledges
that 'Istakhr is a city neither small nor great, but it is more
ancient than any city whatsoever in Farsistan.'[4] Firdausi, in
his epic, presupposes the existence of the city in the age of the
legendary Kei Kaus, for, according to the poet, it had 'a palace
that was the glory of the royal family.'[5] Tabari (d. A.D. 923),
writing in the same century as Firdausi, but earlier, even claims
that it was to a place in Istakhr, called *Dizh-i Nipīsht*, 'Stronghold of Records,' that Zoroaster's patron, Vishtasp, sent the
original copy of the Avesta, which was engrossed in letters of
gold. This tradition, also found elsewhere, seems to agree with
the Pahlavi account of the archetype copy of the scriptures
which was deposited in the 'treasury of *Shapīgān*'[6] and burned

---

[1] See p. 294, above.

[2] Yakut, p. 49. Tahumars, or Tahmuraf, is the same as the Avestan king
Takhma Urupi, the predecessor of
Yima Khshaeta (Jamshid), and, according to legend, his brother. See
on this point Darmesteter, *Le ZA.* 2.
583, n. 13.

[3] Hamdallah Mustaufi, *Nuzhat al-*

Kulūb, cited by Barbier de Meynard,
Dict. géog. p. 48, n. 1; and compare
Le Strange, *Persia under the Mongols*,
in *JRAS.* 1902, p. 519.

[4] Ibn Haukal, tr. Ouseley, p. 100.

[5] Firdausi, *Shāh Nāmah*, tr. Mohl,
2, 428.

[6] The spelling and reading of this
name is various.

RUINS OF STAKHRA

TAKHT-I TAUS, OR RUSTAM'S THRONE

by Alexander the Great; but we are not sure whether this 'Stronghold of Records' was in the city on the plain, or located on the platform itself, as is more probable, having been transferred thither under the later Achæmenians.[1] In Sasanian times the city seems to have been well known as *Stakhr*;[2] but it appears to have lost its prestige with the lapse of time, and the place was in ruins when Pietro della Valle visited it in 1621.[3] Broken columns, bases of pillars, and the remains of an ancient gateway alone now mark its site. To one who is acquainted with the clay-built dwellings alike of the rich and poor in Persia to-day, it is easy to understand how such a city could crumble into dust, with the exception of the few stone columns that mark its site, particularly as Yakut (A.D. 1220) expressly says, 'the houses of Istakhr are built of clay or of stone covered over with plaster.'[4]

The southernmost point of this wide-extended but ill-defined settlement of the past appears still to be marked by a well-preserved small granite staging, which the peasants call *Takht-i Ṭā'ūs*, 'Peacock Throne,' or *Takht-i Rustam*, 'Rustam's Throne,' near the little post-house at Puzah. This raised flooring of stone is between seven and eight feet high and about forty

---

[1] For the statement of Tabari (Leiden edition, p. 675) see the translation by Gottheil in my *Zoroaster*, pp. 97, 224, n. 2. The statement is repeated by Bundari and by Thaalibi, tr. Zotenberg, *Histoire des Rois des Perses*, p. 257. Tabari also says there was 'a fire-temple of Anahedh (Anahita) at Istakhr' (tr. Nöldeke, *Geschichte der Perser und Araber*, p. 4). For the tradition about the archetype copy of the Avesta, see Denkart 3. 3; 7. 7. 3 n.; 5. 3. 4; and compare West, *SBE*. 37. p. xxxi; *SBE*. 47. 82, 127, and my *Zoroaster*, p. 224, n. 1, consulting likewise my article, *Some Additional Data on Zoroaster*, in the volume in honor of Professor Theodor Nöldeke, *Orientalische Studien*, pp. 1031-1033, Strassburg, 1906.

[2] See the Pahlavi works Shatroiha-i Airan, 41, tr. Modi, p. 97 (and notes); Karnamak, 4. 11, ed. Darab D. P. Sanjana, p. 21.

[3] See Pietro della Valle, *Viaggi*, 2. 248; *Travels*, ed. Pinkerton, 9. 101, and cf. Curzon, *Persia*, 2. 134, 136.

[4] Yakut, p. 49. On my journey southward to Persepolis, for example, I noticed an instance where an entire village had been abandoned in comparatively recent times and fallen into a mass of dust and rubbish, but was supplanted by another settlement on a new site half a mile beyond.

feet square, and is composed of two layers of white blocks, some of them ten feet long, laid in terrace fashion. Not a trace of a column or base of a pillar is seen on the floor of the structure, as would have been the case if it were the stylobate of a small audience-hall (for we should hardly expect to look for a true temple among Achæmenian remains); we may presume, therefore, that it was really a throne-platform, as tradition says, like the one mentioned above in the chapter on Tak-i Bostan.[1] As such it was probably not intended for levees like those on the Grand Platform, but may have been designed as a reviewing-stand for great military gatherings, such as the assembly on the muster-field of Castolou Pedion, under the younger Cyrus, alluded to by Xenophon.[2]

The level surface of this granite staging, or platform, near Puzah is broken at the northwest corner by a large block, which might possibly have been a rostrum. About two hundred yards distant from this there rises from the ground a solitary block which looks as if it might have been used as an altar or a pulpit, for in front of it there is a stepping-stone, standing on which I could rest my note-book conveniently upon the top of the block — a statement which will convey some idea of the height. In the light of the sinking sun the adjacent white terrace looked like the purest marble and was outlined in sharp detail against the black tents of the nomad Iliats who were encamped near it.

On the way to the post-house I had time to make a brief inspection of the Sasanian sculptures close by the rocks of Naksh-i Rajab, as a preliminary to a re-examination of them next day. These bas-reliefs, three in number, are carved in a recess in the rocks, and their position is so little obtrusive that they would easily escape notice unless one were looking for them. They belong to the earlier period of the Sasanian dynasty, and two of them represent its founder, Ardashir Papakan (A.D. 226–241), in the act of receiving the crown at

[1] See p. 228, above.   [2] Xenophon, *Anabasis*, 1.1.2; 1.9.7.

SASANIAN SCULPTURE IN THE REAR OF THE RECESS AT NAKSH-I RAJAB

SASANIAN SCULPTURE AT THE LEFT OF THE RECESS AT NAKSH-I RAJAB

the hands of the god Ormazd. In the first of these, the one to the right, or on the western side, Ardashir and the god are mounted on horseback, in a manner similar to that in the seventh bas-relief at Naksh-i Rustam, as shown in the photograph previously given.[1] In the second, that on the rear wall of the niche, both personages are on foot, and there are several other figures in this group. Between the king and the deity stand two small boys, whose statues were originally less sharply carved and are now nearly obliterated. They are supposed to represent sons of the king. Behind the monarch there stands a serious-faced unbearded personage, who points to an inscription back of the king. He is intended possibly to represent a eunuch. Behind him again stands a heavily bearded person who is either a bodyguard or a vizir. On the other hand, to the right and back of the god, there are two smooth-faced figures that look like a queen and her maid retiring from the scene.[2] We do not know precisely the details of the royal incident here depicted, but the names Shahpur and Varahran, given in a Pahlavi inscription to which the unbearded personage points his finger, assigns it to Sapor I (A.D. 241–272) or his son Bahram II (A.D. 276–293).[3] The third panel, the bas-relief on the left, or north, side of the recess, represents Sapor I on horseback and attended by a bodyguard on foot. An inscription in Pahlavi and Greek serves to identify the king.[4]

The night was passed in the tiny *chāpār-khānah* of Puzah, the smallest in all Persia, I believe, and by daylight next morning I was ready to mount for the short ride to the great

[1] See p. 302, above, and the picture of the seventh bas-relief. For a photograph of the Naksh-i Rajab equestrian sculpture, see Stolze and Andreas, *Persepolis*, 2. pl. 100.

[2] They did not look to me like eunuchs, and my guides spoke of them as sculptures of women.

[3] For the inscription and references, see West, *Grundr. iran. Philol.* 2. 77-78.

[4] I have reproduced from my collection photographs of the second and third of these bas-reliefs ; for other photographs of these, including the first, see Stolze and Andreas, *Persepolis*, 2. pls. 100-104 ; Dieulafoy, *L'Art Antique*, 5. pl. 17. The light in the recess is unfortunately not favorable for making successful photographs of the sculptures.

platform of Persepolis, *Takht-i Jamshīd*, 'Jamshid's Throne,' as
the Persians call it, or *Chahal Minār*, 'Forty Columns,' the
name by which it was more generally known in books of
travel three or four centuries ago.   This magnificent terrace
is the foundation upon which stood the palaces of Darius,
Xerxes, Artaxerxes, and their successors ; here Alexander
held revel in the deserted halls of his adversary Darius
Codomannus, the last of the Achæmenians, and in his drunken
orgy, as is believed, burned the lordly edifices and the royal
library that housed the scriptures and ancient records of Iran.[1]
To-day majestic ruins alone crown the height, and the natives
know nothing about the historic associations connected with
the platform and think of it only as one of the scenes of Jamshid's departed glory.

The platform itself lies at the base of a rocky row of hills
called *Kūh-i Rahmat*, 'Mountain of Mercy,' and in former times
apparently also *Shāh-Kūh*, 'Royal Mountain,' the βασιλικὸν ὄρος
of Diodorus,[2] which rises to the east and whose spurs have
been partly cut away in the building of the terraced elevation.
A noble wall, varying from twenty to fifty feet in height and
constructed of stone quarried from the hillside, encloses the
area on the three exposed sides, for no barrier was needed at
the rear because of the natural fortification of the hills, as will
be clear to any one who has visited the scene or consulted the
panoramic photograph by Dieulafoy and the drawings of Flandin.[3] The configuration of the terrace-height is such that three
distinct levels are clearly noticeable, the highest being in the
middle, which is made still more elevated by a mound in its
midst.   Over the surface of the platform are spread the
remains of the architectural glories of the Achæmenians.

We have a general description of the platform, written in

---

[1] See p. 307, n. 1, above. Diodorus
Siculus (*History*, 17. 72) draws a vivid
picture of the orgy and of the burning
of Persepolis, a scene familiar through
Dryden's 'Alexander's Feast.'

[2] See Diodorus Siculus, *History*,
17. 71.

[3] See Dieulafoy, *L'Art Antique de
la Perse*, 2. pls. 4–7 ; Flandin and
Coste, *Voyage en Perse*, 2. pl. 67.

The Grand Staircase at Persepolis

Greek nearly two thousand years ago, by Diodorus Siculus
(c. B.C. 50). Since the passage is important as a means of
identification of the site, I translate the paragraph which relates
to the construction of the terrace and the tombs of the kings,
preserving in my rendering the interchange of tenses, present
and past, that is found in the original Greek.

'The citadel (ἄκρα) is worthy of mention. It had a threefold
wall surrounding it, the first (section) of which was constructed
with stately bastions (ἀναλήμματι πολυδαπάνῳ) and adorned with
battlements (ἐπάλξεσι) and it had a height of sixteen cubits.[1] The
second has a similar arrangement to that of the preceding, but double
its height. The third enclosure is rectangular in shape, and its wall
is sixty cubits high and constructed of solid stone so perfectly set
as to last forever. On each side it has brazen gates and, beside them,
brazen bulls, twenty cubits high,[2] the latter being intended to
inspire awe in the beholder, and the former designed for security.
On the side of the citadel toward the east, and four hundred feet
distant, is the so-called Royal Mountain, in which were the tombs
of the kings. The rock was hewn out and had in its bosom several
sepulchres in which were the vaults of the dead.[3] There were no
specially prepared means of access, but the corpses were hoisted up
by machines (ὀργάνων) devised for the purpose, and thus received
burial.[4] In the citadel itself there were many sumptuously equipped
residences for the king and his officers, and likewise treasuries
well adapted for the safe-guarding of wealth.'[5]

The original plan and the main construction of this noble
platform (which more than a thousand years ago was com-

---

[1] I believe that the 'threefold wall'
refers to the three distinct levels shown
in the terrace rampart, although Blundell (*Persepolis*, in *Transactions of the
Ninth International Congress of Orientalists*, 2. 553) interprets this as referring to actual walls of circumvallation. Instead of 'bastions,' which I
understand as alluding to the various
bays in the rampart, we may perhaps
refer the words ἀναλήμματι πολυδαπάνῳ
to the sumptuous edifices on the terrace.

[2] Reading ταυρούς for σταυρούς, according to Mr. Cecil Smith's excellent
emendation, cf. Curzon, *Persia*, 2.
187, n. 1, and Blundell, *op. cit.* p. 553.
It is possible that the now ruined
bull-flanked portals may have been
actually gilded in ancient times.

[3] Literally 'has in its midst several
houses (οἴκους).'

[4] Literally 'the vaults receive burial
of the corpses that have been hauled up.'

[5] Diodorus Siculus, *History*, 17. 71.

pared with Baalbec and the architectural remains of Palmyra and Egypt,[1] and fabled to be the work of Solomon's *genii*) was due to Darius. In one of his inscriptions he definitely states that he 'built this fortress on a place where no fortress had been built before,' and that he did so by the grace of 'Auramazda and the other gods.'[2] Darius erected at least two of the noblest buildings, but the elaboration of the design was due to Xerxes and its completion to his successors. Though far grander in its magnificence than any ordinary fortress, it must have been easily guarded by armed patrols on the walls and by platoons of soldiers stationed at all points of access, and reasons have been advanced for believing that its strength was re-enforced by walled fortifications or turrets in front of it on the plain.[3] The southerly position of the Palace of Darius and the fact that it faces southward has led, not unreasonably perhaps, to the assumption that there was originally an approach from the south or southeast, whereas the regular means of access, which must have been unchanged since the time of Xerxes, is by a great double staircase constructed in the wall near the northwest angle of the platform.

This Grand Staircase (*A*) consists of a double ramping flight, each series numbering more than a hundred steps, with an angle of ascent so gentle and a width so broad, that a troop of horse-

[1] See the Mohammedan writer Istakhri (c. A.D. 950), ed. De Goeje, *Bibl. Geog. Arab.* 1. 150 and 1. 123, cf. Schwarz, *Iran im Mittelalter nach den Arabischen Geographen*, 1. 13–14, Leipzig, 1896 ; and Mokadassi, or Makdasi (A.D. 984), ed. De Goeje, *Bibl. Geog. Arab.* 3. 420, 435, 446, cf. Nöldeke, *Encyclopædia Britannica*, 9th ed., 18. 558, notes 1 and 10. A still earlier description of Istakhr is given by Masudi (A.D. 944), *Les Prairies d'Or*, ed. Barbier de Meynard, 4. 76 seq.

[2] This statement regarding the 'fort-

ress' (Elam. *halvarras*, the same word that is employed to render OP. *didā* in Bh. 2. 39) is found only in the Elamitic version of the inscription on the side of the rampart, mentioned below, p. 318.

[3] See reference already given to Blundell, *Persepolis*, in *Ninth Internat. Congress of Orientalists*, 2. 547–556. As explained above, I am inclined to explain the threefold wall of Diodorus (17. 71) as referring rather to the three main elevations, and to understand that the bull-flanked portals may actually have been gilded as implied in the 'brazen gates' and 'brazen bulls.'

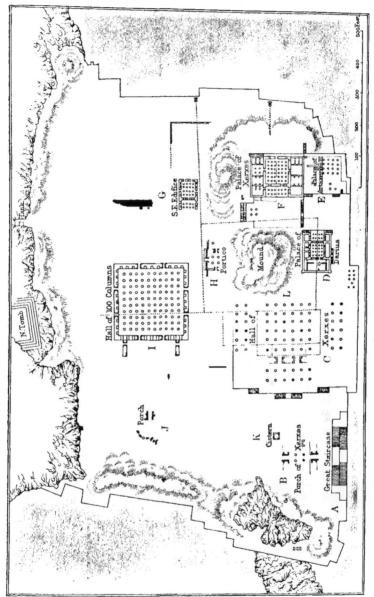

CURZON'S PLAN OF PERSEPOLIS

men, ten abreast, could ride up it.[1] As we surmount the top-most step and cast the eye over the surface of the platform, we are struck by a succession of stately portals, broken columns, capitals, pedestals, stone steps, sculptured friezes, and doorways, spread about in confusion or gathered into disordered groups. So often have these ruins been described, and so fully have they been illustrated that I can do little here except point out the salient features and possibly add a suggestion or two regarding the historic significance of these relics of the past.[2]

Directly opposite the Grand Staircase is the Porch of Xerxes (*B*). This imposing propylæum is guarded at each entrance, back and front, by colossal winged bulls of stone, after the Assyrian manner. Two of these colossi face westward out over the plain; the other two (a photograph of which I have given in the fourth chapter) look eastward toward the hills behind the platform. Near the top of each of the massive pylons of this portico there is a trilingual inscription in cuneiform characters, stating that the portal is the work of Xerxes and ascribing praise to Auramazda for all the blessings of his divine favor.[3] Two of the original four fluted columns are still standing between the stately piers of this triumphal arch, the 'Portal of All Nations,' as Xerxes himself called it,[4] through which at No-Ruz the envoys from tributary lands marched in solemn procession to bring gifts to the Great King, as portrayed on the sculptured stylobate some fifty yards to the south.

---

[1] Attention was called to this fact, centuries ago, in the *Zīnat al-Majlis*, pt. 9, cited by Barbier de Meynard, *Dict. géog.* p. 48, n. 2 ; also by Justi, *Empire of the Persians*, p. 189, and by others.

[2] For the best presentation of all that has been written on this subject, see Curzon, *Persia*, 2. 148–196 ; for illustrative material, consult the standard works of Texier, Flandin and Coste, Stolze and Andreas, Perrot and Chipiez, and Dieulafoy, all of which have been referred to many times before.

[3] See Weissbach and Bang, *Die altpers. Keilinschr.* p. 40, and Spiegel, *Die altpers. Keilinschr.* p. 58.

[4] In the old Persian language, *duvarthi visa-dahyu*, see Xerx. Pers. a. 11. For a conjectural restoration of the Portal, see Perrot and Chipiez, *Histoire de l'Art*, 5. pl. 3, p. 404.

This latter terrace, with its elaborately carved frieze and cuneiform inscriptions on the walls of the four staircases that approach it, served as a stylobate for Xerxes' lofty Audience-Hall (*C*), the ruined columns of which gave rise to the native designation *Chahal Minār*, 'Forty Pillars.' But the original number of columns was seventy-two, and of these only thirteen are standing, to mark with their tall fluted shafts the aisles that led to the spot where Xerxes held levees within its once tapestry-hung walls.[1] The ruin and desolation form a pathetic contrast to the proud vaunt of the king in the cuneiform tablet carved on the stairway of approach, 'I am Xerxes, the Great King, the King of Kings, King of the Nations with their many peoples, King of this Great Earth even to afar,' and a sadder comment on the pious fervor of the words that follow, 'Thus saith Xerxes, the Great King: Everything that has been made by me here and all that has been made for me elsewhere, I have made by the grace of Auramazda; may Auramazda with the other divinities protect both my kingdom and all that I have made.'[2]

Walking about fifty yards to the south we come to the ruins of the Palace of Darius (*D*) situated on the highest part of the platform, and directly before a mound (*L*). Although smaller and less imposing than either of the main edifices raised by his son Xerxes, the Palace of Darius is better preserved than the others. Here, several times repeated, are inscriptions recording the fact that the building was the 'palace '(*tachara*), 'house ' (*vith*), or the 'abode' (*hadish*)[3] of King Darius, whose figure

[1] For the problem of the walls according to Fergusson's architectural ideas, see Blundell, *Persepolis*, in *Ninth International Congress of Orientalists*, 2. 542–547, as opposed to Curzon, *Persia*, 2. 164–165, and the reconstructions by Dieulafoy, *L'Art Antique*, 3. pl. 9, and Perrot and Chipiez, *Histoire de l'Art*, 5. pls. 4, 5, 6.

[2] See Xerx. Pers. b. 12–30 (Weissbach and Bang, *Die altpers. Keilinschr.* p. 40; Spiegel, *Die altpers. Keilinschr.* p. 62).

[3] The word *hadis* is added by Xerxes in two inscriptions on his father's palace, once on a shaft in the southwest corner of the building, and once on the southern wall of the stylobate on which the palace stands (see Dar. Pers. a, c; Xerx. Pers. ca[cb];

PERSEPOLIS

SUBJECT NATIONS BRINGING TRIBUTE TO XERXES

is sculptured in bas-relief, as fighting with some monster, whom he slays, thus triumphing over the power of evil, or as attended by servants who bear the royal umbrella, the fly-flap, and other insignia of sovereignty. To me the most interesting of all the inscriptions was a short device carved around the stone lintels of the windows through which the king looked out upon his people and over the fine panorama that stretched before his view. The cuneiform letters are deeply chiselled and they form a narrow band of text, originally repeated eighteen times because of the number of windows, of which only thirteen now remain. The brief sentence reads, *ardastāna āthangaina Dārayavaush khshāyathiyahyā vithiyā karta,* 'a structure of stone built in the house of King Darius.'[1]

Proceeding again southward, across a space that was once an open court below the palace, we enter the ruins of the Palace of Artaxerxes III, Ochus, (*E*) which faced directly north toward the latter.[2] An inscription, which is thrice repeated on the double stairway that forms the approach on the north, and is reproduced again on the west, bears the name of Artaxerxes III, or Ochus. In this the king gives his genealogy and, after declaring that he has built this stone structure, closes with the words, 'may Auramazda and the god Mithra protect me and my country and all that has been made by me.'[3] These inscribed tablets are separated by handsome panels that are decorated with bas-reliefs of the royal guards; but excepting these stairway-friezes and the bases of a group of columns, there is little to show that the ruins among which we are standing

Weissbach, pp. 6, 8, 32, 43; Spiegel, pp. 50, 62; and compare Justi, *Grundr. iran. Philol.* 2. 451–452).

[1] Dar. Pers. c (Weissbach, pp. 5, 34; Spiegel, p. 50; cf. also Justi, *Grundr. iran. Philol.* 2. 451, and Bartholomae, *Air. Wb.* p. 193).

[2] For the court see Blundell, *Persepolis,* in *Ninth International Congress of Orientalists,* 2. 541–542, and compare Perrot and Chipiez, *Histoire de l'Art,* 5. pl. 9 (p. 644).

[3] Artax. Pers. a[b] (Weissbach, pp. 9, 46; Spiegel, pp. 68, 69). The designation for the stairway, or possibly the stylobate, is *ustašanā aθaⁿ-ga[i]nā,* lit. 'up-building of stone,' cf. also Justi, *Grundr. iran. Philol.* 2. 452, and Bartholomae, *Air. Wb.* pp. 64, 407.

are the remains of a palace.   The small size of the ground-plan and the unfinished appearance of the surroundings have led some scholars to question whether the building was actually intended as a royal residence at all and whether it was ever completed.[1]

Directly to the east, on a large rectangular stylobate formed partly of the natural rock,[2] stand the ruins of the sumptuous Palace of Xerxes (*F*), the grandest of the buildings in design except his own Audience-Hall and the Hall of a Hundred Columns belonging to his father.   The stairways that lead up to it are richly decorated with sculptured panels, slabs, ornamented friezes, inscribed tablets, and pillars.[3]   Fragments of columns, doorways, and windows remain to mark the courts of the king, who still walks in effigy of stone;[4] but like the grandiloquent titles which he hung upon the now crumbled walls they are merely mute witnesses of a dead past.

Crossing some fifty yards eastward over uneven ground behind the palace, we find the remains of a smaller building, the so-called Southeast Edifice (*G*), the identity of which is not positively known.   Apparently it was a royal abode of some sort if we may judge from the images of the king carved on the doorways and representing him in combat with conventionalized monsters or as attended by slaves who carry the royal umbrella and fly-flap.[5]   We may even go further and presume that it was the abode of Xerxes as crown-prince, if we may judge from the physiognomy of the king as portrayed here and on the walls of his palace.[6]

About forty yards north-northwest from this point and

---

[1] On this point compare the remarks of Curzon, *Persia*, 2. 172–173; but see Justi, *Grundr. iran. Philol.* 2. 452, and *Empire of the Persians*, p. 197.

[2] Blundell, *op. cit.* p. 539.

[3] See for example the photographs in Stolze and Andreas, *Persepolis*, 1. pls. 24–25.

[4] For illustrations of Xerxes attended by his servants or in combat with mythical animals, see Stolze and Andreas, 1. pl. 13 seq.

[5] For photographic illustrations, see Stolze and Andreas, 1. pls. 1–4.

[6] Justi (*Empire of the Persians*, p. 198) says 'the portrait of Xerxes is fairly recognizable; it shows a long,

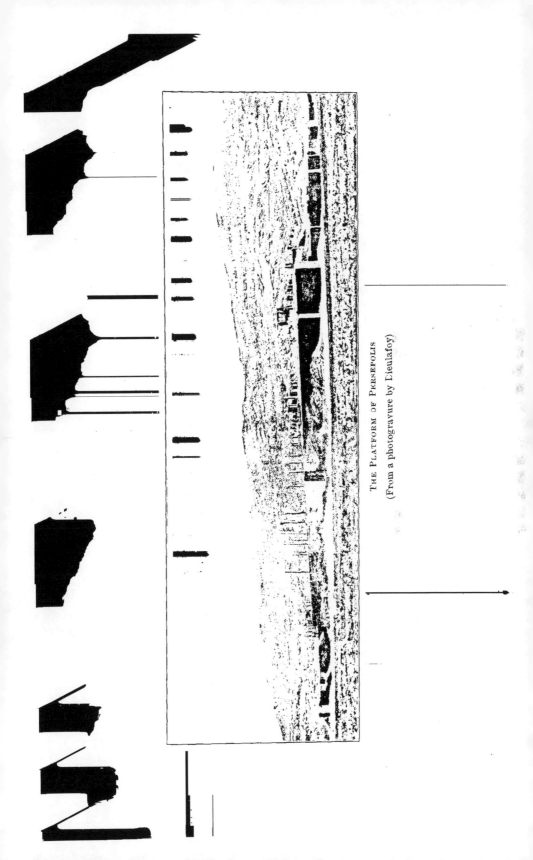

THE PLATFORM OF PERSEPOLIS

(From a photogravure by Dieulafoy)

directly behind the mound in the rear of the Palace of Darius, we see a ruined entrance-hall, decorated with the conventional bas-reliefs of the king seated upon his throne. This small structure is known as the Portico of Darius (*H*), though sometimes called the Central Edifice.

Adjoining it on the east there stands the last and the largest of all the palatial buildings, the Hall of a Hundred Columns (*I*), erected by Darius for holding ceremonial functions. The main entrance was on the north side through a vestibule whose roof was supported by sixteen columns that led the way into the throne-hall itself. This superb edifice covered an area two hundred and twenty-five feet square, and formed a magnificent structure raised on a hundred columns, ten rows each way, but of these not a single one is now standing. The doorways east and west still represent Darius in the act of slaying animals of monstrous shape, and the entrances north and south depict him crowned with a tiara and mounted upon his throne supported by three or even five tiers of subject nations who carry arms in defence of their ruler, over whom hover the wings of his god.[1] The chamber walls of the royal hall were probably of sun-dried brick plastered over with a glaze or coated with enamelled tiles ; but they crumbled into dust ages ago, and only fragments of columns, stone door-jambs, and window-sills remain, together with bits of carbonized cedar buried beneath a mass of débris and ashes, to tell that the pillars once supported a roof with a thousand beams.[2] In this case, as in the case of the Audience-Hall of Xerxes, we are led to wonder whether it was the hand of the drunken

bearded face with a prominent hooked nose.' See also Justi's plan, *op. cit.* p. 187, and compare his remarks in *Grundr. iran. Philol.* 2. 452.

[1] I reproduce a photograph of the North Doorway of the Hall of the Hundred Columns; for a picture of the less imposing South Doorway, see

Stolze and Andreas, 1. pl. 51 ; cf. also Curzon, *Persia*, 2. pp. 176, 178.

[2] The Avesta, by its architectural allusions (Vd.**18**. 28 ; Yt. **5**. 101 ; Ys. **57**. 21) seems to refer to magnificent structures such as this. With regard to the charcoal and decomposed *gach*, or plaster, see Blundell, *op. cit.* p. 540.

Alexander and the torch of his revelling soldiers that brought about the desolation which reigns supreme.

Some sixty or seventy yards north of this famous hall are seen a few blocks and mutilated columns of what was once a bull-flanked propylæum, or Porch, (*J*) that led to the audience-hall itself; but all the rest of its pristine glory is lost forever. In addition to this portal there is near the Porch of Xerxes a rock-hewn Cistern (*K*) which must have fed a fountain whose jets sprang from the midst of a tank like the *hōz* in a modern Persian courtyard. Besides the tumulus, or Mound (*L*), previously referred to, there are beneath the surface of the platform also several underground passages, water-channels, and drains, which have not yet been fully excavated, together with some minor evidences of unfinished work in the past, but they still await the spade of the archæologist.[1]

Before closing the chapter I must add two more paragraphs on matters of historic interest. The first relates to two important inscriptions carved by Darius on mammoth blocks set in the southern retaining wall of the platform and known to scholars as *Dar. Pers. d* and *e*. Each tablet contains twenty-four lines. In the former inscription the king glorifies Auramazda, gives thanks to him for his blessings, and prays that he and the other divinities may ever protect the land. The same idea is repeated in the Babylonian version, which is largely a paraphrase, and partly also in the Elamitic section, which adds, however, some interesting information, not found elsewhere, to the effect that Darius was the first to fortify the place, which was not previously a stronghold.[2] The adjoining inscription on a block to the right is written only in old Persian and

---

[1] For some results from comparatively recent diggings in the mound and some excavations among the ruins, see Blundell, *op. cit.* pp. 537–559.

[2] For a photograph of this inscription, see Stolze and Andreas, *Persepolis*, 2. pl. 95; and for translations, see Weissbach and Bang, pp. 5, 34, and Spiegel, pp. 46–50; and compare Weissbach, *Die Achämenideninschriften Zweiter Art*, p. 76; Bezold, *Die Achaemen. Inschr.* p. 39. Consult likewise, Justi, *Grundr. iran. Philol.* 2. 448.

North Tomb

Middle Tomb

South Tomb

THE TOMBS BACK OF THE PLATFORM OF PERSEPOLIS

enumerates the conquests of Darius, concluding with the prayer that ' Peace may come from Aura.' [1] As I stood at the foot of the rampart to collate the tablets high above and make notes which I hope later to publish, the sun's rays were so scorching and the flies so pestiferous that I could understand the king's need for a *chowri* and an umbrella in ancient days!

The remaining point of historic interest connected with Persepolis is the series of three tombs hewn in the rocky hill of Kuh-i Rahmat behind the platform. They are the sepulchres of three later kings of the Achæmenian line and resemble the four elder tombs at Naksh-i Rustam, which have been already described; but owing to the nature of the hillside where they are cut they differ from the latter in minor details, especially in being less high from the ground and therefore easy of access. The first of the three is hewn in the face of the rock almost directly back of the Hall of a Hundred Columns and is commonly known as the North Tomb and presumed to be the mausoleum of Artaxerxes II, Mnemon (B.C. 404–358). The second lies in a recess in the mountain-side somewhat southeast of the lower end of the platform and is designated as the Middle Tomb,[2] and is believed to be the vault of Artaxerxes III, Ochus (B.C. 358–337). The third is cut in a rock more than half a mile farther to the south and is easily accessible from the ground, but was never finished. It may have been commenced by Darius III, Codomannus (B.C. 335–330), the last of the Achæmenian kings. If that be true, it is reasonable to suppose that his overthrow by Alexander and his subsequent tragic death were the cause of its never having been completed.[3]

---

[1] Dar. Pers. e. 1–24. See also preceding references.

[2] The position of the tombs may best be gathered from Flandin and Coste, *Voyage en Perse, Ancienne*, 2. pl. 65 (reproduced in Perrot and Chipiez, *Histoire de l'Art*, 5. 454).

[3] The assignment of the three tombs, as I have given it, is the generally accepted one. See for example Curzon, *Persia*, 2. 183; Justi, *Grundr. iran. Philol*. 2. 455. For architectural details consult Perrot and Chipiez, *Histoire de l'Art*, 5. 617–638; and for photographs refer to Stolze and Andreas, *Persepolis*, 1. pls. 70–73.

As we gaze upon this tomb and the others, and then cast our
eyes toward the ruins of Persepolis, we can but think with a
heart-pang of Omar Khayyam's lines : —

> ' They say the Lion and the Lizard keep
> The Courts where Jamshyd gloried and drank deep.'

Here stood the palace of Darius, there the throne-room of
Artaxerxes, yonder the pillared halls of Xerxes, and not far
distant the tombs of the kings.   But all are in ruins; all are
relics of glory past.   Yet who knows?   Out of the shadow of
by-gone days, out of the dust of departed ages, out of the ashes
of the Simurgh's fire, out of the fragments of shattered Iran,
there may arise one whose master hand will restore the glory
of the ancient Persian kingdom, illumine again the pages of
Persia's chronicles, recall what was noblest in the Parthian rule
and Sasanian empire, and make splendid once more the land
and people of the Lion and the Sun.

THE PALACE OF DARIUS

A PORTAL AND THE HALL OF A HUNDRED COLUMNS
(The North Tomb in the Background)

CHAPTER XXI

SHIRAZ, THE HOME OF THE PERSIAN POETS

'There's a bower of roses by Bendemeer's stream
And the nightingale sings round it all the day long;
In the time of my childhood 'twas like a sweet dream,
To sit in the roses and hear the birds' song.
The bower and its music I never forget,
But oft when alone in the bloom of the year
I think — is the nightingale singing there yet?
Are the roses still bright by the calm Bendemeer?'

— MOORE, *Lalla Rookh.*

SHIRAZ lies about forty miles south of Persepolis, but the
two stages of the journey are not easy, so I arranged to make
my start from the desolate and ruined halls of the Achæmenians in time to reach the native city of Hafiz and Saadi
before nightfall. The first relay of horses for the journey
I found good, which proved an omen for the second; and a
series of long and hard gallops, with only occasional halts to
adjust the load on the pack-horse, brought my little cavalcade
in two hours to the end of the hill-girt marshy plain of Mervdasht. At no great distance from this point the road crosses
a bridge over 'Bendemeer's stream.' This watercourse owes
its name *Band-i Amīr*, 'Dam of the Amir,' to an arched causeway constructed by Azad ad-Daulah, who governed Fars in
the tenth century, and who also adorned the banks of the river
at various places with parks and palaces.[1] The latter, unfortunately, have vanished generations ago.

A few miles beyond the Bendemeer bridge the village of
Zargan, or Zergun, lies nestled at the foot of a mountain, where

[1] See Yakut, pp. 313, 480.

the *chāpār khānah* is located, and here a change of horses may be obtained. As the weather was warm the post-quarters at the time had been moved out on the main trail in the plain and were lodged in a couple of small tents, so I was saved the extra ride to the halting-place. An unexpected delay, however, occurred. At the moment when we were about to change mounts the horses stampeded and scampered away a mile or more before the muleteer could recapture them. Meanwhile we had time to rest and console ourselves for the loss of time with a good glass of tea. The half hour passed quickly in taking notes of the surroundings and in observing the different types among the natives, for the inhabitants of Farsistan impressed me as being the handsomest Persians I had seen. I was interested also in the primitive tankards of goatskin in which the water for the tea was brought. These rude vessels were made from the undressed hide of a goat, with the animal's hair left on the outside and the skin drawn tightly around a wooden rim and a circular board bottom so as to form a bucket, while three sticks were used as fastenings to give firmness to the whole and as props for the uncouth vessel to stand upon. I presume it was from tankards such as these that the hardy soldiers of Cyrus used to drink, before luxury taught them the use of silver beakers and the accompanying vices which sapped away the vigor that had conquered kingdoms.

Zergun remains clear in my memory because of an accident to the postilion, who was seriously kicked, on the return journey, by my pack-horse, a vicious stallion, as most of the Persian horses are. At first I thought that the man's leg was broken, but on examining the wound I found that the kneecap was not shattered, though I fear that the injury to the bone may have proved in some way a permanent one.

After leaving Zergun the hard stage of the road began. Nature has thrown up a barrier on the north to protect the approach to her chosen city of Shiraz, or perhaps to set bounds to the too enthusiastic admiration that might be bestowed upon

KING DARIUS ON HIS THRONE

BRIDGE LEADING INTO SHIRAZ

its beauty.   This obstacle is in the form of a steep and inde-
scribably stony mountain road winding up and down and
hither and thither, past ruined forts and dilapidated habitations, before reaching the stream of Roknabad.   This small river
was so named after the Buyid ruler, Rokn ad-Daulah Hasan, in
the tenth century, who conducted its water by special courses
to Shiraz and the beautiful suburb Musalla.   It owes its fame,
however, to Hafiz, who sang its praises and compared it with
the rivers of Paradise.   But the Roknabad has now shrunk to
so small a measure that Hafiz seems guilty of a strange hyper-
bole in the verse,

> ' In Paradise thou wilt not find
> The beauteous banks of Roknabad
> And the rose-bowers of Musalla.'

Nevertheless the landscape about the stream is Arcadian, and
the scenery calls forth admiration from the rider as he winds
his way downward through the mountain glade that lies beyond
the stony section of the road.

Suddenly through a great notch in the mountains, Shiraz in
all its beauty bursts upon the view.   It seemed, as I saw it, to
rise like an island in a sea of emerald bordered in the distance
by purple hills.   The coloring was as rich as it was harmoni-
ous, and it seemed no longer a wonder that the proud Shirazis
have given to the city gateway built here at Nature's grander
portal the name *Tang-i Allāhu Akbar*, because the beholder, on
viewing such a scene, instinctively cries out ' God is Most
Great ! ' [1]   The panorama was a magnificent one; plain and
hills, gardens and cypress-groves, towers and walls, domes and
spires, were bathed in a mellow light.   The vision grew in
beauty as I rode forward.   The wayside was lined with myriad
poppies; the gardens were abloom with the jasmine and the
rose, for it was the beginning of May, and the rose had begun
to blush a few days before in obedience to the nightingale's

---

[1] See also the descriptions of   359, and Browne, *A Year Amongst*
Brugsch, *Im Lande der Sonne*, p.   *the Persians*, p. 260.

behest 'her sallow cheek to incarnadine'; the trees were vocal with the note of the *bulbul*: the setting sun threw long shadows from the tall minarets and slender *sarv* trees; and Shiraz for the instant was the realization of that Persian elysium of which the poets sang, and it awaited only the flood of moonlight which swept in after sunset to complete the enchantment.

I confess that this is written in a Persian mood. In calmer moments I can pause to consider that the city is not a Paradise after all. Ahriman has marred its perfection by his blight, as he did in Airan Vej of old. The climate at times becomes extremely hot and exhausting, as the zone is tropical, and fevers are frequent and deadly, since hygienic laws are fatally neglected in the city. The very architecture of the buildings also leaves much to be desired; and the Shirazis, though pleasure-loving and clever, have a traditional reputation for bigotry and conceit — not out of keeping, perhaps, with the official title of the town, which is ·Abode of Knowledge' (*Dār al-'Ilm*).[1] But these are the judgments of a colder moment and foreign to the proper frame of mind for a visit to Shiraz.

Although the city is the capital of the historic province of Fars and by right of inheritance the successor to the glory of Persepolis, the claim which Shiraz can make to eminence by reason of antiquity is not comparable with that of either Hamadan or Rei in Media of old. The general location of the city, it is true, is probably an ancient one, as shown by the vestiges of Achæmenian and Sasanian ruins in the vicinity, and Iranian legend and Mohammedan fable are even ready to ascribe the founding of the city to a son of Tahumars or to a great-grandson of Noah, but the more sober Moslem authors say that Shiraz was 'founded or rebuilt by Mohammed ibn Yusuf Takali after the Rise of Islam' in the seventh century of our era.[2] The Arab traveller Ibn Haukal mentions its

---

[1] On this title see Browne, *Episode of the Bab*, 2. 294, n. 1, 354, n. 2, Cambridge, 1891.

[2] For the statement regarding Tahumars, see Yakut, p. 362, and for the more conservative view, see the re-

THE NEW MOSQUE (MASJID-I NO) AT SHIRAZ

OVERLOOKING SHIRAZ

citadel (*Ḳōhandiz*) in the tenth century, and Yakut (c. A.D. 1220) states that the Buyid ruler Abu Kalanjar Sultan ad-Daulah fortified Shiraz with strong walls in the eleventh century (A.H. 440).[1] These fortifications, however, were of no avail against the Mongol conqueror Tamerlane, when he sacked the town two hundred and fifty years later. Successive rulers restored and embellished the city, but their work was, usually destroyed later by the forces of nature or through the capture of the town by enemies. Shiraz owes most of its architectural beauty to-day to Karim Khan (1751–1779), who governed it as regent under the Safavid dynasty in the latter half of the eighteenth century. Many of the effects of his refining influence were nullified by the eunuch ruler, Agha Mohammed Khan, who razed its stone ramparts to the ground, replaced them by mud walls, and reduced the city to a rank unworthy of its traditional prestige.

Among the architectural monuments of Shiraz, the oldest is a mosque which dates from the latter part of the ninth century and was built by the Safarid dynast Amr ibn Leith. Belonging to a period two centuries later is the New Mosque (*Masjid-i Nō*). Seïd ibn Zangi (1195–1226) reconstructed this out of his own palace, which he is said to have converted to the service of God as the result of a pious vow made in behalf of the life of his son.[2] The flat-roofed cloister around its court is seen in the photograph which I reproduce, while conspicuous in the background is the faience-traced dome of Shah Chiragh, the beauty of which is unfortunately impaired by a popular comparison of its swelling cupola with the head of some gigantic asparagus. Beneath its vaulted roof lie the remains of one

marks of Mustaufi, cited by Barbier de Meynard, *Dict. géog. de la Perse*, p. 362 n.

[1] Ibn Haukal, tr. Ouseley, p. 93, and Yakut, p. 365.

[2] See Curzon, *Persia*, 2. 102, and compare Mustaufi, cited by Barbier de Meynard, *Dict. géog.* p. 362, n., and Browne, *Literary History of Persia*, p. 352. Ethé and Horn, *Grundr. iran. Philol.* 2. 218, 560, 561, give the dates of Amr ibn Leith as A.D. 878–900.

of the sons of Imam Musa, a champion of Islam.[1]   Yet in
architectural merit neither this nor any of the other religious
edifices, madrasahs, mausoleums, or baths can rival those of
several other cities in Persia.   The grand bazaar, *Bāzār-i Vakīl*,
' Regent's Bazaar,' is a fine structure, due again to the munificence of Karim Khan, and it carries on a fairly flourishing trade;
but the caravansarais are not particularly spacious, nor are the
streets of the city beautiful; the Ark, or Citadel, on the other
hand, is rather imposing.   The best-constructed of the modern
buildings in the town is that occupied by the offices of the
Indo-European Telegraph Company.   It was formerly a palace
and has a fine courtyard of stone, while its hallways and roomy
chambers seemed to me Western in their style of architecture
rather than Eastern.[2]   This touch of the West brought me in
another way also nearer home, for I found an opportunity to
send a cablegram to America — a welcome experience after
having been cut off from direct communication with home
since I left Urumiah.

Buildings of brick, mortar, and stone are not the glory of
Shiraz ; it owes its renown rather to the causes which I shall now
enumerate.   In the first place the natural beauty of its environs
is greatly enhanced by cultivation and by art.   The entire
plain surrounding the city is well cultivated, and owing to its
tropical situation (for Shiraz is nearer to the equator than is
the northern part of India) it yields abundantly to tillage and
irrigation.   The vineyards around the city produce the best
wine in Persia, a product for which Shiraz has ever been
famous.   There are two varieties of this wine, a red and a
white; the taste of the white wine reminded me somewhat of a
Marsala.

The gardens and rose-bowers of Shiraz are still more famous.
Within the city and on its outskirts there are dozens of these

[1] On the latter point compare also
Curzon, *Persia*, 2. 102.
[2] For some of the artistic points of
this building, see Weeks, *From the
Black Sea*, p. 116.

VIEW OF SHIRAZ FROM THE ALLAHU AKBAR GATE

(Showing the Chahal Tan, the Haft Tan, and the Tomb of Hafiz)

pleasure-grounds, some of which still retain their beauty despite the neglect into which they have fallen. The Persian garden in general is somewhat different from its counterpart in other lands and is more like an orchard, a horticultural enclosure, than a garden in the narrower landscape sense ; in fact the ordinary Persian word for 'garden,' *bāgh*, may sometimes best be rendered by our word 'orchard,' with little of the connotation of 'flower-garden.' Instead of being winding paths, the walks are usually laid out in straight lines, with brick and tile borders, while terraces also are constructed whenever possible, as in our own gardens, and finished with stonework and masonry. A reservoir of water, even if its basin be only a small tank, necessarily graces the area, and luxury may add a fountain and cascades falling over stone slabs, but water is a precious article, and lavishness in this regard is equivalent to extravagance, even if nature responds liberally to the smallest drop of the precious liquid. Shade trees like the poplar (*ḳalam*), willow (*bīd*), cypress (*sarv*), plane tree or sycamore (*chinār*), line the walks or mark off the grass-plots, while the shrubbery varies considerably according to the latitude.[1]

The main road into Shiraz from the Allahu Akbar Gate, is lined on either side with gardens, two of which on the east, the *Chahal Tan*, 'Forty Bodies,' and the *Haft Tan*, 'Seven Bodies,' are rather large pleasure-groves and a resort for dervishes, and may be seen in the photographic reproduction, with the Tomb of Hafiz in the background.[2] On the western side there are corresponding enclosures, and one of the most characteristic of these is the *Bāgh-i Takht*, 'Garden of the Throne,' to which I paid a special visit. It stands on rising ground overlooking the city from the northwest, and was laid out by the victorious Kajar ruler Agha Mohammed

---

[1] For illustrations of Persian gardens, see Mumford, *Glimpses of Modern Persia*, in *House and Garden*, 2. 175–191, 360–373, Philadelphia, 1902.

[2] See also the comments of E. G. Browne, *A Year Amongst the Persians*, p. 278.

Khan, who constructed it on the site of an older garden admirably adapted for the purpose by its location. Terrace rises above terrace, and fountain, channel, and stream pour their waters in cascades over slabs of marble into reservoirs faced with stone. The watercourses are edged with masonry, and the walks bordered with cypress and orange trees. At the time of my visit the large reservoir in the centre was full, though the cascades no longer flowed, and I understand that in the drought of summer everything dries up and dust prevails everywhere. The walls around the enclosure and leading up the terraces were not kept up and were consequently beginning to crumble, while the pavilion which once graced the upper terrace was deserted and in ruins. Yet there remained enough of by-gone luxury to tell how beautiful this little Luxembourg must have been formerly, and it still offers to the Shirazi an attractive place to visit in the cool of the evening.[1]

The true renown of Shiraz, as I have implied, rests not upon the beauties of nature, which I have been describing, but upon the fame of her poets and the distinguished men she has given to Iran. Not the least known among the latter class is one of recent memory, the Bab, whose religious reform in the past century I have mentioned in an earlier chapter.[2] The list of notable Shirazis was already a long one when Yakut wrote, seven hundred years ago (c. A.D. 1220), yet even he had not lived to be aware of the future greatness of his younger contemporary, Saadi, or to know that one of the world's greatest lyrists, Hafiz, would be born in Shiraz.

Hafiz, whose birth occurred some time in the first half of the fourteenth century, is known almost as well, by name at least, in the West as he is in the East, where every Persian is familiar with his odes, which have made Shiraz a synonym for poetic inspiration. The beauty of his language, the charm of his

---

[1] For descriptions of the gardens, see also Weeks, *From the Black Sea*, p. 116; Browne, *A Year Amongst* *the Persians*, p. 279 ; Curzon, *Persia*, 2. 104.

[2] See pp. 48–50, above.

style, the sweet flow of his verse, and the passionate expression of his feeling, whether it be in the lyrical outpouring of his own love, or in the mystic ecstasy of a spiritual devotion veiled under the guise of material images, entitle Hafiz to rank even in the Occident as a poet's poet and to hold a prominent place in the best literature of the world.[1] His youth may have been Anacreontic, but he must have been a faithful student, as he won by his memory and learning the title *Ḥāfiz*, 'mindful,' a distinction bestowed only upon those who knew the entire Koran and its interpretation by heart, and he received also an appointment as instructor to the family of the ruling House of Muzaffar, as well as a position in the royal madrasah, which was founded expressly for him. Even a prince of India, Mahmud Shah Bahmani of the Deccan, invited him to his court as a permanent guest. Hafiz accepted the invitation and started on the journey, but proved unequal to facing the perils of a journey by sea, and abandoned his plan, excusing himself by writing a handsome panegyric of his would-be patron, and delicately urging his preference for a life amid the enchantments of Shiraz. According to an interesting tradition, furthermore, even the stern conqueror Tamerlane came under the charm of Hafiz's verse, but scholars generally discountenance the legend as they in the same manner reject the fable that he received poetic inspiration from a cup of nectar placed to his lips by an aged man as a reward for his devotion to the love of a beauteous maiden.[2]

Hafiz was prolific as a writer and the manuscripts and printed editions of his works contain more than five hundred *ghazals,* or odes, which have his name deftly woven into the last stanza of each. Regarding the poetic merit of his verses there is no question, but there exists, as there existed even in his lifetime, a diversity of opinion regarding the interpretation

[1] See my article 'Hafiz,' in Warner's *Library of the World's Best Literature*, 12. 6793–6806, New York, 1897.

[2] See Sir Gore Ouseley, *Notices of the Persian Poets*, pp. 35–37, London, 1846.

of his poetry — whether it is to be taken in a literal or in a spiritual sense. Some readers see in his praises of love and wine, of musky tresses and cypress forms, the passion of an Ovid or a Tibullus; but others, especially some of his Oriental admirers, read beneath those physical images the spiritual thoughts of Divine Love and the Soul. Wine is the spirit, not the juice of the grape, and the cup drained in the tavern is but a draught of that self-oblivion which brings one into complete union with the supreme essence. There is undeniable truth in the possibility of so interpreting the verses according to the doctrines of Sufiism, just as there is in the mystic interpretation of the Song of Solomon, and parallels might even be cited from the poems of Donne, Vaughan, and Crashaw, in the English literature of the seventeenth century; but it is equally true that some of the verses of Hafiz, perhaps those of his youth, can hardly allow of anything but a material and passionate interpretation. As an illustration of his lyrical style I choose an ode translated by the late Professor Cowell, who taught 'Omar' FitzGerald his Persian.

> 'The fairest of roses no longer is fair,
> If she who possesses my heart is not there;
> If wine, the bright ruby, be ever forgot,
> The spring hath no charms and delighteth us not;
> The walks of the garden are lonely and drear,
> If the song of the nightingale strikes not my ear.
> The cypress may wave, and the roses may bloom,
> But in vain if the queen of my heart does not come;
> The wine and the roses are charming, I own,
> But if *she* is absent, the charms are all gone.
> The most lovely designs which art can devise,
> Without my fair mistress delight not my eyes.
> O Hafiz, thy life is but useless at best,
> Scarce worth a *nivār* to be thrown to a guest.' [1]

The peculiar structure of Hafiz's verse and his repetition of rhymes has been well imitated in some English renderings by Mr. Walter Leaf. I reproduce the latter's translation of one

[1] See Professor Cowell's *Life and Letters*, p. 24, London, 1904.

CULTIVATED FIELDS AROUND SHIRAZ

GARDENS AROUND SHIRAZ

of the poet's best-known odes, a favorite especially because of
its refrain *tāzah bah tāzah, nō bah nō.*

'Minstrel, awake the sound of glee, joyous and eager, fresh and free ;
Fill me a bumper bounteously, joyous and eager, fresh and free.

O for a bower and one beside, delicate, dainty, there to hide ;
Kisses at will to seize and be joyous and eager, fresh and free.

Sweet is my dear, a thief of hearts; bravery, beauty, saucy arts,
Odours and unguents, all for me, joyous and eager, fresh and free.

How shall the fruit of life be thine, if thou refuse the fruitful vine?
Drink of the wine and pledge with me, joyous and eager, fresh and free.

Call me my Saki silver-limbed, bring me my goblet silver-rimmed;
Fain would I fill and drink to thee, joyous and eager, fresh and free.

Wind of the West, if e'er thou roam, pass on the way my fairy's home,
Whisper of Hafiz am'rously, joyous and eager, fresh and free.' [1]

The opponents of Hafiz maintained that his philosophy of
life was too much akin to free-thinking and his scorn of the outward semblances of piety too undisguised, to say nothing of lax
verses on wine-bibbing and odes perfumed with the tresses of
his loves, so that when he died, in 1389, this feeling found open
expression among the Mullahs, who refused to accord to his
remains the last rites due to a true Mohammedan. A contro-
versy arose, and to settle the question it was agreed to leave the
solution to the poet's own writings. A number of his verses
were taken at random and a child was selected to draw one of
these out of an urn. Happily the stanza read: —

'Forbear thou not to shed a tear
Compassionate on Hafiz' bier,
For know that though now deeply 'mersed in sin
To Paradise he yet shall enter in.' [2]

The omen was favorable ; Hafiz was granted a Mohammedan
burial, and his tomb, the Hafiziah, has since become a shrine
for pilgrims from far and near.

[1] Leaf, *Versions from Hafiz, an Essay in Persian Metre*, p. 23, London,
1898; cf. also Payne, *Hafiz*, 1. 45.
[2] Ode **60**. 7; cf. Payne, *Hafiz*, 1. 76.

The sepulchre lies about two miles northeast of the city, and a short gallop, after we leave the outskirts of the town, brings us to the walled enclosure that surrounds it.   Passing through the gateway we find ourselves within a spacious square bordered on three sides by low buildings, which afford shelter for priests, dervishes, and pilgrims ; the area is shaded by poplars, cypresses, and maples, and beneath their shadows a small reservoir is seen.   The tomb of Hafiz stands in the middle of the garden and is surrounded by a number of graves, since burial near the poet's dust is now a special privilege.   The place is well kept up, being no longer neglected as when Ker Porter described it in the last century,[1] and the increasing number of pilgrims that yearly visit the shrine speaks for the growing fame of the poet, if not of orthodox Islam.   A handsome oblong block of marble covers the grave and takes the place of the original slab, which Karim Khan is said to have placed in the Jahan Namah Garden when he replaced the stone by the present sarcophagus.[2]   The block is beautifully carved with verses from the poet's writings and at the top is an Arabic inscription, the tenor of which is the transitory character of human things and the eternal nature of God; while at the bottom is added the date of the poet's death, which is given as the year 1389 (A.H. 791).[3]   The present governor of Shiraz has taken pains to have the sepulchre protected by a large iron grating which is more imposing than the old metal cage that formerly enclosed it, and the scroll-work and design show some artistic taste.   The stanchions and corner-posts, however, are iron telegraph poles, received from the Indo-European Telegraph Company, and the Shirazis seemed to be almost as proud of these and of the little metal flags that decorate the top, as of the inscribed slab over the poet's dust.

[1] See Ker Porter, *Travels*, 1. 694–695. Sir Gore Ouseley (*Notices of the Persian Poets*, p. 40, London, 1846) spoke of the grave as being 'in excellent order' when he saw it in 1811.

[2] See Curzon, *Persia*, 2. 109.

[3] For the inscriptions see Browne, *A Year Amongst the Persians*, pp. 280–281.

THE TOMB OF HAFIZ

The tomb of Saadi lies about a mile farther northward in a slight hollow of the plain and is called the Saadiah. Like the tomb of Hafiz, it is in an enclosed garden, and a grove of poplars, cypresses, fragrant shrubs, and rose bushes surrounds the building which contains the remains of Persia's great moralist and poet. It is a fitting resting-place for one who gave the titles of 'Rose Garden' (*Gulistān*) and 'Garden of Perfume' (*Bōstān*) to his two chief works. Within this precinct Saadi alone is buried — at least I saw no other graves — and the sepulchre itself is now enclosed within a building. The chamber in which the sarcophagus stands is entered through a stout door, and the poet's remains lie in a heavy stone case surrounded by a metal network. The room itself is without decoration, but is richly carpeted with a Persian rug, on which the foot falls noiselessly as one moves about the sarcophagus to do homage to the memory of the dead. The same Arabic inscription about the immutability of God, as on the grave of Hafiz, is chiselled on the stone, and verses are added from Saadi's own poems, a handsome manuscript of which is preserved in the building.

Saadi's life was a long and eventful one. Born in 1181 or 1184, or nearly a century and a half before Hafiz, he is said to have rounded out a full fivescore and more of years, as his death is recorded as having taken place in A.D. 1291. Although we may be uncertain with regard to dates, we know that his life was one of many experiences, and that he was a man widely travelled. He had journeyed east, west, north, and south throughout his own country, and had made more than a dozen pilgrimages to the shrine at Mecca, besides travelling in India, Asia Minor, and Africa. On one occasion he was taken prisoner by the Crusaders in Tripolis, enslaved, and set to digging in the trenches. The story goes that a wealthy merchant of Aleppo took compassion on his wretched plight, ransomed him for ten *dīnārs*, and later gave him his daughter in marriage with a dowry of a hundred *dīnārs*. The marriage did not prove a happy one, owing to the wife's bad temper, and once she reviled him with the reproach: 'Art thou not the slave whom my father bought for ten *dinārs?*' 'Yes,' replied Saadi, 'he ransomed me for ten *dinārs* and sold me to you for a hundred.' And he added in verse : —

> 'I've heard that a man of high degree
> From a wolf's teeth and claws a lamb set free.
> That night its throat he severed with a knife,
> When thus complained the lamb's departing life:
> "Thou from the wolf didst save me then; but now
> Too plainly I perceive the wolf art thou."' [1]

As Saadi in the Gulistan tells the story about himself, it can hardly be thought gossipy to repeat it.

As a literary work Saadi's Gulistan is a storehouse of anecdotes as well as wise maxims, good counsel, and poetic thought. In this didactic work of mingled prose and verse the author himself says that 'the discourse is combined with pleasantry and cheerful wit, the pearls of grave counsel are strung on the thread of diction, and the bitter medicine of advice is blended with the honey of mirthful humor.' Some of the stories are truly amusing, and the substance of one or two is worth giving as an example of Oriental humor, for the Persians possess a sense of humor, with which they are not always credited. Almost modern in its point is the anecdote of the man whose disagreeable voice in reciting his prayers in the mosque was annoying to everybody. One day some one asked him how much he was paid for reciting. 'Paid!' he responded, 'I am not paid! I recite for the sake of Allah!' 'Then,' replied the other, 'for Allah's sake don't!'

A sequel in the same vein is told by Saadi to prove the occasional value of a disagreeable voice. A certain muezzin in the mosque had so harsh a voice that his call to prayer only kept the worshippers away from service. The prince who was the patron of the mosque, being tender-hearted and not wish-

---

[1] Saadi, *Gulistān*, tr. Eastwick, pp. 101–102, 2d ed., London, 1880.

The Tomb of Saadi

ing to offend the man, gave him ten *dīnārs* to go somewhere else, and the gift was gladly accepted. Some time afterward the fellow returned to the prince and complained that an injustice had been done him by the smallness of the donation: 'for,' said he, 'at the place where I now am, they offered me twenty *dīnārs* to go somewhere else and I'll not accept it.' 'Oh,' laughed the prince, 'don't accept it, for if you stay longer they will be glad to offer you fifty.'

A single other illustration of Persian humor from Saadi may be added. The point of the story is this: A man who was suffering from inflamed eyes went to a horse-doctor for treatment. The veterinary gave him some of the salve that he used on animals and the man lost his eyesight. He then brought a suit in court to recover damages. The judge, after weighing the evidence in the case, handed down his decision as follows : 'There are no damages to be recovered ; the man would never have gone to a veterinary if he had not been an ass!'

This and a score of other instances might be cited to show the light touch of Saadi's wit beside his acknowledged poetic talents. His rare gift as a poet is seen particularly in the Bostan and in the Divan, a collection of his short poems in the lyrical strain, which justify his title of the 'Nightingale of Persia.' Some of the metrical stanzas in the Gulistan are gems of poetic thought, and as an example of Saadi's fancy I quote from it the following lines, which show his fineness of imagination and delicacy of touch.

> 'I saw some handfuls of the rose in bloom,
> With bands of grass suspended from a dome.
> I said, "What means this worthless grass, that it
> Should in the roses' fairy circle sit?"
> Then wept the grass, and said, "Be still! and know,
> The kind their old associates ne'er forego.
> Mine is no beauty, here, or fragrance — true;
> But in the garden of the Lord I grew." ' [1]

The hills beyond the grave of Saadi and to the east of the

[1] Saadi, *Gulistān*, tr. Eastwick, p. 115.

Allahu Akbar Gate possess one or two points of interest that
may be mentioned.   One of these is a large hollow in the rock,
partly natural and partly artificial, called from its shape the
' Cradle of the Demon' (*Kahvārah-i Dīv*), although its precise
origin is not known; the other is a ruined structure situated
somewhat east of it and known as ' Bandar's Fortress' (*Ḳalʿah-i
Bandar*), which is supposed to be the remains of a Sasanian
castle.   Near this are two very deep wells, one of which is
known as ' Ali's Well' (*Chāh-i Murtazah Alī*) and described as
a pool at the bottom of a series of steps surmounted by a building which gives the place the character of a shrine.   It is said
to occupy the place of an old fire-temple, and the story goes
that the well sprang up as a miracle to quench the flame of the
old Zoroastrian faith when the true religion of Mohammed
came into Persia.[1]   There are also some Achæmenian remains
about four miles southeast of Shiraz and still farther beyond
there are some sculptures of Sasanian kings who were Zoroastrians, but I did not inspect them.[2]

My allusion to Zoroastrianism leads me to speak of the so-
called Gabars, or fire-worshippers, of Shiraz, as the city knew
only their religion in Sasanian times, whereas scarcely fifty of
their faith now live there.[3]   I took the earliest opportunity of
sending to Rustam Shah Jahan, the leading merchant among
them, the letter I carried from his brother in Isfahan.[4]   He
occupied a shop adjoining the main bazaar, and as I entered the
room behind the outside booth, I found a number of persons

[1] See Browne, *A Year Amongst the Persians*, p. 286 ; Curzon, *Persia*, 2. 108 ; Ker Porter, *Travels*, 1. 698.

[2] The earliest notice that I have seen of these ancient monuments is in Masudi (A.D. 943), *Les Prairies d' Or*, ed. Barbier de Meynard, 4. 79. They have been described by various writers, among them Ker Porter, *Travels*, 1. 698–706, and Curzon, *Persia*, 2. 95, n. 2, and have been drawn by Flandin

and Coste, *Voyage en Perse, Ancienne*, 1. pl. 55, and photographed by Stolze, *Persepolis*, 2. pl. 96 ; cf. also Perrot and Chipiez, *Histoire de l' Art*, 5. 754.

[3] The precise number at the time of my visit was 42, according to the statistics I subsequently obtained at Teheran from the Secretary of the Society for the Amelioration of the Persian Zoroastrians.

[4] See pp. 274–275, above.

gathered there. Remembering my Isfahan experience and knowing that Shiraz was Islamitic to the extreme of fanaticism (so much so, that some of my friends later expressed surprise that my body-servant did not meet with persecution there, as he was a Christian convert from Mohammedanism), I began by making commonplace observations and inquiries in Oriental style, until I should be surer of my ground, and only indirectly indicating my interest in the religion. In this case, however, I found there was not the slightest occasion for reserve, as my host Rustam had been prepared by his brother's letter, and he told me that all the persons who were present were Zoroastrians, so that we could speak without hesitation on religious matters.

From the conversation I learned that the Zoroastrian community in Shiraz keep up their religious observances and beliefs, in a general sort of way, but not so strictly as at Yezd and Kerman. They have no regular *dastūr*, or High Priest, nor have they any fire-temple, whereas in antiquity there must have been at least one pyræum at Shiraz, as is shown by the remains of an ancient Atash Kadah which a Mohammedan pointed out to me on the hill overlooking the city. No dakhmah, moreover, is kept up by the Zoroastrians of Shiraz, although this could hardly be expected in so small a community and it is their practice to inter the body in the earth, placing stones around it and over it. They possess no manuscripts of the Avesta, so far as I could learn, but they encouraged me in my hope of finding copies at Yezd, the chief centre of the Persian Zoroastrians, and told me that I would there meet the Chief Priest of the Faith and be able to learn from him more about religious matters. Despite their lack of knowledge concerning their creed — and it would be unreasonable, perhaps, to expect merchants and traders to possess technical information on theological points — I was favorably impressed by these believers in Ormazd. They seemed honest and thrifty, and fairly prosperous, considering the fact that they

z

have had to live for over a thousand years under restriction and persecution, and they appeared also to cultivate the sterling virtues which their prophet of old enjoined. This fact made me more anxious than ever to visit Yezd, so I began my preparations for departure on the third day, bidding adieu to them and to my Christian hosts at the English mission, as well as to other friends.

CHAPTER XXII

FROM SHIRAZ TO YEZD

'From Shiraz to Yezd is seventy-four farsakhs.'
— Ibn Haukal, *Geography*, tr. Ouseley, p. 111.

IT was toward mid-day on the sixth of May, and the sun was scorching hot, when I set out from Shiraz on my way to the city of Yezd to visit the Zoroastrians in that ancient stronghold of the faith. I was provided with a letter from the Persian governor of Shiraz, directing that certain privileges and attentions be extended to me on the journey, and was furnished with an authorization from the Director General of the Persian Customs and Post, enabling me to procure horses or other means of transport over portions of the route that had not yet been formally laid out. As I knew on my southward journey that I should have to travel for three days over the same route by which I had come from Pasargadæ to Shiraz I had taken the precaution to pave the way with silver. The investment was expensive, but it proved to have been worth making, for it quickened the pace of the post-horses and hastened the movements of the men at the halting-places, and haste is a rare thing in Persia. By this expenditure, by liberal use of whip and spur, and by reducing the time of sleep at night to three or four hours, with cat-naps stolen at odd moments during the day, I was able to shorten the ordinary time of ten days between Shiraz and Yezd to five days and a quarter.

Toward evening of the first day, as I retraced my route northward, I reached once more the ruins of Persepolis. The desolate terrace looked picturesque in the moonlight, but I did

not halt again to wander through its crumbled palaces and
deserted halls. On the next day, however, I paid another
visit to the sepulchres of the Achæmenian kings at Naksh-i
Rustam and the Magian altars and rock-hewn tables on
the cliff that overlooks them, and I reached Pasargadæ and
the tomb of Cyrus that same afternoon, spending the night
once more at Meshad-i Murghab. After a hard march of
seven farsakhs in six hours over rough hills and stony ways
I rested for an hour at Deh-Bid, and then resumed the journey and arrived, about five o'clock, at Khan-i Khorah, where
the night was to be passed and I could at last strike eastward
on the trail to Yezd. From my previous experience I remembered Khan-i Khorah as a desolate place at which I was held up
for two hours and a half because the post-horses had roamed
miles away over the plain to graze. The interval till their
return I had spent in a wretched hovel surrounded by natives
in a dazed condition from opium-smoking, the unfortunate
effects of which common vice are only too frequently seen in
Persia. My present impression was more pleasant, as I was
conducted to a fairly comfortable little house, not far from
the caravansarai, where I could spend the night.

There was a small but pretty garden at the rear of this simple
abode ; the fruit trees were in full blossom, and everything
looked cheerful in the light of the setting sun. I hardly had
time to dispose of my pack and arrange my camp-bed for the
night, before the head man of the village paid me a visit. He
had come for medical aid, he said ; his wife was suffering
from toothache. I prescribed as best I could from my limited
stock of drugs, but I soon became convinced that the real
patient was my visitor himself and that he hoped he might
have some arac and tobacco added to the prescription. I
yielded to his broad hints so far as the tobacco was concerned,
for I had one or two cigarettes left in my case, but I omitted
the spirituous part of the remedy, probably to my visitor's
regret.

FROM DEH-BID TO KHAN-I KHORAH

OPIUM-SMOKERS

The night was short, as Persian nights are in the spring, and when one is trying to make time, it is necessary to rise long before three o'clock in order to start from the caravansarai by daylight. In fact, I saw more sunrises in Persia than I ever expect to see again in all my life. Darkness was melting into dawn when I found myself again in the saddle, with a cavalcade of five horses and three footguards to accompany me over the barrier of mountains that lay between Khan-i Khorah and the sandy deserts of Abarkuh and Yezd. The scenery for a time was superb. Steep ascents, deep ravines, narrow gorges, and wild passes succeeded each other in great variety. One welcome excuse for rest and refreshment was found at the foot of a rocky height, where a crystal spring pulsed up with cool water, offering the last chance for a drink before crossing the desert to Abarkuh. Leaving the great ridge behind us and dismissing most of the guards, as they were no longer needed, for Persian highwaymen operate chiefly in the mountain passes, we entered upon the arid tract marked on the maps as the Sandy Desert, whose barren stretch as far as Yezd is broken only by the oases of Abarkuh and Deh-Shir and the mountains beyond the latter.

The town of Abarkuh, or Abarguh, (*Abarḳūh*) is evidently of great antiquity. The Persians in earlier and later times have commonly pronounced the name as *Barkūh* or *Warkūh*, understanding it to signify 'upon the mountain,' or 'over the mountain,' especially when speaking from the standpoint of the desert towns that lie beyond it and are separated from it by hills.[1] The tenth-century geographer Istakhri (c. A.D. 950) describes the town as follows :—

'Abarkuh, or Warkuh, is a fortified city, densely populated, and of about one-third the size of Istakhr. The houses are lattice-worked,

[1] So my informant, Khodabakhsh Raïs of Yezd ; see also the statement of Yakut, p. 8, 'the Persians say *Varkūh* for *Barkūh*, "upon the mountain."' Cf. likewise (in De Goeje, *Bibl. Geog. Arab.*) Istakhri, 1. 126 (*Abarḳūh*), Mokaddasi, 3. 437 (*Barḳūh*), and Al-Hamadhani, 5. 203 (*Abarḳūiah*) ; see also Schwarz, *Iran im Mittelalter*, p. 17.

and most of the buildings, as well as the buildings at Yezd, are built with colonnades (or vaulted domes).[1] It is a barren place; there are no trees or gardens around it except at a distance, but the soil is productive and the living is cheap.' [2]

On the right of the road as we approach from the southwest there is a large fortress-like ruin called *Dakhmah-i Dārāb*, 'Structure of Darab,' after the name of Darius Codomannus, the last of the Achæmenians. The term *dakhmah*, which is applied to it, is used, as also in Turkish, for a structure in general, and is not to be confused with the usage of the word *dakhmah* in the technical sense of 'Tower of Silence.' The ruin looks like a deserted stronghold of considerable antiquity.

On the left of the road, upon an elevation, stands the *Dakhmah-i Gabrahā*, 'Structure of the Gabars,' another ruined edifice of mud and sun-dried bricks, closely resembling the *Ātash Kadah*, or 'Shrine of Fire,' near Isfahan, which I have already described.[3] Adjoining this so-called Gabar structure stands another building, evidently an old temple, but, like the shrine, a crumbling ruin. The site of these ancient Iranian structures appears to be a historic one, as is shown by some allusions in Mohammedan writers. Ibn Haukal, for example, in the tenth century, says: —

'In the vicinity of Abarkuh are considerable heaps of ashes. The common people say that here was the fire of Nimrod (into which he caused Abraham to be thrown), but this is not true; the fact

---

[1] The Arabic expression *muštabekat al-binā*, 'of netted-work buildings,' seems to allude not to the crowding together of the houses, but to the open or trellis-work style of architecture seen in the front of the building. The second term (Arabic word *āzāj*, note i, p. 351) appears to allude to colonnades or arched galleries. See the pictures of Yezd in Malcolm, *Five Years in a Persian Town*, pp. 134, 184, 216. But 'vaulted domes' is the rendering of Barbier de Mey-nard, *Dict. géog. de la Perse*, p. 8 ('cintrée'), and of Schwarz, *Iran im Mittelalter*, p. 18 ('mit gewölbter Decke'). Such domed mud roofs are common in Persia, as is shown also in some photographs that I have of Yezd and Kashan, but this explanation seems to me not so good.

[2] Istakhri, ed. De Goeje, 1. 126. The Persian version adds to the Arabic a note on the export of fruits from Abarkuh.

[3] See pp. 252–261, above.

is that Nimrod and the kings of Canaan dwelt in the land of Babylon.'[1]

This statement of Ibn Haukal is evidently based on older authorities, for he re-edited Istakhri, whom Yakut (c. A.D. 1220) briefly cites. Yakut has a somewhat similar legend, but differs from this account in certain noteworthy details.

'At Abarkuh there is a large hill of ashes, which the inhabitants claim was the fire of Abraham, lighted by Bardah and Salamah.[2] But in the Book of the Avesta, which is the book of the Magi, I have read that So'da (Sudabah),[3] the daughter of Tubba, wife of Kei Kaus, fell in love with his son Kei Khosru (Siavash).[4] She endeavored to seduce him, but he rejected her, whereupon she told his father that he had tried to dishonor her, which was a lie. Thereupon Kei Khosru built a large fire at Abarkuh for an ordeal and said: "If I am innocent the fire will not harm me; if I am guilty, as claimed, the fire will devour me." At this he entered into the fire and came out of it unhurt, without having suffered any harm. In this way he dispelled the entire charge against him. The ashes of that fire are to be seen at Abarkuh in the shape of a large hill, and to-day it is called the Mountain of Abraham. But Abraham never saw the land of Fars, nor entered it; he abode in Kutharabba, in the land of Babylon. I have read elsewhere, however, that Abraham came to Abarkuh and prohibited its inhabitants from employing cows in farming; consequently they do not employ cows in this way, although there are plenty in the country. Abu Bekr Mohammed, who is known as al-Harbi of Shiraz, . . . states: "I was in Abarkuh three times, but I never saw rain fall within the walls of the city, and the people said that this was owing to the prayers of Abraham."'[5]

---

[1] Ibn Haukal (c. A.D. 975), tr. Ouseley, p. 130.

[2] The Arabic seems to mean 'which Bardah and Salamah lighted upon it (*i.e.* the hill)'; but Barbier de Meynard, *Dict. géog. de la Perse*, p. 8, renders 'qu' Abraham alluma pour Berdeh et Selamah.'

[3] Sudanah, as well as Sudabah, is found as a variant form of the name. For references, see p. 344, n. 1.

[4] Firdausi (tr. Mohl. 2. 164-195) and the author of the Haft Iklim narrate the story not of Khosru, but of Siavash, which is apparently more in accordance with the facts.

[5] Yakut, *Geographisches Wörterbuch*, ed. Wüstenfeld, 1. 86, Leipzig, 1866; cf. also the translation of Yakut by Barbier de Meynard, *Dict. géog. de la Perse*, pp. 8–9. For assistance with the Arabic I am indebted to

This legend of the fire-ordeal, as preserved in Yakut, is sufficient to prove the sacred associations of the place and its right
of title to having been the site of a pyræum, even if Firdausi
and Thaalibi, in their accounts, do not give the precise locality
where the ordeal took place.[1]   We may consider, therefore,
that still another identification has been added to the list of
sites of ancient fire-temples in Persia and that the ruined
shrine at Abarkuh commemorates, in its location at least, the
place where the honor of Siavash was vindicated.

In this connection I may mention a legend connected with
a Mohammedan saint at Abarkuh, as told by Hamdallah Mustaufi (A.D. 1340).   This author narrates that there was in the
town the tomb of a saint of Islam, named Taus al-Haramein,
which literally means 'Peacock of the two Sanctuaries' (that
is, of Mecca and Medina), and he reports that the walls of the
building would not allow a roof to enclose it, for if a roof was
erected over the tomb, some supernatural power always destroyed it.   He likewise adds that no Jew could exist in Abarkuh for more than forty days.[2]

When I entered the town, I went at once to the Reis of
Abarkuh and presented my letters from the Governor of
Shiraz and from the Director of the Post.   The town is only a
small place nowadays, and the Reis could not obtain horses for
me, but he managed to procure four mules to make up a caravan for crossing the desert, and arranged that the start should
be made soon after midnight.   This gave me time to rest in
the afternoon, which I spent looking out from the window
upon a little stream bordered with sycamore trees whose
branches rang with the song of birds.   When evening came,
I fell asleep and did not wake until midnight.   After some

the kindness of my colleagues Yohannan and Gottheil.

[1] For the well-known account of
Sudabah and Siavash in Firdausi's
Shāh Nāmah, see the translation by
Mohl, 2. 153–195 ; and compare

Thaalibi, *Histoire des Rois des
Perses*, tr. Zotenberg, pp. 171–186.

[2] See Hamdallah Mustaufi, *Nuzhat
al-Ḳulūb* (L. 174 *g*), cited by Le
Strange, *JRAS.* 1902, p. 519, n. 1.

مترتب بماه قافلهٔ خروف اُنس قراولداه اوراتی راقیم کو عالیا همسیوِر کن اُنس آبراه

منزلم هست دبغرم رحمت یزدِ میره از نوری تا شهار ماکنک دارانخنه نفر

نشگم باماً راییه هراه باریینه که اودا سلما باکنک یزدِ دربنتر ولاره ات

۱۲۲۱

.: و جسترام زا اد اودم عی دللاد که سلامت دخنژو قرس های لتعقدیقو شر صلوالملو

delays we finally got our company of mules, muleteers, and guards under way and resumed the journey. The moon was flooding the sky with a soft Oriental light and the nightingale was singing in the tamarisk bush behind the mud walls as we threaded our course through the narrow streets. The outskirts of the town were presently left behind, the roads began gradually to merge into sandy trails, and an hour later the swiftly rising sun had brushed aside the silvery veil of night and gleamed over the desert, upon which we had entered.

From this point on, for fourteen farsakhs, or nearly fifty miles, the track led straight across an arid waste marked only by hoof-prints in the snowy sand and by skeletons of beasts of burden that had fallen by the way. The air was warm, but not excessively hot, and every now and then a breeze sprang up, sweeping powdery whirlwinds off into the distance to perish in the sand that gave them birth. Mirage after mirage arose to surprise the eye and give play to the fancy, thus relieving the tedium of the march. Once in a while the beaten track forked for a mile or more, but the two branches always rejoined, pointing again toward the oasis town of Deh-Shir, which, though miles away, was our nearest goal. There was little need for guides and none for guards, so we dismissed a part of our company of attendants, but could not spare the muleteers, who found plenty to do in keeping our unruly animals in order. The pack-mule kept bolting from the track at the most unexpected moments, and had constantly to be recaptured and brought back to the train. My own beast was always ready for rebellion at the slightest provocation, and I narrowly escaped having my skull fractured by his heels. A halt had been made in the ankle-deep sand, and, as I was remounting, the badly girt saddle slipped and I was thrown under the beast's heels, with my foot caught in the stirrup. A shower of terrific kicks, resembling those seen in comic pictures of the Mississippi mule, filled the air. I was bruised, dragged, and torn, but I managed to shield my head from the vicious animal's hoofs, and he was finally reduced to subjection.

The sun was well on its way in the western sky when our long, heated march of nearly fourteen hours, without a drop of water to drink, ended at the green oasis of Deh-Shir. The lord of the town extended a kindly welcome in Oriental fashion and provided a hearty meal, served by his Persian servants, one of whom was a eunuch slave. He then conducted me to the terrace on the roof to show me the view over the oasis, the desert, and the hills beyond, expressing a doubt whether any land could compare in beauty with Iran. I appreciated his enthusiasm, even if I did not fully share in it. He inquired about my own country, the location of which I could best convey to his mind by describing it as a far-off land, many thousand farsakhs distant, and explaining that eight days of the journey had been across 'the black water,' whereupon he at once exclaimed ' *Yankī Dunyā*,' [1] which means literally ' New World ' in Persian, whereas the term America conveyed nothing to him. He commented upon my tanned face, which was almost as dark as his own, and talked about the life at Deh-Shir, which, it appeared to me, must be rather monotonous. He knew the surrounding country well, but the main fact that I elicited regarding antiquities was that some stone coffins with human remains had once been found in the vicinity. Our view over the landscape was enjoyed through a telescope, of which he was the proud possessor, having inherited it from a father or grandfather, to whom it had been apparently presented many years ago by its original owner, an English officer, if I may judge from the inscription engraved upon the brass. As I was a foreigner, he expected me to be equipped with tobacco, and I was sorry not to have any American cigars to offer him as samples of ' the weed ' in our country, but I tried in other ways to return his hospitality and to reciprocate his acts of courtesy.

---

[1] Pronounced ' Yankee Doonya.'

When I was taking my leave and asking directions and information, he told me that the road through all his district was safe ; there had been bandits operating recently in the hills, he said, but he had attended to the last of these about a fortnight previously. The closing sentence was accompanied by a significant gesture with his hand drawn like a knife across his throat to indicate the punishment he had inflicted upon the thieves. Nevertheless, to make my safety assured, he accompanied me himself, after the Persian manner, some distance beyond the town and gave a guide and guard to conduct me across the Shir Kuh Mountains.

The road led over wild and jagged hills, and the rocks took on fantastic and picturesque shapes in the rich moonlight as our little caravan clambered up and down the rough ways to the pretty hamlet of Deh-Zeresh. After a few hours' sleep we pushed forward again over the hills to Aliabad, where our pack-mule was exchanged for two small donkeys, and we enjoyed a half hour's rest and breakfast under the trees near a little brook. We had not proceeded far after resuming the march, before one of the donkeys had a severe fall and received a cruel cut in his chest. I urged the muleteer to send the animal back to Aliabad, as I would pay for a substitute, but he gave no attention to the poor beast's suffering, for animals seem to have no rights in Persia, where a society for the prevention of cruelty would have an ample field for activity, and he seemed almost amused that I should consider the matter of an animal's pain. I was obliged, therefore, to postpone my sympathy until I could reach Yezd and there have the donkey's wound properly treated.

As we proceeded on our way the signs of increasing civilization and comparatively fair prosperity grew more and more marked, and about an hour after noonday we reached Taft. This is a well-to-do suburb of Yezd and a place that counts among its population a considerable number of Zoroastrians, mostly gardeners. We halted here long enough to have one

of the mules shod, as its shoes had been loosened and lost on
the hard journey over the rocky hills and pebbly roads of the
Shir Kuh.   This gave the muleteer and the guides a chance to
rest ; they had been walking forty miles a day, yet without
apparent fatigue, for when called upon for a spurt, they were
always ready to set off at the pace of a sprinter.   These men
have evidently kept up the tradition of the ancient Persian
couriers, and I was told by English residents in Yezd some
remarkable stories of the feats of endurance and speed these
desert runners were able to accomplish.

Most of the remainder of the afternoon was spent in
reaching Yezd, ever tantalizingly near because of the clearness of the atmosphere, yet still remote because of the
expanse of desert around it.   This encircling tract of sand,
which is nearly thirty miles broad and many more miles long,
is bounded on the south and west, and partly on the north, by
ranges of rugged hills, while a belt of sand-dunes on the east
reaches almost to the walls of Yezd, but is kept back by
gardens, whose green tinge affords a welcome contrast to the
brown and parched aspect of all around.

Yezd is a city of considerable antiquity, since its name
apparently occurs, under the form of Ἰσατίχαι (*Isatichai*), in
Ptolemy's Greek geography, where it is named among the few
towns of the desert of Carmania.[1]   According to Persian
tradition, moreover, it must have been known in Alexander's
time, having been used by the victorious invader as a place
of confinement for his prisoners of war.[2]   The common view
associates the name Yezd, or Yazd, with Yazdagard I (A.D. 399–
420), father of Bahram Gor, probably as the rebuilder rather
than the original founder.[3]

[1] Ptolemy, *Geography*, 6. 6. 2. This
name is not to be confused with Istakhr
(Curzon, *Persia*, 2. 239).

[2] On this latter point (drawn from
Hafiz) and for the common view regarding Yezd (Yazd) and Yazdagard,

see Sykes, *Ten Thousand Miles in
Persia*, pp. 419–420.

[3] For remarks on the name of Yezd
and Kathah, see note i at the end of
this chapter, p. 351.

VIEW OF YEZD

A STREET IN YEZD, SHOWING A WIND-TOWER

During the earlier years of Mohammedan rule Yezd became a place of refuge and stronghold for the Zoroastrian Gabars, probably because of its remote situation in the desert, although it was never out of touch with the rest of Persia. The first European known to have visited it was Marco Polo in 1272, who calls it 'the good and noble city of Yasdi.'[1] The Italian friar Odoric of Pordenone, who came here about fifty years later than Marco, speaks of the town as 'Geth,' 'Gest,' or 'Iest,'[2] and Josafa Barbaro, the Venetian (1474), writes the name as 'Ies' or 'Jex.'[3]

Notwithstanding the earlier and later importance of the city, Yezd has little to offer in the way of sight-seeing, and it certainly cannot lay any claim to natural beauty. One rides for hours through narrow winding streets, with nothing to see but walls of clay, the backs of houses, a streak of sky (which blazes as soon as summer begins), and a glimpse of high wind-towers rising from the roofs of the better dwellings. These lofty air-shafts (*bād-gīrs*, 'wind-collectors') resemble square chimneys with slat-openings above to catch the slightest breeze. They are rendered necessary by the long continuance of the heat during the summer months, and are characteristic of Yezd.

The area of the city is considerable; Odoric spoke of the town as 'walled and of V myles in circuite,' and the same is practically true to-day, except that the circuit may be somewhat larger and the walls have fallen in some places. The fort within the city was erected or reconstructed in the year 1137, and is built of sun-dried bricks and mud, but neither this nor the citadel of the Governor inside its walls would afford any material defence at the present time.[4] In several

[1] Marco Polo, ed. Yule, 1. 88.

[2] Odoric de Pordenone, ed. Cordier, p. 451.

[3] Josafa Barbaro, 49. 59, 73, 82.

[4] On this point see Curzon, *Persia*, 2. 240; Landor, *Across Coveted Lands*,

1. 381; Sykes, *Ten Thousand Miles in Persia*, p. 421. The Arabic allusions in note i at the end of this chapter show that the citadel must have existed before 1137 and that it was probably rebuilt in that year.

parts of the town there are public squares, the one near the Governor's palace being somewhat effective,[1] and among the features of Yezd are numerous arches over the narrow streets ; but the only public building that has any claim to consideration is the Friday Mosque (*Masjid-i Jum'ah*). It was built in 1119 by Sultan Allah ad-Daulah Garshasp, who thus won for Yezd the cherished title *Dār al-'Ibādat,* 'Abode of Worship,' a dignity which was rendered still further assured in after centuries by the pious munificence of some of the later rulers, traces of whose donations, especially two beautifully carved wooden doors, are still to be seen.[2]

The population of Yezd is estimated at between thirty and forty thousand, or at nearly sixty thousand if the villages in the district be included in the count. A large part of the population is engaged in silk-weaving, which is one of the chief industries of this region. But this was a matter of minor interest to me at the moment, nor did I pay much attention to the manner in which Yezd meets the difficult problem which it has to face in securing an adequate water-supply, nor again was I especially interested in the bazaars, or in the trade and commerce of the city, except that I found it very convenient that Yezd had a branch of the Imperial Bank, from which I could draw upon my letter of credit. My real interest in Yezd was to see the Zoroastrians, and I shall devote the next chapter to the visit that I paid to this interesting community.

[1] For a picture, see Malcolm, *Five Years in a Persian Town*, p. 184.

[2] For notes upon this subject, together with quotations and a description of the mosaic dome near the fort, see Sykes, *Ten Thousand Miles*, p. 421.

I. Note on Yezd and Kathah

There is good reason for claiming that an old name for Yezd or a collateral title for the main quarter of the city was Kata, judging from the article *Kathah* in Istakhri and other Perso-Arabic geographers. Istakhri (ed. De Goeje, *Bibl. Geog. Arab.* 1. 125) writes as follows: 'One of the most famous cities in the district of Istakhr on the confines of Khorasan is Kathah. It is the chief place (*haumah*) of Yezd and Abarkuh ... ,' and he continues: 'Kathah, the chief town of Yezd, is a city located on the edge of the desert. It has good and healthy air from the desert and possesses also the comforts that belong to large cities. Its districts are noted for their fertility, and living is cheap. The houses are generally built of clay and have colonnades (or, 'vaulted domes' — *āzāj*, plur. from *ăzāj*, see p. 342, n. 1, above). It has a fortified citadel, with two iron gates, one of which is called the 'Gate of Izad' (it would be tempting to compare Ptolemy's 'Ισατίχαι, as a possible corruption from 'Ισατ-τείχεα, if not for the Persian variant *Bāb-i Andar*, 'Inner Gate'); the other is called 'Gate of the Mosque' (*Bāb al-Masjid*), on account of its proximity to the chief mosque. The mosque of the city is located in the suburbs. The water for the city comes through *kanāts*, but there is also a river which comes from the vicinity of the Kalah, or citadel (*i.e.* the Kal'at al-Majūs, or Kal'at-i Zard), near a village where there is a lead-mine. It is very delightfully located and has fertile and extensive districts. The town and its districts abound in fruit, so much so that it is exported to Isfahan and other places. The mountains have many trees and plants, which are also exported. Outside the city there is a suburb which has fine houses and bazaars. For the most part the inhabitants are men of education and letters.' Ibn Haukal (ed. De Goeje, 2. 181, cf. also 2. 196) repeats this statement verbatim and adds: 'As regards the district of Istakhr, the division of Yezd is the largest division in it, and in this there are the following cities: Kathah, which is the citadel, and Maibud, Naïn, and Al-Fahraj, and in all the divisions there is none that has four pulpits (*minbars*) except this one.' In his list of fortified places (taken from Istakhri, 1. 112) Ibn Haukal (2. 187) mentions Kathah directly after Istakhr (Persepolis), saying, 'The city of Kathah has a fortress.' Yakut has two separate paragraphs devoted to Kathah and Yezd. In the first (ed. Wüstenfeld, 4. 239) he says: 'Kathah, a place of Fars; it is the chief city (*haumah*) of the district (*kūrah*) of Yezd and belongs to the district (*kūrah*) of Istakhr.' In the second paragraph (ed. Wüstenfeld, 4. 1017) he states: 'Yezd, a place midway between Nisapur, and Shiraz, and Isfahan; it is reckoned to the province of Fars and belongs to the district of Istakhr; it (Yezd) is the name of the region and its citadel is called Kathah ; between it and Shiraz the distance is seventy farsakhs.' Compare also the French translation by Barbier de Meynard, *Dict. géog.* p. 475 (Kathah), p. 611 (Yezd); likewise Schwarz, *Iran im Mittelalter*, p. 19. (For help in translating the Arabic passages I am indebted to the kindness of my colleagues Gottheil and Yohannan.) With the name *Kathah*

(Old Iran. *Kata*) we may compare the first part of the Latin name *Cetrora* for the corresponding place in the geographical list of the Tabula Peuting-eriana, as Tomaschek (*Sb. Akad. Wiss. zu Wien.* 102. 105, Vienna, 1883) derives that name from the Old Iranian word *kata*, used in the Avesta to designate an 'excavation,' house dug to receive corpses, and the presumably Iranian element *ravara*, found in the Mod. Pers. *Rūdh-rāvar* (cf. Ptolemy's 'Ροάρα, *Geog.* **6**. 5. 2). This suggestion is plausible in the main, since it is reasonable to suppose that Istakhri, who was a native of Stakhr, would have been well acquainted with the territory around Yezd. The details which he gives regarding Kathah and the river that flows from a village near a citadel where there is a lead-mine, would answer in general to the region about the modern village *Kattū* near the 'Yellow Castle' (*Kal'ah-i Zard*), as described by Browne, *A Year Amongst the Persians*, p. 358. [I find the identity of Kathah and Yezd accepted also by Le Strange, *Lands of the Early Caliphate*, p. 285, Cambridge, 1905; but Khodabakhsh Bahram Raïs writes me that the name Kathah seems to be absolutely unknown in Yezd, although there is a large village called *Kahtū* or *Kathū* about 20 farsakhs south of the city.—Proof-sheet addition.]

II. NOTE ON TWO OLD ITINERARIES FROM SHIRAZ TO YEZD

I add two old itineraries, the one by an Oriental, the other by an Occidental, covering in part at least the route followed in this chapter. The first is by the Arab geographer Istakhri in the tenth century and reads as follows (ed. De Goeje, 1. 129–130): 'Route from Shiraz to Kathah, the chief town of Yezd, along the Khorasan route: From Shiraz to the village of Zarkān (Zargān) 6 farsakhs; from Zarkān to the city of Istakhr 6 f; from Istakhr to the village of Bīr (v.l. Bīn, Pīr, Gīz) 4 f; from Bīr to Kahmand (v.l. Kīhandah, Kīhandaz; Ouseley reads Kahndaz) 8 f; from Kahmand to the village of Bīd (Deh-Bīd, 'Willow Village') 8 f; from the village of Bīd to the city of Abarkūh 12 f; from Ab-arkūh to the village of Al-Asad ('Lion Village,' v.l. Deh-Shīr) 13 f; from the village of Asad to the village of Al-Jūz (or Jauz, v.l. Al-Khūr, Deh-i Khvar) 6 f; and from the village of Al-Jūz to the village Kalah al-Majūs 6 f; and from Kalah al-Majūs to the city of Kathah, the chief place of Yezd, 5 f.' The second is the memorandum of the route of Josafa Barbaro, in the fifteenth century, from Persepolis to Yezd (ed. Hakluyt, 49. 81–82), and it reads as follows: 'From thense, iij daies io'ney, yoᵂ come to a towne called Dehebeth (Deh-Bīd), wheare they vse tillaige and making of fustians. Twoo daies io'ney further ye cõe to a place called Vargari (or Vargan), which in tyme past hath been a great and a faire towne; but at this pñt it maketh not aboue mⁱ houses, in the which they also vse tillaige and making of fustians, as is aforesaid. Foure daies io'ney thense ye come to a towne called Deiser (Deh-Shīr), and iij daies io'ney further an other towne called Tafte (miswritten as Taste), from whense following that waie another daies io'ney ye come to Jex, of the which I haue made sufficient mencõn before.'

CHAPTER XXIII

THE ZOROASTRIANS OF YEZD

'From Yezd's eternal Mansion of the Fire.'
— MOORE, *Lalla Rookh.*

SITUATED amid a sea of sand which threatens to ingulf it, Yezd is a symbolic home for the isolated band of Zoroastrians that still survives the surging waves of Islam that swept over Persia with the Mohammedan conquest twelve hundred years ago. Although exposed to persecution and often in danger from storms of fanaticism, this isolated religious community, encouraged by the buoyant hope characteristic of its faith, has been able to keep the sacred flame of Ormazd alive and to preserve the ancient doctrines and religious rites of its creed.

When the Arab hosts unfurled the green banner with the crescent and swept over the land of Iran with cry of Allah, shout of Mohammed, proclamation of the Koran, fire, sword, slaughter, enforced conversion, or compulsory banishment, a mighty change came over Persia. The battle-grounds of Kadisia and Nihavand decided not Iran's fate alone, but Iran's faith. Ahura Mazda, Zarathushtra, and the Avesta ceased almost to be known, the temple consecrated to fire became a sacrifice to its own flame, and the gasp of the dying Magian's voice was drowned by the call of the Muezzin to prayer on the top of the minaretted mosque.

In a way the Moslem creed was easy of acceptance for Persia, since Mohammed himself had adopted elements from Zoroastrianism to unite with Jewish and Christian tenets in making up his religion. The Persian, therefore, under show of reason or exercise of force, could be led to exchange Ormazd for Allah, to acknowledge Mohammed, instead of Zoroaster, as the true prophet of later days, and to accept the Koran as the inspired word of God that supplanted the Avesta. The conqueror's sword, inscribed with holy texts in arabesques, contributed its share, no doubt, to making all this possible, but many a Gabar stubbornly refused to give up his belief, and consequently sealed his faith with his blood. The few that sought religious liberty by accepting exile in India became the ancestors of the modern Parsis of Bombay, so often spoken of already; but the rest of the scanty handful that escaped the perils of the Mohammedan conquest found a desert-home at Yezd and in the remote city of Kerman, not to mention the straggling few that are found elsewhere in Persia, to prove the exception to the now universal rule of Islam in Iran.

Almost immediately after my arrival at Yezd I inquired for the home of Kalantar Dinyar Bahram, the head of the Zoroastrian community, which numbers between 8000 and 8500 in the city and its environs,[1] but it took me some time to find his house. For nearly two hours my tired mules and donkeys threaded their way through dusty, crooked lanes, across camel-filled squares, and in and out of closing bazaars, until we reached the Kalantar's door just as the sun was going down. The dwelling was unpretentious on the outside, as all Persian houses are. Several servants answered the summons of my man, who announced the arrival of a *farangī*, and I was then ushered into a large, oblong room carpeted with fine Persian rugs. The walls of the apartment were almost without decoration, and the furnishing was confined chiefly to divans and cushions, as in many Oriental dwellings; but on one side there were arranged in Occidental manner a table and some chairs, made and upholstered after European models. The front of

---

[1] These are the figures given me at Tcheran by Mr. Ardeshir Reporter, Agent of the Society for the Amelio- ration of the Zoroastrians in Persia. See also p. 336, n. 3, above; p. 376, n. 1, and p. 425, below.

SCENE IN YEZD

THE RESERVOIR IN THE MEIDAN AT YEZD

the room seemed almost open to the air, because of the broad doorways and deep windows that ran from floor to ceiling and looked out upon a covered veranda and a court which enclosed a pretty garden with roses and potted plants. My Gabar host entered the room a few minutes later.

He was a man somewhat over fifty years of age, with a roundish face and grizzled beard, and was dressed in a robe of grayish cloth with a large white cotton sash about his waist. Upon his head he wore the low rolled turban which is characteristic of the Persian Zoroastrians ; I had seen the same style of head-gear worn by an Iranian priest from Kerman when I was in Bombay. With genuine courtesy and manifest cordiality my host extended a welcome, and turned aside with a light touch the apologies I offered for my dusty appearance and for entering his room wearing riding-leggings — as one has to do often in Persia. In the best *Fārsī* phrases that I could command I explained the purpose of my visit. In Eastern fashion he immediately placed his house and his all at my disposal, and this I found to be no empty phrase of courtesy in his case, even though I could not accept the generous invitation to lodge under his roof, because I had already promised to be the guest of the English missionaries.

As soon as the Kalantar learned in more detail the reason for my coming to Yezd, he sent for a member of the community named Khodabakhsh Bahram Raïs, who had studied in Bombay and spoke English fluently, and who was known in Yezd as ' Master ' because of his attainments. The style of dress of this scholar was similar to the Kalantar's, even in the waistband and turban, and his features were of the same general cast, although somewhat sharper. The nose, as in the case of all the Persian Zoroastrians that I met, was rather prominent, but well shaped. In manner he was modest and courtly, and his face lighted up when he recognized the name he had heard from common friends in Bombay, where my Zoroastrian interests were known. He held a hurried consultation with the

Kalantar, and they at once proposed a plan for a conference on the morrow with the High Priest and with the spiritual and secular leaders of the Zoroastrian community, setting the time in Persian fashion at so many hours 'after sunrise.' Gifts of flowers were brought in and presented to me as a sign of welcome, and the hospitality of supper was extended in Zoroastrian style.

At this meal the host himself declined to take a seat at the table, but moved about, standing now at the doorway and again withdrawing to give directions, but returning to see them carried out. He explained that this was regarded among his people as the true manner of hospitality in olden times, when the master of the house was supposed to be ever ready to serve his guests in person, and he thought that I would best like to have the time-honored custom observed. The number of dishes was perhaps ancient Median in its variety, rather than early Persian — in other words, the abundance of Astyages and not the frugality of his grandson Cyrus, if we may accept the picture in Xenophon's Greek romance as accurate. A hearty broth as first course was followed by lamb, vegetables, and some dishes characteristic of Yezd, with sweetmeats and tea for dessert and some mild wine such as 'the house of the Magian' produced in the days of Hafiz. To converse at table was, I knew, contrary to the Avestan code, but I preferred not to observe this prescription, even in the house of a Zoroastrian, as I wished to use every possible moment to learn more concerning the interesting people among whom I had come. We talked about matters of home life among the Zoroastrians, the size of their community, their relations with Kerman, and the communication they had with their co-religionists in India, until it was time for me to leave for the English Mission, where I found a hearty welcome awaiting me.

At an early hour the next morning I returned again to the house of my Zoroastrian host. The Anjuman, or synod of leading men in the Gabar community, was assembled to the number of eighteen. The Chief Priest, *Dastūr-i Dastūrān*, who was named Namdar, happened to be absent in India at the time, but the Acting High Priest, Tir Andaz, who was his father-in-law, was at home and entered the assembly a few minutes later. He was a tall, handsome man, dressed in robes of pure white, and his flowing beard of snow lent the dignity of age to his kindly face. A brownish turban set off his dark, intelligent eyes, which had the gleam of youth and were in keeping with his manly frame, erect bearing, and clear voice.

The formal reception in Oriental manner now began, and I was reminded of the description in the Zartusht Namah of the ceremonies when Zoroaster first appeared before his patron Vishtaspa. Settees and chairs were placed in a large open hall that faced upon the garden court. They were arranged in the form of a widespread V, in much the same manner as in the council of Ormazd described in the old Iranian Bundahishn.[1] I was formally conducted to a seat at the apex of this V. My host took the place on the right, the High Priest sat on the left ; the other members of the assembly were arranged in order of seniority or rank. When all were seated there was a moment's pause. Then those sitting on the right turned toward me and made a solemn bow, to which I responded ; the same salutation was formally repeated on the left. A servant next entered with a tray of confectionery, a ewer of rose-water, and a hand-mirror. From the hospitality of the Parsis in India, I was familiar with the rose-water and sugar candy, but I had not previously seen the mirror used in ceremonies, although I was told it was an old Zardushtian custom in receiving a guest. My momentary embarrassment was relieved when the mirror was handed to the High Priest. He looked gravely into it, slowly stroked his white beard, on which he poured a few drops of rose-water, and then with perfect dignity passed

---

[1] See my article in *Archiv für Religionswissenschaft*, 1. 364. I have also been told that the Talmud somewhere speaks of this as the Parsi manner of sitting at meals, in contrast to the Jewish fashion.

the glass to the next, who did likewise, and so did the others. The sugared bonbons, for which the Zoroastrians of Yezd are renowned, proved very refreshing and served to satisfy that craving for sweets which is felt by travellers in hot and dry climates. Meanwhile a number of the company regaled themselves with snuff, as there seems to be no objection to the use of tobacco in that manner, but only to its being smoked, as that is regarded as a defilement of the fire.

The formalities finished, the real conference began, and for three or more hours I asked and answered questions relating to Zoroaster and his faith, and concerning the condition of his followers in Persia. Two manuscripts of the Avesta and some fragments were first shown me. One of these was a fine large copy of the Vendidad Sadah, seen by Professor E. G. Browne, when he visited Yezd in 1888; the other was a text of the Yasna. The copy of the Vendidad Sadah was much the older of the two, and was said to date back about three hundred years. The Yasna manuscript belonged to the middle of the last century. The third text, incomplete, was a good transcript of the Vishtasp Yasht, which is a comparatively late compilation devoted to the praise of Zoroaster's patron and other worthies of the religion. These were all the manuscripts that could be produced at the moment, and the best-informed members of the assembly stated that all their more important manuscripts had been sent to India for safe-keeping or for use, and they feared that the chances of obtaining hitherto unknown copies were growing yearly less.[1] I urged upon them the importance of making a careful search, especially among the older families, who might possibly have texts that had not found their way to Bombay, and I have since corresponded

---

[1] A number of these manuscripts which are now in Bombay had already been used by Professor Geldner in the preparation of his edition of the Avesta. I communicated afterward to the Parsi Panchayat in Bombay the facts about the manuscripts I had seen at Yezd and also in Mr. John Tyler's possession at Teheran, as the Secretary of the Panchayat had requested from me a report regarding any copies of Avestan texts I could find.

with them on the subject; but I am hardly more sanguine about the results of the search than was Westergaard, who visited Yezd and Kerman in 1843.[1] The members of the assemblage naturally ascribed the loss of their texts largely to the persecutions that followed after the Moslem conquest, an instance of which I gathered from an oral tradition current among them. It is worth repeating.

About a century and a half after the Arab conquest, or more accurately in the year A.D. 820, there was a Mohammedan governor of Khorasan, named Tahir, who was the founder of the Taharid dynasty and was called 'the Ambi-dextrous' (*Zū'l-Yaminein*). He was a bigoted tyrant, and his fanaticism against the Zoroastrians and their scriptures knew no bounds. A Musulman who was originally descended from a Zoroastrian family made an attempt to reform him and laid before him a copy of the book of good counsel, *Andarz-i Buzurg-Mihr*, named from the precepts given by Buzurg-Mihr, the prime minister of Anushirvan the Just, and he asked the governor for permission to translate it into Arabic for his royal master's edification.[2] Tahir exclaimed, 'Do books of the Magians still exist?' On receiving an affirmative answer, he issued an edict that every Zoroastrian should bring to him a *man* (about fourteen pounds) of Zoroastrian and Parsi books, in order that all these books might be burned, and he concluded his mandate with the order that any one who disobeyed should be put to death. As my informant added, it may well be imagined how many Zoroastrians thus lost their lives, and what a number of valuable works were lost to the world through this catastrophe. A variation òf the story, but told of Tahir's son, named Abdullah (A.D. 828–840), and applied to the romance of *Vāmik and 'Adhrā*, which is described in its title as 'a pleasing story (*khūb hikāyat*) compiled by

---

[1] See Westergaard, *Zendavesta*, preface, p. 21, n. 4, and p. 11, n. 3, Copenhagen, 1852-1854; see likewise his letter to Dr. Wilson, quoted by Karaka, *History of the Parsis*, 1. 60.

[2] This work corresponds to the Pahlavi treatise Pandnamak-i Vazborg-Mitro-i Bukhtakan, which has survived. See on this point West, *Grundr. iran. Philol.* 2. 113.

sages and dedicated to King Anushirvan' (A.D. 531–579), is given by the Persian biographer Daulatshah in his literary notices.[1] The story as it exists to-day among the Zoroastrians is an interesting illustration of their pertinacity in keeping up the tradition regarding the loss of much of their literature after the Mohammedan conquest as well as during the invasion of 'Alexander the Accursed.'

Inquiries regarding legends of Zoroaster did not result in bringing out anything particularly new, but it was interesting to obtain their views on some of the debated questions in connection with the prophet's life. Zoroaster, they believe, came from Rei, the ancient ruined city of Ragha near Teheran, long associated with his mother's name.[2] They knew nothing of the tradition that connects him with Urumiah.[3] They associate his home, or rather his father's house, which is said in the Vendidad to have been located on the Drejya, Darejya, or Daraj, with the region about the river Karaj on the road from Teheran to Kazvin. The village, they said, corresponds to the modern Kalak near the Karaj River which flows from the mountain Paitizbara, as they interpret the words *paiti zbarahi* in the Avestan text.[4] The resemblance between the letters *D* and *K* in Avestan *Darejya, Drejya*, Phl. *Dareji*, Pers. *Daraj*, if written in the ancient script, does make this ingenious comparison seem plausible for a moment, especially as the river Karaj itself, a photograph of which I took three weeks later when I

---

[1] See Daulatshah, *Tadhkirat ash-Shu'ara*, ed. Browne, p. 30, London, 1901, and compare Browne, *Literary History of Persia*, pp. 12, 346–347.

[2] See p. 430, below, and compare my *Zoroaster*, pp. 17, 85, 192, 202.

[3] See pp. 87, 103, above.

[4] See Vd. 19. 3, 11. The view that the text contains an allusion to a mountain called 'Paitizbara' (*paiti zbarahi*) from which the Darejya flows, is found in an essay in English by Ervad Sheriarji Bharucha, *Zoroastrian Religion* *and Customs*, p. 3, Bombay, 1893, and this treatise has been translated into Persian by Master Khodabakhsh. The same interpretation appeared to be found in a lithographed work from which they quoted, and which was a compilation by Mirza Tath-ali-khan Zanganahi (so far as I could catch the name). The comparison of the Daraj with Karaj is due to this latter writer. There are some incidental references to the Karaj in Yakut, pp. 65, 478, 488 ; see also p. 443, below.

THE ZOROASTRIAN ANJUMAN AT YEZD

crossed it, also shows precipitous banks that would answer to the conditions supposed to be required by the phrase *paiti zbarahi* in the Vendidad;[1] but in spite of this the identification seems fanciful, and I have given reasons elsewhere for believing that the river Darejya, Drejya of the Avesta, is the modern Daryai in Azarbaijan.[2] I may add in passing that a number of persons in the assembly knew that Zoroaster's name was associated by tradition with the city of Balkh in eastern Iran.

For Zoroaster's name, which appears in the Avesta as *Zarathushtra* and in Modern Persian as *Zartusht* or *Zardusht*, which is believed in reality to mean some sort of a camel (Av. *ushtra*, see p. 89, above) they offered nearly a dozen fantastical interpretations or attempted etymologies. Dastur Tir Andaz, after the Oriental manner, suggested that the name, if divided as *Zartusht*, might be explained as 'pure gold,' or 'washed gold,' as if the latter element were connected with *shustan*, 'to wash.' Another member of the company proposed 'enemy of gold,' as if the final member of *Zar-dusht* were *dushman*, 'foe.' Finally my host turned to the lithographed book that he held in his hand, and which seemed to be a compendium of the various Persian and Arabic writers who mention Zoroaster and are already known to Western scholars.[3] The work contained no less than nine different explanations, part of them cited from Persian lexicographical works, and I subsequently learned that it was handed down by Farzanah Bahram ibn Farhad, a disciple of Azar Keivan, who lived in the time of Akbar the Great, about A.D. 1600.[4] The value of the book was most highly

---

[1] I have reproduced the photograph in Chap. 28, below. For *paiti zbarahi*, see Bartholomae, *Air. Wb.* p. 1699.

[2] See my *Zoroaster*, pp. 194–195.

[3] For the main sources, see my *Zoroaster*, pp. 280–286.

[4] According to the *Parsi Prakash*, ed. Bamanji Bahramji Patel, p. 10, Bombay, 1888, the above-mentioned Dastur Azar Keivan bin Azar Go-shasp was a learned and well-known Persian priest who believed in a universal religion. After spending twenty-eight years of his life in meditation he came to India and settled at Patna, where he became known as a teacher of a universal creed. He wrote the Makashifat-i Azar Keivan and died at Patna in 1614, at the age of eighty-five. For this information from the

thought of by my best-informed critic, Khodabakhsh Raïs, who referred to it as an imaginative work and branded the etymologies as 'fanciful and invented by the disciples of the aforesaid Azar Keivan, who was a half-Brahman, half-Zoroastrian, a believer in metempsychosis.' Scholars will certainly agree with the estimate as to the philological value of the interpretations, but I give the list as I noted it.

1. *āfarīdā-i avval,* 'first created being.'
2. *nafs-i kull,* 'universal soul.'
3. *nafs-i nātikah,* 'spirit of speech.'
4. *'akl-i falak-i 'utārid,* 'genius of the heaven of the planet Mercury.'
5. *nūr-i mujarrad,* 'incorporeal light.'
6. *'akl-i fa"āl,* 'active genius.'
7. *rabbu 'n-nau'-i insān,* 'lord of all mankind.'
8. *rāst-gū,* 'truth-speaker.'
9. *nūr-i khudā,* or *nūr-i yazdān,* 'light of God.'

From the same historical compilation the reader cited a passage to the effect that the Mohammedans believed that there were several Zoroasters—a view which I had heard propounded also by some of the Zoroastrians in India—and that the Zardusht of Vishtasp's time was the ninth in order, the first of them being Hoshang;[1] but this view, according to my host, was due to a mistaken reading of a verse in the Shah Namah.

From questions relating to Zoroaster we turned to religion and philosophy. The discussion led to the problem of dualism, the relation of Ormazd (*Ahura Mazda,* 'Lord Wisdom') and the archangels and angels (*Amesha Spentas* and *Yazatas*) to

Parsi Prakash I am indebted to my pupil and friend, Ervad Maneckji Nusservanji Dhalla, of Karachi, India, a student at Columbia University. For a note on Farzanah Bahram ibn-Farhad, see Shehriarji Bharucha, *The Dasātir,* in *Zartoshti,* 3. 122, Bombay, 1905.

[1] In the Dasatir (see Shehriarji Bharucha, *op. cit.* p. 121) Zartosht is the thirteenth in the line of prophets. Such is the view held also by some of the theosophists among the Modern Parsis of India, certain of whom regard him as the seventh of the name. See Bilimoria, *Zoroastrianism in the Light of Theosophy,* p. 4, note, Bombay, 1896.

Ahriman (*Angra Mainyu*, 'Evil Spirit,') and the arch-fiends
and fiends (*Daēvas* and *Drujes*), who war against the soul of
man. I found that the most enlightened of these Zoroastrians
look upon Ahura Mazda as comprising within himself the
conflicting powers of good and evil, designated respectively as
Spenta Mainyu, 'Holy Spirit,' and *Angra Mainyu*, 'Evil Spirit,'
and that their views in this respect, and possibly under the
influence of Bombay, would agree with the monotheistic tenets
upheld by the Parsis of India to-day, who stoutly deny the
allegation that Zoroastrianism teaches pure dualism.[1] They
believe also in the resurrection of the dead, or are acquainted,
at least, with this doctrine, which their faith has taught since
early times ; and my informant promptly gave me the technical term (Pahlavi *rīstākhēz*, Mod. Pers. *ristākhīz*) for the
'rising of the dead.' The Messianic doctrine of a Saoshyant,
or Savior, appeared likewise to be well known.

When hearing the High Priest recite passages from the
Avesta and when listening to a Mobed as well as a layman read
from the sacred texts lying before us, I was struck by certain
peculiarities of pronunciation that are worthy of note. For
some of the striking features I was prepared through a previous study of the variations in the Iranian manuscripts of the
Avesta, used by Geldner for his great edition of the Avesta, and
through my observation of the pronunciation of the Parsi
priests in India ;[2] but some of the peculiarities and certain phonetic inconsistencies in reproducing the words were
quite unexpected. What I noticed most was the fact that the
Avestan letters *th*, *ph*, *dh*, *gh*, and generally *kh*, which are
presumed historically to have been spirants, as in English *kith*,
burthen (for *burden*), and German *hoch*, were pronounced as
ordinary *t*, *d*, *g*, *k*, or occasionally as aspirates *tʿ*, *dʿ*, *gʿ*, *kʿ*, (*tʰ*,

[1] On the whole subject of dualism,
see the views expressed in my article
in *Grundr. iran. Philol.* 2.626–631,
647–649, 663.

[2] Many of the phonetic features are
common in the ordinary pronunciation
of the Indian Parsis, except among
the trained scholars.

d^h, g^h, k^h) : for example, *athā*, 'so,' sounded as *atā* or *at'ā*, *at^hā*; *vĕrĕt^hrag^hna*, 'Victory.' The consonant *t̲* was given everywhere as *d* ; for example, *cvat̲*, 'as many as,' was pronounced like *c^awad*. The secondary nasal *ṅh* (*ṇh*) arising in Avestan from an original sibilant was pronounced like *nk* (*vank-ē-osh*, *vank-hi-osh*, or *vank-i-ash*, for *vaṅhéush*, 'of good,' and *ank-i-ush* for *aṅhéush*, 'of the world'). The voiced sibilant *z* was pronounced like the English *z*, and the Avestan letter for *zh* could not be distinguished from our *j* (or from *j̇*, *j^h*), while the previously mentioned *th* occasionally interchanged with *s*, as in the Avestan manuscripts (*sĕrish* for *thrish*, 'thrice'), thus coming near to the earlier spirant character of the sound *th* than does the pronunciation *t* or *t'* in vogue among the priests as indicated above. The vowels *a*, *o*, *u*, were frequently confused with each other, and *i* was shaded in the direction of *ĕ* (*vĕhĕshta*, 'best,' for *vahishta*), while certain of the diphthongs were merged into simple vowels (*ao* in *mraot̲*, 'he spoke,' pronounced as *ū*, *m^arūd*). The anaptyctic and epenthetic vowels were clearly marked : thus, *pa-i-ti*, 'against.'

A few illustrations of the general characteristics of the pronunciation will suffice. The name of the prophet Zoroaster, in the nominative form *Zarathushtrō*, was pronounced as *Zarat(^h)ushtrū*, *Zarat(^h)oshtrū*, or even *Zarat(^h)ashtrū*. The opening lines of the well-known Profession of Faith, *nāismī daēvō fravarānē mazdayasnō zarathushtrish vīdaēvō ahura-t̲kaēshō*, 'I abjure being a Demon-Worshipper, I profess myself a Worshipper of Mazda, a foe to the demons, and a believer in the faith of Ahura,' were sounded like ' *nāismī dīvū fravarānē mazdayasnū vīdīvū ahura-d-kīshū.*' The sacred formula of the Ahuna Vairya sounded on their lips quite different from the pronunciation generally given to it in the Occident, at least as indicated in the accepted philological works. This will be clear from a comparative transcript, first in the ordinary transliteration with which we are familiar, and then in the transliteration reproduced from the memoranda I made of the Yezd pronunciation, supplemented by notes from Master Khodabakhsh.

AHUNA VAIRYA STANZA AS ORDINARILY WRITTEN

yathā ahū vairyō athā ratush ashāṭcīṭ hacā
vaṅhéush dazdā manaṅhō shyaothananām aṅhéush mazdāi
khshathremcā ahurāi ā yim dregubyō dadāṭ vāstārem.[1]

AHUNA VAIRYA STANZA AS PRONOUNCED AT YEZD
(with the variant pronunciations in parentheses)

yatā (yat^hā) ahī vaireyū atā (at^ha) ratosh (ratāsh) ashād^acīd hacā
vaṅk-e-osh (vaṅke-hī-osh, vaṅh-ī-ash) dazdā manaṅkahū she-yū-tananūme
aṅke-hī-osh (aṅk-ī-ash) mazdāe
kashatramcā (khashatremcā) ahorāe (ahārāe or ahurāe) ā yem dare-
gābe-yū (dargābyu) dadad vās-e-tāram (vāwstārĕm).[2]

For a fuller collection of material to illustrate the pronunciation I must refer to a monograph on the subject which I hope soon to publish in one of the Oriental journals.

While on the subject of pronunciation and the reading of the sacred texts, I may add an observation which will not, however, surprise specialists; I refer to the fact that the Acting High Priest and also the more scholarly members of the assembly were unaware that a great part of the Younger Avesta is composed in metre. The idea of verse and verse-structure appeared wholly new to them, when I read for them a portion of the Hom Yasht metrically in the manner that is familiar to students in the West. In all such matters it is manifest that ages of persecution and of neglect of their sacred lore have not been without a detrimental influence upon their technical knowledge; on the other hand, certain points in their pronunciation appear to deserve the consideration of linguistic scholars, because the Persian Zoroastrians are not affected by any philological bias and have remained practically free from the Indian influences

---

[1] For the sake of parallelism I have here retained, with trifling modifications, the older transliteration of Justi.

[2] The *ā* is sometimes labialized to *aw* (Eng. *law*).

that may have affected, in some respects, the pronunciation of the Parsis of Bombay.[1]

By this time it was considerably past mid-day, and nearly an hour more was spent in examining the manuscripts and in photographing specimens of the text. A rare privilege was now accorded me ; I was invited by Tir Andaz to visit his fire-temple early that afternoon after I had enjoyed the repast spread by our host. I was glad to accept at once this opportunity to become acquainted with a place of worship used by the Persian Zoroastrians. It was the temple of the *Ātash-i Varahrān*, or *Ātash Bahrām*, 'Fire of Victory,' situated in the Parsi quarter and located next to the house of Dastur Namdar, the priest who was absent in India at the moment. It is the chief Zoroastrian sanctuary of Yezd, although there are three other fire-shrines or chapels, designated either as *Dar-i Mihr* or *Ādariān*, besides one such minor place of worship in every Zoroastrian village in the vicinity of the city.[2]

Upon reaching the temple I found it to be a simple, unpretentious building. From its exterior and from the entrance it would hardly have been possible to recognize it as a temple at all. Mohammedanism allows no rivals to its beautiful mosques with turquoise domes, arabesque arches, and slender tessellated minarets. The splendor of the ancient temple of Anaitis at Ecbatana, from which, as I have described above, conquerors carried off untold wealth in gold and silver plate, the grand ruins of Kangavar and the gorgeous display at the Shrine of Fire in Shiz, under the Sasanian kings, belong to ages long since dead.[3]

Before reaching the main room of the sanctuary at Yezd it

---

[1] It is only the younger generation of Zoroastrian students at Yezd that has come into close contact with the Zoroastrians of India, through the influence of Master Khodabakhsh and a few other scholars who have been in Bombay.

[2] The name *Dar-i Mihr*, 'Shrine of Mihr' (used also in India) contains a reminiscence of the ancient Mithraic worship, but is now used (like *Ādariān*, 'pyraea') merely as a designation for a small chapel or shrine of fire.

[3] See pp. 131–143, above.

Two Zoroastrian Priests at Yezd

A Wind Tower at Yezd

was necessary to pass through several corridors and an ante-chamber, all of which help to render the shrine safer from desecration. On one side of the last passageway I observed a pile of short logs, one or two feet long and several inches thick, that were used as fuel for the holy flame ;[1] it appeared to be 'well-dried and well-examined wood,' as the Avesta enjoins.[2] From the anteroom I entered the large oblong chamber, or chapel, adjoining the sanctum sanctorum in which the fire was kept. My ear caught at once the voice of the white-robed priests who were chanting in the presence of the sacred element a hymn of praise sung by Zoroaster of old. It was a glorification of Verethraghna, the Angel of Victory, in the Bahram Yasht, and I felt a thrill as I heard the Avestan verses — *verethraghnem ahuradhātem yazamaide*, 'we worship the Angel of Victory, created by Ahura' — ring out from behind the walled recess where the fire was hidden. The door was open and I stood within a few feet of the fire, so as to listen, but I made no attempt to see the flame, as I knew such a step would be regarded as a profanation and might bar the way to other privi-leges which I wished to enjoy. It seemed an unusual experience thus to be standing in a fire-temple in Zoroaster's own land and listening to the priests of his hereditary line chanting verses from the sacred texts as had been done for nearly three thousand years. The voice of the *zōt*, or officiating priest, was high, nasal, and resonant, and his intonation was so rapid that he had to pause at times to catch his breath ; while his assistant, the *raspī*, chanted in a lower key or accompanied his recitation in a nasal minor key with great rapidity of utterance.[3] Each of the cele-brants wore over his mouth the *paitidāna*, a small white veil prescribed by the Avesta to be worn over the lips when before

---

[1] Cf. Vd. **3.** 1.

[2] Cf. Vd. **14.** 2; **18.** 27, 71.

[3] The intonation of both the priests was loud and resonant and more swift than that of the Parsi dasturs I had heard in Bombay and Udvada, and I observed the same peculiarities in pro-nunciation that I had observed in the conference of the forenoon.

the fire, in order to prevent the breath and spittle from defiling the hallowed flame.

I almost fell into a revery as I listened to this monotonous chanting of the Yasht; but the hymn was soon ended, and the veiled priests came out from the presence of the fire and were kind enough to allow me to take their photograph, although the light was too dim to secure a good picture.

While speaking of pictures I may mention a so-called portrait of Zoroaster hanging on the wall of this main chamber. I had heard of it a number of years before, and when writing my book on the Prophet of Ancient Iran I had expressed a keen desire to see it.[1] My conference with Tir Andaz in the forenoon, when he gave me the meagre information that he had about its possible remote connection with Balkh, had prepared me for disappointment as to its value, but I did not expect to find it of so little importance. The picture is merely a modern colored print, apparently a cheap Parsi chromolithograph from India, perhaps not twenty years old, and of no historic interest. It is a variety of the familiar representation based on the Tak-i Bostan sculpture;[2] but the staff is not fluted, as in the sculpture, the top is capped with a symbolic flame, as in other modern representations current among the Parsis in India, and the lower end of the staff rests upon the ground. This colored picture was the only decoration I noticed on the bare, whitewashed walls.

At the rear of the chamber there was a gallery used on occasions when a considerable number of the Zardushtian community come together, as at the Gahanbar season, the Farvadin festival, on some commemorative day, or at some special celebration. The gatherings on such occasions are the nearest approach that the Zoroastrians have to the assembling of a congregation in church, for they have nothing that corresponds precisely to our general Sunday worship.

The Acting High Priest now opened a door leading into a small side-chamber to the right of the sanctum where the fire

---

[1] See my *Zoroaster*, pp. 288–289.   [2] See pp. 216–218, above.

was kept. It was a room arranged as an *Izashnah Gāh*, a place set apart for the performance of religious ceremonies and priestly rites. The floor was built of stone and was cemented and marked off into little channels (*pāvi*) or grooves (*kash*), to enclose the space within which the priest sat while conducting the ritual, as I had witnessed in the halls adjoining the Parsi temples in India.[1] A lambskin, used apparently as a seat, was lying on the floor, and there were small, low stone stools such as are generally employed in the Izashnah Gah, besides a number of sacrificial utensils. Among the latter were the cups for holding consecrated water, milk, and the juice of the *hōm*-plant (Av. *haoma*), from which the sacred drink was prepared in ancient times, as nowadays, and partaken of by the priest as a part of the ceremony.

The *haoma*, as is well known, corresponds to the *sōma* of Vedic India, which grows on the mountains,[2] and the two branches which the priest gave me came from the mountain heights some distance from Yezd. In addition to this and the *urvarā hadhānaēpatā*, or pomegranate,[3] there is still another plant employed in the sacrifice, and it has been used in the Magian ritual since time immemorial. It is the barsom (Av. *baresman*), the twigs or sprays of which are tied in a bundle at a certain point in the sacrifice, corresponding in a distant manner to the *barhis*, or straw, strewn as a seat for the divinities in the Vedic ceremonies of old. In Yezd the tamarisk bush is used to form this bundle, and it is bound with a slender strip of bark from

[1] I refer to the so-called *urvis-gāh* connected with the fire-temples at Udvada, Navsari, and Bombay. For a photograph and a description of the latter, together with a representation of the various implements and utensils employed in the sacrifice, see Darmesteter, *Le ZA.* 1. introd. p. 72 (pl. 4), and compare the interesting notes descriptive of some Parsi ceremonies, by Haug, *Essays on the Parsis*, 3d ed., pp. 392–409 ; cf. likewise my note in *JAOS.* 22. 321.

[2] See Ys. **10**. 3, and Rig Veda **5**. 85. 2 ; **10**. 34.1.

[3] The Zoroastrians of Yezd, like the Indian Parsis, agree in regarding the pomegranate as the representative of the Avestan *urvarā hadhānaēpatā* ; on the latter, compare Haug, *Essays on the Parsis*, pp. 251, 399, and West, *SBE.* 37. 186.

2 B

the mulberry tree, probably in exactly the same manner as it was in Zoroaster's day.[1]   Brass rods are sometimes substituted for the twigs, as is done by the Parsis in India, but at Yezd this substitution is made only in winter, when it is impossible to procure the branches, or at some particular time when it is impracticable to obtain them.   It was the use of these very branches, perhaps, that the Prophet Ezekiel denounced as an abomination to God when he saw in a vision 'about five and twenty men, with their backs toward the temple of the Lord, and their faces toward the east, and they worshipped the sun toward the east, . . . and, lo, they put the branch to their nose.'[2]

I saw the large tamarisk bush from which the sprays were cut for use in the *barsom* ceremony; it was of a light green color, twelve or fifteen feet high, and stood in the garden adjoining the rear of the temple.   A high wall shut in the garden at the back; a gallery ran part of the way around the enclosure ; a flight of steep steps led down from this to the ground, where there were blossoming rose bushes, sweet-scented shrubs and plants, a pomegranate tree, and the tamarisk bush. Tir Andaz cut off from this three handsome sprigs, each nearly two feet long, and presented them to me.   They were slender and delicate, covered with downy fibrous leaves, and look graceful even in the dried form in which I now have them.[3]

Besides the sacred plants, perfumes (*baodhi*), bread-offerings (*draonah, myazda*), consecrated water, the *haoma*, and milk, the Avesta frequently refers to the cow (*gao*) in connection with the Yasna ceremony.   Like their Parsi brethren in India, the Zoroastrians of Persia interpret the Avestan words *gao jīvya*,

---

[1] The Avestan words employed in connection with the *barɔsman* indicate that the twigs were originally spread (*star-, frastɔrɔta-*), then gathered into a bundle and bound (*yāh-, aiwyāsta-, aiwyå̄ṇhana-*); see the references under each of these words in Bartholomae, *Air. Wb.* pp. 98, 947, 1290, 1595.

[2] Ezekiel 8. 16, 17.

[3] My friend Mr. Percy Bodenstab, of Yonkers, has made a drawing of the sprays (here reproduced) in a reduced size ; to convey a clearer idea it would be necessary to reclothe the branches with the softest green color imaginable.

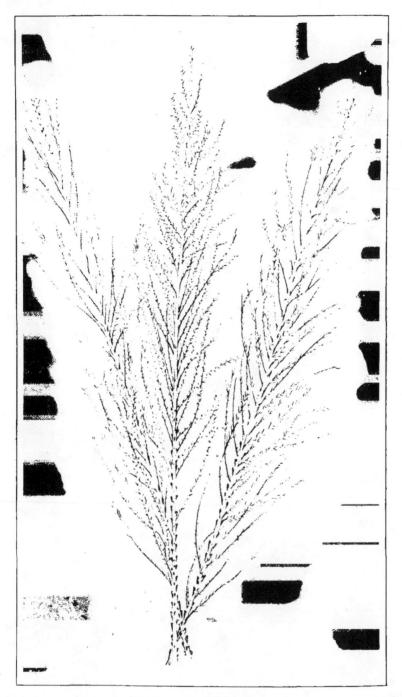

SPRAYS OF THE BARSOM PLANT

lit. 'living cow,' as goat's milk (Pers. *shīr*), and similarly employ an egg and melted butter to represent the *gao hudhāh*, lit. 'beneficent cow,' in the ceremony. The faithful of both communities agree in regarding the true Zoroastrian sacrifice to be a bloodless sacrifice, an offering of 'good thoughts, good words, good deeds,' accompanied by praise and thanksgiving, with appropriate ceremonies. Such was the sacrifice offered by Zoroaster himself in the Yashts, after the manner of Ahura Mazda,[1] although the Avesta does allude to the sacrifice of animals, once, for example, in the Yasna, and several times in the Yashts, which represent Vishtaspa and the heroes of old as sacrificing thousands of animals, some of which must have been slain as a blood-offering.[2]

A possible survival of the ancient custom of animal sacrifice may survive at Yezd, down to the present, in the celebration of the *Jashn-i Mihrgān*, ' Sacrifice to Mithra,' although the views on this subject may differ.[3] This festival falls on the day of Mihr, in the month of Mihr (February-March), and is an important one among the Persian Zoroastrians, as they prolong it for five days, till the day of Bahram, or Verethraghna. According to the account I received, it commemorates the victory gained by Feridun (Avestan *Thraētaona*) over the Babylonian tyrant Zohak (Avestan *Azhi Dahāka*), whose cruel rule oppressed Iran for a thousand years. 'The Persian Zoroastrians used to believe, and some of them still believe,' as my authority informed

---

[1] See Yt. **5.** 17, 104 ; **9.** 25 ; **17.** 44 (rendering *gava* each time as 'milk').

[2] See Ys. **11.** 4 ; Yt. **5.** 21, 25, 33, 108 ; Yt. **9.** 25 ; compare also the description of the Magian sacrifice given by Herodotus, *History*, 1. 132. Observe likewise that on the eve of battle (Yt. **5.** 68) Jamaspa himself offers an animal sacrifice.

[3] The notes which I present on the Jashn-i Mihrgan are given on the authority of Khodabakhsh Bahram Raïs, who, it should be noticed, attributes the origin of the custom to Mohammedan influence after the Arab conquest, like the sacrifices at the feast '*id-i kurbān*, referred to above, p. 162, n. 1. The opinion of the Parsis in India would also be in favor of his view. See Modi, *Meher ane Jashne Meherangan* (*Mithra and the Feast of Mithras*), Bombay, 1889 ; cf. also Marquart, *Untersuchungen zur Geschichte von Eran*, 2. 132-136, Leipzig, 1905.

me, 'that at this festival Feridun sacrificed sheep and bade his subjects to follow his example in this respect, and to eat, drink, and be merry, because of the overthrow of their arch-enemy. It was accounted meritorious, therefore, to celebrate the occasion joyfully and to sacrifice a sheep or a goat in every house, or, if the family were poor, to kill a chicken. The priests themselves at first used to kill the animals, but the people afterward did this at home, sprinkling some of the blood on the door-posts and over the lintel, and cooking the rest of the blood with suet and onions, as a dish to be eaten with unleavened bread.[1] Since it was regarded not merely as a sacrifice but as a burnt-offering unto *Mihr-i Īrān-dāvar*, 'Mithra, Judge of Iran,' the flesh of the sheep and goats, when roasted, was carried to the fire-temple, prayers were said over it by the priests, to whom a share of the flesh was given, a portion was set aside for distribution among the poor, and the remainder was taken home to be eaten by the family and their friends.' Such is the account I received from my informant, who added, 'this custom is now dying out; the people are becoming wiser and saner, and outgrowing this cruel practice and bloody rite, which the Parsis of India do not recognize and like which they have nothing.'

After leaving the fire-temple I asked if I might visit the Barashnum Gah, a place set apart for the performance of the ablution for nine nights, as I shall describe in the next chapter. Since it was situated in another street I had an opportunity, both when going and returning, to see more of the Parsi quarter of the town and make further observations as to the community and its general condition. As there are about eight thousand Gabars in Yezd, they occupy a not inconsiderable section of the city. It is known as the *Mahallah-i Pusht-i Khān-i Alī*, or *Mahallah-i Pusht-i Khānah-i Alī*, 'the Quarter in the Rear of Khan Ali, or of Ali's House,' and I subsequently learned

---

[1] It is interesting to note the resemblance between this old-time Persian custom and the observances of the Jewish Passover.

that they have a tradition current among them as to the origin of this name. The common belief is that the designation by Ali's name is due to a device resorted to by the worshippers of Mazda in order to escape persecution at the hands of their Mohammedan enemies after the Arab conquest. They pretended, it is said, that Ali, the cousin and son-in-law of Mohammed, had a house in this part of Yezd and that he settled the Zoroastrians here, in order to shield them from persecution; and that they were Ali's cowherds. In support of this claim they cleverly urged the plea that the name *Gabr-ān,* 'Infidels,' by which they were stigmatized, and the modern pronunciation of which among the Parsis of Yezd would be *Gavr-ūn* or *Gavr-ān,* really meant *Gav-rān,* 'cow-keeper,' and that as Gabars the Zoroastrians were therefore worthy of Moslem protection. As I know through Khodabakhsh Bahram Raïs, the better educated among them regard this explanation of the name of the quarter as a mere fiction, a piece of popular etymology, and they suggest a more probable interpretation. The name Ali, they say, is not an uncommon one among the Persians, and this was probably the name of a land-owner, or wealthy Khan (Pers. *Khān*), who had a caravansarai outside the old part of Yezd, near where the Parsi quarter now is, and the Zoroastrians settled there, 'back of *Khān* Ali' (not *khānah,* 'house'), so that the designation has nothing to do with the house of Ali, the successor of Mohammed.

Some details regarding the general condition of the so-called Gabars in Yezd and its environs may be of interest. A large proportion of the Zoroastrians who live outside of the city itself, especially in the neighborhood of the flourishing town of Taft, are occupied in gardening and the cultivation of the soil. According to the Avesta, as I have already stated,[1] agriculture is one of the noblest of all employments, because he who sows grain, sows righteousness, and one of the most joyous spots on earth is the place where one of the faithful sows grain and

[1] See p. 246, above.

grass and fruit-bearing trees, or where he waters ground that
is too dry and dries ground that is too wet.[1]

The Zoroastrians who dwell within the city are largely occupied in trading.[2] This privilege was not accorded them until
about fifty years ago, and they are even now subject to certain
restrictions and exactions to which no Mohammedan would be
liable. They are not allowed, for instance, to sell food in the bazaars, inasmuch as that would be an abomination in the eyes of
the Moslems, who regard them as unbelievers and therefore
unclean. Until 1882 they were oppressed by the *jazīa* tax, a
poll tax imposed upon them as non-believers, and this gave an
opportunity for grinding them down by extortionate assessments
and trading-tolls. The *jazīa* was finally repealed by Shah
Nasr ad-Din, who issued a firman to that effect, September 27,
1882. It was largely owing to influences brought to bear upon
him by the Parsis of Bombay that the Shah was led to make
this liberal-minded move. They worked through the agency of
the Society for the Amelioration of the Zoroastrians in Persia,
which they had founded with an endowed fund in 1854, sending at the same time a representative to Iran to look after the
interests of their co-religionists.[3] Up to the time of the Shah's
firman, a Zoroastrian was not allowed to build an upper story
on his house, or, in fact, erect a dwelling whose height ex-
ceeded the upstretched arm of a Musulman when standing on
the ground.[4] Even within a year after the firman was issued,
a Zoroastrian in one of the neighboring villages is said to have
had to flee for his life because he had ventured to go beyond
the traditional limits and add an upper room to his abode,

---

[1] See Vd. **3**. 31 and Vd. **3**. 4.

[2] The Zoroastrians in general appear
to have an especial aptitude for business, and they appear rather to accept
than reject the designation 'Jews of
the East' that is sometimes applied to
them because of their commercial
activity.

[3] For an account of the efforts for
the abolition of this tax, see Dosabhai
Framji Karaka, *History of the Parsis*,
1. 72–82, London, 1884; cf. also p. 397,
below.

[4] The comparative scarcity of upper
stories on the houses in the Gabar
quarter is still noticeable.

A ZOROASTRIAN CON-
VERT TO ISLAM

SCHOOLBOYS AT YEZD, MOSTLY ZOROASTRIANS

YEZD TYPES
(1 and 2, Parsi women; 3, English woman in
Parsi dress; 4, Armenian girl)

and another Gabar, who was mistaken for him, was killed by the enraged Musulmans.[1]

As regards their dress, moreover, the Zoroastrians have always been obliged to adopt a style that would distinguish them from the Mohammedans, and it is only within the last ten years that they could wear any color except yellow, gray, or brown, and the wearing of white stockings was long interdicted. The use of spectacles and eye-glasses, and the privilege of carrying an umbrella, have been allowed only within the same decade, and even now the Gabars are not permitted to ride in the streets or to make use of the public baths (*hamām*); but the latter prohibition, as they told me, is no longer a hardship, because they have built a bathing-establishment for their own use. A score of petty annoyances that they have to undergo might be cited in addition to the more serious disqualifications; but enough have been given to show the disadvantages under which they labor and the persecutions to which they are exposed.

In 1898 the present Shah, Muzaffar ad-Din, sought to relieve their condition further by issuing a firman revoking the formal disabilities from which they suffered. While imperfectly observed, this decree has contributed, in spirit at least, to bettering their position. The spread of Babist doctrines, which favor religious liberty and toleration, has possibly contributed also by lessening intolerance on the part of the Mohammedans. The presence of Europeans has likewise had a salutary effect and aided considerably in the general advance. But the most has been done by the Bombay Society for the Amelioration of the Zoroastrians in Persia, whose funds have helped the Gabars and whose reform measures have tended to their general good, so that their numbers have increased considerably within the

[1] For this point and the next, see Malcolm, *Five Years in a Persian Town*, pp. 46, 49, London and New York, 1905. This interesting book on life at Yezd appeared after the present chapter was written, but I have been able to incorporate one or two references, and I would recommend to the reader's attention Mr. Malcolm's remarks on the restrictions in general upon the Gabars (pp. 44–53).

last fifty years.[1] Nevertheless, they still do not feel themselves
free from oppression, and they constantly have to avoid trouble
and persecution by yielding to Moslem prejudice.   In fact, their
lives are in danger whenever the fanatical spirit of Islam
breaks out, as was the case about a month after I was in Yezd.
A general Musulman rising then took place against the Babis,
a large number of whom belonging to the Behai branch
are found at Yezd.   These Babis were massacred by scores,
and even hundreds, or were subjected to shocking outrages
and cruel indignities.   The Zoroastrians feared that they
would suffer the same fate, and I was informed on the authority
of one who had witnessed the horrors that such might have
been the case if the fanatical wave had not been broken in its
course by the prompt and energetic intervention of the Europeans in telegraphic communication with the authorities in
power at Teheran.

The organization of the Zoroastrian community at Yezd has
already been indicated in a general way.   The spiritual guidance is in the hands of the priesthood (dasturs, mobeds, and
herbeds), but the authority which they exercise is greatly limited by the fact that those who do not wish for any reason to
accept it can simply throw it off and act in accordance with
the rule of the Moslems around them.[2]   In civic matters the
community is under the leadership of a synod, the *Anjuman*
(Av. *hanjamana*, ‘assembly, convention’), headed by a *kalāntar*,
or mayor, the present incumbent of that office being Kalantar
Dinyar Bahram, whose hospitality I have described, and whose

---

[1] In 1854 the number of Zoroastrians
in the vicinity of Yezd was given at
6658 souls (Karaka, *History of the
Parsis*, 1. 55) ; in 1882 as about 6483
(Houtum-Schindler, *Die Parsen in
Persien*, in *ZDMG*. 26. 54) ; in 1903
as between 8000 and 8500, including
the environs of Yezd (these last figures
being given to me in Teheran by Mr.

Ardeshir Reporter, Secretary of the
Society for the Amelioration of the
Zoroastrians).

[2] For the relations between the spiritual and temporal powers in ancient
times, see Wilhelm, *Kingship and
Priesthood in Ancient Eran*, pp.1–21,
Bombay, 1892 (translated from his German treatise in *ZDMG*. 40. 102–110).

official duties often take him to Kerman, Anar, and other towns in this region where there are Zoroastrians.

With the Kalantar's young son Bahram I formed a friendship in the short time of my stay, for he acted as my guide round the city and through the mazes of the bazaar. He was a bright, intelligent fellow, straightforward and honest, manly in his bearing, and agreeable in his manners. I could picture from him what might have been the type of youth in Zoroaster's day, since the blood of the ancient faith flowed in his veins by direct descent. I liked his naturalness and lack of affectation, and certain of his characteristics were charmingly naïve, for when I took his photograph he instinctively plucked a rose to hold in his hand (for a true Persian portrait would be artistically incomplete without a rose), and in the other hand he held up to view his European watch. I could understand his pride in this respect, since a Zoroastrian would not have been allowed some years ago to carry a watch or even to wear a ring.

Benevolence is a Zoroastrian characteristic, and the Avesta inculcates the virtue of generosity. Many of the Parsis of Yezd live up to this doctrine so far as their limited means will allow. As an instance of this I may cite the following example. When the English Christian Mission at Yezd was in need of quarters for its hospital — a branch of their work with which the Parsis especially sympathized — a prosperous Gabar merchant, named Gudarz Mihrban, came forward and donated to the cause a large caravansarai and its property, including a house that adjoined it. The structure of this erstwhile halting-place for caravans lent itself in a remarkable manner to the uses to which it was now to be put : the central court that once was filled with camels, asses, and pack-mules was turned into a pretty garden ; and the old-time lodgings of the camel-drivers and muleteers were transformed into chambers and wards for the Good Samaritan work.

CHAPTER XXIV

ZOROASTRIAN RELIGIOUS CUSTOMS AT YEZD

'Ev'n them who kept thy truth so pure of old.'
— MILTON, *Sonnet on the Massacre in Piemont.*

IN the preceding chapter I have touched upon the religious rites of the Zoroastrians as connected with the temple ; in the present chapter I shall speak of the religious aspect of their home life, the ceremonies and customs observed in connection with birth, bringing-up, marriage, and death.[1]

In respect to ceremonies connected with birth, the Iranian Parsis differ from their co-religionists in Bombay chiefly in the scarcity of such observances. A few Zoroastrians in Persia, like their Parsi brethren in India, call in the services of an astrologer (*nujumī*) on the occasion of a birth in their family, and the wiseacre makes up the horoscope of the infant's nativity. The custom, if resorted to, has the advantage at least of preserving a record of the child's day of birth, for most Zoroastrians, as I was informed, do not know the age of their children, or even the day, month, and year of their own birth. As a rule the astrologer is a Mohammedan ; a Parsi astrologer is far to seek, and if found, he practises his calling on the lines of the Moslem astrologer,[2] but with less skill and cunning in making his superstitious forecast. Charms and amulets are commonly worn by children, and it is probable that this custom is very ancient, antedating Islam by ages.[3] In order to avert

[1] I have been able to add largely to the notes taken at the time through correspondence with Master Khodabakhsh Bahram Raïs, whose kindness I wish again to acknowledge.

[2] The same is true in India, where the method adopted is that of the Hindu astrologer (*joshi*).

[3] For the usage of talismans in early times, including the Avesta (Yt.

the influence of the evil eye or to cure a child of some disease, a parent will occasionally hire the mobeds, or Zoroastrian priests, to read from the Yasna, the Yashts, or the Khordah Avesta ;[1] and when women are childless, they will sometimes pay to have the Vendidad Sadah recited by the priests, in order that the curse of sterility may be removed. With reference to birthday anniversaries, it is needless to say that they are not observed with any particular attention, for the obvious reason already given. This is in contrast to what must have been the custom in ancient days, for Herodotus says : 'The Persians honor their birthday above all other days, and on this day they prepare a feast more abundant than usual ; the rich serve up on such an occasion an ox, a horse, a camel, and an ass, roasted whole in ovens, and the poor set on the table smaller cattle.'[2] The custom now is practically forgotten, although a few Zoroastrians who have been in Bombay, where birthdays are festively celebrated, do observe the natal anniversary (*sāl-girih*) of their children by dressing the child in new clothes, preparing savory dishes, and inviting their friends and relatives to the feast.

The present education of the Zoroastrian youth is meagre as compared with what it might be, but all such statements are relative, of course, and depend upon the standard that is used.[3] Until half a century ago the Zoroastrians were even worse off in the matter of education than the rest of the Persians, because they either had no schools or were not allowed to have them. Happily in the year 1857 certain moneys from the Persian Zoroastrian Amelioration Fund were devoted to establishing

---

14. 34-40), see Jivanji Modi, *Charms or Amulets for Some Diseases of the Eye*, in the *Journal of the Anthropological Society of Bombay*, 3. 338-340 (1894), and *Nirang-i Jashan-i Burzigarān*, ibid. 5. 398-405 (1900), and *An Avesta Amulet*, ibid. 5. 418-425 (July and October, 1900).

[1] The Ardabahisht Yasht (Yt. **3.** 1-19) is regarded by the Parsis in India as especially efficacious in this respect.

[2] Herodotus, *History*, 1. 133.

[3] For the status of education in pre-Mohammedan times see Modi, *Education among the Ancient Irānians* (reprinted from *The Parsi*, vol. 1, nos. 2-9), Bombay, 1905.

and maintaining Parsi schools in the districts of Yezd and Kerman.[1] This progressive move was brought about by the energy of the Bombay Parsis and has been carried on with varying success ever since. It is to be hoped that even more ample funds will be subscribed for this purpose and still greater educational facilities afforded the Zoroastrians in Iran. The value which such increased advantages would have for them is recognized by those among their number who have studied in Bombay, and it is an encouraging sign to note that members of the priestly class are now going to India for advanced education and bringing back the seed of knowledge to sow once again in the Zoroastrian soil which originally produced it.

When the Zoroastrian boy or girl passes from childhood into the period of full youth, it is customary for each to assume personal responsibility in religious matters and be initiated into the community of the faithful. This confirmation of faith, if I may so call it, takes place between the ages of seven and fifteen. In contrast to the formal ceremonies performed by the Indian Parsis when the young novitiate puts on the sacred thread and shirt, there is practically no religious ritual performed in Persia.[2] The Iranian boy or girl simply puts on the

---

[1] See Karaka, *History of the Parsis*, 1. 83-89, and Malcolm, *Five Years in a Persian Town*, p. 47, and for a favorable estimate of the Parsi school at Yezd compare Landor, *Across Coveted Lands*, 1. 388-389.

[2] The modern name for the sacred cincture, or thread, is *kostī, kusti,* or *kushtī*; the Avestan designation was *aiwyåṅhana,* 'girdle' (Yt. 1. 17; Ys. 9. 26; Vijirkart-i Denig, 12, 18, 20; Nirangistan, 95). The consecrated shirt is now called *sudrah, sedrah,* or *sadarah*; its Avestan designation is not known, but it is presumed to correspond to *vastra,* 'garment,' and it is alluded to, together with the *kustī,* in Nir. 85-96; Vd. **18**. 54 (*anaiwyāsta,*

anabdātā). The wearing of the shirt is also alluded to (by implication) in the old Parsi Patits, or formulas of confession, see for example Patit Adarbat 19, in Spiegel, *Avesta Übersetzt,* 3. 213, Leipzig, 1863 = tr. Bleeck, p. 157, London, 1864. For the usage of the shirt and girdle in India and the ceremonies connected with assuming them, see Dastur Jamaspji Minocheherji, *Navjot Ceremony,* Bombay, 1887; Modi, *Religious System of the Parsis,* in *Parliament of Religions,* 2. 912, Chicago, 1893; Sheriarji Bharucha, *Zoroastrian Religion and Customs,* pp. 35-36, Bombay, 1893; Darmesteter, *Le ZA.* 2. 243, n. 13; 251, u. 54.

kushtī, kustī, or *kōsti,*[1] the sacred thread of the religion, as soon as he or she can recite the so-called 'Four Avestas'; that is, the *Srōsh Bāj,* 'prayer to the angel Sraosha,' *Kushtī-bastan,* 'tying the thread,' *Pa Nām-i Stāyishn,* lit. 'in the name of praise,' and *Birasād,* 'may it come.'[2] No priest is invited to the house to conduct this rite, as in India, nor are the Zoroastrian Scriptures recited. Instead of that, the kusti is merely put on at home without formality, although occasionally the youth goes with the kusti in hand to the house of the person who has taught him the four Avestan formulas, and there puts on the thread in his presence, making, at the same time, a gift of a sugar loaf to his preceptor. The wearing of the consecrated shirt, *sudrah, sedrah,* or *sadarah* (as the word is variously written), and formal investiture, which is scrupulously observed in Bombay, as prescribed by the religion, is not common at Yezd; but some of the Indianized Zoroastrians in Persia imitate their Parsi brethren of Bombay in keeping up this orthodox custom.

After assuming religious responsibility by putting on the kusti, the person is qualified for receiving the rites of the faith, and should, in theory at least, be subject to its regulations, especially to the rules of purification that are inculcated by the Avesta. Throughout the religion, Zoroaster enjoins purity of body as well as of soul, and the Avesta prescribes an elaborate set of lustrations and ablutions to remove any defilement that may have been incurred by contact with unclean matter. The greatest pollution comes from touching anything that is dead, since death is Ahriman's greatest triumph over Ormazd's creation. For that reason the code of the Vendidad gives elaborate rules for an 'Ablution of Nine Nights' (*barashnūm nū-shaba, nō-shva*), to be gone through with the most scrupu-

---

[1] In India *kustī* is the current pronunciation, and I have adopted that form.

[2] For a translation of the first two (*Nīrang Kustī* and *Srōsh Bāj*), see

Darmesteter, *Le ZA.* 2. 685–688 ; Spiegel, *Avesta Übersetzt,* 3. 4–7, Leipzig, 1863 = tr. Bleeck, 3. 4–5, London, 1864.

lous care in order to restore the ceremonial purity that may
have been lost by contact with the dead. It consists in a
series of sprinklings with bull's urine (a supposed disinfectant)[1]
and consecrated water, accompanied by an endless amount of
ritual that is thought to aid in exorcising the spirit of contamination.[2]

Originally, as in the Avesta, the rite appears to have been
used only in cases of great defilement, when a man had actually
touched a corpse, or when a woman had given birth to a
dead child, or it was employed to insure the absolute ceremonial purity of a priest who is to perform a sacrifice ; later
its usage appears to have become more extended, so that it was
resorted to as a means of securing purity in general, and it is
so used by the Indian Parsis, both in the abridged form of a
mere ablution and in its full form of a lustration covering nine
nights. According to the Persian treatise entitled Sad Dar,[3]
'it is strictly incumbent on mankind, on man and woman, to
perform the Barashnum ceremony ' at least once in a lifetime
in order to purify the soul for entrance into heaven, for other-

---

[1] The urine of beef was thought to
possess great purifying and medicinal
qualities and is called *gaomaēza*,
'beef's urine,' in the Avesta (Vd. **9.**
14 ; **19.** 21, 22) and *gōmēz* in Pahlavi
and Modern Persian. When consecrated by special prayers it is called
nīrang and is generally spoken of by
that name. See the treatise of Wilhelm, *On the Use of Beef's Urine
according to the Precepts of the Avesta*,
Bombay, 1889.

[2] See Vd. **9.** 1–46 ; **8.** 35–72 ; compare also the discussion of the Barashnum ceremony by West, *SBE*.
18. 431–454, and the notes by Darmesteter, *Le ZA*. 2. 159–172, and *SBE*.
4. 122–134. The Greek writer Lucian
alludes to this prescription when he
says, in one of his humorous dia-

logues, that his hero, Menippus, was
washed in the Tigris at Babylon for
twenty-nine days ' by the Magi, the
disciples and successors of Zoroaster.'
It is probable that this was the way in
which the Magian ' Zabratas,' or
' Zaratos,' according to Porphyrius
(*Vita Pythagorae*, 12) cleansed Pythag-
oras of all the sins he had committed
in his life. For the Greek texts of
these passages, see my *Zoroaster*, pp.
237, 242 ; Nauck, *Porphyrii Opuscula
Tria*, p. 18, Leipzig, 1860 ; and cf.
Kleuker, *Zend-Avesta, Anhang*, vol. 2,
pt. 3, pp. 104, 117, Riga, 1776–1783.

[3] See Sad Dar, **36.** 1–8, tr. West, *SBE*.
24. 296–298, and compare Darmesteter,
SBE. 4. 123. The treatise Sad Dar,
in its oldest form, dates back to the
time of the Arab conquest.

TWO PICTURES OF KHODABAKHSH BAHRAM RAÍS
(The Kalantar's young son in the background)

PARSI WOMEN AND GIRLS
(1 and 2, English; 3 and 4, Armenian)

wise the natal impurity contracted by being in the womb and sucking at the mother's breast will not be removed.[1]

When I visited the Barashnum Gah at Yezd, which is located within easy walking-distance of the fire-temple I found a primitive mud-walled structure, circular in form and differing greatly from the somewhat elaborate rectangular enclosure I had seen at Udvada in India. There were a few heaps of stones placed at certain intervals around the edge of the circuit, intended to serve as standing-places for the person undergoing this purification, since, according to the Vendidad, he must move from spot to spot within lines specially drawn in the sand and be sprinkled by the priest with the drops of bull's urine and water. The liquid is poured from a ladle fastened to the end of a stick 'nine knots' long, or long enough to allow the officiating priest to stand outside the circles that have been drawn. I observed a number of niches in the wall, precisely like the ordinary *tākchahs*, or sunken recesses, in the walls of a Persian room; they were used, I was told, as receptacles for food and drink to be taken by the person undergoing purification. The whole place looked dilapidated and neglected,[2] and from what I observed, as well as from conversation on the subject, I infer that less attention is given in Yezd to keeping up this ceremony than I should have expected in the centre of Zoroastrian orthodoxy in Iran. From the remarks of Khodabakhsh Raïs I conclude that certain of the more advanced Zoroastrians are opposed to insisting upon the importance of keeping up this rite, especially in the case of women, although the Avesta prescribes it under certain

[1] Sad Dar, **37**. 1–6. According to Khodabakhsh Raïs, the cleansing from the natal impurity is technically called *šustan-i sar-i šīr*, lit. ' washing of the head of milk,' milk being regarded as blood turned white and therefore impure, since blood defiles. For the comparative frequency with which the Barashnum ceremony is employed in India, see the account of the initiatory ceremony called *nāvar*, by Modi, *Zoroastrian Priesthood*, in *Zartoshti*, 1. 94, Bombay, 1903.

[2] This was perhaps to be expected from its nature as a place of isolation, but I could not help contrasting it with the Barashnum Gah at Udvada.

circumstances for women as well as men.[1] I inquired further
about the subject from Bahram, the son of Kalantar Dinyar,
and I found that the youth himself, for example, had never
undergone the ceremony, a fact which shows that it is not
regarded as obligatory for removing the original taint incurred
at birth, whatever may be the custom with regard to priests.

I shall now turn to the subject of marriage among the followers of Zoroaster. The age at which the Iranian Zoroastrians
marry is usually between twenty-five and thirty in the case of
men, and between fourteen and nineteen in the case of women.
Yet boys sometimes marry at the age of fifteen, and girls are
given in marriage when only twelve. Instances have also occurred where a widower of sixty has married a girl of fifteen or
has taken a widow of twenty for a wife. I was also informed
that in the case of families closely connected by ties of friendship, it has happened that a two-year-old daughter in one family
has been betrothed by her parents to a three-year-old son in
the other household; but such contracts are looked upon by
the community with disfavor.[2]

Parents, as a rule, arrange the marriages of their children,
since a son cannot take a wife, nor a daughter be married, without the consent of the parents or guardians, and the mother has
as much to say as the father regarding the choice that is to be
made. When the consent of all concerned has been obtained,
a formal betrothal of the young couple takes place; gifts of ornaments and money are frequently exchanged; and the marriage
banns are then publicly announced by the High Priest, without
whose consent a Parsi cannot marry, unless he disregards the

---

[1] See Vd. 9. 21, and compare Sad
Dar, 36. 1 (quoted above) and connect
with it the custom of segregation in
the *Armēsht Gāh*, Vd. 5. 45-62, or in
the *Dashtānistān*, Vd. 16. 1-18; cf.
Darmesteter, *Le ZA.* 2. x-xv.

[2] The same is true in India, where
such infant marriages formerly took
place occasionally among the Parsis,

but now are forbidden. See Karaka,
History of the Parsis, 1. 171–172.
For valuable statistics of the mar-
riage ages of the Parsis in India, by
Bamanji Behramji Patel, see the inter-
esting chapter on marriage, in Mlle.
D. Menant, *Les Parsis*, pp. 154–
155, Paris, 1898.

authority of the priest and marries according to the law of Islam.

The ceremonies connected with the marriage itself differ from those in use among the Parsis of India, especially in being much simpler. In India the bride sits by the side of the bridegroom, and after the marriage witness for each has formally given sanction to the union, the two priests stand before the young couple, recite an address of prayer, admonition, and benediction, a part of which is in Sanskrit and accompanied by rites borrowed from the Hindus.[1] In Persia the bride does not take part formally in the ceremony except by renewing her consent to the bridegroom's representative, who comes again for that purpose to her house on the marriage day, before the wedding begins. In Yezd only men are regularly present at the matrimonial service, but the bride and her female relatives and friends are usually near enough to hear the texts recited, and sometimes they stand on the roof of the house to watch the proceedings. When the male relatives and friends of both families are assembled, the priest (not two, as in India) takes a seat, and the bridegroom and a representative of the bride, her father, or some one who has helped to arrange the match, are seated on his right, the groom's party being on the other side. Sugar candy is placed in the hand of the bridegroom by the bride's marriage witness and is formally accepted, and after a few minor ceremonies the officiating priest recites the marriage address, *Andarz-i Gavāh*, lit. 'Admonition of the Witness,' composed partly in the Dari dialect, the language current among the Iranian Zoroastrians, and partly in Pazend and Zend.[2] It contains wholesome advice and admonitions and

---

[1] In India this address is called *Paivand-Nāmah* or *Ashirvād*. See Modi, *Marriage Customs of the Parsis*, pp. 34–39, Bombay, 1900 ; Karaka, *History of the Parsis*, 1. 189–192.

[2] The text of the *Andarz-i Gavāh* may be found in the *Persian Khordah* *Avesta* (lithographed), pp. 435–450, Bombay, 1900. Mr. Khodabakhsh Raïs (who compares *gavāh* with Skt. *vivāha*) has given an interlinear version of the Dari words in Modern Persian.

2 c

a benediction invoking blessings upon the two that are now married and upon all mankind.   When the Andarz is finished, gifts of Kashmir hats and presents of sugar loaves are freely exchanged by both parties, good cheer is the order of the hour, and the guests partake of the viands provided for the occasion.   When the supper is finished, they accompany the bride, who is veiled from head to foot in a robe of green silk, to the bridegroom's house, where she enters upon her new life.

In the home the wife occupies a freer position than the women in the Mohammedan household, and despite the Moslem influence, which would tend to make the Zoroastrian regard his wife as his inferior, she enjoys more of the old Persian law of equality 'and sometimes even gets the better of her husband,' as the statement was frankly made to me.[1]   The women whom I saw appeared to be dignified without reserve, and modest without diffidence, although, of course, they do not enjoy the greater advantages of the Parsi women of Bombay, whose opportunities have been many.

In their domestic relations the Zoroastrians of Yezd are monogamists, as a rule, but bigamy and even polygamy, which they attribute to the influence of their Mohammedan surroundings, were not uncommon in former times.   The sentiment of the Zoroastrian community, as was evident from two particular instances which they cited, is distinctly against dual marriages, even in cases where the first wife has borne no child to the husband, and for a woman to commit . bigamy would mean death.   The cause of the difficulty of enforcing the standards of the Zoroastrian faith and preventing infringements of the marriage law is found in the force of the Moslem example that prevails around them.   A Zoroastrian who is unwilling to abide by priestly regulations in such matters

---

[1] On the law of equality of the wife in Ancient Iran, see Darab Dastur Peshotan Sanjana, *Position of Zoroas-* *trian Women in Remote Antiquity, as illustrated in the Avesta,* pp. 35–42, Bombay, 1892.

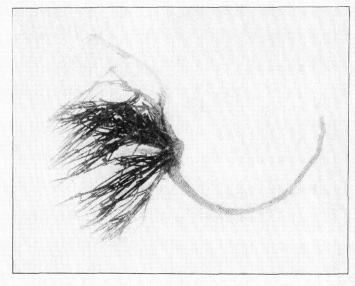

A BRANCH OF THE SACRED HOM PLANT

(One fifth natural size)

ZOROASTRIANS OF KERMAN

(The dress is typical of the Persian Zoroastrians)

simply rejects them, or, if he chooses, goes over to Islam. For that reason, as I learned, cases of breach of promise and divorce occur even in the circle of the faithful, and certain other vices, which I need not mention, also exist ; but the main body of the Zoroastrian community is making earnest efforts to eradicate these evils from their midst and to uphold the high ideals set by their religion.

The funeral rites of the Zoroastrians in Yezd are practically a continuation of the ancient customs of the Avesta and substantially the same as those of the Parsis in India, but with minor points of difference due either to local conditions or to present circumstances as contrasted with the past. Since nothing in detail has been written in English regarding these mortuary ceremonies of the Modern ' Gabars ' in Iran, I shall devote some space to the subject, making occasional comparisons with the more familiar Parsi customs in India and the ancient rites of the Avesta.[1]

When a person is at the point of death, a mobed, or priest, is usually summoned to administer the last rites. He recites the prayer of repentance for sins (*patit pashīmānī*, 'penitential office') and performs the ceremony of extreme unction by pouring on the lips of the dying some drops of consecrated bull's urine (*gōmēz*, Av. *gaomaēza*). When the person is dead, the priest goes to the fire-shrine or to the temple and performs the *srōsh-drūn* ceremony for the repose of the soul of the departed. In Persian this ceremony is called *ravān barsm*.

---

[1] For detailed information on the Zoroastrian funeral rites at Yezd I am again indebted to the kindness of Khodabakhsh Bahram Raïs. I have supplemented my material by notes from an interesting article, written in Gujarati, by Dastur Khudayar Sheheryar, *A Zoroastrian Death in Persia*, in *Zartoshti*, 1. 169–181 (Bombay, 1904). For a translation of the main points of this Gujarati article, I thank my pupil, Mr. Maneckji Nusservanji Dhalla. In comparing the rites of the Parsis in India, which I knew also by experience, I have referred to Modi, *Funeral Ceremonies of the Parsees*, Bombay, 1892 (reprinted from *Journ. Anthropolog. Soc. of Bombay*, 1891) ; Karaka, *History of the Parsis*, 1. 192–213 ; Mlle. D. Menant, *Les Parsis*, pp. 179–235, Paris, 1898.

Shortly after death has taken place the corpse, which henceforth must not be touched, except by those who have to do so, is placed at one side in the room and washed. This task is performed by a *murdah-shūr*, 'corpse-washer,' or *pāk-shūr*, 'clean-washer,' accompanied by an assistant, since, according to the Avesta,[1] one is never allowed to be alone with a dead body. The two corpse-washers also constantly hold a *kustī*-thread between them to signify their joint action (*paivand*, lit. 'union, connection') in the work. The person who washes the body wears on his hand a fleecy glove of wool (*pashm*), over which, as he rubs the body, his assistant pours beef's urine (*gō-mēz*)[2] from a brass bowl with a long-handled spoon. Water is never used for this purpose. It is a rule, moreover, that men should wash the corpse of a man, and women that of a woman, after which they clothe the body in a clean, but worn-out, white garment, including the sacred thread (*kustī*), but they do not put anything new on the body, as the Avesta forbids such an act.[3] When their task is completed, they wash themselves thoroughly in order to remove the defilement caused by contact with the dead.

The ceremony of the *sag-dīd*, 'glance of a dog,' is now performed for the first time. This ancient rite, which dates back to the period of the Avesta, consists in making a dog look at the dead body, since its gaze is believed to have a peculiar efficacy for driving away the *nasu*, or spirit of defilement. Various explanations have been suggested to account for the origin of this custom, from the mythological idea of the four-eyed dogs of Yama in the Veda, all the way down to the rationalistic theories that it is due to the instinct which the dog has for discerning whether any life remains in the body, or owes its origin to the time when the corpse was devoured by dogs as well as birds.[4] No special dogs are employed in

---

[1] Vd. 3. 14.

[2] Av. *gaomaēza*, Vd. 9. 14 ; 19. 21, 22.

[3] Cf. Vd. 5. 61 ; 8. 23–25 ; see also Sad Dar, 12. 1–2, and cf. Vd. 6. 51.

[4] For the role of the dog in connec-

Yezd for performing the sag-did;[1] the ordinary street-dog is called in for the purpose. Morsels of bread are strewn around the corpse, or, according to the older usage, laid on the bosom of the dead, and the dog eats these.[2]

The corpse-bearers now come to remove the body, first to a sort of mortuary chapel or charnel-house (*zād-ō-marg*, lit. 'birth and death'), as I shall explain, and then to the *dakhmah*. These carriers (*nasu-kashas*), or pall-bearers (*pīsh-gāhān*, lit. 'before the bier'), convey the body on an iron bier (*gāhān*).[3] The men who perform this office do not as a rule belong to a special class, but any one who may volunteer or be hired for the purpose may do this service; some tend, however, to make it a part of their livelihood. The number of bearers varies from twelve, sixteen, twenty-four, to thirty-two, according to the weight of the body and the distance to be traversed, but in no case can they be less than two, since the Avesta forbids that one man alone should carry a corpse.[4] They always hold a kusti between them to keep up the mystic union in their task, and must be prepared afterward to wash their persons and their clothes thoroughly before again associating with other people.

A procession (*pādāsh*) is now formed to conduct the body to the temporary receiving-vault. A man walks in front, holding a fire-vase in which incense is burning. He is followed by the relatives and friends; and after them the dead is carried,

---

tion with death, see Modi, *Funeral Ceremonies*, pp. 8–10, and Bloomfield, *Cerberus, the Dog of Hades*, pp. 27–31, Chicago, 1905. For the dog in the Avesta, see Hovelacque, *Le Chien dans l'Avesta*, Paris, 1876, and Kuka, *The Dog in the Vendidad*, in *Zartoshti*, 1. 271–280.

[1] See p. 78, above.

[2] This information I have directly from Khodabakhsh Raïs.

[3] In India they are generally called khāndhiahs, 'shoulder-men,' and are not to be confused in either case with the bearers who carry the corpse inside the dakhmah; cf. Modi, *op. cit.* p. 12.

[4] Vd. **3.** 14–21; **8.** 10. For the numbers twelve to thirty-two, see Dastur Khudayar Sheheryar, *op. cit.* p. 172. Anquetil Duperron (*Zend-Avesta*, 2. 584, Paris, 1771) said that forty was the number at Kerman.

lying on the iron bier and followed by the mobeds and some more members of the family of the deceased.[1]

They all march in solemn manner to the *zād-ō-marg*, or *parsish-khānah* (*pursish-khānah*), the charnel-house, which serves as a receiving-vault before the body is finally carried to the dakhmah.[2]

The use of this mortuary building can be traced directly back to the *kata* of the Avesta, since the Vendidad commands that ʻin every house and in every village they shall erect three *katas* for the dead.'[3] The present charnel-house is of larger dimensions evidently than the small structures described in the Vendidad, for there is a separate room for the women, a compartment for the corpse, and one for the bier, besides the room where the relatives and friends gather. The building, as now constructed, has two doors, through one of which the corpse is brought in and through the other of which it is carried out, symbolizing the idea of birth and death (*zād-ō-marg*) given in a Persian couplet:—

> ʻ What is the world? It is simply a halting-place, with two gates.
> By the one ye enter; by the other ye depart.'[4]

But the custom of carrying the corpse out by a way different from the entrance by which it came in, appears to be as old as

[1] In former times it was customary in the villages and outlying districts to have the procession led also by some one blowing a horn, beating a drum, or making doleful music, but this custom has almost died out. For the substance of these two or three particular paragraphs I am indebted to Dastur Khudayar Sheheryar's article already referred to.

[2] The name *zād-ō-marg*, ʻ birth and death,' is explained directly below; the designation *pursish-khānah*, lit. ʻhouse of inquiry,' is from the custom of coming to inquire (*pursī-raftan*) and condole with the family of the deceased.

[3] See Vd. **5**. 10–14. Anquetil Duperron (*op. cit.* 2. 583) alludes to the ʻzād marg' in India, and its use is said still to linger in the Gujarat provinces, but in general the Parsis have abandoned it and convey the body within twenty-four hours directly to the dakhmah, as necessitated by the hot climate. A partial survival of the zad-o-marg among the Indian Parsis is the *nasā-khānah*, ʻ dead house,' where the bier and other funeral equipments are kept by the *nasā-sālārs*. See also Modi, *Funeral Ceremonies*, p. 7, n. 9, and Darmesteter, *SBE*. 4. 53, n. 2 ; 97, n. 1.

[4] The Persian text is given by Khudayar Sheheryar, *op. cit.* p. 171.

the Avesta, since the Vendidad alludes to making a ' breach ' in the wall to take out the body.[1]

When the corpse is brought within the zad-o-marg, it is removed from the iron bier and laid on a raised platform of mud paved with stone, about nine feet long and four feet wide, and the bier is carried into a separate room.[2] The friends gather to pay their last respects to the dead; this is called *pursī-raftan*, lit. ' coming to ask,' or *sez* (*saj*).[3] The mobeds then begin the *Gāhān Srāyishn*, or chanting of the Gatha Ahunavaiti (Ys. 28–34), which treats of various subjects relating to piety, faith, and the future life. When the recitation is half over, the priests cease chanting,[4] the sag-did is performed once more, and the body brought from the room where it was laid, and replaced upon the iron bier, to which it is fastened by a thick kusti, and a white sheet is thrown over the whole.

The procession is then re-formed and leaves the building, reciting verses from the Avesta in memory of the dead (*iris-tanām*).[5] After going a short distance a halt is made, the women and those who do not desire to follow the body all the way to the dakhmah, pay their parting tribute to the dead, and then the near relatives and friends go on in procession. As the main dakhmah at Yezd is about nine miles from the city, many in the procession ride on horses or donkeys, but the priests go the entire distance on foot. It sometimes happens also, especially in the case of hamlets and villages far remote from the

[1] Vd. **8**. 10. Compare the Pahlavi commentary on this passage and the notes by Darmesteter, *Le ZA.* 2. 121, n. 15, and *SBE.* 4. 97, n. 6.

[2] For these special details I have combined my notes from Khodabakhsh Raïs with material from Khudayar Sheheryar.

[3] See note above and compare the *sejdo* of the Indian Parsis; cf. Modi, *op. cit.* p. 15.

[4] The pause is made at the words *tat̲ mōi vičidyāi*, Ys. **31**. 5 (so Khudayar

Sheheryar, *op. cit.* p. 172), and the same is true in India (cf. Modi, *op. cit.* p. 14).

[5] See Sheheryar, *op. cit.* p. 173. I am not quite certain which particular verses are referred to, but (if not Ys. **26**. 7) I presume that the passage may be Ys. **16**. 7, ' we praise those bright abodes of Righteousness in which dwell in happiness the souls of the dead (*iristanām*), which are the spirits (*fravashayō*) of the righteous. We praise the best world (Paradise), holy, brilliant, and all-glorious.'

dakhmah, that the corpse is placed upon a cow or a donkey, instead of being carried [1]—a procedure which would be in no way striking in Persia, because there corpse-caravans convey dead bodies for long distances to Mohammedan shrines.

Upon reaching the dakhmah, the sag-did is repeated for the third and last time, the final preparations made, and the corpse is given over into the charge of two other men whose special office it is to convey it within the tower. They are called *nasā-sālārs*, 'chief of the dead,' a designation also applied to them in India.[2] They must be men well advanced in years and of a high moral character. Owing to the nature of their occupation they are obliged to live apart from men and are not allowed to mingle with other members of the community or to enter a house where religious rites are being performed or any special festival is being celebrated, and if possible they must also refrain from tilling the earth. They are obliged, moreover, to wash themselves thoroughly after having carried a corpse into the tower, and if they should ever wish to resign from their office, they must undergo the ceremony of the 'Nine Nights Washing' (*barashnūm nō-shva, nō-shaba*), as already described.

As soon as they take the corpse into their charge at the door of the dakhmah they make the *paivand*-bond, by holding a kusti between them, and they recite the Srosh Baj. One of them next takes a piece of metal or an iron key and, beginning near the left ear of the corpse, draws three furrows (*kash*) around it, reciting the Ahuna Vairya formula, or Avestan paternoster, as he draws each circle.[3] The two nasa-salars now take up the body and carry it into the dakhmah, laying it down with the head toward the south, and removing the clothes, in

---

[1] A reference to this custom is even found in the Pahlavi commentary on the Vendidad (Phl.Vd. **3**. 14).

[2] My statements in this paragraph are based on the authority of Khoda-bakhsh Raïs. For the Indian customs in this respect, see Modi, *op. cit.* pp. 12–18.

[3] For the material in this and the next five paragraphs I am indebted to the Gujarati article by Dastur Khudayar Sheheryar, *op. cit.* pp. 169–181.

accordance with the ordinances of the Avesta.[1] They then recite in Persian the following prayer to the angels (*yazatas*): —

'O victorious and holy Srosh, we have removed N or M[2] from the earth, Spendarmad, and have committed him (or her) to the stone Ayokhshust.[3] O Angel Srosh, we turn our backs upon him (her), but do thou turn thy face towards him (her); into thy keeping we have given him (her); do thou take his (her) hand.'

[To the corpse.] 'Do not thou, N or M, be afraid, do not tremble, because this place is thousands of years old; it is the resting-place of our fathers and mothers and our ancestors.'

[To the Angels.] 'O Srosh, Mihr, and Rashn the Just, we have delivered him (her) into your keeping; take his (her) hand, and lead him (her) to the abode of our forefathers and the righteous and the pure. So be it, in accordance with the will of the Angels and Archangels (*izad u amshaspandān*); so be it; so, verily, let it be.'[4]

The corpse-carriers withdraw from the tower after this, and the body is left exposed for the birds of prey to devour the flesh. When the bones have been denuded and become dry they are usually laid in a separate place in the dakhmah and turn to dust.[5] In no instance nowadays is the corpse torn by dogs or wild beasts as it was in ancient days, nor in any case is burial in the ground lawful, since it was prohibited by Zoroaster. If a dakhmah is not accessible, the body may be disposed of after the manner known as *sang-chīn*, 'heap of

---

[1] The removal of the clothes is implied in the Avestan phrase *raočā-aiwi-varena*, 'clothed with the light of heaven' (Vd. 6. 51). In the Avesta (Vd. 19. 1; Yt. 22. 7) and throughout the Zoroastrian Scriptures the southern region is auspicious, the northern region the abode of Ahriman and the demons.

[2] Here the name is to be inserted and the rest of the prayer made to conform to it.

[3] This expression, 'stone Ayokhshust' (Pers. *sang Ayokhshast*), is not quite clear; but it appears to answer to Avestan *ayōkhshusta*, 'molten

metal,' see my article in *JAOS*. (*Proceedings*, p. lviii), 1890.

[4] See Khudayar Sheheryar, *op. cit.* p. 174.

[5] See what I have said below (p. 439) regarding the dakhmah at Rei near Teheran. Compare likewise the description of the dakhmah at the village of Shah Ali near Yezd, which was examined by Westergaard in 1843 (*JRAS*. 8. 352); furthermore the account of the dakhmah near Isfahan, which Chardin in the seventeenth century described as round with a central pit (*Voyages*, 3. 131). In the Bombay towers this central well is called the *bhandār*.

stones.' Under these circumstances the corpse is carried to some remote place in the hills or mountains, is then piled around with stones and covered with a slab, but not interred.[1]

It is customary, after the body has been exposed upon the dakhmah, for the friends and relatives to partake of some refreshment after their long march ; the simple meal consists of bread, cheese, potatoes, or eggs, as the case may be, with some wine, but no meat or melted butter is eaten. Prayers are again offered for the dead and sympathy is expressed for those in affliction, and then all those present perform the *kustī*-ceremony and return home.[2]

According to the ancient and present Zoroastrian belief, the soul hovers near the earth for three days after death, before departing to the other world. During that time the family observe certain rules, pray for the dead, abstain from eating meat and from any act that might cause distress to the soul or detain it longer on earth. On the spot where the body lay before it was removed from the house, it is usual to place three bricks in the form of a little arch and to thrust an open pair of scissors into the ground to drive away any evil spirits that may be lurking near. The ceremony of the Yasna is performed each morning, between sunrise and noon (*Hāvani Gāh*), the Srosh Yasht is recited in the evening after sunset (*Aiwisrūthrima Gāh*), and the Vendidad ritual is celebrated at midnight, unless for some reason the corpse must remain in the house over the first night, in which case the Vendidad observance is omitted.

On the afternoon (*Uzayeirina Gāh*) of the third day the priest is invited to recite some texts from the Avesta,[3] with accompanying ceremonies, and some food is prepared for the

---

[1] This is practically the method pursued at Shiraz (see p. 337, above) and wherever there are not enough believers to justify a dakhmah.

[2] Minor variations in the funeral rites are found, of course, but the general description here given presents all the more important details.

[3] Selections from the Khordah Avesta (*e.g.* Khurshed Nyaish, Uzeirin Gah, and Patit Pashimani) are used for this purpose.

evening. At midnight, in the presence of the assembled company, religious rites in honor of the deceased (*yasht-i sedush*) and the dedication of a white muslin garment takes place at this vigil (*shab-girih*), so that the soul may not be naked in paradise.[1]

At dawn (*Ushahin Gāh*), when the soul is believed to be crossing the Bridge of Judgment (Av. *Chinvat Peretu*, Mod. Pers. *Chinvad Pul*) the ceremonies of the *chahārōm*, 'fourth day,' are carried on. These rites are believed to be efficacious in facilitating the difficult passage of the soul over the Bridge. Invocations are made to the angels Sraosha, Rashnu, Arshtat, Rama Hvastra, and to the Fravashis, and prayers are offered for the dead. After the completion of this requiem mass all those who are present, with the exception of the priest, partake of a slight repast of food previously consecrated, and the priest, with a rosary of beads, asks each of the mourners how many prayers he will offer in memory of the deceased, and after announcing the number and reciting some texts of absolution and benediction, dismisses the assembly.[2]

[1] The designation *shab-girih* apparently means 'night-watch, vigil for the dead, wake,' and is then applied to the garment that is dedicated to the deceased and thus answers to *shiyāv* among the Indian Parsis. This custom, with others that are still kept up by the Zoroastrians, is alluded to in Sad Dar, **87**. 1–11, see West, *SBE.* 24. 350–352.

[2] In performing the rites of the third night and the fourth day (*chahārōm*), when the soul is crossing the Bridge, the offices of a son and heir are particularly important. For that reason, in the case of an adult of fifteen years or more who has died without leaving a child, it is appropriate to appoint an adopted son who assists in the crossing of the Bridge and is therefore called *pul-guzār*, 'bridge-crossing.' Nowadays the appointment of an adopted heir is made only in cases where the person dies absolutely childless ; but in former times it was done even if daughters were left, but no son. Formerly only a boy was eligible, but now even a girl may be chosen, although such a choice is rare. The age of the person adopted is generally over fifteen years, but nowadays an infant may be nominated to the office, its father acting for it during the years of its minority. As is natural, the one chosen to serve in the office of *pul-guzār* is selected from the nearest relatives and acts like an executor to an estate, dividing the property among those who are of kin to the deceased, and distributing a large part of it in charity, especially in funds for the annual celebration of the Gahanbar festivals. (This note is from memoranda furnished me by Khodabakhsh Raïs.)

Some additional rites are observed on the tenth day (*dahah*), the thirtieth (*sīrūzah* or *sīrūzhah*), the return of the day (*rūzah* or *rūzhah*) each month, and again on the anniversary (*sāl* or *sar-i sāl*) of the death, and these observances are to be kept up as long as possible, besides remembering the dead during the Fravardigan Festival of ten or eighteen days at the end of the Parsi year.[1] There are likewise several other observances which, though not directly connected with death, have nevertheless a bearing on the subject of the repose of the soul hereafter. They are enjoined by the priests and performed by the orthodox, but by no means without exception. Among them are the recitation of a thousand prayers of repentance (*hazārah-i patit*) to gain absolution from sins; likewise a thousand prayers to fire and water (*hazārah-i ātash-nyāish, hazārah-i āb-nyāish*) in atonement for sins committed against those elements; or again, an invocation of the earth (*yasht-i bīn-i Sipandārmīz* or *Spandārmad*) to pardon any defilement of the ground, which may have been committed in life, even by going barefoot; and lastly the consecration of several fires (*ātash-i mas kartvun* or *ātash buzurg kardan*, lit. 'aggrandizing the fire') as an act of merit and atonement. Mention may also be made of the so-called rite of *sahm-astah*, lit. 'dread of bones,' offered by a widow who marries a second time and desires to appease the soul of her former husband; and finally, of prayers recited near the dakhmah for the repose of the dead (*yasht-i daur-i damah*), together with the 'Nine Nights Ablution' (*barashnūm nō-shva, nō-shaba*) already described.[2]

It is interesting to note that, according to information I received, a recent convert (*jadīd*) from Zoroastrianism to Islam sometimes still maintains his old-time orthodoxy sufficiently

---

[1] The Fravardigan Festival is a perpetuation of the Avestan *fravashi*-worship, or commemoration of the souls of the departed, somewhat like our All Saints' Day.

[2] For the subject-matter of this and the preceding paragraph I am indebted to notes given me by Khodabakhsh Raïs. I am not certain as to the precise meaning of the words *daur-i damah*, although he explains *damah* as *dakhmah*.

to desire his funeral services to be performed according to the Avestan ritual. It has likewise happened that the body of such a convert after being buried has been stolen by night from the grave and carried under cover of darkness to the dakhmah. No precise investigation of the matter is afterwards made. The Parsis give out that angels have come down from heaven and borne the dead on high to the throne of God, and the Moslems believe that the angels have come and taken the body to Najaf in Arabia, to lie by the side of the holy Ali, *Shāh-i Najaf*, ' King of Najaf.'

I shall conclude this sketch with some notes regarding the the dakhmahs in the vicinity of Yezd. There are two such towers in the hills west of the city, and both are in use. One of these is old and is called *Dakhmah-i Jamshīd*, ' Tower of Jamshid '; the other, which is round in shape like the Indian Towers of Silence, is situated opposite to this and is of comparatively recent date. It was erected by Manakji Limji Hoshang Hantaria, who came from Bombay to Persia in the beginning of the year 1854 as representative of the Persian Zoroastrian Amelioration Fund.[1] Still farther to the west of Yezd, at a distance of twelve or fifteen miles in the direction of Taft, there are the ruins of an ancient tower, called *Dakhmah-i Kuhnah*, ' Old Dakhmah,' which is now used only as a place for exposing the bodies of still-born or abortive children and of persons who have died by suicide or in some violent manner.

There are several other dakhmahs located at various points north of Yezd. One of these is situated on a hill called Zarch Kuh, near the village of Ilahabad, about ten miles from the city; it was built in memory of a rich childless merchant, Khosru-i Mihrban-i Rustam, by his adopted son, Ardeshir Mihrban Irani, a philanthropic Zoroastrian of Yezd. Still farther

[1] An interesting account of this agent of the Indian Parsis and of his efforts in behalf of his oppressed co-religionists in Persia is given by Kar- aka, *History of the Parsis*, 1.72, where his name is recorded as Manakji Limji Antaria.

north, near the village of Sharafabad, are several other Towers of Silence, which are referred to in the next chapter. [1]

Most of my details regarding the dakhmahs I received directly from Khodabakhsh Raïs, from whom I also learned that the Parsis had a tradition, handed down from antiquity, that when Persia was under the rule of Zoroastrian kings and the country was rich and prosperous, each worshipper of Ormazd built for himself during his lifetime a dakhmah to be used at his death, and that individual dakhmahs of this kind were called *dakhmah-i tan bah tan,* 'dakhmah for a single body.'

It is furthermore reported that the large structures, like those in use at present, were originally called *dakhmah-i lashkarī,* 'dakhmah for soldiers,' because they were put up for the corpses of those slain in battle, and their use became general after the Arab invasion, as the Zoroastrians were no longer able to keep up their religious rites with all the former detail and were obliged to resort, therefore, to the common large towers and discontinue the practice of building individual receptacles for the bodies. The tradition of individual dakhmahs is certainly interesting because of its bearing on the Vendidad, where dakhmahs are alluded to as if very numerous. It is worth adding that Khodabakhsh is of the opinion that the original dakhmahs were built with mud walls, like those of the old one near Sharafabad.

From all that has preceded, it will be manifest how closely the Zoroastrians of Yezd still follow the injunctions of the Vendidad. A further illustration may be gathered from the following amusing incident in daily life. The cook of my English hosts at Yezd was a Gabar, and on one occasion, as they told me, he had made some wine and purchased an earthen jar in which to store it, but he first filled the vessel with water and let it stand over night before placing the wine in it. A mouse accidentally fell into the jar and was drowned. The

[1] See p. 403, below.

A Zoroastrian Merchant

A Gabar Family

receptacle was henceforth unclean in the eyes of the Zoroastrian, because it had been polluted by contact with dead matter, and was therefore unfit for use.[1] The man's business sense, however, and his regard for thrift — since the Avesta prohibits wasting anything[2] — would not allow him to throw the jar away, so he sold the vessel at a reduced price to an Armenian, who had no scruples against using it.

This combination of thrift and practical sense, united with a tenacious adherence to the faith of their forefathers, is a characteristic of the Zoroastrians of Yezd. The impression which I gained of them was very favorable, on the whole, considering the conditions under which they live in Persia, as contrasted with the advantageous environment of their Parsi brethren in India. From the latter they have much to learn in the way of progress, enterprise, and intellectual activity, and they have little to offer in return, even in the way of religious customs and observances or gifts of ancient manuscripts relating to the faith.

Nevertheless, so far as my limited observations allowed me to judge, there are some of their customs and certain of their methods of conducting religious ceremonies that deserve further study from the specialist, as such observances may actually be nearer the ancient forms, and therefore historically valuable, even if it be no longer practicable or desirable to follow them.[3] In any case the Parsis of India are thoroughly justified in taking an active interest, as they have done, in their Zoroastrian kinsmen in Iran, whose motto, wherever they be, whether in Yezd, Kerman, Teheran, or elsewhere, is

[1] The laws which underlie the Zoroastrian Vendidad are largely sanitary in their origin and these rudimentary attempts at sanitation take on a new complexion when viewed in the light of modern hygienic theories.

[2] Cf. Vd. 5. 60.

[3] I am not unmindful of the existence of Mohammedan influence upon the Zoroastrians in Persia, nor do I on the other hand forget the presence of Hindu, Mohammedan, and European influences on the Parsis in India; it is a task for some thoroughly versed scholar to estimate the relative extent and proportion of these outside influences in each case.

the same as their own — ' good thoughts, good words, good deeds '; and they will likewise do well to promote, as heretofore, all causes that may tend to improve the condition of these Persian brethren and to enable them to live up to the standards of the ancient creed which they both possess in common.

CHAPTER XXV

FROM YEZD TO TEHERAN

'They have ridden the low moon out of the sky,
    Their hoofs drum up the dawn.'
            — KIPLING, *The Ballad of East and West*, 39.

IT was the morning of May 13 when I bade adieu to Yezd
and its Zoroastrian community and to my English hosts, and
started on the journey northward to Teheran. The distance
to be covered was about 375 miles over a trail through plains
alternating with deserts which now and then encroach on the
track if the hills on either side do not hold them back. Some
day the journey will be made in seven hours by an Occidental
express-train, but it took me seven days to accomplish the
weary march, most of it on the back of animals only less tired
than myself.

As I mounted my horse at the door of the Mission and rode
out through the gates of Yezd into the desert, I was warned
that, if a heavy sand-storm should break, I was to take my
bearings by means of the compass and head toward the nearest
haven of refuge, as the path might be wholly obliterated by
the sand. There was happily no occasion to necessitate this
measure, and as the horses were good, I enjoyed ' chaparing ' at
a brisk gallop for a number of miles.

Safar, all this while, kept up a spirited conversation with
the little postilion (*shāgird-chāpār*), a bright lad who did
not allow the horses to lag, but kept whipping them up from
time to time with a thin metal chain that served as a whip,
so that we reached before long the vicinity of the Gabar dakhmah, which crowned a high sand-dune in the distance. Here

I halted for an instant to take a photograph of our youthful
postilion holding in his hand the chain, which he sold me as
a memento at a price (thanks to Safar's dealings) far below
the figure which my *farangī* extravagance might have offered
him.[1]

The hamlet of Hojatabad, about twelve miles from Yezd,
was the first station for changing horses, and I rested in its spacious caravansarai for about an hour, from one to two in the
afternoon.   My luncheon consisted of raw eggs (*tukhmahā
na pukhtah*) ; these formed my staple food when 'on the road'
in Persia, because I always found them good and nutritious, and
I could save time, when hastening to make long stages of
twelve or thirteen hours in the saddle, by not even waiting to
have them boiled.   For dessert on this occasion I had some
sharbat, which was sickishly sweet in taste, but was served in
an antique brass saucer engraved with a tracery so artistic in
design that I bought the dish as a curio and had Safar wrap up
the sticky receptacle and place it in his capacious saddle-bags.
Sundown found us in Maibud, which Yakut and other early
Oriental geographers, who wrote before the thirteenth century,
locate at a distance of 'ten farsakhs from the borders of Yezd
and the same distance from Akdah.'[2]   Like most of the ancient farsakh measurements, these numbers have remained unchanged and are still given as the respective distances to these
places when reckoning the pay by farsakhs for post-horses.
Even if we do not go back to the Persian and Arabic geographers, we have more or less precise records of the route
dating from the time when Marco Polo traversed a part of it

---

[1] At the time of the purchase I
thought that this thin metal chain
might be the modern representative
of the ancient *aspahe aštrā*, 'horse-
goad,' of the Avesta (Vd. 4. 19 ; **6.
5 ; 14.** 2, etc.), but I have since become
convinced that the *aspahe aštrā* is
represented rather by the ordinary
whip with leather thong and wooden
handle, one of which I had purchased
near the Tomb of Cyrus, and that
the chain represents rather the *sraošō-
čarana*, as seen also in the chain
whips at Modern Merv in Turkistan.

[2] Yakut, p. 555 ; cf. also p. 404.

SHOEING A DONKEY

THE ZOROASTRIAN DAKHMAH AT REI NEAR TEHERAN

in the latter part of the thirteenth century.[1]   The Italian friar
Odoric of Pordenone rode over it from Kashan to Yezd early
in the fourteenth century (about 1325),[2] and in the latter part
of the fifteenth century (1474) Josafa Barbaro, the Venetian
envoy to the court of Usun Cassan, describes Kashan and
Kum, two of the most important towns on the line.[3]

The second day's march, as my diary shows, was a plodding
ride of fourteen hours, with two brief breaks before the goal,
fifty-six miles distant, was reached.   A mid-day halt on this
journey was made for an hour at Akdah, or Agdah, which is
described by Yakut as 'a town on the borders of the desert of
Yezd.'[4]   Somewhere in the hills in this vicinity there is said to
be a shrine sacred to the memory of Banu-i Fars, or Khatun
Banu, the mother, or more probably the daughter, of the last
Sasanian monarch Yazdagard, with whose death the line of
Zoroastrian rulers in Persia came to an end.[5]

In this same region, in the Zoroastrian village of Sharafabad,
in the district of Ardakan, there is an old mud-walled Tower
of Silence (*dakhmah*), and the story goes that seven charitable
sisters built seven different dakhmahs at various points on the
plain of Ardakan, and the sites of these structures are indicated by mounds of earth which are still pointed out by the
aged Parsis of Sharafabad.[6]   There is also a modern Zoroastrian
dakhmah between Sharafabad and Mazra-i Kalantari, in Ardakan; it was erected by Manakji Limji Hoshang Hantaria, the

---

[1] See Marco Polo, ed. Yule, 1. 88 ;
cf. also Sykes, *Ten Thousand Miles in
Persia*, p. 155.

[2] See *Odoric de Pordenone*, ed. Cordier, p. 41, Paris, 1891.

[3] See Josafa Barbaro, *Travels in
Persia*, 49. 73.

[4] Yakut, pp. 404, 555.   The older
form of the name is generally given as
'*Ukdah* in the Arab geographies.

[5] The legend of her flight and the
cow which kicked over the pail of milk
that was to quench her thirst, and the
consequent traditional sacrifice of
cows on the spot by Zoroastrians (now
discontinued), is recorded by Karaka,
History of the Parsis, 1. 85–87 ; Sykes,
Ten Thousand Miles in Persia, p. 156.

[6] For this information regarding
the dakhmahs I wish again to thank
Khodabakhsh Bahram Raïs of Yezd.
On the Zoroastrian village of Sharafabad, see Sykes, *Ten Thousand Miles
in Persia*, p. 156, n. 1.

same person that built the new tower near the dakhmah of
Jamshid at Yezd.[1]

The survivals of Zoroastrianism noticeable throughout this
entire district were evidently observed centuries ago by Josafa
Barbaro when he halted at a town called ' Guerde,' the identity
of which is not clear, although its general location is undisputed.
He says : —

'Thense [from Yezd] ye go to Meruth, a little towne, and twoo
daies io'ney further is a towne called Guerde, in the which there
dwell certein men called ABRAINI, which in myne opinion either
be descended of Abraham orells haue Abrahams faith, and they weare
longe heare.'

The association of Abraham with Zoroaster by the Mohammedans is a familiar fact,[2] and the identity of the two religious
leaders is assumed by many of the Mohammedan Seïds in this
district, who are really converts from Zoroastrianism to Islam
and regard the Parsis as their kinsmen.[3]

My journey continued for some distance along the line of
the Persian telegraph, whose posts and wire became welcome
company as a reminder of civilization and an assurance of
safety in case of accident.   The feeling of security is marked
when one is within reach of the wire, not because a station is
near, for they are miles apart, but because, if anything happens, the traveller can get assistance by simply cutting the
wire, as some one will be sent from the nearest station to discover the cause of the broken current.   The element of civilization also comes in strongly, because one meets with hospitality
from the few European telegraph-employees along this benighted
route, and I felt grateful that afternoon for an hour's rest and
a cup of tea at the temporary camp they had set up, some miles
south of Nu-Gumbaz.   Darkness was falling and a storm approaching when I reached the *chāpār-khānah* at Nu-Gumbaz —
a dreary and desolate place.   I felt too tired to wait for any-

---

[1] See p. 397, above.

[2] See p. 343, above ; p. 438, below.

[3] For this latter point, see Sykes,
Ten Thousand Miles, p. 156.

thing to be cooked for supper, but I enjoyed a hearty meal of thirteen raw eggs (adding the extra one to the dozen for good measure) and then threw myself on my camp-cot for a short night's rest.

My foot was in the stirrup again at 3.45 A.M., and after a stretch of six short farsakhs, or eighteen miles,[1] part of them over plain and desert, we filed slowly into the town of Naïn, called 'Naim' by Josafa Barbaro, who found it 'evill enhabited, not exceeding V^c houses.'[2] A century earlier (1340) the Persian geographer Mustaufi described it as surrounded by 'a rampart 4000 paces in circumference,'[3] and Yakut, a hundred years before him, spoke of the theological reputation of Naïn, as having produced a number of eminent students of the Koran and scholars versed in Mohammedan lore.[4] I was struck by the evident antiquity of the place, and I find Naïn mentioned by the Arab geographers in the ninth and tenth centuries,[5] but I have not yet been able to trace its history back to the Sasanian period, although the designation of the ancient citadel as *Ḳal'ah-i Gabar*, ' Gabar Castle,' and the retention of Zoroastrian names in some of the local designations point to a very early age.[6]

All went well on the journey until Neïstanak (Barbaro's 'Naistan ') was reached on the same day, two hours after noon. There I found that the outgoing post, north and south, had taken all the horses of the *chāpār-khānah*, and that not even a

[1] The *farsakh*, or ancient *parasang*, a variable measure derived from convenient stages in the day's march of a caravan, differs considerably in different parts of Persia, especially according to the nature of the country to be traversed. In the region of Yezd the farsakhs are short.

[2] Josafa Barbaro, *Travels*, ed. Hakluyt, 49. 82.

[3] See Barbier de Meynard, *Dict. géog. de la Perse*, p. 561.

[4] See Yakut, p. 561.

[5] See, for example, Mokaddasi, ed. De Goeje, 3. 51 (mere mention) ; Istakhri, 1. 100, 135, 136, 155, 202, 229, 231, 232 ; Ibn Haukal, 2. 182, 203, 204, 289, 291, 296.

[6] On this latter point see Sykes, *op. cit.* p. 157. It is even possible that the *Ḳal'ah-i Gabar*, ' Castle of the Gabars,' may represent Marco Polo's *Cala Ataperistan*, 'Castle of the Fire-Worshippers,' whence one of the three Magi is said to have come to worship the infant Christ, as I have pointed out in *JAOS*. 26. 79–81, but Kashan has a stronger claim, as I shall state below.

mule could be hired in the neighborhood.   There was consequently nothing to do but wait until one of the post-relays
returned, and we were thus delayed until midnight.   We
started at 1.00 A.M., but the horses were so tired that we could
not urge them off a walk, and since no fresh relay was found
at the next station, we were obliged to use the same jaded
animals all the way to Ardistan.   This single day's journey of
forty miles occupied sixteen hours! [1]

Ardistan is a flourishing town, abounding in streams and
orchards, and counting some twelve thousand inhabitants, a
number notably larger than the estimate given in the fifteenth
century by Josafa Barbaro, who calls ' Hardistan a little towne
that maketh a V^c howses,' [2] but more in accordance with the
statement made in the tenth century by Mokaddasi (Makdasi).
The latter says : ' Ardistan is larger than the other cities in the
region of the desert.   It is well populated, and has fine bazaars
and numerous mosques.   There are many sages and learned
men residing there.   The region of Ardistan abounds in
white flour, whence it derives its name (*ārd*, ' white flour,'
and *stān*, ' place ').' [3]

Historically the place is of considerable interest to the student
of Zoroastrianism, as may be gathered from information in the
older Mohammedan writers.   Ibn Rostah (c. 900) speaks of Ardistan as a fine city, and says that Anushirvan (*i.e.* the Sasanian
king Chosroes I, A.D. 531–579) was born there. [4]   Istakhri (951)
states, ' Ardistan is a walled city, every quarter of which is

---

[1] Two days was the time occupied
by Josafa Barbaro in the fifteenth century, for he says : ' From thense [*i.e.*
from Neïstanak] two other daies ior-
ney is Hardistan, a little towne that
maketh a V^c howses ' (ed. Hakluyt, 49.
83).

[2] See preceding note, and for the
present estimate of 12,000, cf. Sykes,
op. cit. p. 157.

[3] Freely rendered from Mokaddasi,

ed. De Goeje, *Bibl. Geog. Arab.* 3. 390.
The etymology is not correct; see below, p. 407.   In contradistinction to
Mokaddasi's praise of the people of
Ardistan I may cite a Persian writer of
the seventeenth century, Sadik Isfahani
(p. 62), who reports that ' the people of
this place are, it is said, prone to excessive anger and violence.'

[4] Ibn Rostah, ed. De Goeje, 7. 153,
275.

My Donkey-Caravan in the Desert near Khalatabad

The Little Shagird
(The Gabar Dakhmah in the background)

fortified, and there are in it some ancient traces of such Magians as Anushirvan and Khosru, and it has a large and wonderful underground aqueduct (*ḳanāt*); its people are men of culture and letters, and they have a knowledge of the traditions of Islam.' [1] Mustaufi (1340) says that 'Isfendiar (the son of Zoroaster's patron, King Vishtasp) built at Ardistan a fire-temple which enjoyed great fame during the ages of idolatry and attracted many pilgrims.' [2] Yakut expands Istakhri's account by speaking of the vaulted roofs of Ardistan and its beautiful gardens, and naming the distinguished men that the city had produced. [3] The name *Ardistān* argues for the antiquity of the place, because *ardastāna*, or more precisely *ardastāna āthangaina*, was a designation for a stone construction in Achæmenian times and was applied, for example, to the windows in the Palace of Darius at Persepolis. [4] Traces of the wonderful water-courses, referred to by Istakhri, were still plainly to be seen, as I remember, when I walked through the town between rows of gardens in full bloom, to which Yakut alludes. Careful investigation would probably give more information also regarding the fire-temple which Isfendiar is said to have founded here, and Ardistan should be added to the list of places already recommended as inviting sites at which to pursue archæological investigations.

My attention at the moment had unfortunately to be devoted more to the question of transportation than to archæology, so I was obliged to direct my steps to the telegraph station, which was situated in an attractive garden, filled with blossoming fruit trees, and was in charge of a Persian telegraph operator. Although he was not able to procure a post-relay for me, he kindly placed his own horse at my disposal and provided donkeys to make up my caravan so that I might start at mid-

[1] Istakhri, ed. De Goeje, *Bibl. Geog. Arab.* 1. 202, n. 1.   p. 22, n. 1 ; cf. also Le Strange, *JRAS.* 1902, p. 243.

[2] Mustaufi, *Nuzhat al-Ḳulūb*, cited by Barbier de Meynard, *Dict. géog.*   [3] Yakut, pp. 22–23.

[4] See p. 315, above.

night, besides wiring a message in advance to have horses meet me at Khalatabad on the morrow.   As I returned to the post-quarters, a messenger, looking like a mounted arsenal, galloped in on a fine horse, with a rifle across his shoulder and two enormous holster-pistols on either side of his saddle.   I thought that he might possibly allow me to hire his horse to add to my limited cavalcade for the next stage of the journey, but his errand was urgent, and he dashed onward over the plain, leaving us to watch the sunset and retire.

After four hours' sleep I gave the signal at 1.15 A.M. for my caravan of donkeys and the horse to start, and the company of half a dozen beasts of transport moved slowly out on the plain and gradually into the desert.   The gait was a snail's pace, but I had long before become accustomed to taking naps in the saddle, waking from time to time to watch the progress of the stars, particularly glorious in Persia, and to count the long hours, till the brightening hues of dawn ushered in the day with a burst of sunlight.   Forward through the sand trudged our little cavalcade until, about the time when one would ordinarily be breakfasting in America, we were approaching the small town of Moghar, on the edge of the desert, having been six hours already in the saddle.   The outskirts of the settlement were rich in grain-fields, and the gleaners were already at work with the sickle.   The Persian sickle curves far more beyond the semicircle than does our own, so that the blade resembles an immense steel hook.   In using it, the gleaner squats on the ground in Oriental fashion, gathers an armful of the tall barley, deftly cuts it, and lays it down to be bound afterwards into a sheaf.

The stretch of desert from Moghar to Khalatabad seemed interminable at our slow pace.   The sun beat down pitilessly, and I could feel its scorching rays penetrating through the white cotton covering that I wore over my hat.   The sand was dazzling and in many places was encrusted with a coating of salt that looked like ice or snow.   From time to time we encountered a row of sand hillocks that looked as if some gigantic mole had been burrowing beneath the surface of the earth. These high-heaped mounds, which are a familiar sight in the arid districts of Persia, are made from the sand thrown up around the mouth of the *ḳanāts*, or deep wells, dug at intervals and joined by a succession of underground tunnels which carry the water sometimes several miles. Wherever moisture had gathered and had been evaporated by the sun, the sand was baked into huge cakes like clay, across the cracks of which myriads of lizards darted, while every suggestion of humidity on the desert gave rise to mirages so deceptive that it was often impossible, a few feet away, to tell whether we were looking upon a pool or not. The unceasing stretch of sand made the stage seem endlessly long. Now and then I varied the monotony by giving the horse to Safar to ride and taking one of the donkeys ; my particular choice was a beast that was easy to ride, but had a provoking habit of lying down in the sand at the most unexpected moments.

Khalatabad was reached at last after a ride of fourteen hours, and we found to our joy that the *chāpār* horses had arrived. After an hour's rest I vaulted again into the saddle for a ride which proved to be one of the keenest pleasures I experienced in Persia. The horse assigned me was a splendid animal, one of the three truly fine mounts I had ridden since leaving Urumiah (and I had ridden more than fifty), but it was evident that he was not used to a Western bit, for he took the iron at once between his teeth and ran away with me, galloping for nearly three miles before I could bring him down. The plain was as smooth as a cinder path, his mettle was superb, and the speed delightful after the crawling pace at which we had proceeded all day. Again and again he became unmanageable and ran, leaving the rest so far behind that I had to gallop back again for fear of losing the servants and my baggage. After three hours of this exhilarating sport, which the horse enjoyed as much as I, he suddenly bolted, being frightened by a flock

of sheep running in confusion before an approaching thunderstorm ; but I was in too good training to be unseated, and we
galloped at full speed beneath the *bālā khānah* of the post-house
at Abuzaïdabad at 7.30 P.M., just as the rain began to pour
down. The day had been one of almost incessant riding for
seventeen hours, and the journey, which ordinarily takes four
days, had been made in one. My mettlesome steed, however,
paid for his speedy gait, for I found his high spirits gone the
next morning, and sheer fatigue made him quite docile by the
time we caught sight of the blue domes of the mosques at
Kashan that rose with a glimpse of color over the brown plain.

Kashan, pronounced in Persian as *Ḳāshān*, is flanked by
mountains and hills on the south, west, and northwest, but on
the other sides it lies open to the plain. The city looks low
and level as one approaches it, but the outline is broken by the
characteristic vaulted mud roofs of the houses, the domes of
the mosques and madrasahs, and by a lofty minaret, over one
hundred feet high (seen in the left of the picture),[1] which looks
in the distance as if a modern factory with a high chimney had
been set up to give occupation to the inhabitants, who number
over seventy thousand.

The history of Kashan, like that of its rival city Kum, is
wrapped in obscurity, but Firdausi assumes that it was in
existence in the time of Kei Khosru, the legendary king who
is supposed to have reigned about eight centuries before the
Christian era, for the great warrior Kamus is frequently alluded
to as the hero ʿof Kashan.ʾ[2] Persian history also records that
Kashan and Kum furnished about twenty thousand men to the
army that fought in vain against the Caliph Omar, at the time

---

[1] This is the leaning tower of Zein
ad-Din, a picture of which is given
by Mme. J. Dieulafoy, *La Perse*,
p. 198, Paris, 1887; see also Landor,
Across Coveted Lands, 1. 263, and compare the description of Kashan by
Curzon, *Persia*, 2. 12–16 (who repro-
duces the picture of the leaning tower

from Mme. Dieulafoy's work), and the
valuable account of the province of
Kashan by Houtum-Schindler, *Eastern Persian Irak*, pp. 109–118, London, 1897.

[2] Firdausi, *Shāh Nāmah*, ed. Vullers-Landauer, 2. 870, 918, etc., and
transl. Mohl, 3. 1, 58, 97, etc.

DOMED ROOFS OF KASHAN

KASHAN

of the Arab conquest.[1] A common report assigns the building
of the city to Zobeidah, the wife of Harun al-Rashid (A.D. 800),
but this is incorrect, as it was in the case of Tabriz, already
cited,[2] although Zobeidah may have rebuilt the city.

Mustaufi's brief but interesting account of the city of Kashan,
which was written about the year A.D. 1340 and based on older
sources, is in substance as follows : ' This city was built by
Zobeidah, the wife of Harun al-Rashid.. The heat is intense
here in summer, but the winters are very pleasant. The water,
which is not very abundant, is brought from a reservoir at Fin,
which is fed by the Kuh Rud.[3] Rain water is also collected in
cisterns by the inhabitants. The people of Kashan are intelligent
and well informed, and belong to the Shiite sect of the Mohammedan faith ; but the inhabitants of the eighteen villages in the
vicinity, on the contrary, are Sunnites. The melons and figs of
Kashan are held in esteem.'[4] The European traveller Josafa
Barbaro, a century later, speaks of it as the ' well enhabited citie
called Cassan, wheare for the moste parte they make sylkes and
fustian in so great quantitie that he who wolde bestowe x^{ml}
ducates in a daie may find enough of that merchaundise to bestow
it on. It is about iij myles in compasse, walled, and w^{t}houtfoo^{rth}
hath faire and large subvrbes.'[5] Barbaro resided in Kashan for a
time and was visited here by his fellow-countryman Contarini,
the Italian traveller, who arrived at 'Cassan' on October 25,
1474, and calls it a finer city than Kum (' Como ').[6]

All modern travellers speak of the heat of the place and
re-iterate the statement that the town is noted for three things:

[1] See Ouseley, *Travels in Persia*,
3. 3, n. 3, and 3. 100. Ouseley cites
as his authority ' The Book of Conquests,' a chronicle history (*tārīkh*)
by Ibn Aasim of Kūfah, who flourished
in the eighth century A.D.

[2] See p. 39, above.

[3] Fin is located on the mountain
slopes about five miles southwest of
Kashan. Its garden and groves, well
supplied with water, were once a
favorite place of resort for the Persian
kings, including Shah Abbas and Fath
Ali Shah ; but Fin is now deserted.
See Curzon, *Persia*, 2. 12 ; Landor,
Across Coveted Lands, 1. 265–266.

[4] Mustaufi, cited by Barbier de Meynard, *Dict. géog.* p. 434, n. 1.

[5] Josafa Barbaro, *Travels*, 49. 73.

[6] Contarini, *Travels*, 49. 129.

its manufacture of porcelain tiles, brasswork, and silk, its black
scorpions, and the cowardice of its inhabitants. The latter
stigma is constantly put upon the Kashanis by the other Persians,[1] but I was glad not to have any occasion to judge whether
it is true. The silk, however, I found good, judging from the
samples brought me by a vender, who followed me from the
bazaar to the telegraph quarters and showed the same enterprising spirit and business energy for which the Kashanis were
praised hundreds of years ago.[2] As for the scorpions, I saw
some formidable specimens, as the manager of the telegraph
station was making a collection of them.

I regretted that during my short halt at Kashan I did not
know of a Western legend which connects this city with the
Three Kings of the Orient who went to Jerusalem to worship
the infant Christ. It is a known fact that a majority of the
Church Fathers agree in regarding Persia as the native country
of the Wise Men, without expressly locating their place of
origin.[3] The Italian traveller Marco Polo (1272) and the
Venetian envoy Odoric of Pordenone, who traversed this
route, the latter about 1320, record traditions that definitely
attach the Three Wise Men to certain cities. Odoric expressly
says that Kashan, or ' Cassan,' as he calls it, was ' the city of
the Three Kings ' and that these worshippers set out from
there to Jerusalem, which they reached by divine aid in thirteen days.[4] The passage in the account of Odoric de Pordenone reads as follows : —

' DE LA CITÉ DE CASSAN. — De ceste cité m'en alay vers la grant
Inde par mer. Si vins par maintes journées a une cité des trois roys
qui firent offrande à Jhesu Crist nouvel né. Et appelle on ceste cité
de Cassan, cité royal de grant honneur mais Tartre l'ont moult de-
struite. De cette cité de Cassan jusques en Jherusalem a plus de L

---

[1] On this point, see Sykes, *Ten
Thousand Miles in Persia*, p. 158.

[2] See Barbier de Meynard, *Dict.
géog.* p. 434, n. 1.

[3] See my article in *JAOS*. 26.
79–83.

[4] See Odoric de Pordenone, ed. Cordier, p. 41, Paris, 1891.

Kum

Persian Gleaners

journées dont on puet clerement appercevoir que ly troy Roy qui de ceste cité de Cassan furent en xiii journées amené en Jherusalem par vertu divine et non humaine. En ceste cité a moult grand habondance de tous biens, de pain, et de vin et de toutes autres choses.'

According to a legend given by Marco Polo, two of the kings came from 'Saba'[1] and 'Ava,' both of which places are located about fifty miles southwest of Teheran, and the third is said to have come from 'a place three days' journey' from Avah, and Marco Polo states that he 'found a village there which goes by the name of Cala Ataperistan (i.e. *Ḳalʿah-i Atashparastān*), which is as much as to say 'The Castle of the Fire-Worshippers.' And the name is rightly applied, for the people there do worship fire.' In an article entitled *The Magi in Marco Polo* I have given various reasons for identifying the so-called 'Castle of the Fire-Worshippers' with Kashan, which Odoric mentions, or a village in its vicinity, the only rival to the claim being the town of Naïn, whose Gabar Castle has already been mentioned above,[2] but I may refer to the discussion in the article without repeating it here.[3] I should like to have had time to visit Gabarabad, a deserted town on the Isfahan road about twenty miles distant from Kashan, as its name (lit. 'Gabar Town') shows that there was once a settlement of fire-worshippers in its vicinity, and the ruins of a magnificent caravansarai are still to be seen there.[4] In Kashan to-day there are some Zoroastrians, for the statistics which I gathered in Persia show that about forty-five of them do business in this city.[5]

Most of my short stay in Kashan was occupied in purchasing articles which I needed, and in securing some sort of a vehicle to convey me to Kum. I had been riding uninterruptedly for weeks and was very tired and anxious to procure some means of conveyance on wheels. With the aid of the manager of the

[1] On 'Saba' (= Sāvah) cf. also Sykes, *Ten Thousand Miles*, p. 264.

[2] See p. 405, above.

[3] See my article, *The Magi in Marco Polo*, JAOS. 26. 79–83, and cf. Marquart, *Untersuchungen zur Geschichte von Eran*, 2. 1–19, Leipzig, 1905.

[4] Cf. Bishop, *Journeys in Persia*, 1. 232.

[5] See p. 425, below.

telegraph station I was able to hire a lumbering cart; it had no springs, but it could at least be driven, and I was able to lie down as we travelled. Four horses were hitched to it, and away we jolted for hours over ruts and hollows, till we caught sight of Kum towards nightfall and were passing through its bazaars and shops about as they were closing.

Kum is little less than a city of mosques, minarets, madrasahs, and corpses, for, next to Meshad, it is the most famous burial-place in Persia. Its special sanctity is due to the fact that it is the proud possessor of the shrine of Fatima, sister of Imam Riza, the eighth Imam. She was interred here in A.D. 816, and honors are accorded her that Mohammedanism rarely vouchsafes to a woman. Kings have chosen the city as a final resting-place for their bones, and the great Kajar monarch Fath Ali Shah is among the Persian monarchs buried there. Burial near Fatima's shrine is in fact almost equivalent to a viséed passport for heaven, although Kum cannot quite rival Kerbela and Meshad in this respect.[1]

The city did not attract or interest me enough, however, to make me wish to stay longer than was necessary, and I was content to remember it by two photographs which I purchased afterwards. The *mahmān-khānah*, or hostlery, at which I put up showed signs that we were approaching a more civilized region. The building had a veranda, a large sleeping-room furnished with a table and a bed, and there was a kitchen, where I found a saucepan and tried the experiment of making an omelet, which proved quite a success. My most vivid impression of the *mahmān-khānah*, however, is associated with my first taste of arac. I needed spirits for medicinal purposes, and the servants could procure only arac in the bazaar. I should not like to repeat the dose of this particular brand, for the taste resembled what I could imagine a combination of gin, whisky, and furniture-varnish might be!

---

[1] For valuable details concerning Kum, consult Houtum-Schindler, *Eastern Persian Irak*, pp. 56–77, London, 1897.

Shrine of Fatima at Kum

A Persian Vender of Sherbet

To transport me to Teheran I found that a so-called ' diligence' could be procured as a substitute for the wretched cart I had used all day. I felt happy when I heard at midnight the announcement that it was 'ready' (*ḥāẓir*), but in spite of this assurance another hour was wasted before the horses were hitched and the rumbling vehicle rolled to the door. It was a ramshackle conveyance, threatening each moment to fall to pieces, but deserving, I suppose, the respect due to advanced age. Despite the discomfort of my cramped position and the distressingly raw rainy weather, I managed to fall asleep, and I slept during most of the journey of twenty hours, until, about nine in the evening, after seven days' travelling from Yezd, we arrived at Teheran. A note of the itinerary of the journey may be of some interest.

ITINERARY FROM YEZD TO TEHERAN

WEDNESDAY, MAY 13, 1903

			FARSAKHS	MILES
10.10 A.M.	leave YEZD			
	Pass Gabar Dakhmah			
1.20 P.M.	arr.	Hojatabad	4	
2.20 P.M.	lv.			
5.20 P.M.	arr. **Maibud**		6	

Time: 7 hrs. 10 min. (6 hrs. 10 min. in saddle + 1 hr. halt)
Distance: 10 farsakhs = about 36 miles

THURSDAY, MAY 14

			FARSAKHS	MILES
4.00 A.M.	lv. Maibud			
7.15 A.M.	arr.	Jaftah (or Chiaftah)	6	18
7.30 A.M.	lv.			
	Poor horses; very slow progress			
10.15 A.M.	arr.	Akdah (or Agdah)	4	12
11.30 A.M.	lv.			

Frequent mirages
Halt in afternoon for nearly an hour at construction-camp of Persian Telegraph Company
Road mostly over a brown plain

			FARSAKHS	MILES
6.10 P.M.	arr. **Nu-Gumbaz**		9	27

Time: 14 hrs. 10 min. (11 hrs. 40 min. in saddle + 2 hrs. 30 min. halts)
Distance: 19 farsakhs = 57 miles

Friday, May 15

		FARSAKHS	MILES

3.45 A.M. lv. Nu-Gumbaz
Plain and desert ; frequent mirages

8.00 A.M. arr. ⎤
9.20 A.M. lv. ⎦ Naïn   6   18
Remains of an old town in the vicinity

1.55 P.M. arr. **Neïstanak**   6   19
Delayed here because of lack of horses
Time : 10 hrs. 10 min. (8 hrs. 50 min. in saddle
+ 1 hr. 20 min. halts)
Distance : 12 farsakhs = 37 miles

Saturday, May 16

1.00 A.M. lv. Neïstanak
Moonlight ; horses very slow

8.20 A.M. arr. ⎤
11.45 A.M. lv. ⎦ Jokand   7   24
No fresh horses ; 3½ hrs. delay ; proceed with
same horses

5.00 P.M. arr. **Ardistan**   4   15
Time : 16 hrs. (12 hrs. 35 min. in saddle + 3 hrs.
25 min. halt)
Distance : 11 farsakhs = 39 miles

Sunday, May 17

1.15 A.M. lv. Ardistan
No post relay ; make up a caravan of 1 horse
and 4 donkeys

7.15 A.M. arr. ⎤
9.30 A.M. lv. ⎦ Moghar   5   18
Desert

3.10 P.M. arr. ⎤
4.50 P.M. lv. ⎦ Khalatabad   5   16
Excellent post-horses waiting ; fast time ; slight
thunderstorm

7.30 P.M. arr. **Abuzaïdabad** (or Abuzadabad)   6   17
Time : 18 hrs. 15 min. (14 hrs. 20 min. in saddle
+ 3 hrs. 55 min. halts)
Distance : 16 farsakhs = about 51 miles

Monday, May 18

4.30 A.M. lv. Abuzaïdabad
7.30 A.M. arr. ⎤
9.10 A.M. lv. ⎦ Kashan   6
Hire a cart (*gari*) instead of post-horses
11.10 A.M. Kasimabad (?)
2.20 P.M. Shurab

A VIEW OF TEHERAN

A PERSIAN GARDEN

		FARSAKHS	MILES
5.15 P.M.	Pasangun		
9.30 P.M.	arr. **Kum**	12	

Time : 17 hrs. (3 hrs. in saddle, the rest in *gari*)
Distance : 18 farsakhs, estimated at about 70 miles

TUESDAY, MAY 19

1.00 A.M.	lv. Kum		
	Travel in a diligence, sleeping most of the way		
9.00 P.M.	arr. TEHERAN	25	85

Time : 20 hrs.
Distance : 25 farsakhs = 85 miles

Time of the journey : 7 days
Total cost : 125 tomans (about $120)

2 E

CHAPTER XXVI

TEHERAN, THE MODERN CAPITAL

'Where in sunshine reaching out
Eastern cities, miles about,
Are with mosque and minaret
Among sandy gardens set,
And the rich goods from near and far
Hang for sale in the bazaar.'
— ROBERT LOUIS STEVENSON,
A Child's Garden of Verses.

'ISFAHAN is fair, Shiraz is beautiful, but Teheran — *Ṭahrān khailī khūb ast* — Teheran is very beautiful,' this is the encomium which I heard bestowed, over and over again, upon the modern capital of Iran as I journeyed northward from Yezd. During a week's stay in the metropolis I found the city sufficiently attractive to make me sympathize, in part at least, with the enthusiasm of the Persians, even if Teheran cannot boast of many of the natural beauties of such a city as Shiraz.

East and West combine imperfectly in its mixed civilization, with a far greater preponderance of the Orient, as is natural. Landau carriages in the public square, a post-office with bilingual notices in Persian and French, well-equipped telegraph headquarters, an imposing Imperial Bank, a so-called Boulevard des Ambassadeurs, along which the ministers of the foreign legations ride in official dress, not to speak of shops with European goods, two 'hotels,' a claim to the use of gas, and a pretense of having a jingle-bell tramway, all these tell something of the influence of the Occident. But all the rest — mosques, minarets, and madrasahs, camels and caravansarais, bazaars crowded with scuffling men and veiled women,

418

THE MEIDAN-I TOP KHANAH AT TEHERAN

with the survival of many a custom that seems to antedate the time of Cyrus — are characteristics that belong to the Orient and make Teheran as Oriental as any capital in the East, although I missed those signs of national greatness which belonged to the days of Persia's by-gone glory and are visible at Persepolis even in the ruins.

Looked at from the historic standpoint, Teheran may be considered to be the inheritor of the ancient honors of Pasargadæ and Persepolis, and the successor to the imperial rank held a few centuries ago by Shiraz and Isfahan. With the rise of Teheran to power, Media has been able once more to reclaim the supremacy she lost to Persis in the time of Cyrus, and the present capital occupies a site that is almost identical with the ancient city of Rages (Avestan *Raghā*, Old Persian *Ragā*), now Rei, its ruined suburb, which shared with Ecbatana in antiquity the honors of supremacy over Iran. And yet, comparatively speaking, Teheran is a modern town, a city that came into existence less than seven hundred years ago, about the time when Ragha began to sink into oblivion ; its rank, in fact, as capital has been held only since 1788, when the present Kajar dynasty came into power. Of so little importance was Teheran at the beginning of the thirteenth century that Yakut (c. 1220) spoke of the place merely as ' a stronghold, one farsakh distant from Rei,' adding that the inhabitants lived in dwellings dug beneath the ground and were rebellious to all authority and in a constant state of warfare.[1] If then unimportant, the place must have grown extensively during the next four hundred years, as we may judge from the accounts by the different European travellers who visited it during that period; and so important had it become by the end of the eighteenth century, that Agha Mohammed Shah made it his capital and bestowed upon it the laurels won by the overthrow of the Zend dynasty of Isfahan.

The present size and appearance of the city are largely due

[1] Yakut, p. 399.

to the late Shah Nasr ad-Din, who devoted himself with genuine enthusiasm, after his first visit to Europe, to developing
and beautifying his chosen seat of government.   The old walls
were torn down for the most part, the moat filled up with
the débris, and an entirely new rampart was constructed,
fully a mile outside the older enclosure, thus making the compass of the city vastly larger.   This wall, over ten miles in
circuit, is entered by a dozen gates, the more important of
which are capped by gayly decoráted towers with glazed minarets, whose shining tiles are seen at a long distance.

As the city lies rather low in a sandy plain, its location is not
commanding, but a line of hills to the north, behind which
towers the Alborz range crowned by the magnificent crest of
Damavand, 19,400 feet high, forms an imposing background in
that direction, in contrast to the miles of level tracts that stretch
southward over the territory traversed in coming from Yezd.
The mountains temper the wind from the north in winter,
and the foot-hills, with their gardens and orchards, afford
a pleasant place of resort during the heat of summer.

Descriptions of Teheran are so numerous that I may be allowed to confine myself merely to the principal features without going into details.[1]   This is not due to a lack of interest in
the capital or to a scarcity of material at hand, but it is owing
to lack of space for a more extended account of the place.

A plan of the city, if we had a sketch-map before us, would
show that Teheran is laid out in octagonal form, roughly speaking, and the heart of the town lies considerably north of the
middle point of this walled enclosure.[2]   The principal square
in this section is called *Meidān-i Tōp Khānah*, ' Arsenal
Square,' a handsome quadrilateral, about 300 yards long and
150 broad, with its larger side running east and west and its
surface paved in a rough sort of way with cobble-stones.   The
central portion of this extensive parallelogram is occupied by a

---

[1] The description given by Curzon,   ous accounts and should be consulted.
Persia, 1. 300–353, supplants all previ-   [2] Cf. Curzon, *Persia*, 1. 305.

THE SOUTHWEST GATE OF THE MEIDAN AT TEHERAN

THE AMERICAN LEGATION AT TEHERAN

large basin of water fenced in by an iron railing and lined
on all sides by old mounted cannons. The eastern end of
the plaza is practically devoted to the building and grounds
of the Imperial Bank of Persia, a rather imposing white
edifice, in Perso-European style, with an arched gateway at
the left leading into an attractive garden, where the English
members of the bank find an opportunity on holidays to indulge
in tennis. Out from the north side of the great plaza runs the
principal driveway of the city, *Khiābān-i 'Alā ad-Daulah,*
'Boulevard des Ambassadeurs,' along which are built the
residences of the foreign legations and some of the finer houses
of the city. On the west side of the square is the Arsenal
(*Tōp Khānah*, lit. 'Cannon-House'), with quarters for the
soldiers and some small buildings of the same character as those
on the northern and southern sides of the parallelogram. The
arched gateways that are raised over the half-dozen avenues
which lead from the square are conspicuous because of the
gaudy effect they produce by their glazed tiles and fancy decorations. The most noticeable of these portals is the one that
guards the entrance to the *Khiābān-i Almāsiah*, or 'Avenue of
Diamonds,' leading from the southwest corner of the plaza to
the palace, and the royal flag floats from the top of this gateway
when the Shah is in Teheran.

By this exit we leave the main square to visit that portion of
the city which lies to its south and which is the most interesting section for foreign visitors, because it is the oldest and
most characteristic, containing minor public squares, the original fortifications, the palace grounds, and the bazaars. The
first point to engage our attention is a small square, outside
the palace enclosure and somewhat to the south; it is the *Meidān-i
Ark*, ' Citadel Square,' or *Meidān-i Shāh*, ' Place de l' Empereur.'
Here, by the side of a large tank of water, is mounted a huge
cannon, known as the *Tōp-i Murvārīd*, 'Cannon of Pearls.'
According to some accounts, its muzzle was originally decorated with a string of pearls, but other explanations are like-

wise given. The history of the gun is also variously related. But whatever the case may be, this large piece of artillery has now a semi-sacred character, because it affords a place of refuge (*bast*) for criminals who seek shelter beneath its shadow, and superstition has further endowed it with miraculous powers, even with the gift of granting children to barren women who touch its brass mouth. Facing one side of this square is a stately arched portal, the *Naḳārah Khānah*, ' Band-Tower,' or 'Hall of the Royal Music,' from whose chambers sunrise and sundown are signalled by the same noisy accompaniment that I have described in speaking of Urumiah and Isfahan.[1]

The second place of interest to the south of the Top Meidan is the area of the old fortified enclosure, nearly a quarter of a mile square, known as the *Arḳ*, or ' Citadel,' within whose mud walls is located the Palace of the Shah. It is needless to say that the royal residence and the various buildings and grounds which belong to it, the courtyards, pavilions, fountains, and gardens are a source of pride to the imperial heart. The Museum of the palace contains, among other objects of interest, the sword of Tamerlane and the mail-coat of Shah Abbas, as well as a priceless collection of crown jewels, together with much that is tawdry, according to the judgment of those best entitled to speak on the subject. The most often described among the treasures, because the handsomest from the artistic point of view, are the magnificent jewelled globe — a geographical study in emeralds, diamonds, and turquoises — and the famous Peacock Throne (*Takht-i Ṭā'ūs*), which is said to have been brought from Delhi in India by Nadir Shah, the Great Mogul, about the middle of the eighteenth century; but, according to Lord Curzon's claim, it is not the original Peacock Throne, but was made for Fath Ali Shah, more than half a century later than Nadir Shah.[2]

---

[1] See pp. 104, 267, above.

[2] See Curzon, *Persia*, 1. 317–322, to whom I must refer the reader for details, as I neglected the ordinary 'sight-seeing' duty of a visit to the palace and museum.

A Graduating Class of the American School for Boys at Teheran

A Persian Family

The chief bazaars of the city are located also to the south
of the Top Meidan. They are similar to the vaulted, covered
structures that I have already described in other cities, with
the customary shops, booths, mazy passages, and courtyards for
caravans, but all on a larger scale than elsewhere in Persia.
The opportunities which I found in them for shopping were excellent, but I sought in vain for one object which I wished to
purchase; it was a flag with the Persian emblem of the Lion
and the Sun. The flag has little significance in Persian patri-
otism; for that reason it is not commonly on sale, so I had
to have the banner made to order. I may add, however, that
it was handsomely painted, and it now hangs in my study
as a memento of my journey to Iran.

Regarding the other native edifices in the older part of the
city there is little to say. The mosques of Teheran are of
minor importance, considering that they are in the capital, and
none of them can compare in sanctity with the shrine of Shah
Abdul Azim near its ruined suburb, Rei. There are a number of madrasahs, or religious colleges, and several educational institutions on royal foundations, including the Shah's
College, which is supported by funds from the Crown and
employs European instructors as well as native teachers; but,
although this institution furnishes free instruction, clothing,
and food, many young Persians go to the schools established
by the foreign missions, and over a hundred are in attendance
at the American School for Boys in Teheran.[1]

As we return from the older part of the town to the southeast entrance of the chief Meidan, we pass the large building
occupied by the Indo-European Telegraph Company, where
there is an opportunity to send a communication home by
cable, and then we again enter the main square. Crossing
to the northwest of the great quadrilateral, we leave it by
the gateway that arches a street leading to another grand

[1] See *Sixty-seventh Annual Report of the Board of Foreign Missions of* the Presbyterian Church in the U. S. A. p. 238, New York, 1904.

enclosed area, the largest, although not the most important, plaza in Teheran. It is the city's great parade-ground, more than a quarter of a mile long and nearly as wide, and is called *Meidān-i Mashk*, 'Drill Square.' This vast area is one of the largest enclosed grounds for manœuvring that there is in the world,[1] and here the Shah's troops go through their military exercises, having been trained in Occidental tactics by European drill-masters. But this immense *Champ de Mars* is comparatively little used, and it served as an admirable playground for boys, when I saw it, or as a place where stray animals that had died from disease or some other cause were allowed to lie until devoured by dogs.

The northernmost section of Teheran is largely European, as I have already intimated. A short distance from the great parade-ground there are to be found the grounds and buildings of the American Presbyterian Mission, with its dozen or more laborers in evangelistic, medical, and educational work. From the Mission it is an easy walk to the English Hotel. This small hotel is the place where foreigners usually stay when on a brief visit. It is conveniently located near the principal thoroughfare, the Avenue of the Ambassadors, along which we drive past the various diplomatic residences. The Legation of the United States is pleasantly situated, and its grounds are attractive and have been occupied for about twenty years, as the Legation was established in 1883. As I passed through its gateway and entered the enclosure, I remember the thrill which I felt when I raised my hat to salute the Stars and Stripes, and I was welcomed by our American Minister, Mr. Richmond Pearson. To our Secretary of Legation, Mr. John Tyler, who has resided in Teheran for more than thirty years, I was indebted, besides other favors, for the privilege of a visit to the Persian Minister of Foreign Affairs, whose two sons I had met at Berlin and St. Petersburg, where each occupies a position as Minister from the Persian Court.

[1] Pekin alone can claim a larger one, if I understood my informant aright.

THE PARSI SCHOOL AT TEHERAN

ZOROASTRIAN SCHOOLBOYS AT TEHERAN

I found in him the grace of manner and polished behavior that belongs to the cultivated Persian, for a gentleman is a gentleman all the world over. There was no oppressive formality, the conversation proceeded easily, aided by Mr. Tyler's skill, and turned eventually to the subject of travelling in Persia. My host expressed an interest in my journey, especially in my experiences on the Behistan Rock. He requested me to pronounce some of the Ancient Persian words in the inscription of Darius in order to compare them with the Modern Persian form, and we conversed also about the platform of Persepolis, a magnificent representation of which in tapestry completely filled one wall of the large room in which we were sitting. Sweetmeats, tea, and cigarettes were served, and a gracious word at parting completed the visit.

Because of my interests and because of the many associations of Zoroaster's name with Rei, the suburb of Teheran, I was anxious to meet the Zoroastrians, and was happy that among the first visits I received was one from the secretary of the Zoroastrian Amelioration Society, Ardeshir Edulji Reporter, agent in Teheran for the Parsis of Bombay. This gentleman, whose brother I had previously known, gave me excellent opportunities for becoming acquainted with the circumstances of his co-religionists at the capital, and he added material to my stock of information concerning the Zoroastrians throughout Iran. His statistics show that the number of Zoroastrians is increasing slightly and not declining. The figures are as follows : —

Yezd and vicinity . . . . . between 8000 and 8500
Kerman . . . . approximately 2400
Teheran 324
Kashan 45
Shiraz 42
Kum 8
Isfahan 6
Sultanabad 4
Total number of Zoroastrians in Persia about . 11,000

The Zoroastrians of Teheran, taken as a whole, are in better circumstances than those in any other city of Persia, because of the more liberal conditions that prevail in general at the capital. The most prominent member of the community is a rich banker, Arbab Jamshid Bahman, whose wealth is estimated in the hundreds of thousands of tomans, and to whom recognition at Court is also accorded — a fact which helps the position of the Zoroastrians considerably, since an appeal to the Shah is possible through his mediation. His integrity is of the highest order, and his esteem, even in the eyes of the Mohammedans, who would naturally despise him as an 'infidel,' is so great, that the Persians place implicit faith in his honesty — a tribute paid to no other native banker as yet, so far as my knowledge goes. This is a tribute not alone to his uprightness (*arshtāt* in the Avesta), but also to the teachings of Zoroaster, who made truth and honesty a watchword of the religion and whose creed was 'good thoughts, good words, good deeds.'

Arbab Jamshid called upon me shortly after my arrival and invited me to visit his home and his beautiful garden — a privilege of which I availed myself twice. The garden-court adjoining his house in the city is laid out in the characteristic Persian manner with fruit trees, flowering shrubs, trellised arbors, pathways, and a fountain, and in addition to this a door opens into a small chamber on one side that is used as an Izashnah-Gah, or chapel, in which the rites of the Zoroastrian faith are occasionally conducted by a priest. We spent some time comfortably seated beneath the fruit trees, chatting on general topics, eating sweetmeats and dates that had been sent by the Zoroastrians of Yezd, and drinking tea, but not smoking. The business quarters of Arbab's banking establishment form a part of his own residence, and a large staff of clerks and assistants are occupied in conducting his affairs. Some idea of the number of this corps of employees may be obtained from the picture of the group which I reproduce. The Zoroastrian banker himself sits in the second row, to the right

ARBAB JAMSHID AND HIS STAFF

of the middle as we face the picture, with a scarf thrown over
his shoulders, and with his two little sons squatting in front
of him, in Oriental fashion, near the fountain.

The Teheran Parsis, as I learned, take an interest in education, and I am able to present also a photograph of their Boys'
School, with the teacher, Kayomars Vafadar, in the foreground
and some of the members of Arbab Jamshid's staff of assistants
standing by the side of the scholars. The attendance at the
school, so far as my information goes, is fair, and is proportionately larger than that at the Jewish schools in Teheran, considering the relative size of the respective communities, there
being 5100 Jews, in all, as against 324 Zoroastrians. Out
of the five thousand Jews, statistics in 1904 show a total of only
372 attending the two schools for boys and girls established
at Teheran in 1898 by the Alliance Israélite Universelle — a
matter for the consideration of both the amelioration societies
engaged in the betterment of their co-religionists in Iran.[1] It
would be interesting and instructive, if it were possible, to draw
a comparison between these two isolated religious communities
and show the results accomplished in each case by the special societies which have their interests in charge. Such a comparison
should include also the work of the schools of the various Christian missions in Teheran, and should be summarized in connection with the Mohammedan institutions, before a final conclusion
is drawn.

But that is a matter about which I am not now qualified
to speak, nor have I time to devote more attention to the
subject at present, but must turn rather to the theme of the
succeeding chapter, closely connected with Zoroastrianism and
Teheran — Rei, the ruined suburb of the capital.

[1] See *Bulletin de l'Alliance israélite
universelle, deuxième série*, no. 29, p.
126 (cf. also pp. 168–169), Paris, 1904,
where the school-attendance is given as
242 in the boys' school, 130 in the girls'
school. Compare likewise my article
'Teheran' in the *Jewish Encyclopedia*,
12. 73-74, New York, 1906.

CHAPTER XXVII

RUINS OF REI, THE ANCIENT RAGHA

'How doth the city sit solitary that was full of people !
How is she become as a widow, she that was great among the nations.'
— JEREMIAH, *Lamentations*, 1. 1.

SOME Iranian Jeremiah might well find cause to lament over that vast heap of ruins, six miles southeast of Teheran, which once formed the city of Ragha, or Rages, the metropolis of ancient Media and one of the oldest centres of civilization in Iran. Sanctified as the cradle of Zoroastrianism, hallowed for a day by the presence of the angel Raphael, exalted by princes and cast down by conquerors, this city that was great among the nations is now but a mass of crumbling walls, mounds, hollows, and ruined watercourses, with but few signs of life amid the dust of ages. If marked on the map at all, it is designated as the Ruins of Rei, or Rhey (pronounced like English *ray*), for Rei is the modern form of Ragha, Rhagæ, or Rages. Treasure-hunters dig for coins and pottery amid its deserted tumuli, and brick-hunters demolish its walls for building-materials to be used in Teheran. In a few places, it is true, the irrigator has restored an ancient aqueduct or cistern and thus converted a sand-heap into a cultivated plot of ground, but otherwise desolation reigns everywhere.

To the modern Persians Rei is known chiefly as the place adjoining the shrine of Shah Abdul Azim, which is visited annually by thousands of pilgrims and within whose precincts the late Shah, Nasr ad-Din, was assassinated in 1896. Within the confines of Rei itself there is also a renowned spring, *Chashmah-i Alī*, 'Fountain of Ali,' named after the cousin and son-in-law of Mohammed and therefore more or less sacred.

REI, THE ANCIENT RAGHA

(Towers of Abdul Azim near the left edge)

Upon a hill in a northeasterly direction from Rei is the
Zoroastrian Tower of Silence, where the Gabars expose their
dead. Among the ruins at Rei there are some which have a
special interest, and I shall therefore describe them in detail;
but one of the chief distinctions of Rei nowadays is that it
forms a terminus of Persia's only railroad, an insignificant line
running from Teheran to the mosque of Shah Abdul Azim.
Over the six miles of track, with little attention to regularity
or punctuality, a train of a few cars is drawn by a ʻmawsheen,'
as the natives call the engine, having Persianized the French
word *machine*. In visiting Rei, however, experience proves
that it is better to rely on a good horse as a means of transportation rather than trust to this uncertain conveyance, since the
distance can be covered in an hour's canter. The road, lined
with caravan after caravan, all on their way to or from the
capital, is not uninteresting, and I felt I had been but a short
time in the saddle when I found myself dismounting with my
friends to enjoy a morning cup of tea beneath the ruined citadel and the huge moundlike walls that mark the northern outline of this ancient city.

The date of the founding of Ragha, or Rei, is lost in oblivion,
although tradition assigns it to Hoshang, the first king of Iran,
in the fourth millennium before Christ.[1] According to the
Bible, Rages, or Ragau, as the name is given, must have been a
flourishing city in the eighth and seventh centuries before the
Christian era, since the books of Tobit and Judith mention it
as an important contemporary of Nineveh and Ecbatana, and
the strange story of the angel Raphael's visit to Rages is
familiar to all who know the Apocrypha.[2] The Avesta twice

---

[1] See the legends cited by Barbier
de Meynard, *Dict. géog.* p. 273, n. 1.

[2] See Tobit 1. 14 ; **4.** 1, 20 ; **5.** 5 ; **6.**
12 ; **9.** 2 (and for ʻ Rages ' in Tobit **6.** 9
read ʻ Ecbatana,' which is rightly given
in two texts, the Codex Vaticanus B
and the Codex Sinaiticus K) ; see also

Löhr, in Kautzsch, *Die Apokryphen
des Alten Testaments*, Freiburg, 1898.
The correct reading is also given in the
old Latin version, Itala, in the Hebrew,
and in the Aramaic; cf. Neubauer,
Book of Tobit, introduction, pp. 36,
55, 78, Oxford, 1878.

alludes to Ragha in connection with Zoroaster's name, the Pahlavi texts do likewise, and tradition makes Rei the home of his mother.[1] The Old Persian inscriptions speak of the district and city of Raga, and the Greek and Roman classics refer to it in connection with Alexander and his successors; the later Persian and Arabic writings have much to say of its importance, one of its claims to renown being the fact that Harun al-Rashid was born at Rei in 763. With a fair degree of completeness we can trace its annals down to the fifteenth century, by which time it appears to have fallen into its final decay, as Clavijo, the Spanish ambassador to the court of Timur Lang, in 1404, describes it as ' a great city all in ruins.'[2] A detailed history of the city I shall reserve for publication elsewhere,[3] but I shall reproduce here from the Arabic an account of Rei, its gates, and its market-places, given by the Mohammedan geographer Istakhri in the tenth century. He says : —

'Rei is the largest of all the cities in its vicinity; it is located on the route which runs from Arak to the east, and there is no city more populous, more prosperous, or larger than it throughout all Islam, except Nishapur. The latter has a greater area and has lattice-work buildings,[4] a palace, and other advantages, but Rei is superior to it. Its length (like Nishapur) is a farsakh and a half, and its buildings are of clay, although plaster and brick are also employed in it. The city has several famous gates; among them is the Gate of Tak, which leads out toward Jabal and Arak; the Gate of Balisan, which leads to Kazvin ; the Gate of Kuhkin, toward Tabaristan; the Gate of Hasham, toward Kumis and Khorasan; and the Gate of Sin, toward Kum. The chief market-places, or bazaars, are Ruzat, Balisan, Dahak-i Nu, Nasarabad, Sarbanan, and the Bab-i Jabal, Bab-i Hasham, and Bab-i Sin. The most important of these is Ruzat, which does the principal business and has the

---

[1] For the passages, see my *Zoroaster*, pp. 202–205.

[2] See Clavijo, *Narrative of an Embassy*, Hakluyt Society, 26. 99 ; cf. also Curzon, *Persia*, 1. 349.

[3] See *Spiegel Memorial Volume*, edited by Jivanji Jamshedji Modi. I do not agree with Rawlinson's view that the ruins at Veramin represent ancient Ragha.

[4] Or does it mean ' a network of buildings ' ? See p. 342, n. 1.

CRUMBLING WALLS OF REI

MOSQUE OF SHAH ABDUL AZIM, NEAR REI

largest caravansarais; it is a broad street with lattice-work caravan-sarais and buildings.[1] The citadel is in one quarter of the city and in it there is a mosque. Most of the city is in ruins, and the palace is in the rampart.[2] The water comes from wells, and there are water-conduits (*ḳanāts*). One of the two streams for drinking-water in the city is named Surakani, and it flows toward the Ruzat quarter; the other is named Jilani (or Gilani), flowing toward the Sarbanan quarter. These streams furnish the drinking-supply, but as there are many canals (*ḳanāts*), the people distribute over their farms the water that is not needed for drinking purposes. The coins that are current in the city are the *dirham* and the *dīnār*. The inhabitants resemble the people of Arak in appearance and are of refined manners. They are chiefly occupied with trade and commerce.'[3]

The description of Rei given by Ibn Haukal, whose work (about 975) is based on Istakhri, but whose description, especially of gates, is sufficiently independent to deserve quotation in full, reads : —

'The most considerable city of those we have mentioned is Rei. After Baghdad there is not in the eastern regions any city more flourishing. Its gates are much celebrated; one of them is called the Darwazah Natan, facing the mountainous country, or the Kohistan of Arak; another leads to Kazvin; another, called the Darvazah Gerhak,[4] is in the direction of Kum. And there are many remarkable streets and quarters in this city, such as Rudah, Kalisan, Dahak Nu, Nasarabad, Sarbanan; Bab al-Jabal, or the Mountain Gate; Dar-i Hasham, or Hasham's Gate; the Dar-i Ahanin, or the Iron Gate; and the gate called Dar-i Athab: but the quarter of Rudah is the most populous and flourishing of all. In this place (Rei) are many bazaars, caravansarais, and market-places. In the suburbs there is a mosque. The citadel is in good repair, and there is a wall round the suburbs, which is, however, falling to decay and

---

[1] See preceding note.

[2] Judging from the description of Yakut (tr. Barbier de Meynard, *Dict. géog.* p. 277), the palace, like the mosque, must have been situated within the rampart of the citadel ; but the text is not absolutely clear to me.

[3] Istakhri, ed. De Goeje, 1. 207

(thanks again to Dr. Yohannan and Professor Gottheil for assistance with the Arabic). For a briefer description of Rei by Istakhri, see De Goeje, 1. 202.

[4] The precise reading of these names in the Arabic letters is not certain, and this probably accounts for some of the seeming variations from Istakhri.

almost desolate. Here they have both river-water and water brought by canals or trenches; one of these is called the Kariz Shahi, or Royal Aqueduct; it passes by Sarbanan; another, called Gilani, also passes through Sarbanan. For the most part the inhabitants drink the water of these aqueducts. There are many canals besides. Here they cultivate the land and practise husbandry, and traffic for gold and direms. The people of this place are hospitable and polite. Here they manufacture fine linen, cotton, and camelots, which are sent to all parts of the world.'[1]

The northern wall, which I have mentioned, is the best-preserved portion of the entire circumvallation, and the mound rising before it is the site of the ancient citadel. The natives call the mound *Ḳal'ah-i Rei*, ' Castle of Rei,' and it is evidently this elevation to which Yakut refers when he speaks of the height as *Rei-bandī*, 'Stronghold of Rei.'[2] According to Yakut, who quotes liberally from his predecessors in his long article on Rei, the citadel was situated outside the 'city' itself and formed a part of the so-called 'exterior town,' or suburb, named Mohammadiah.[3] Its walls and moat, he adds, were completed by al-Mahdi in A.D. 775 (A.H. 158), and the great mosque was also built by this same ruler.[4] Yakut's description of the 'outer city,' the 'citadel,' and the 'city' itself — to repeat again his own designations — would be worth quoting in full if there were space, because his remarks make us more sure of our ground when endeavoring to trace among the ruins the main features of by-gone Rei. By far the best description of these remains, however, was given by an Englishman, Ker Porter, nearly a century ago. His account was also accom-

---

[1] Ibn Haukal, *Oriental Geography*, tr. Ouseley, pp. 176–177. In this quotation, I have made insignificant changes in punctuation and spelling, so as to conform with the rest of the book.

[2] Yakut, p. 277. The name *Zobeidiah* given to the citadel in the text of Jafar ar-Razi, which Yakut (p. 517) cites, is a misreading of the Arabic letters for *Rei-bandī*.

[3] See the French translation of Yakut's long article on ' Rei,' and ' Mohammadiah ' in Barbier de Meynard, *Dict. géog. de la Perse*, pp. 273–280, 516–518.

[4] Yakut, pp. 277, 517.

MOUNT DAMAVAND

panied by a well-sketched plan, which will remain authoritative until careful archæological surveys and researches point out the changes that have occurred since his day owing to the lapse of time, excavations by the natives, and the building of the rail-road to Rei.[1] Ker Porter's description is so excellent and his book so little accessible nowadays, that I regard it worth while to reproduce the main paragraph here, making such changes in punctuation as would be required to-day, and including his excellent map of Rei, which may be helpful in locating the gates mentioned by the Arab geographers, and adding explanatory footnotes of my own.[2]

'The ruins lie about five miles southeast of Teheran, extending from the foot of the curving mountains and running in that direction across the plain in an oblique line southwest. The surface of the ground, all over this tract, is marked by hollows, mounds, mouldering towers, tombs, and wells. The fabric of all being chiefly of that burnt and sun-dried material which seems to bid defiance to the last oblivious touch of time. A very strong citadel appears to have occupied a high and rocky promontory that juts out considerably beyond the other huge buttresses of nature which here start from the different clefts in the mountains.[3] Along the perpendicular sides of this height we easily discovered the foundations of its embattled works. And directly from its base a line of massy fortification appeared, reaching southward and apparently defending the eastern face of the city, till it terminated in an immense square bulwark, flanked with towers and making a fortress in itself.[4] Thence the wall curved round in an irregular oblique sweep towards the northwest till it met another enormous square tower flanked in like manner with six round ones.[5] This tower terminated not only that line of wall, but another, which had also started from the base of the

[1] It is to be hoped that some future student or traveller, or an investigator like M. de Morgan, may undertake a series of careful researches at Rei, because the field is a promising one.

[2] Ker Porter, *Travels in Persia*, 1. 358–360.

[3] This is marked A on Ker Porter's

plan; it is the citadel alluded to by Yakut, as I have already described.

[4] This is the eastern outline marked ACCD in the plan.

[5] On the plan this is the broken line running upward toward the northwest, past the village of Shah Abdul Azim and the tomb of the Imam Abdullah.

promontory and formed the northern front of the city;[1] the whole
fortified space between the three walls taking the shape of a triangle, its vertex [A] touching the citadel-promontory, its base [DD]
stretching southwest from the one large, square tower to the other.
These walls are still many feet in height, of prodigious thickness,
and have been additionally strengthened by proportionably sized
towers connecting the wall and placed at point-blank arrow-distance
from each other.   The two enormous fortress-like towers before
mentioned [DD], which terminate the southeastern and northwestern points of the triangle, are united with the walls; but in
going along the outer side of the longest line which stretches from
the one square tower to the other, we find a third tower about the
middle of the wall, but standing out at some distance from it.[2]   It is
nearly of the same dimensions with the others and supported in the
same way with round flanking towers.   Probably a ditch and a bridge
lay between this great bulwark and the principal gate of the town, this
entrance lying in almost a direct line with the citadel.   The remains
of other fortifications are near it, as if still more to protect this
ingress which opens to the southwestern side of the plain.   I have
no doubt that these three square towers [DDD] commanded the
three great entrances to the city, the northern holding the communication with Azerbijan and Mazanderan, the southern that
toward Khorasan, and the southwestern pointing to Hamadan, the
ancient Ecbatana.[3]   Therefore, by this last gate, it is probable that
Tobit's celestial messenger entered on his embassy to Gab[a]el.[4]
At the foot of the great promontory [A] which crowns the apex
of the fortifications, and projecting within their area, is another
range of equally strong walls, embracing a considerable space and
forming a lower citadel [B], within which, in all likelihood,
were the royal palace and other buildings of state.[5]   Another

[1] That is, running from A westward
to D. The outlines of the northern
wall are best preserved.

[2] It is also marked D and is near the
tomb of the Imam Abdullah in the
southwest part of the plan.

[3] With these remarks on the entrances it is interesting to compare the
notes on the city gates made by the
Mohammedan writers quoted above,
whose statements antedate Ker Porter
by nearly a thousand years.

[4] Through the same approach Darius
Codomannus probably entered when
fleeing before Alexander.

[5] Ker Porter's inference is borne out
by Yakut, pp. 277, 517, who cites older
authorities also to the effect that the
citadel, where the Khalif resided during his stay at Rei, dominates the
grand mosque of Mahdi and the palace
of the governor. Both of these buildings, together with the city prison,
were situated in the 'exterior city,' or

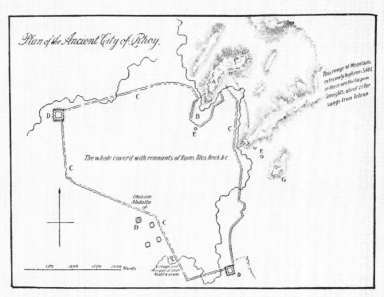

Plan of the Ancient City of Rhoy.

This range of Mountains, extremely high runs S.60E. in these are the Caspian Straights, about 19 far sungs from Tehran

The whole coverd with remnants of Ruins, Tiles, Brick &c

Imaum Abdalla

500   1000   1500   2000 Yards

Village and Mosque of Shah Abdul Azem

KER PORTER'S PLAN OF REI

TOWER ON A HILL NEAR REI

wall,[1] exterior to the city-rampart, connects the height on which the first great citadel stands, with another rocky projection of the mountain, where every tenable spot has been strongly guarded by outworks,[2] linking themselves across the gorge of a deep ravine to the side of a third citadel, or fortress, finely built of stone and on the summit of an immense rock which commands the open country to the south.'[3]

Some idea of the size and sweep of the massive ramparts may be gathered from my photographs. In several places the moldering walls are fully fifty feet high, and the sun-dried bricks which composed them can still be seen plainly in outline, and they reminded me of the bricks used in the old Zoroastrian fire-temple near Isfahan, although somewhat larger, since some of the specimens measured 17 by 7 inches (44 by 18 cm.) along the face.[4] I was afterward told in Teheran that they are known as 'Gabar bricks,' a designation that would seem to confirm my impression of their antiquity.

Everywhere about the walls and within the desolate area that once formed the city there are scattered fragments of pottery and shards of earthenware. Several of the pieces closely resembled the bits of a rough yellow jar I had picked up on the hillside of the Atash Gah near Isfahan and probably dated from the same period.[5] I found also a few specimens of finer ceramic art which showed the exquisite lustre or glint known to porcelain-connoisseurs as the *reflet métallique*, and I added them to my collection of mementos. The natives are aware of the value of these curios, and they treasure up for sale the more artistic specimens unearthed in digging new wells or restoring the old canals that still run from the active stream which flows through Rei to restore life

suburb, of Mohammadiah (Yakut, pp. 277, 517).

[1] This wall is shown by the curved line running from the citadel A toward F in the plan.

[2] The outworks are indicated by circles running from the hill toward the tower F in the plan. A photograph of the tower F may be seen in Curzon, *Persia*, 1. 351.

[3] The position of the fortress is indicated by G in the plan.

[4] See pp. 253, 255, above.

[5] Cf. p. 253, above.

to the gardens within and without its otherwise desolate walls.

Within the compass of the ancient city, and nearly midway between the citadel and the central point, there rises a high brick tower which the natives say is 'old' (*ḳadīm*), but whose claim to antiquity cannot exceed a thousand years.[1] Some writers have supposed it to be the burial-place of the grandson of Tamerlane, Khalil Sultan, and his beloved consort, Shad al-Malik, 'Joy of the King,' in the fifteenth century; others ascribe it to a date four centuries earlier and see in it the mausoleum of Tughral Beg, who died A.D. 1063. I am not yet prepared to pronounce judgment as to which view may be nearer the truth.[2] I can only say that the tower is not mentioned in Istakhri, Ibn Haukal, or Yakut, and that it reminded me of two similar towers I had seen in Hamadan.[3]

This structure, cylindrical in form, but corrugated in outline because of its many angles, rises to a height of about seventy feet, is fully forty feet in diameter, hollow within, and open at the top. The arrangement of the bricks of the outer casing is such that they form a succession of huge perpendicular prisms, some twenty in number, and the cement is curiously indented in a honeycomb fashion, attention to which was called years ago by a Presbyterian missionary from the United States, the Rev. Dr. J. Perkins, in an unpublished letter to the American Oriental Society. · A paragraph in his 'Diary of a Visit to Teheran, the Capital of Persia,' dated Dec. 2, 1845, on p. 58 of the manuscript, briefly describes the tower and concludes as follows : 'Another peculiarity which I noticed is, that the mortar in the interstices between the ends of the bricks is curiously indented and wrought into honeycomb sections, which imparts to the whole an exquisite delicacy, con-

---

[1] The position of this tower (which is roughly indicated by E in Ker Porter's plan) may be seen from the photograph that I have reproduced. I have added also an older photograph of the tower, which was taken before the structure was restored.

[2] For the views, see Benjamin, *Persia*, 1. 59; Curzon, *Persia*, 1. 350.

[3] See p. 162, above.

TOWER AMONG THE RUINS OF REI, AFTER RESTORATION

TOWER AMONG

nected with durability.'[1]   The entrance to the tower is through a high, arched doorway surrounded by a square portal, as will be seen in a photograph that was taken before the two were restored, some fifteen or twenty years ago.   The picture shows why the Kufic inscription, which Ker Porter says encircled the top, has disappeared, no attempt being made to restore it when the new cornice was added.   Care, however, was taken to develop a garden around the tower and to plant numerous *ḳalam* trees, whose slender and straight lines harmonize admirably with the perpendicular outlines of the structure.

An ascent to the summit of the edifice is worth making, as the view of Rei from its top is one of the best that can be obtained.   Far to the north is seen the lofty crest of Damavand. In the near foreground the broken outline of the northern wall of ancient Ragha may easily be traced from east to west. As one looks toward the hills on the northeast, the Gabar Dakhmah, or Tower of Silence, appears like a white speck against a rocky background, while on another hill to the east is a small tower ('old Gabar,' the guide suggested), and again somewhat beyond it to the east-southeast rise the walls of an elevated fortress.   Far to the southeast and south, one notices on the plain a series of mounds of earth and elevations that are said to be a farsakh's distance apart and are explained (for lack of a better interpretation) as 'signal towers' for pilgrims making the journey to and from Kerbela.   To the south and southwest, in the nearer foreground, the hamlet of Shah Abdul Azim nestles amid green trees, and the western line of Rei is skirted by the railway that approaches the shrine.

While resting and taking luncheon near the gateway that forms the entrance to the tower garden, we had a chance to converse with the natives and to ask them some questions to see whether they knew anything of Zoroaster or were even acquainted with his name as Zardusht in Modern Persian.   In

---

[1] This honeycomb effect in plaster is familiar in a larger way in the Mohammedan architecture of Merv, Bokhara, and Samarkand.

answer to the inquiry as to who was the prophet of the Gabars, two of the Mohammedans with whom we spoke replied, wholly independently of each other, that 'the prophet of the Fire-Worshippers was *Ibrahīm*,' that is, Abraham. This response is of interest because of the frequent association of Zoroaster with Abraham by the Moslems.[1] Somewhat later there came along a bright-faced young Mullah wearing a white turban; on being interrogated, he promptly replied: 'Zardusht was the prophet of the Gabars and lived about six thousand years ago; to find out more about him, one must consult the Gabar books, for the Gabars have books.'[2]

Although there would have been time for a special visit to the Shrine of Shah Abdul Azim, I decided rather to devote it to continuing my survey of the ancient ruins. Returning to the upper section of Rei, I first examined a sculpture, carved in a space something less than ten feet by twenty, on a rock to the east of the ancient citadel. It has something of a history, as the rock is really a palimpsest, an old carving having been chiselled away in the first part of the nineteenth century to give place to a new one. In its present form the monument represents Fath Ali Shah in the act of spearing a lion, and has little, if any, historic value. The old sculpture which the monarch caused to be obliterated in order to afford a space for his own picture was really a historic one and dated back to Sasanian times. Fortunately it had been sketched by Morier (1809), W. Price (1811), and Sir William Ouseley (1811–1812), and described also by Ker Porter (1818), so that it has not been lost entirely, and I reproduce here the drawing by Ouseley, because of its archæological interest.[3] The sculpture

---

[1] See p. 404, above, and my *Zoroaster*, p. 157; cf. also Hyde, *Historia Religionis Veterum Persarum*, pp. 28–31, Oxford, 1700.

[2] The Moslems always lay stress on any religion that has books, even if they despise the believers as infidels.

[3] Sir W. Ouseley, *Travels*, 3. plate 65; compare also Morier, *Second Journey*, 2. 190, London, 1818; W. Price, *Journal of the British Embassy to Persia*, p. 37, 2d ed., London, 1832; Ker Porter, *Travels*, 1. 363; and see the remarks by Curzon, *Persia*, 1. 351–352.

SASANIAN SCULPTURE NOW DESTROYED
(From the drawing of Sir William Ouseley)

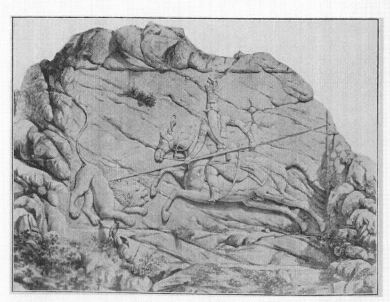

MODERN BAS-RELIEF REPLACING THE SCULPTURE SHOWN ABOVE

represented a mounted warrior charging at full speed with a couched spear against an antagonist, the head of whose horse was roughly indicated in outline on the stone. The figure with the spear was undoubtedly a Sasanian king, as was shown by the balloon-like head-gear and other typical accoutrements of Sasanian times, but we no longer know which particular monarch may have been intended. Ker Porter thought it probable that Ardashir, the founder of the dynasty, was the hero, and that the combat was against the last of the Parthians; Sir William Ouseley, on the contrary, was inclined rather to attribute it to Ardashir's son Shahpur, but both scholars were of the opinion that the entire sculpture had never been finished. We can but regret that it is no longer possible to solve such a problem, and we must deplore the destructive zeal of Fath Ali Shah, which has robbed us of a monument of antiquity.

The sculptural activity of Fath Ali Shah was not confined, however, to making palimpsest records; he has left us another carving which is chiselled on a huge panel that was specially prepared for the purpose on the face of the volcanic rock overhanging the waters of the holy and much frequented Chashmah-i Ali, or 'Spring of Ali.' The sculpture represents the long-bearded monarch seated upon his throne, surrounded by his sons and viziers, in the same manner that he is portrayed in the painting on the walls of the picture-gallery of the Nagaristan in Teheran.[1]

Riding some distance beyond the intrenchments of Rei toward a spur of the mountains that surround the ruins on the easterly and northeasterly side, I ascended the barren hill on whose rocky side stands the old Zoroastrian Tower of Silence. Because of the historic association of Ragha with the Zoroastrian religion, it is probable that this dakhmah is located on one of the oldest known sites for a Tower of Silence, and its situation fulfils all the requirements of the Vendidad canon, which enjoins that the dakhmah shall be placed on a hill, far

[1] For a reproduction of the Nagaristan paintings, see Curzon, *Persia*, 1. 338.

from human habitations, but accessible to ' the corpse-eating dogs and birds.' The location recalled that of the dakhmah at Ajmere in India, and the structure resembled the Parsi Towers of Silence at Bombay in being round in shape, about thirty feet in height, and covered with a cement which gives it the whitish color noticeable in the Bombay towers.[1] It was repaired some years ago, as were the dakhmahs at Yezd, through an expenditure of funds supplied by the Parsis of India for the amelioration of the Zoroastrians in Persia.[2] Unlike the Bombay towers, it has no door, because, as the Zoroastrians in Teheran told me, they are afraid that the Mohammedans may desecrate the place.   The corpse is lifted over the wall by means of ladders and ropes or a chain, as I learned from the Rev. L. F. Esselstyn, a missionary, who had helped to lift into it the dead body of one of his servants, who was a Zoroastrian.

I ascended higher up the hill to a point where I could see the interior of the tower. The *pāvis*, or receptacles for the bodies, were arranged after a rectangular method and not radiated in the wheel-like fashion of the Parsi dakhmahs. I could see no *bhandār*, or central pit, in which to deposit the skeleton after the flesh had been stripped from the bones, but I was told by those who had been inside the dakhmah that there was a place to which a few steps led down, and this might have served as an *astodān*, or repository for the bones.   The whole arrangement appeared to me rather primitive and less systematic and up-to-date than in the Bombay Towers of Silence.   I may add that there was no evidence anywhere of a *sagri*, or shrine, for a perpetual lamp to burn near the place of the dead.

As we galloped homeward toward Teheran, the sun began to cast long shadows from Mount Damavand, the great peak of Alborz, the Avestan Hara Berezaiti, whose snowy cap and frowning front loomed skyward to the height of nearly twenty

---

[1] See the accompanying photograph of the tower and also the distant view of this dakhmah given above, p. 403.
[2] See p. 397, above.

SCULPTURED PANEL OF FATH ALI SHAH, ABOVE THE 'SPRING OF ALI'

THE ZOROASTRIAN TOWER OF SILENCE AT REI

thousand feet.   No wonder it looked sullen at its ceaseless task in crushing beneath its ponderous bulk for ages, as legends tell, the giant monster Zohak, or Azhi Dahaka, lest he escape from his chains and tyrannize the world.   Only in the eleventh millennium will the mountain be relieved from duty, for then the hero Sama Keresaspa will waken from his sleep, slay Zohak, and usher in the dawn of a new era.

But soon we were entering the gates of the capital, and my thoughts were turned from ancient legends and ancient ruins to themes of the present.

CHAPTER XXVIII

THROUGH MAZANDARAN TO THE CASPIAN SEA

'To the sea-shore he gan his way apply,
To weete if shipping readie he mote there descry.'
—SPENSER, *Faerie Queene*, 5. 12. 3.

I HAD been a week in Teheran and had especially enjoyed my visit because I had accomplished most of the immediate purposes I had in view. Though loath to depart, I found the time demanded my leaving if I were to carry out my plans for visiting Central Asia. The official calls had been made, and the requisite papers obtained from governmental sources to enable me to travel freely in Transcaspia and Turkistan; the adieus to my friends had been said ; and the minor arrangements for the journey had been completed. Yet to say farewell to Persia without delays is always impossible, and although the carriage, horses, and driver were at the door, it took an endless amount of time and ado before the baggage was lashed to the wagon and the start made for the Caspian Sea which we hoped to reach on the second day — *inshăllah*, ' God willing ! '

Another hour had elapsed before we came to the outer post-station of the city, near the Kazvin gate. A long delay occurred here to remind me again that we were still in Persia. Each piece of luggage had to be taken off the rickety vehicle, weighed with a precision that could come only from a desire to exact the utmost *shăhī* for every ounce of baggage and extract an additional bakhshish, and then the packages were slowly lashed in place again upon the conveyance.

The fare and toll rate for this uncomfortable journey of some 240 miles in a rattle-bang old brougham was about 70 tomans (dollars), a sum that seemed exorbitant considering the dis-

THE KAZVIN GATE, TEHERAN

THE MEIDAN-I MASHK, DRILL SQUARE, AT TEHERAN

comforts, but I was promised a prompt and safe arrival (again *inshállah*), and away we started.

The road was the best I had seen in Persia, because built and managed by the Russians, and it was therefore marked off in *versts*, not *farsakhs*, as a measure of distance. The weather was warm, as it was the end of May ; the way was hot and dusty; and the plain flat and uninteresting. Nothing special engaged my attention until we came to the river Karaj. This active stream rushes out from a deep gorge in the mountains, with high precipitous banks that recalled to my mind the suggestion I had heard from the Gabars in Yezd, that the Karaj might be the Darejya of the Avesta.[1] I photographed the scene to fix it firmly in my memory, but I felt no more convinced of the accuracy of the suggested identification than I did when the Zoroastrians proposed it to me. Without halting longer we proceeded again and travelled all through the night, jolting, lurching, lunging in our cramped vehicle, which stopped at irregular intervals for fresh relays of horses, until we rumbled into Kazvin shortly before eight the next morning after a tour of nearly twenty hours.

Kazvin was once one of the most important cities of northern Persia and was sufficiently well known in England in Milton's day to be mentioned in *Paradise Lost*.[2] The city's long history is said to have begun in the fourth century A.D., when it was founded by the Sasanian King Shahpur II. Four centuries later Harun al-Rashid showed it distinguished marks of favor, and so far had Kazvin advanced by the beginning of the thirteenth century that Yakut, in his Arab geography, devotes several pages to the town. In the sixteenth century it became, for the first time, an imperial city, as Shah Tahmasp I then made it his chosen residence; but Isfahan and Teheran in turn supplanted it as the nation's capital, so that Kazvin is no longer a city of the first rank, although the number of its inhabitants is variously estimated from 50,000 to 100,000 persons.

[1] See p. 360, above.   [2] See Milton, *Paradise Lost*, 10. 435.

Despite its level and unimposing situation, Kazvin makes a pleasant impression upon the eye because the main avenue leading through the city to the Governor's Palace is richly lined on either side with shade-trees. The principal inn, *mahmān-khānah*, at the other end of this boulevard, is the best of its kind in all Persia and has spacious quarters for fairly comfortable lodging and ample accommodations for numerous relays of post-horses, but it does not possess sufficient attraction to induce the stranger to prolong his stay more than is necessary. The rows of single-storied bazaars on the main streets gave me the impression of being reasonably prosperous, and in one of the semi-European shops I replenished my supply of certain necessaries for the voyage which one best knows how to appreciate after long travel in Persia. I was not sorry, however, when the time came to resume the journey toward the Caspian, although I should have liked to visit the mosque which was originally built by Harun al-Rashid.[1] I also regret that I did not know at the time that the distant hills that I saw rising back of Kazvin were once the stronghold of the *Sheikh al-Jabal*, 'Old Man of the Mountains,' the head of the Assassin Band in the twelfth century, for I am sure I should have noted the outline of these hills more closely than I did and should have sought for local legends regarding the picturesque though villanous outlaws whose name, *hashshāshīn*, 'hashish-eaters,' corrupted by Europeans into *assassin*, has become synonymous with murderer.

The next stages of the journey were devoted to sleeping as best I could in the uncomfortable conveyance, but I awoke in time to enjoy the grand mountain scenery of the Kharzan Pass. This lofty roadway crosses the Alborz range at a height of seven thousand feet, or more, above the Caspian, and in winter it is one of the bleakest and most desolate places in all Persia, a pathway of death where many a beast of burden falls by the way. The descent to the village of Peichanar was slow and

[1] See Yakut, p. 443.

The Mahman-Khanah at Kazvin

The River Karaj

winding. The entire region interested me because it lay on the borders of Mazandaran, the abode of the *Māzainya Daēvas,* 'Demons of Mazandaran,' in the Avesta, and I confess that some of the natives of the rude villages looked like the veritable *dīvs,* 'devils,' of Firdausi's Shah Namah.

Early on the second morning we crossed the Safid Rud, literally 'White River,' which I believe to be identical with the Daitya River of Zoroaster, and I wondered whether its waters shimmering in the light of sunrise preserved any memory of the prophet's glorification or of the sacrifice offered on its bank by his patron Vishtaspa.[1] At nine o'clock we were in Resht, a flourishing but unattractive town of possibly 100,000 inhabitants.[2] I did not stay here more than two hours before engaging another conveyance to carry Safar and myself to Piri Bazaar, the landing-place where one hires a rowboat as a transport to Enzali, the main port.

Piri Bazaar is a filthy hole, a place where it is almost impossible to avoid a conflict with the shameless watermen who seem to have all the vices of dishonesty and fraud that belong to boatmen at insignificant ports. Bargains in such cases are usually treaties of peace after prolonged warfare in which the foreigner comes off worst, at least in his own estimation. The bags and packages were finally bestowed somewhere in the bow or in the stern of the boat, after an extra bakhshish had been paid to insure more careful handling, and we rowed and poled for several hours through the lagoons and river until landing at Enzali. Here I spent two nights waiting for the steamer *Constantin* of the Kavkas-Merkur Line to sail, and I enjoyed the company of the British Consul at Isfahan, Mr. J. R. Preece, who was on his way to England after a long residence in Persia.

To reach the steamer, which lay several miles from shore,

[1] See my *Zoroaster*, pp. 40, 42, 45, 49, 52, 196, 197, 211, 221.

[2] See *Sixty-seventh Annual Report* of the Board of Foreign Missions of the Presbyterian Church in the U.S.A. p. 231, New York, 1904.

it was necessary to embark in a lighter, a huge scow almost as unseaworthy as the one in which I had crossed the Persian Styx at Julfa on entering Iran, but much more unsafe because of the distance to be traversed and the danger from the surf and waves of the Caspian, which were running high at the time. I could not help thinking what an irony of fate it would be to be lost in this wretched hulk of a scow after climbing Behistan and going through various hardships on the journey now drawing to its close. But all went well. On board the *Constantin* I found good accommodations and excellent company, the Austrian Minister and his wife being among the passengers on their way from Teheran to Europe. The sea journey proceeded pleasantly.

But Persia all this while was fading gradually from view. The steamer called next day at Astara, where I bade adieu to my faithful Safar, who had served me so well and whom I would gladly, if possible, have taken with me to Central Asia. I felt certain it was not easy for him, too, to say good-by. As his yawl-boat pushed off from the steamer's side and headed toward the shore, I could see Mount Ardabil, where Zoroaster once preached the law, raising its lofty brow, no longer mitred with snow, but turbaned in green. The color may have been emblematic of the change of faith from Zarathushtra to the Prophet of Islam, but perhaps, like the green bay tree that has sprung from the roof of the Tomb of Cyrus at Pasargadæ, it symbolized the fact that florescence in Persia is still possible, when the season of national greatness once again returns.

The wheels of the steamer began to revolve ; I waved good-by once more to Safar and said a long farewell to the Land of the Sun as we sped forward toward Baku, whence I was to continue my journey into Central Asia, a description of which I shall give in another volume, supplemented by a historic account of Susa and of Eastern Persia, which I hope also to visit at some future time.

PEICHANAR, BETWEEN KAZVIN AND RESHT

ENZALI

INDEXES

GENERAL INDEX

Small superior numbers after the page-numbers refer to the footnotes.

Iranian words are printed in italic type, and when they are not modern Persian the language is indicated.

In the alphabetic arrangement of Arabic names the prefix *al-* has been disregarded, but not the elements *Ibn* and *Abu*.

A

Abadah, village, 277.
Abarkuh, town, 341–4.
Abbas, Shah, 27, 37.
    made Isfahan capital, 265.
    founded Julfa, a suburb of Isfahan, 270.
    mosques erected by 5, 267.
    mail-coat of, 422.
Abbasid dynasty, 27.
Abdul Azim, Shah. shrine of, 428.
Abdullah, governor of Khorasan, destroyed Zoroastrian works, 359.
ablution of nine nights, 381, 392, 396.
Abraham, legends of, 342, 343.
    associated with Zoroaster, 404, 438.
Abu Ali ibn Sina, tomb of, 165–7.
Abu Dulaf Misar, described Tak-i Bostan, 224.
Abu Kalanjar Sultan, fortified Shiraz, 325.
Abu Saïd, tomb of, 167.
Abuzaïdabad, village, 410, 416.
accipenser huso, 9.
Achæmenian dynasty, 26.
Achmetha, Aramaic form of Hamadan, 152.
Adarian, Zoroastrian chapel, 366.
Adhargushnasp (Adharakhsh), fire-temple of, 133–42.
Aena, name of Anahita, 153.
aësha (Av.), plow, 246.
Afghans, invaded Persia, 27.
Afrasiab, conflict with Hom and Kei Khosru, 137–9, 142.
    legend of defeat by Rustam and Kei Kaus, 264.

Agamatanu, Babylonian form of Hamadan, 150.
Agha Mohammed Shah, 27.
    sacked Hamadan, 155, 159.
    razed the ramparts of Shiraz, 325.
    laid out a garden at Shiraz, 327.
    made Teheran capital, 419.
Aghri Dagh (Ararat), 17.
agriculture, implements of, 85–6, 246–8.
    praise of, in the Avesta, 246, 373.
Ahmadabad, 122–3.
Ahmat, ash-hill at, 94.
Ahriman, 63, 363.
Ahuna Vairya stanza, as pronounced at Yezd, 365.
    recited in the funeral rites, 392.
Ahura Mazda (Ormazd), 65–6. 362.
    Zoroaster converses with, 62.
    in the inscriptions of Darius, 181–2.
    represented on a sculpture at Naksh-i Rajab, 309.
    possibly represented at Tak-i Bostan, 220, 225.
Airyema Ishyo, a prayer, 87.
Aiwisrûthrima Gâh, a time of day, 394.
Akdah, village, 402, 403, 415.
Akhuri, Akori, Armenian village, 17.
Alborz, Mount, 58.
Alexander the Great, at Ecbatana, 157, 158.
    vanquished Darius III, 26, 319.
    burned the archetype copy of the Avesta, 306–7.
    legends of, 5, 163–5.
Aliabad, village, 347.
Allah ad-Daulah Garshasp, Sultan, built mosque at Yezd, 350.
altars, Achæmenian, 303.
Alusjird, river, 147.

Paivand-Nāmah, a formula, 385[1].
pāk-shūr, washer, 388.
palace of Darius, at Persepolis, 312, 314.
of Xerxes, at Persepolis, 316.
of Artaxerxes III, at Persepolis, 315.
pālān, saddle, 106.
Pandnamak-i Vazhorg-Mitro-i Bukhtakan, Pahlavi work, 359[2].
paradise, derivation of the word, 30.
Parsa-karta, probable ancient name of Persepolis, 294.
Parsis of India, departure from Persia of the, 67.
efforts of, in behalf of Zoroastrians in Persia, 379, 397, 399, 440.
parsish-khānah, mortuary chapel, 390.
Parthian dynasty, 26.
Parthian sculpture of Gotarzes, 209.
Pasangun, village, 417.
Pasargadæ, location of, 279.
platform at, 280.
square building at, 280.
sculpture of Cyrus at, 282.
inscribed column of Cyrus at, 175, 281.
tomb of Cyrus at, 283–93.
pashm, wool, 388.
patit pashīmānī, repentance, 387.
pāvi, channel, 369, 440.
Peichanar, village, 444.
perfumes, in Zoroastrian rites, 370.
Persepolis, name of, 294.
ruins of Stakhra near, 306–7.
great platform of, 310–8.
Old Persian inscriptions at, 312–315, 318–9.
royal tombs at, 319.
Persian history, survey of, 25.
literature, 30.
words in English, 29–30.
Persian Tales, fictitious work, 31.
Persis (Persia proper), 26, 419.
Petrorvsk, town, 4.
Phraaspa, possibly Takht-i Suleiman, 137.
Phraortes, Median ruler, 25.
Pietro della Valle, see della Valle.
pigeon-towers, at Isfahan, 262.
pipes, for smoking, 51, 88.
Piri Bazaar, landing-place, 445.
Piruz, Sasanian king, fire-temple near Isfahan assigned to the reign of, 261.
Pishdadians, legendary founders of Stakhra, 306.
pīsh-gāhān, pall-bearers, 389.

platform of Persepolis, 310–8.
at Kangavar, 238.
at Tak-i Bostan, 228.
mortuary, at Naksh-i Rustam, 304.
near Puzah, 307.
Pliny the Elder, mentions the tomb of Cyrus, 287.
plows, Persian, 85–6, 246.
Plutarch, describes the tomb of Cyrus, 286.
describes the death of Clitus, 164.
Polo, Marco, visited Yezd, 349, 402.
relates a legend of the 'Three Kings,' 413.
Polvar (Medus), river, 279, 295, 305.
Polyænus, mentions the death of Cyrus, 284.
Polybius, describes Hamadan, 153–4.
pomegranate, in Zoroastrian ceremonies, 369.
population of Erivan, 17.
of Hamadan, 148.
of Kermanshah, 231.
of Resht, 445.
of Tabriz, 40.
of Urumiah, 104.
of Yezd, 350.
Portal of Xerxes, at Persepolis, 313.
Portico of Darius, at Persepolis, 317.
pottery, found at Degalah, 92.
found at Diza-Takiah, 98.
found at Termani, 93.
found at the ruined temple near Isfahan, 253.
fragments of, found at Rei, 435.
Prexaspes, vizir of Cambyses, 43.
priests, Zoroastrian, 376.
read from the Avesta to cure disease, 379.
summoned at death, 387.
Prometheus, legend of, 3.
pronunciation of Avestan at Yezd, 363–5.
Ptolemy, Greek geographer, mentions Yezd, 348, 351.
mentions Isfahan, 264.
mentions Nakhichavan (Naxouana), 22.
punishments, cruel, 157, 201, 271–3.
pursī-raftan, condolence, 391.
pursish-khānah, mortuary chapel, 390.
Puzah, halting-place, 305, 309.

Q

Quintus Curtius Rufus, describes the tomb of Cyrus, 287.

legends of Zoroaster at, 360–1.
pronunciation of Avestan at, 363–5.
verse in the Younger Avesta unknown to the Zoroastrians of, 365.
fire-temple at, 366–70.
Barashnum Gah at, 372–3.
animal sacrifice at, 371–2.
dakhmahs in the vicinity of, 397–8.
Yezdikhast, village, 276.
Yezidis, devil-worshippers, at Tiflis, 10–14.
Yima, see Jamshid.
yuyō-semi (Av.), yoke of a plow, 247.

Z

zād-ō-marg, charnel-house, 389–91.
zairimyāka, zairimyañura (Av.), tortoise, 234.
Zangi, river, 19.
Zarathushtra, see Zoroaster.
Zarch Kuh, hill, 397
Zargan (Zergun), village, 321.
Zendah Rud, river. 255, 265, 269.
zgeresnō-vaghdhana (Av.), suggested explanation of, 247.
Zindan, Mount, description of, 124–126.
  possibly the ancient Asnavand, 139[5], 141.
Zobeidah, wife of Harun al-Rashid, said to have founded Tabriz, 39
  said to have founded Kashan, 411
Zofian (Sofian), village, 37.
Zohak, monster, legend of, 264.
Zoroaster, 5, 53.
  probable explanation of the name, 89, 361.
  fanciful etymologies of the name, 361–2.

life and teachings of, 57–67.
legends of, at Yezd, 360–2.
associated with Urumiah, 87.
said to have come from Shiz, 133–136.
thought to have come from Rei, 360.
seclusion of, on Mount Savalan, 134.
cave near Urumiah connected with, 103–4.
vision of, on Mount Asnavand, 38.
supposed sculpture of, at Tak-i Bostan, 216–20.
associated with Abraham, 404, 438.
the Three Kings guided by a supposed prophecy of, 102–3.
Zoroaster, story by Marion Crawford, 31.
Zoroastrian ceremonies, general, 367–71.
  at the birth of a child, 378–9.
  of initiation into the faith, 380–1.
  of purification, 381–4.
  of marriage, 385–6.
  connected with death and burial, 387–97.
Zoroastrianism, 26, 28.
Zoroastrians in Persia, 25.
  number of, 425.
  restrictions on, 374–6.
  religious ceremonies of, 367–71, 378–97.
  formerly numerous near Isfahan, 252.
  at Isfahan, 273–5.
  at Kashan, 413.
  at Miandoab, 119.
  at Shiraz, 336–8.
  at Teheran, 425–7.
  at Yezd, 354–400.
zōt, officiating priest, 367.

INDEX OF PASSAGES

As in the General Index, footnotes are designated by small superior figures after the page-numbers.

AVESTAN

VEDIC

For convenience of reference a list of the more important Avestan and Old Persian words explained or referred to in this work is here given. The General Index should, however, also be consulted, especially for Phl. and Mod. Pers.

AVESTAN

OLD PERSIAN

Made in the USA
Lexington, KY
22 August 2013